C000051631

HISTORY OF THE PEOPLE OF TRINIDAD
AND TOBAGO

HISTORY OF THE PEOPLE OF TRINIDAD AND TOBAGO

Eric Williams

On August 31st, 1962, Doctor Eric Williams became the first Prime Minister of the country which he had led to independence. As an historian and the long acknowledged authority on the West Indies, he viewed the transformation of the former colony into a nation from the perspective of its historical development. His aim in writing this book in the months before the Declaration of Independence was to provide his countrymen with a national history, with a basic document about their past which could serve as a guide for their future.

Beginning with an account of the Amerindian cultures existing in Trinidad and Tobago at the time of their discovery, Doctor Williams goes on to analyze the failure of Spanish policy in the territory, the period of French influence in Trinidad and occupation of Tobago, and the century and a half of British rule, giving a detailed picture of the islands' slave-based economy and showing how, in effect, this structure was maintained after Emancipation both by the conditions imposed on African labor and the ordinances governing indentured labor imported from India in the nineteenth century. He then describes in full the methods of Crown Colony government, and concludes with the story of the coming of Independence.

continued on back flap

PRINTED IN GREAT BRITAIN

History of the people of
Trinidad and Tobago

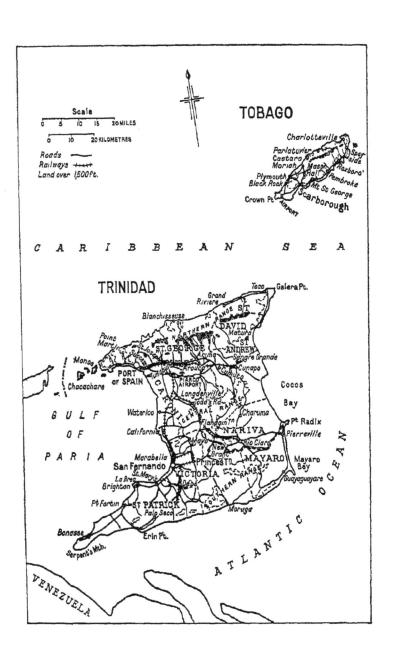

HISTORY OF THE PEOPLE

OF

TRINIDAD AND TOBAGO

BY

ERIC WILLIAMS

FREDERICK A. PRAEGER, *Publisher*

NEW YORK

Published in the United States of America in 1964
by Frederick A. Praeger, Inc., Publisher
64 University Place, New York 3, N.Y.

All rights reserved

© 1962 by Eric Williams IN TRINIDAD

Library of Congress Catalog Card Number: 64–13390

.

Printed in Great Britain

Contents

.

THIS BOOK IS DEDICATED TO ALL THOSE WHO
HAVE GONE BEFORE IN THE STRUGGLE FOR
INDEPENDENCE AND AGAINST COLONIALISM, A
STRUGGLE WHICH—AS ANTONIO MACEO, THE
GREAT NEGRO CUBAN GENERAL IN THE WAR OF
INDEPENDENCE AGAINST SPAIN, RECOGNISED OF
THE CUBAN REVOLUTION—HAS NO COLOUR.

Introduction to the London Edition

This book tells the story of the travails and tribulations of a British Colony which, after a hundred and sixty-five years of crown colony rule, achieved its independence on August 31, 1962.

It is the story of the misrule of metropolitan bureaucracy and the indifference of metropolitan scholarship. Trinidad and Tobago attracted metropolitan attention only in periods of riot and disorder (1903 and 1937), only when the discovery of oil made it an object of interest to the British Navy and British capitalism, only when its invaluable natural harbour, Chaguaramas, made it a useful pawn to be traded by Britain against American aid in the Second World War.

These developments apart, Trinidad and Tobago was merely a crown colony, forgotten and forlorn. No British statesman of substance was ever distracted by it from larger and more important issues, unless it was Joseph Chamberlain, and his connection with Trinidad and Tobago is probably the least reputable phase in his career. No British scholar found it worth his while to pay any attention to the history and potential of Trinidad and Tobago, unless it was Froude who came and went on a tourist visit leaving only froudacity behind.

To metropolitan officialdom and the metropolitan press, Trinidad and Tobago emerged, after the revelations of the bankruptcy of colonialism by the Royal Commission of 1938, merely as a colony with a higher national income than its neighbours which, by imperialist criteria, did not need the economic aid provided under Development and Welfare by the United Kingdom.

Colonial nationalism, in India, Africa and elsewhere, has given high priority to the rewriting of the history purveyed by metropolitan scholars and to writing that history where the metropolitan country has ignored or bypassed it. The very fact of National Independence, therefore, made this history of Trinidad and Tobago mandatory. Its publication, moreover, throws light on one of the dark crannies of the long West Indian association with Britain which British scholarship has seen fit to leave unexplored.

This history of the People of Trinidad and Tobago will, it is hoped, explain to people, within and outside the Commonwealth the policy of the new Independent Commonwealth country. That policy can be very simply stated – to remove the vestiges of colonialism and change the colonial pattern and mentality in every sphere.

As this introduction to the London edition is being written, a Commission of Enquiry comprising international experts is assessing the legacy left behind by British policy which, in law and in lease, in finance and in operation, ignored the interests of Trinidad and Tobago.

The nationalist movement in Trinidad and Tobago has in the past five years re-examined all the postulates and policies of colonial education, in the primary school, in the secondary school which is now free, and in the teacher training college. The University of the West Indies, that British *damnosa hereditas* which sought to export St Andrews to Jamaica, is being steadily West Indianised and made to serve West Indian needs and aspirations.

The Prime Minister of Trinidad and Tobago, currently on an extensive tour meeting the people to ascertain their grievances, receives daily first hand evidence of the distortion and injustice of the crown colony agricultural system and the exploitation of the villages. The small man, a pariah under the British régime which, true to its slave-owning antecedents, emphasised the latifundia and the plantocracy, is coming into his own as a citizen as of right and not of grace in his independent country.

Hookworm and malaria which debilitated the population in crown colony days and were responsible for their low productivity have now been exorcised in the nationalist wind of change. The water supply, a feature of one of the greatest financial scandals in the crown colony era, is being rapidly improved. The telephone system, handed over to a British company through one of the more brutal uses of the imperial power, is now the property of the People of Trinidad and Tobago. What passed in the colonial catalogue as roads are now being opened up and made accessible to the expanding population. Tobago, transferred to Trinidad by metropolitan fiat for a paltry £4,000, now holds pride of place among the smaller islands of the Caribbean as a result of the unaided development efforts of the Government of Trinidad and Tobago.

All this has taken a mere six years, from the absurd constitution of 1956, approved by the Secretary of State for the Colonies, to the Independence Constitution, worked out by the two political parties on the basis of proposals submitted by the People in their organisations in 'constituent assembly'. If, in this transition to orderly and rational progress, we have erred, it is to the British People above all that we would look for sympathetic understanding, for, after all, we are merely trying, unaided by Britain, to succeed where Britain has hopelessly failed.

Port-of-Spain   ERIC WILLIAMS
Trinidad and Tobago
August 31 1963

Foreword

This book originated in a personal conviction that it would be an unfortunate handicap in the field of international relations and a great mistake in respect of affairs and domestic relations, if Trinidad and Tobago were to enter on its career of Independence without a history of its own, without some adequate and informed knowledge of its past, and dependent solely upon amateur outpourings in the daily press.

The writing of this book began on July 25 and was completed on August 25, except for the index. With such haste in composition and in writing, and the attendant haste in printing, it would be surprising if there were no typographical errors or failure in some instances to make the necessary comparisons and indicate the necessary sequences. In addition, the book is twice as long as originally planned but it has been thought better, partly for the education of the people of Trinidad and Tobago, partly to forestall uninformed challenges, to let the documents speak for themselves and to quote them rather than to summarise or condense.

The aim in writing the book, however, was not literary perfection or conformity with scholastic canons. The aim was to provide the people of Trinidad and Tobago on their Independence Day with a National History, as they have already been provided with a National Anthem, a National Coat of Arms, National Birds, a National Flower and a National Flag.

This history of the people of Trinidad and Tobago, in seeking to inform them of their past as an essential guide to their future action, places them and their problems at all times in international perspective. There has been no hesitation in drawing extensively upon, where necessary, the author's knowledge of Caribbean history as a whole, in respect of which he had the advantage of an incomplete and unfinished history of the West Indies begun some eleven years ago and put into cold storage until more leisured times.

Two principal objects have been kept in view in the preparation of this National History on the occasion of the Independence of the people of Trinidad and Tobago. The first is the author's passionate conviction that it is only in unity on essential national issues that future progress can be made. Division of the races was the policy of colonialism. Integration of the races must be the policy of Independence. Only in this way can the colony of Trinidad and Tobago be transformed into the Nation of Trinidad and Tobago.

The second principal object that has been kept in view is the integration of the separated Caribbean Territories. Separation and fragmentation were the policy of colonialism and rival colonialisms. Association and integration must be the policy of Independence. Here the other countries of the Caribbean suffer from the same handicap that faced Trinidad and Tobago before the preparation of this National History; they do not know their past history. As the completion of a history of the entire Caribbean area is a task of too vast magnitude to be contemplated in these days of intense political activity, it is the author's intention to follow up this history of the people of Trinidad and Tobago with similar historical monographs for several Caribbean countries. It will be no easy task to determine the priorities on which this new assignment should be based. But the author is satisfied that similar historical monographs must be prepared as a matter of urgency for at least five Caribbean countries—British Guiana, Jamaica, Cuba, Barbados, and either Martinique or Guadeloupe. To this assignment he proposes to dedicate himself in the next few months; if only as a hobby, if only to get out of his system some of the poison which is perhaps unnecessarily imbibed in political activity in countries which have learned only too well the lessons of colonialism.

It is with this philosophy that the history of the people of Trinidad and Tobago is presented, first to the people of Trinidad and Tobago, then to their Caribbean colleagues who loom so largely in these pages, and then to the colleagues of Trinidad and Tobago on the international stage. No apology is made either for its form or its content, or its timing. It is the work of a private citizen, whatever his political affiliation or his governmental responsibility, and neither Party, nor Government, nor individual has any responsibility for its contents for which the author alone is responsible. Many will praise the book, and some will censure it. The author wishes to make it clear that he seeks neither praise nor blame, that his particular concern is with the people of Trinidad and Tobago with whom he is identified in aspirations and achievements, and that he has always regarded it as his special responsibility to pass on to them the knowledge which would have been unobtainable without them and for which they in fact paid.

If some do not like the book, that is their business. The author is not responsible for the calamitous mistakes of the past; when he was in a position to advise in a small field, his advice was rejected; now that he is in a position to help to make the history of Trinidad and Tobago, efforts are made to frustrate him from abroad. Those who make their bed must lie on it. The author has made his and is lying on it. This book is not conceived as a work of scholarship. It is a manifesto of a subjugated people. Designed to appear on Independence Day, August 31, 1962, it is the Declaration of Independence of the united people of Trinidad and Tobago.

INDEPENDENCE DAY   ERIC WILLIAMS
August 31 1962

Our Amerindian Ancestors

At the time of their discovery, the archipelago of islands which have
become known as the West Indies was inhabited principally by two
Amerindian tribes which had close links with the Amerindians of
Guiana on the South American mainland. The first of these was the
Arawaks, one branch of which, the Tainos, was concentrated in the
Greater Antilles and the Bahamas, while the second, the Igneris, dominated the Lesser Antilles Apart from the Arawaks, there was a second
principal group, the Caribs. A third variant of the Amerindian pattern
was located on a small scale in Western Cuba, the Siboneys, possibly
representing a pre-Arawak strain originating in Florida.

The outstanding general work on the Amerindian culture is a
Swedish publication, *Origins of the Tainan Culture, West Indies*, by
Sven Loven, the 1935 English translation and expansion of his Swedish
treatise of 1924. In respect of Trinidad itself, our knowledge comes
from a little masterpiece, *The Aborigines of Trinidad*, by J. A. Bullbrook, Associate Curator of the Royal Victoria Institute and Museum,
in 1960, representing the results of his excavations in the middens –
which were both refuse dumps and burial grounds – of the Amerindians in Cedros, Palo Seco and Erin. Useful information is also
available from Surinam, not only from archaeological investigations –
a brief account of which is available in English, the work of D. C.
Geijskes – but also from a direct study of living Arawak tribes which
have retreated with the onset of Western civilisation further and
further into the interior of the country. Examples of the arts and
crafts, of the life and work of the Amerindians can be seen in the
Royal Victoria Museum in Trinidad and the Surinam Museum in
Paramaribo.

Except for the Siboneys with their primitive shell culture, ignorant
of stone, pottery and axe blades, and using vessels of shell, the
Amerindian civilisation of Arawaks and Caribs was essentially agricultural, representing an important advance in the scale of civilisation
over the paleolithic period of human history. They cultivated the soil
by constructing round heaps or mounds of earth, firstly to loosen the
soil, secondly to protect the roots against the dry season, and thirdly
for composting with shovelled ashes.

The national food was cassava. The Arawaks developed the tech-
nique of changing the poisonous prussic acid of cassava juice into
a kind of non-poisonous vinegar by cooking it. They called this
cassareep, and the cassareep, together with one of the known spices,
the chili pepper, made possible the pepperpot, the Carib *tomali*, which
stabilised the alimentation in a high degree and made easier the consumption of cassava cakes. The Arawaks further developed the grater

1

for making cassava cakes. In their development of graters, juice squeezers, large flat ovens of coarse clay on which the cassava cakes were baked, as well as in the development of cassareep and the pepperpot, the Arawak culture represented essentially an annex to the Amerindian civilisation of Eastern Venezuela and Guiana.

Our Amerindian ancestors in the West Indies were also familiar with a variety of other crops. One of the most important was maize, from which in certain places a species of beer was brewed. They also knew the sweet potato and a variety of tropical fruits such as the guava, custard apple, mamey apple, papaw, alligator pear, star apple and pineapple. Columbus has stated that he saw beans cultivated in Hispaniola, and the Amerindians knew also, among the spices, cinnamon and wild pimento. They introduced peanuts to the Spaniards, and it would appear that they were eaten regularly with cassava in Hispaniola.

The Amerindians also knew and cultivated two additional crops which facilitated a further development of what we would today call civilised existence. They cultivated cotton, which they used on the one hand for petticoats, and on the other for the manufacture of hammocks for sleeping purposes. Dr Bullbrook found a bone needle and buttons in his Trinidad researches. The Amerindians knew also tobacco which was exceedingly popular among them; possibly in its origin it was connected in some way with religious rites The Arawaks used it both for snuff and for smoking, generally in the form of cigars, though the pipe was not unknown, while in the form of chewing tobacco in rolls it was used as currency by the Caribs.

Fishing played some part in the economy of Amerindian society, and the Amerindians developed the canoe and the pirogue which enabled them to move from island to island. In the sheltered waters of the Gulf of Paria, the canoes appeared even to have cabins for the women. Molluscs or shell fish figured prominently in the Amerindian diet, and particularly the chip-chip, as Dr Bullbrook's investigations of the middens indicate. But bones representing fish and tortoise have also been found. As compared with the shellfish and the fish, bird bones, however, are extremely scarce.

These Amerindians had no knowledge of metals Their tools were of polished stone, bone, shell, coral, or wood – some of their wooden artifacts have been fortunately preserved through accidental burial in the Pitch Lake of Trinidad. They made pottery and wore ornaments. Dr Bullbrook's exhumations of over twenty burials indicate evidence of arthritis and a high incidence of dental caries, but not of rickets. Their age would appear not to have exceeded forty years, and their height no more than five feet seven inches. They seem to have been, however, a people of great physical strength.

The Amerindians had a simple but well-established family life, in which, as in most underdeveloped societies, there appeared to be some sexual differentiation of labour. Possibly for religious motives, Arawak men alone could collect gold. The women prepared the cassava, cared for the poultry, brought water from the river, wove cloth and mats, and shared in the agricultural work using the primitive implement of the Amerindians, *the digging stick.*

It is not too clear whether the Amerindian women of Trinidad and Tobago displayed as much readiness as has been noticed of the Amerindian women in Hispaniola to promiscuity in their sexual relations as some form of welcome to strangers. Nor is it clear whether in Trinidad, as in Hispaniola, there was the same accentuation of the feminine tendency among male Amerindians which has been noted of them in comparison with the Negroes of Africa. And the records do not permit us positively to involve Trinidad in the 470-year old argument as to whether syphilis was an export from the Old World to the West Indies or an importation from the West Indies into Spain and thence into Europe. Dr Bullbrook found evidence of syphilis in his exhumations. What is certain is that syphilis would appear to have been as prevalent in Guiana and Venezuela as in the Greater Antilles and Mexico and that the Arawaks developed a peculiar remedy for the disease.

The Amerindian tribe was governed by a cacique, very much as a father governed his family. If Columbus is to be believed, fighting between two Amerindians was rare, and so was adultery. The only crime punished by the community was theft, for which the punishment on Hispaniola, even where petty thefts were concerned, was death, the culprit being pierced to death with a pole or pointed stick.

The Arawaks were a relatively peaceful people, the Caribs essentially warlike. While both painted their body with roucou, partly no doubt to present a terrifying appearance in time of war, the Caribs were distinguished from the Arawaks in their use of poisoned arrows. The Caribs also have conventionally been described as cannibals.

As far as Trinidad is concerned, there would appear to have been several distinct tribes of Amerindians present in the island towards the end of the 15th century. The Caribs tended to settle for the most part in the North and West, around what is today Port-of-Spain; two of their principal settlements were located in Arima and Mucurapo. The Arawaks seem to have concentrated above all in the south-east, and it is recorded that on one occasion the Arawaks took Tobago from the Caribs.

Dr Bullbrook, however, challenges the view that there were any Caribs in Trinidad. He bases this on the absence of two facts customarily associated with the Caribs. First, he found no evidence of the use of bow and arrow, which, in his view, is confirmed by the relative scarcity of bird bones in the middens. But he admits the possibility that the spines of the sting ray and eagle ray, found in large numbers in the middens, in some cases obviously improved by man, might have been used as arrow or lance heads. In the second place he emphatically denies any evidence of cannibalism in the remnants of the animal foods found in the middens. Not a single human bone was found.

Trinidad's strategic situation, tending to make it a meeting point of different cultures, was apparent even in Amerindian days. Sven Loven, the outstanding authority on the prehistory of the West Indies, has written as follows:

'By the scanty information that we have concerning Trinidad at least one thing is brought out clearly, namely that Trinidad, through the arrival of Carib elements and cultural influences from different directions that never reached the Greater Antilles, had attained a development richer in many respects and visible above all in their warlike culture, than that which must have characterized the forefathers of the Tainos, before, their emigration to the Antilles.'

It is possibly for this reason that Columbus was able to write on his discovery of the island, and at first sight of a group of twenty-four Amerindians in a large canoe, that they were well-proportioned, very graceful in form, tall and lithe in their movements, whiter than any other Indians that he had seen, wearing their hair long and straight and cut in the Spanish style. Their heads were bound with cotton scarves elaborately worked in colours and resembling the Moorish headdress. Some of these scarves were worn round the body and used as a covering instead of trousers.

This was the people who, six years after their discovery in the Greater Antilles, were to be brought by Columbus' third voyage into the whirlpool of modern colonialism.

CHAPTER 2

The Coming of the Spaniards

The discovery of the West Indian islands by Christopher Columbus, acting as agent of the Spanish monarchy, in 1492 and subsequent years was the culmination of a series of dramatic events and changes in the European society in the 15th century.

Behind the voyages of Columbus lay the urge to the East with its fabled stories of gold and spices popularised by the famous travelogues of Marco Polo and Ibn Battuta and the persistent legend of Prester John. The disruption of the conventional Mediterranean-cum-overland route by the Turks, followed by the domination of the Mediterranean by the Italian cities of Venice and Genoa, stimulated the desire to find a westerly route to the East.

The development of nautical technology brought this desire within reach of realisation. New maps of the world and new theories of the nature of the universe exploded ancient beliefs, fallacies and superstitions. The compass and the quadrant had been devised, making possible longer voyages out of the sight of land and outside of sheltered seas. Larger ships had appeared, notably the Venetian galleys; as early as 1417 Chinese junks, of a colossal size for those days, had sailed all the way from China to East African ports.

In the economic sense Europe in 1492 was ready for overseas expansion; it had the experience, the organisation, or to use the contempory vulgarism, the know-how.

Europe in 1492 knew all about colonialism. The Italian republic of Genoa had long before established colonies in the Crimea, the Black Sea and on the coasts of Asia Minor. A Catalan protectorate was established over Tunisia in 1280. The Portuguese had conquered Ceuta in 1415, an inversion of the Moslem conquest of the Iberian Peninsula. Thereafter they had penetrated all along the coast of West Africa until, in 1487, Diaz made his memorable voyage rounding the Cape of Good Hope. The Portuguese were thus set for their long colonial reign in Asia which ended only with their expulsion from Goa by India in 1961.

Europe in 1492 knew, too, about slavery, which was the normal method of production in the medieval colonies of the Levant. Slavery existed also on European soil, in Portugal, Spain, and in southern France, and the African slave trade in its origins was a transport of slaves from Africa to Europe. The slaves were used in agriculture, industry and mining. To such an extent did slavery dominate Portuguese economy before the voyages of Columbus that the Portuguese verb 'to work' became modified to mean 'to work like a Moor'. When the Spaniards enslaved the Amerindians in the West Indies and later introduced Negro slaves from Africa, they were merely continuing

5

in the New World the slavery with which Europe was sufficiently familiar.

The European society of 1492 was also conversant with sugar cultivation and manufacture. Sugar manufacture originated in India, whence it spread to Asia Minor and, through the Arabs, to the Mediterranean. The early literature of India is full of references to sugar – for example, the Ramayana; and a sugar factory and its machines are used to illustrate maxims of Buddhist philosophy. The Law Book of Manu, some two centuries before the Christian era, prescribed corporal punishment for stealing molasses with fasting for three days and nights as penance; a Brahmin was not to be forced to sell sugar; a man caught stealing sugar would be reborn as a flying fox.

With Arab expansion, the art of growing cane and manufacturing sugar spread to Syria, Egypt, Sicily, Cyprus, Spain, Crete, Malta and Rhodes. But the Arab sugar industry was differentiated in one important particular from that of Christian Europe – it was not based on organised slavery.

The European sugar industry in the Mediterranean, developed after Europe's contact with sugar during the Crusades, contained from the outset the germ of the colonial system familiar to all West Indians. It was an industry established in a distant country and financed by local bankers. One of its principal centres was Sicily, where we find the University of Palermo in 1419 studying and advising on irrigation of the cane, and it was dominated by Italian financiers. Another important centre was Cyprus; a 1449 account of the sugar industry of Cyprus anticipates the wealth and prosperity of the early West Indian sugar planters. Large merchant houses in Italy distributed the sugar throughout Europe.

Europe, too, was politically ready for overseas expansion. The European State, with its theories of protection and its grants of charters and monopolies, developed the economic doctrine of the balance of trade and the need for conserving bullion and the precious metals by encouraging exports and either reducing imports of luxury goods or developing its own local production of such luxury goods. The Monarchy, with the aid of the great commercial cities and foot soldiers, had established control of the feudal aristocracy with their mounted armies, and the Nation State had begun to emerge. Generations of war between Christians and non-Christians in the Crusades had developed a militant crusading Church not yet split by schism and not yet reformed into dissenting sects.

Of all the countries of Europe in 1492, apart from Portugal which preceded it, Spain was best fitted, physically and psychologically, for the initiation of overseas colonialism. The heirs of the rival Crowns of Castile and Aragon had brought peace to the country and developed the centralised monarchy, backed by the cities and the lawyers. The expulsion of Jews and Moors demonstrated the Church militant and triumphant. Undoubtedly secure, the Spanish monarchy was ready to

receive Columbus when he arrived with his new theories and his
discovery proposals.

There was nothing strange in the approach by Columbus, an
Italian from Genoa, to the Spanish Monarchy. The Genoese were no
strangers in Spain. From the 12th century they were established in a
quarter in Seville, whence they would be well placed to participate in
Spain's subsequent trade to the West Indies. Convoys of Genoa, as
well as of Venice, Florence and the Kingdom of Naples, called regularly at Spain on their way to England and Flanders.

The Genoese, and the Italians generally, were equally well known
in Portugal. They served as Admirals in the Portuguese navy, and
they served also, like Columbus' father-in-law, in the Portuguese trade
with the Canary Islands. Columbus himself approached, without success, the Portuguese Court, and the great Italian geographer, Paolo
Toscanelli, was consulted by the king of Portugal on Columbus' proposals. These proposals were ultimately rejected by Portugal, either
because it had no faith in Columbus, or because it had evidence –
which Diaz was soon to confirm – that the true route to India was
by way of Africa.

Thus did Columbus turn to Spain and to the service of Spain. In
those days adventure and geographical scholarship knew no national
boundaries. The Cabots, Venetians, served England. Verezzano,
Florentine, served France. Magellan, Portuguese, served Spain.
Hudson, English, served Holland. Columbus was ready to serve either
England or France or Portugal or Spain. Spain accepted his proposals; the others temporised or studied them or rejected them.

The sovereigns of Spain signed the discovery contract with Columbus in 1492 by which they agreed to finance the voyage in return for
royal control of the lands discovered and a high proportion of the
profits of the voyage. This contract opened the door to the introduction of the medieval society into the West Indies, with its grants of
titles and large tracts of land. Columbus was the mouthpiece of the
medieval tradition, which was to be followed in the seventeenth century by French concessions inspired by the feudal system in France
and by the wholesale grants of islands to favourites of the British
Monarchy.

The Spanish Monarchy, after the success of Columbus had been
established, secured a religious title to the entire Western Hemisphere
by the Papal Donation of 1493, ratified by the Treaty of Tordesillas
between Spain and Portugal in 1494. This Treaty was a diplomatic
triumph for Portugal. Spain, led astray by Columbus' delusions,
agreed to rectify the Papal boundary in a way that confirmed to Portugal not only the true route to India but the whole of the South
Atlantic with Brazil.

It was against this background that Columbus set out on his third
voyage on May 30, 1498 and sighted the island, which he christened
Trinidad, at noon on Tuesday, July 31. He touched at a harbour
which he called Point Galera and then sailed westward until he

entered the Gulf of Paria through the entrance which he named the Serpent's Mouth Searching for an exit from the Gulf of Paria in which he sailed north, south and west, he identified the narrowness of the strait separating Venezuela from Trinidad. After running the danger of the furious currents both north and south, he eventually managed to find an exit into the Caribbean Sea which he called the Dragon's Mouth. One can well understand today the difficulties encountered by the sailing ships of Columbus' day in these tricky passages when one reads, in a Dutch report on Trinidad as late as 1637, 139 years after Columbus, that the Spaniards, before going through the Dragon's Mouth, promised a Mass to St Anthony so that he might guard them as they passed.

On this same voyage Columbus is alleged to have sighted Tobago. What is certain is that he did not land in Tobago but proceeded from Trinidad to Hispaniola. Tobago remained therefore virtually isolated and undiscovered, an Amerindian island untouched for many decades by any Europeans, retaining its name, 'Tobaco' (whence the corruption Tobago), signifying the importance of tobacco in the Amerindian economy.

The arrival of the Spaniards in Trinidad entailed the same clash of cultures that had been induced by their arrival in Hispaniola and the other islands of the Greater Antilles. The Spanish conquest of Trinidad represented the victory of armour over roucou paint, of the sword and lance over the bow and poisoned arrow, of horsemen over foot soldiers who had never seen a horse, of a society whose diet was wheat over a society whose diet was cassava.

The inevitable conflict developed, in Trinidad as in Hispaniola before it, between the European desire for surplus production and the subsistence economy of the Amerindians, between the Spanish settlements copied from Spain and the Amerindian village, between the Spanish Viceroy or Governor representative of the royal autocracy and the paternal rule of the cacique, between imported European diseases like smallpox and the tropical diseases like malaria and yellow fever, and between the mining economy based on the Spanish obsession for gold and the agricultural economy of the Amerindians.

In this setting, in this clash of cultures, in this conflict between two different ways of life and two different philosophies of existence, the Spanish conquest of Trinidad, like the Spanish conquest six years before of Hispaniola, and like the Spanish conquest of Mexico and Peru in the 16th century, developed a tremendous irreconcilable contradiction between the greed for wealth and the conversion of the Amerindians, between the lust for gold and the salvation of souls. Trinidad was a part of that internal conflict in Spain itself which could not make up its mind whether the Spaniards should compel the Amerindians to work or should leave them free to be idle if they so chose; and the further conflict, if they were to compel the Amerindians to work without which there could be no gold or no production, how were they to organise this exploitation of Amerindian labour so that the Amerindians should not be decimated by a way of life and by physical exertions to which they were unaccustomed?

These two practical economic questions gave rise to two philosophical conflicts which ran right through the period of Spanish colonialism: the first, what was the nature of the Amerindians? Were they men like other men, capable of living, as the Spaniards were very fond of saying, like rational human beings, or were they an inferior species? And the second, what was the nature of the Spanish title to the West Indies and to America?

Spain's conquest of Trinidad formed a part of this economic and intellectual conflict in the Spanish Empire, and Spanish colonialism in Trinidad developed amidst the reverberations of that conflict as fought out in Spain and America by the four great protagonists.

On the one side was the Roman Catholic theologian, Bartolome de las Casas, who openly and flatly stated that the Amerindians should be allowed to live in peace and that the purpose of the conquest was to convert them to Roman Catholicism. Las Casas was ably supported by the international jurist, Francisco de Vitoria, who attacked the question of Spain's title to the Indies.

On the other side were the conquistadors, Francisco Pizarro, who openly and flatly stated that he had not gone to the Indies to preach the faith to the Amerindians, he had gone to take away their gold, and Hernan Cortes, who openly and flatly stated that he had gone to the Indies to get gold and not to till the soil like a peasant. The conquistadors were ably supported by the international jurist, Gines de Sepulveda, who attacked the capacity of the Amerindians, denied that they were men like other men, and alleged that they were closer to the monkey than they were to man.

This was the background, political, economic and intellectual, to Spanish colonialism in Trinidad.

CHAPTER 3

The Bankruptcy of Spanish Colonialism

Trinidad remained in Spanish hands from July 31, 1498, until it was surrendered by the Spanish Governor to a British naval expedition on February 18, 1797. During these three centuries Spain was able to develop what, more modern examples notwithstanding, has become a byword in the history of colonialism for its inefficiency and incompetence.

Spanish colonialism, in Trinidad and elsewhere, rested on certain well-established principles and well-defined practices.

The first was that the colony existed for the benefit of the Spanish monarchy and for no other reason. The Spanish monarchy, engrossed in its battle for European hegemony, was interested in gold and silver and in very little else.

The second foundation of Spanish colonialism was that the native population, the Amerindians, were to be compelled to work for their Spanish masters, preferably in mines. When the Amerindians were decimated by colonial exploitation, their place was taken by imported African slaves who had the same obligation to work as their Amerindian predecessors.

The third principle of Spanish colonialism was, to borrow the explicit phrase developed subsequently by the French, the Exclusive. This meant that the colony could trade only with the metropolitan country. It could buy only from the metropolitan country and sell only to the metropolitan country, and all commercial relations with foreigners were rigorously prohibited. As refined by the Spaniards, this essential principle of European colonialism throughout the West Indies further required that this import and export trade with the colonies should be concentrated in a single port in Spain – Seville was the port selected – that it should be controlled by a special organisation known as the Casa de Contratacion or House of Trade in Seville, that only such ships as were authorised by the House of Trade should participate in colonial trade, and that the ships engaged in colonial trade should, whether on their outward or inward voyages, proceed in convoys, protected by Spanish galleons against pirates, buccaneers, and rival European countries.

The fourth principle of Spanish colonialism was that the Governor ruled supreme, though he was assisted by a Council of local notables who, like the cities in Spain, had certain well-defined rights and privileges.

And the fifth principle of Spanish colonialism was that it was closely associated with the Church, and that the Church, whether by direct

10

spiritual methods or by its economic activity, shared in the responsibility for civilising the Amerindian or slave population.

Spanish colonialism, with these principles, proved inadequate all over America for the work of developing the colonial areas. But few Spanish colonies suffered as much as Trinidad did from Spanish colonialism.

After the discovery by Columbus in 1498, Trinidad remained almost completely neglected by Spain until in 1530 a Governor was appointed from Puerto Rico by the name of Antonio Sedeno. Little was accomplished in the way of effective possession of Trinidad by Sedeno and thereafter the island lapsed into virtual oblivion until in 1595 a new beneficiary of the Spanish crown arrived as Governor, Antonio de Berrio. Throughout the 17th and 18th centuries Trinidad languished, a Spanish colony in name, a forgotten and underdeveloped island in fact. Governors came and went, but Trinidad continued to languish.

A former British Colonial Governor once complained to an Under-Secretary of State for the Colonies in England of the rubbish sent out by Britain for departmental service in the Crown colonies. The Under-Secretary of State replied: 'It is true that we send out a great deal of rubbish, but it is mostly in the form of Governors.'

Trinidad suffered in this way not only from England but also from Spain. No real progress was made until the last fourteen years of Spanish rule and the régime of the last Spanish Governor, Don Jose Maria Chacon.

Spain experienced two fundamental weaknesses in the implementation of its plans for colonial expansion and of the basic principles underlying Spanish colonialism. The first was its inability to maintain the Exclusive.

Spain lacked the production organisation in Spain either to satisfy colonial import needs or to handle colonial exports. It lacked the ships which had been prescribed as the sole carriers of colonial trade. It lacked the warships to give the prescribed protection to the merchant vessels engaged in colonial trade. Spanish shipping engaged in trade with the New World amounted to between 3,000 and 4,000 tons around 1500. By 1565 this had increased to 15,000 tons. Just before the Spanish Armada of 1588 was defeated by England, the tonnage amounted to between 25,000 and 30,000. At its peak in 1608, the Spanish shipping engaged in trade with the New World amounted to 45,000 tons.

From 1564 two armed fleets were despatched from Spain annually, one to Mexico, the other to Panama. They reassembled at Havana in the following spring for the return voyage. Each fleet consisted of from 20 to 60 sail, with an escort of from two to six warships. The system was supported by cruiser squadrons based at Santo Domingo and Cartagena and protected by such defences as those at Havana. The protection thus afforded was reasonably effective, but the colonials paid a high price for it, in the delay in obtaining metropolitan supplies and in the consequent enhancement of prices.

Spain's second weakness was its inability to provide the manpower needed for its vast colonial dominions which existed not only in the Caribbean but also in all of South America with the exception of Brazil. It had no real surplus population for export, this small country of some eight million people at the end of the 16th century. In this respect Spain was no worse off than its neighbours. If France's population at the end of the 16th century was 16 million, England had only five million, the Netherlands less than three, Portugal one million only. Large scale emigration would have been rigorously opposed. In the European State of that time, soldiers (seamen in the case of islands) ranked next in importance only to bullion.

Neither in fact nor in theory could the New World have been peopled from the Old. Actually, the influx of American treasure into Spain created a tremendous labour shortage and Spain could neither prevent immigration nor her neighbours prevent emigration. In Valencia in 1548 there were 10,000 Frenchmen; hostile Spaniards called them 'fleas living on Spain'. But Spain's population problem where her colonies was concerned was aggravated by her religious exclusivism Spain rigorously prevented all non-Catholics and all heretics from participation in colonial development.

Those Spaniards who did proceed to the Indies went, like Cortes and Pizarro, lured by gold and silver. Spain's overseas revenue increased from 35,000 ducats a year in 1516 to between two and three millions by 1588. The imports of treasure into Spain from the New World, in pesos equal to 42.29 grams of pure silver, were 371,055 in 1503 and 34,428,500 – nearly one hundred times as much – in 1596.

A whole society in miniature accompanied Columbus on his second voyage in 1493. The total of 1,200 persons included soldiers, artisans, farmers, priests. They took with them seeds, tools, animals. The object was not trade but conquest. The goal was a farming and mining colony in Hispaniola producing its own food, paying for the costs of transport by remitting gold, and serving as a base for further explorations.

The dazzling grandeur of the conquests of Mexico and Peru, and the discovery of the silver mines of Potosi in what is today Bolivia, wrecked all this. What impressed was the rebuilding by Cortes of the ancient Aztec capital of Tenochtitlan, which he renamed Mexico City; its population in 1520 was around 100,000, larger than that of Toledo or Seville or any Spanish city in Europe. Pizarro, in his turn, destroyed the ancient Inca capital of Cuzco and built an entirely new capital, Lima, the City of Kings. The land grants in Mexico and Peru corresponded to this viceregal splendour. Cortes arrogated to himself, in Oaxaca Valley in Mexico, a land area comprising officially 23,000 heads of households required to work his lands.

This was what attracted the Spaniards who emigrated – the magnificence of the conquistadors, the wealth of Potosi, the chimera of

El Dorado with its cities whose streets were paved with gold. A benighted, poverty-stricken island like Trinidad could never hope to compete with this.

These two fundamental weaknesses made the Spanish Empire, on paper a formidable proposition and a grandiose achievement, in fact a vast conglomeration of poor, undeveloped and defenceless territories open to any invader with adequate resources in ships and manpower. One early British imperialist, writing from Port-of-Spain in 1611 to the Lord High Treasurer of England as he was engaged in the trade with Trinidad prohibited by Spanish laws, asserted that Spain's force was reputation and its safety opinion. Spain's empire was protected, in other words, by a reputation which was not justified and an opinion of Spanish strength in the colonies which was without foundation.

Thus it was that, a mere century or so after Columbus' memorable voyage, a Spanish ambassador in London could say piteously to the British Government that 'God has committed the Indies to the trust of the Spaniards that all nations might partake of the riches of that new world; it is even necessary that all Europe should contribute towards supplying that vast empire with their manufactures and their merchandises'.

Spain came to depend on a trade system in which she bought her requirements, domestic and overseas, from the rest of Europe and paid for them in treasure from the New World. French vessels dominated the Seville – New World Market Antwerp became the great beneficiary of Spanish trade. The Spaniards in Seville, with their monopoly of colonial trade, became nothing more than commission agents for Genoese, Jewish, Flemish and German business houses.

The whole history of Trinidad under Spanish colonialism demonstrated Spain's inability to organise and develop the colony.

Consider, for example, the operation of the Exclusive in practice.

On January 1, 1593, Antonio de Berrio, in a letter to the Council of the Indies, requested that two ships of 200 tons each should be provided for Trinidad for a period of five years. The ships were not provided.

The people of Trinidad had to live – if not with Spain, then without Spain. If Spanish ships did not arrive with Spanish goods, then, law or no law, they would trade with foreign ships and send their exports elsewhere. Thus it was that the English adventurer referred to above was able to see in the harbour of Port-of-Spain in 1611 fifteen ships, English, French, and Dutch, 'freighting smoke' as he put it, that is to say engaged in the tobacco trade. It is probable that these included the three English ships which, according to the Spanish Ambassador in London, arrived in London later in the year 1611 with Trinidad tobacco, the smallest of them bringing a cargo valued at half a million ducats

If Spanish colonialism was based on the exclusion of foreigners from colonial trade and the restriction of colonial trade to Spaniards and Spanish vessels, the obvious way to stop illegal foreign trade was to provide the essentials for the legal Spanish trade The only remedy that the Spanish Ambassador in London could suggest, however, was that the Governor of Trinidad should be punished, in much the same way as a royal official in Trinidad had two years earlier advised the King of Spain that the fountainhead and author of all the colonial transgressions against the Exclusive was the Governor of Trinidad himself.

It was not the poor Governor's fault. Everybody in Trinidad was a lawbreaker. It was not a question of smuggling. It was an open trade, conducted in broad daylight, in which all participated, men and women, young and old, adults and children.

The Spanish Government had a system whereby an investigation was instituted into the conduct of a colonial Governor at the end of his term. This was called *a residencia*. One Sancho de Alquiza was designated to conduct a *residencia* in Trinidad in 1611. This is the report that he sent to one of the highest colonial courts in the West Indies, the Audiencia of Santo Domingo, on January 13, 1612 from Trinidad:

'I have begun to conduct this residencia and find generally that everyone here is guilty without exception.

'I have not taken action against anyone because they all freely confess their fault and ask for mercy in such a way that I could only pity them and considering what I have learnt in the past three days, I have pardoned these people . . . The petition was in the names of all the vecinos asking mercy for all who, from the highest to the lowest, admitted that they were guilty of trading with the enemy. As the petition was being read, all the women and vecinos fell on their knees in front of my house confessing their fault and asking forgiveness.

'This was very painful and I told them to rise from the ground and consoled them as best I could. I was alone in the Town and the people had done all that they could; to arrest all those guilty was not possible, I had neither the soldiers nor a prison large enough

'I am reporting all this to His Majesty and asking that a general pardon be given to all in this place, otherwise all would have to be punished down to the children of ten years old.'

The bankruptcy of the Exclusive was revealed in all its nakedness. It was universal guilt, guilt without exception. The very basis of Trinidad colonial society was illegality, a complete violation of metropolitan law. The investigator was absolutely powerless. He had no troops, he had no jail. He would have had to arrest the whole population. Thus powerless, he could only recommend a general pardon.

But the very recommendation of a general pardon meant that the illegal trade would continue, since no one in his senses believed that Spain could either produce goods in adequate quantity to render the illegal trade unnecessary or could provide the soldiers who would enforce the metropolitan legislation. It was a typical illustration of the well-known Spanish attitude in the colonies to metropolitan legislation, expressed in the colonial proverb, 'Let it be obeyed but not enforced'.

As for actual remedies to the metropolitan problem, those suggested were absurd in the extreme. As far as the King himself was concerned, all he could propose was that the Armada proceeding to Central America to collect the royal silver should alter its course and proceed to Trinidad to capture, burn or sink the foreign vessels. He thought that a mere two days would be sufficient for this assignment, but warned in the strongest language that the safety of the galleons was not to be delayed.

This was the fountainhead of Spanish colonialism, which passed a law and organised a system, but could not enforce the former or maintain the latter. Its incompetence and inefficiency led to universal disregard of the law and the system. So the solution? Take a little time out and destroy the illegal ships. But what then would happen? Two foreign ships would replace every one that was burnt or sunk And the needs of the population, which had given rise to the illegal trade, would continue to patronise the illegal trade once the galleons had departed.

The Governor of Margarita off the coast of Venezuela, which was part of the entire Province that included Trinidad and Guiana, therefore proposed another solution which was, if possible, even more absurd than the solution proposed by the King Noting that after the visit of the galleons, ten or eleven English and Dutch ships had visited Trinidad, he recommended that the King should prohibit the cultivation of tobacco in Trinidad so that the enemy traders would obtain nothing there, give up the trade, and cease visiting Trinidad. Tobacco was at the time the basis of Trinidad's economy. If ships could not be authorised to go to Trinidad to take its tobacco exports, and if foreign vessels insisted on going to Trinidad to take its tobacco exports, and if foreign vessels insisted on going to Trinidad to buy the tobacco and take it to foreign countries, then the Governor's solution was to destroy the economy of the island in order to maintain an ineffective metropolitan system which the metropolitan country could not implement.

Yet a third absurdity was propounded. A royal official in 1613, in pleading once more with the House of Trade in Seville to send annually to Trinidad two ships of about 200 tons, to bring to Trinidad food and other necessaries and to take in return Trinidad produce, perhaps realising that he was beating his head against a wall of metropolitan indifference and incompetence, had this more to offer:

'The only remedy is to make the Spaniards afraid to trade with the enemy and of dealing with them in the produce of these lands. Any who would thus trade should not be allowed into this island

which has cost our people so much blood and which is so much
wanted by the enemies of our faith.'

And so the dismal story goes on, the story of the colonial struggle
for survival in the face of metropolitan ineptitude. Take, for example,
the year 1653. The people of Trinidad made representations to the
monarchy that it was twenty years since an authorised Spanish vessel
had been sent to Trinidad. They claimed that they were in great want
of clothing and other necessities and that their crops were worthless
as they had no market for them. They petitioned the King therefore
to grant them in perpetuity one authorised ship a year If eternity
was too long, they were ready to compromise on one authorised ship
a year for ten years. The Council of the Indies advised the King that
he should send to Trinidad one authorised ship a year for four years.
What was to happen after the four years? Absolute silence.

But even one authorised ship a year for four years was beyond
the capacity of the Spanish Government. Nine years later, in 1662,
when the Governor of the Province attempted to enforce the Exclusive in Trinidad to forbid trade with a Dutch ship in the harbour of
Port-of-Spain, the Spanish settlers decided that they would welcome
the ship and sent an emissary as their spokesman before the Spanish
authorities in Trinidad. The spokesman urged that the order enforcing
the restriction of trade with the Dutch ship should be set aside on
account of the great poverty of the people of the island. He asserted
that it was more than thirty years since a ship from Spain had arrived
in Trinidad, so that the Spaniards lacked not only clothes but knives,
hatchets, cutlasses and other tools for cultivation. The spokesman
threatened that if the wishes of the inhabitants were not acceded to,
they requested permission to leave Trinidad and serve His Majesty
in some other part of his dominions.

Thus the bankruptcy of the Exclusive was made complete and the
wheel came full circle. Trade only with Spain and not with foreign
countries. But Spain cannot really serve us Then sink the foreign
vessels, destroy the tobacco, banish the lawbreakers. Then permit us
to emigrate. It was the Exclusive with a vengeance. There were only
two alternatives: on the metropolitan side, the Exclusive or banishment; on the colonial side, no Exclusive or emigration.

It was not only that Spain was incapable of developing Trinidad
economically. What aggravated the situation was that Spain was
incapable of defending the colony. Defence involved both a local
militia, a national guard in the territory composed of settlers, and
the military, Spanish troops from Spain. Spain was unable to provide
military reinforcements, whether soldiers or ships or to supply the
necessary white population on which the national guard would have
been based. Thus the history of Trinidad under Spanish colonialism
is a dismal record of reports on its defenceless state, piteous pleas
for help, and inability to defend itself either from local enemies, or
from Carib invaders, or from rival foreign powers.

The most hysterical of all the pleas for help and the most exasperated of all the analyses of Trinidad's defenceless state came from the Governor, Antonio de Berrio, in a letter to the King of Spain on November 24, 1593. The Carib menace was uppermost in his mind. De Berrio had, he said, only 70 men against 6,000 hostile Amerindians. Order Puerto Rico to send 100 of the 400 idle paid soldiers of the King in Puerto Rico to patrol the coast. Order Puerto Rico also to supply 20 quintals of powder, an equal weight of lead, 6 culverins and 50 muskets.

The metropolitan country failed the colony militarily as it failed it economically. A piteous plea to the King of Spain was made by the Cabildo of Trinidad, the assembly representative of the Spaniards presided over by the Governor with little real power, on September 30, 1625. The Cabildo emphasised the general poverty of the place, illustrating it by the thatched building which served as Church because there were no funds to erect a proper structure, and emphasising it by the Cabildo's need to beg for a supply of oil in order to light the building for Church services. According to the Cabildo, there were only 24 Spanish settlers in the whole island, without arms or ammunition, 'completely defenceless against their many enemies'.

If on the economic problem the King's solution was to reduce it to absurdity by ordering the destruction of the foreign vessels, on the defence problem he literally exploded with rage In 1638 the House of Trade emphasised the defenceless state of Trinidad and the impossibility of putting up any resistance to enemy attack. The House of Trade stressed that Trinidad's inability to resist was the result of the metropolitan failure to assist over the years with arms, supplies, clothing, and authorised ships. This was too much for the King who, as the ruler of vast European dominions and a huge transatlantic empire, saw Trinidad in its international context. The royal indignation was expressed in a memorandum to the House of Trade on their representations:

'You make reproaches about the money I have used as though I had taken yours or some private person's without compensation, or as if I had ordered it to be taken for the purpose of making presents to certain people, or as though, if I had not taken it, a great portion of the State of Milan and of Flanders with the whole of Burgundy would not now have been lost; so you may see with what slight reason you advise repeatedly on this matter.

'If the trade would voluntarily pay one per cent, or two, or had been made to pay for the public cause on any of the many occasions on which I have so ordered, there would have been a totally different result, and what has happened and is feared would never have occurred, nor would so tardy a remedy as a visit by the ships of the Brazil route be proposed, for they can only be a very small fleet and cannot arrive for four months, nor can they alone effect

anything of importance against those who may have taken possession over there.

'What might be done is to send direct at once to the Island of
Trinidad, in tenders and caravels or light vessels, 200 men with
munitions and clothing and some provisions for the people there
and a couple of good soldiers as leaders to ensure success, and when
this assistance has been despatched, as I have resolved, this matter
can be discussed to some purpose and on a firm basis.'

The King proposed but the Spanish economy disposed. Spain
simply could not provide the men. Thus it was that the Governor of
Trinidad, writing to the Secretary of the Council of the Indies
in 1671, could state that he had only 80 settlers and 80 'domesticated'
Amerindians insufficient for the defence of the island. He therefore
urged that a garrison of 50 men should be sent to Trinidad. Nothing
was done. Therefore the Cabildo in 1700, warning the King of
mortality among the settlers in the national guard, as a result of which
families were left without support, urged that 25 soldiers should be
transferred to Trinidad from the garrison in Guiana.

Nothing came of this. Nothing. On January 18, 1776, the Governor
of Trinidad reported simply of Trinidad and Margarita: 'There is
nothing of importance about these islands to record.'

Spain's Exclusive policy was bankrupt. Spain's defence policy was
bankrupt Spanish colonialism on its death bed had ended in nothing.

It was therefore totally impossible for Spanish Trinidad to defend
itself from either Caribs, pirates or buccaneers. Sir Walter Raleigh was
able to land with impunity in Trinidad in 1595, to travel up and down
the island, to arrest the Spanish Governor, to burn the capital St
Joseph, and openly to challenge Spanish authority in a speech which,
through an interpreter, he made to the Amerindians, as follows:

'I made them understand that I was a servant of a Queen, who
was the Great Cacique of the North, and a virgin, and had more
Caciques under her than there were trees in their Island, and that
she was an enemy to the Castillians in respect of their tyranny and
oppression, and that she delivered all such nations about her, as
were by them oppressed, and having freed all the coast of the
northern world from their servitude had sent me to free them also,
and withal to defend the country of Guiana from their invasion
and conquest.'

Two years later a fleet of pirogues sailing from Trinidad to Guiana
with stores and men was attacked by a Carib fleet from Dominica
and Grenada and totally destroyed. In 1637 the Dutch attacked St
Joseph so suddenly and unexpectedly that the women in the town
hardly had time to leave their houses and escape into the forest. The
Dutch burnt the town including the Church and nothing escaped.
They then left the island with plans to return.

Eighty years later the Dutch had yielded to the French, and the
Governor of Barbados, writing to the Commissioners of Trade and

Plantations, stated that the French behaved in the West Indies like Lords Paramount and treated the Spaniards as they pleased.

The English contempt for Spain and Spain's title to Trinidad was illustrated by the grant which Charles I made on February 25, 1628, to the Earl of Montgomery of Trinidad, Tobago, Barbados and other islands.

Spain's European rivals simply refused to recognise or admit Spain's claims to a monopoly of the New World and the West Indies. King Francis I of France gave voice to the general view when he said he would like to see the clause in Adam's will which excluded him from a share of the world, and he sent Verezzano, the Florentine in his service, to make discoveries with the instruction: 'God had not created these lands for Spaniards only.' The British Government refused to abide by the Papal Donation. Sir William Cecil asserted to the Spanish Ambassador in London in 1562: 'The Pope had no right to partition the world and to give and take kingdoms to whomsoever he pleased.'

The French and British countered the Spanish monopoly with the doctrine of effective occupation. France, challenging Spain's interpretation of international law, stated boldly:

'In lands which the King of Spain did not possess they ought not to be disturbed, nor in their navigation of the seas, nor would they consent to be deprived of the sea or the sky.'

The British view on effective occupation and on freedom of the seas was even more specific. Queen Elizabeth I expounded it to the Spanish Ambassador in London as follows:

'Her Majesty does not understand why her subjects and those of other Princes are prohibited from the Indies, which she could not persuade herself are the rightful property of Spain by donation of the Pope of Rome, in which she acknowledged no prerogative in matters of this kind, much less authority to bind Princes who owe him no obedience, or to make that new world as it were a fief for the Spaniard and clothe him with possession: and that only on the ground that Spaniards have touched here and there, have erected shelters, have given names to a river or promontory; acts which cannot confer property. So that this donation of alien property (which by essence of law is void), and this imaginary proprietorship, ought not to hinder other princes from carrying on commerce in these regions, and from establishing Colonies where Spaniards are not residing, without the least violation of the law of nations, nations, since prescription without possession is of no avail; nor yet from freely navigating that vast ocean, since the use of the sea and the air is common to all men; further that no right to the ocean can inure to any people or individual since neither nature or any principle of public user admits occupancy of the ocean.'

While the Governments did not feel free to take positive action against Spain, they did nothing to restrain their subjects from doing so. The sixteenth century in particular was the great age of the buccaneers, the foreign captains who waylaid the Spanish treasure fleets, who sacked and plundered the Spanish cities in the New World, who violated the Spanish Exclusive by force of arms. Fleury intercepted the first treasure sent by Cortes from Mexico. Sir Francis Drake plundered Nombre de Dios, the treasure house of the New World. Sir John Hawkins forced the Spaniards in Hispaniola to trade with him. So persistent were the Dutch free traders that the Spanish Governor of Venezuela recommended that they should be kept out of the Spanish colonies by poisoning the salt pans to which they were in the habit of resorting

There was, as the saying went in Europe at the time, no peace below the line. This doctrine was written into the Treaty of Cateau-Combresis in 1559

'West of the prime meridian and south of the Tropic of Cancer . . . violence done by either party to the other side shall not be regarded as in contravention of the treaties.'

Thus did Trinidad and the West Indies live under Spanish colonialism – disregard and violation of metropolitan law in Trinidad itself, disregard and violation of international law in West Indian waters. Spanish colonialism was cradled in illegality, violence and disorder.

No Spanish ships for trade, no Spanish soldiers for defence. And there were no Spanish settlers for economic development. Spain was simply unable to provide the manpower. The early attempts of Columbus in Hispaniola to attract small white settlers, either by liberal grants of land or other concessions or by metropolitan remission of penalties for various crimes, had been a failure.

Two decades later Las Casas failed in his attempt to set up a colony of white Spanish farmers in Venezuela. Privileges and liberties were granted to Spanish farmers to go to the Indies to develop the land, thus providing the opportunity for improvement to those who lived in poverty in Spain, and for occupation of the discovered territories in order to prevent foreign invasion. The inducements offered by the King were free passage to the New World, free medical care and medicines, free land and animals, exemption from taxes for twenty years except the tithe for the Church, assistance in the building of their new homes, and prizes to farmers who produced the first dozen pounds of silk, cloves, ginger, cinnamon or other spices, and the first hundredweight of rice or of olive oil. Las Casas went up and down Spain making speeches, seeking to recruit workers for America. He failed dismally, running into the hostility of the feudal lords who wanted to preserve their own labour supply, and he dropped the project quietly in April 1519.

It was therefore never likely that there would be any large-scale migration of Spaniards to Trinidad. But Spain's basic inability to provide manpower, or ships, or soldiers was unnecessarily aggravated by its exclusive policy in respect of population. In 1630, for example, the King protested to the Governor of Trinidad against the concessions granted to certain Portuguese who had arrived in Trinidad without his permission, who had been allowed to settle there, and who had been granted land and Amerindian workers to cultivate the land. The King ordered that these Portuguese should be required to leave or be ejected by force, and instructed the Governor to grant in future no lands to Portuguese without his expressed permission. If ever a colonial system was mad, the Spanish colonial system was mad.

Spain was interested not in Trinidad but in gold. If Trinidad had gold, then Spain would show an interest in Trinidad. Gold was a positive obsession with King Ferdinand who had signed the contract with Columbus, and on February 23, 1512, he wrote to the authorities in Puerto Rico, under which jurisdiction Trinidad then fell, as follows:

'It is of importance to me to know definitely whether or not there is gold in Trinidad as you were told by the five Indians who came to your ship when you anchored there; you should proceed to find out all you can about this and determine the truth of this statement.'

There was really no gold in Trinidad, notwithstanding early reports that gold had been found in some of the rivers. There being no gold, Spain was not impressed, and Spaniards were not interested Trinidad's importance, and lack of importance, therefore revolved around El Dorado, the rumour of gold in Guiana. It proved as impossible to keep Spaniards in Trinidad with the lure of El Dorado as it had proved to keep them in Hispaniola because of the gold and silver of Mexico and Peru. As early as 1530, the Governor of Puerto Rico had reported that the prayer on the lips of every Spaniard on that island was 'May God take me to Peru'.

Similarly, de Berrio's principal interest in his settlement in Trinidad in 1592 was that it would be a base from which to enter and settle El Dorado. Writing to the Council of the Indies on January 1, 1593, he stated that 'if God aids me to settle Guiana, Trinidad will be the richest trade centre of the Indies', for if Guiana was one-twentieth of what it was supposed to be, it would be richer than Peru.

This is the explanation of the metropolitan failure to send ships, the metropolitan failure to send soldiers, the unwillingness of Spaniards to settle in Trinidad. The Spanish conquest of Trinidad was a conquest in name only, and the prospects of the island under Spanish colonialism, never bright as we have indicated, were ruined by the lust for gold in El Dorado. This is what the Governor of Sante Fe wrote to the King of Spain about Trinidad on January 20, 1608:

'We have heard how weak is the foundation of that conquest which is only sustained by vanity and with vanity.'

'Let His Majesty be pleased to consider that though it is not carried on (and even because it is not carried on) at the expense of the Royal Treasury, it touches your most Christian conscience nearer, for the price of pursuing the chimera of this discovery is the free and licentious lives led by the soldiers who without spiritual and temporal leading run headlong into every kind of vice.

'From that place which is the chosen resort of secular criminals, irregular priests and apostate friars and in general a seminary of rascals, nothing is to be expected except some seditious scandal when they despair of finding what they seek or tire of the delay in its discovery.'

Trinidad, such as it was, underpopulated, defenceless, victim of metropolitan indifference, turned to tobacco and the tobacco trade with foreigners. By 1718, however, the first real indication of Trinidad's future place in the world economy emerged Cocoa trees were found in Trinidad, and thereafter the cocoa economy developed slowly until collapse came in 1733. One of the clergymen in Trinidad blamed the collapse on the refusal of the Spanish planters to pay the tithes to the Church. The Abbé Raynal, the well-known French authority on the West Indies, writing many years after the event, attributed the failure of the cocoa crop to the north winds More plausible reasons have been advanced for the collapse. One, the severe drought in that year; two, that the cocoa variety then planted, whilst of the highest quality, was far more tender and less hardy than the forastero variety from Brazil generally cultivated after 1756 Whatever the cause, the effects of the failure of the cocoa crop were ruinous to Trinidad. Many of its inhabitants emigrated, and the King was forced to remit for several years the annual tribute exacted from the Amerindian workers.

The Amerindians constituted the labour supply of the Spaniards. This was in accordance with the Spanish policy in conquered territories in assigning a stipulated number of Amerindians to each Spaniard for the double purpose of providing labour for the Spaniards and of being instructed in the principles and the teachings of the Roman Catholic faith. In other parts of the West Indies and South America the secular purpose had superseded the religious, and it was this that formed the foundation of the unrelenting struggle of Las Casas for some sixty years for justice for the Amerindians and for taking them out of the care of secular landlords and putting them under the jurisdiction of the Church. Las Casas had been able, by the promulgation of the New Laws in 1542, to secure recognition of the principle that the Amerindians were a free people, were not to be enslaved, were to be paid prescribed wages, and were not to be compelled to work beyond prescribed hours One result of this was a growing conflict between landlords and Church which spread to Trinidad, where it was claimed that the Church had too much economic influence and that, by the labour of Amerindians on Church estates, the Church was in competition with the secular planters.

In Trinidad, however, Spanish colonialism began with the enslavement, direct or indirect, openly avowed or casuistically concealed, of the Amerindians and even of a slave trade in Amerindians. From both ends of the archipelago, from the Bahamas in the northwest and Trinidad in the southeast, the policy developed of transporting what the Spaniards called useless Amerindians to the mines of Hispaniola Las Casas has recorded that this slave trade reached such alarming proportions that it was possible for a ship to sail from the Bahamas to Hispaniola being guided solely by the trail of dead Amerindians thrown overboard.

It was against this background that the King of Spain, on June 15, 1510, in a letter to Columbus' son and successor Don Diego Columbus, placed a ban on the Amerindian slave trade from Trinidad The ban was neither humanitarian in its motives nor permanent in its intention. The King was of the opinion that Spanish interests would be better served at that time by the ban as there were other islands much nearer Hispaniola from which Amerindian slaves could be carried, whilst he was also interested in preserving the Amerindian population in the islands and along the coast of the mainland where the pearl fishery seemed to be promising. He was also concerned, in a letter about a year later, with the possibility that there was gold in Trinidad, because, if so, it would be better to utilise the Amerindians in their native locality than to transport them to another place.

Thus there was no real prohibition of the enslavement of the Amerindians in Trinidad. Sedeno in 1535 planned, as part of his development of the fishing industry in Trinidad, to capture some Amerindians in Trinidad and send them to Cubagua to be sold as slaves, fishing nets being bought with the proceeds. The royal officials at Cubagua, however, refused to authorise such transactions. And the King himself, in 1511, specifically permitted both the slave trade and slavery in respect of Caribs, on the ground that the Caribs refused to allow Christians to enter the islands they inhabited and in the process of resistance had killed several Christians. He therefore specifically authorised war against the Caribs of Trinidad, Dominica, Martinique, St Lucia, St Vincent, Tobago, Barbados and other islands, and their enslavement and transport to any other place on the one condition that they were not sold outside of the West Indies. This was an open invitation to any and everybody to capture Amerindians, all and sundry, and merely plead afterwards that they were Caribs.

In the course of his long career as protector of the Amerindians, Las Casas fought many legal battles, engaged in many polemics and much disputation, wrote innumerable books and travelled up and down the West Indies and the north coast of South America and Central America. One of his greatest polemical achievements, which laid the basis of either his fame (to some) or his infamy (to others) in the

B

outside world depending on the point of view, was his *Very Brief Narrative of the Destruction of the Indies*, published in 1559. It was at one and the same time an impassioned defence of the Amerindians and a tremendous indictment of his Spanish contemporaries. This world-famous document includes a section dealing with the Spanish attitude to the treatment of the Amerindians in Trinidad, which is reproduced here as indicating one redeemable feature in the history of the inefficiency and ineptitude of Spanish colonialism:

'In the island of Trinidad which is much larger than that of Sicily and more beautiful and which is linked to the mainland by the Province of Paria, the Indians are as good and kind as any to be found in all the Indies.

'A marauder went there in the year 1516 with some 60 or 70 other villains who represented to the Indians that they had come to settle there and live in the Island with them. The Indians received them as if they were their friends and relatives showing every mark of respect and affection, supplying them every day with food, the best that could be got. It is the generous custom of all the Indians in the New World to give liberally to meet the needs of the Spaniards from whatever they may have.

'These men began to make a large house of wood in which they could all live as this was what they had alleged they had come to do. When the time came to apply palm leaves to the supports and some way up the walls had been covered so that those without could not see within, the Spaniards said that they wanted to finish the house quickly and so put many Indians inside to help while the Spaniards went outside and drew their swords to prevent any Indians leaving. Then they began to threaten the defenceless Indians with death should they attempt to escape. They bound the Indians as prisoners while some, forcing their way out, were cut to pieces by the Spaniards.

'Some who had managed to escape though wounded, and others from the pueblo who had not entered the house, seized their bows and arrows and retired to another building in the pueblo to defend themselves. When one or two hundred of the Indians were inside holding the gate, the Spaniards set fire to the house and burnt them all alive. With the prisoners who amounted to about 180–200 men whom they had been able to catch, they returned to their ship and set sail for the Island of San Juan (Puerto Rico) where they sold half of them for slaves; thence they went to Hispaniola where they sold the remaining half of the Indians.

'Having reprimanded the Captain for this dastardly treachery and evil attack when I met him at this time in the said Island of San Juan, he replied: "I did, Sir, what I was ordered; those who sent me instructed me to take them how I could either by war or in peace." He also told me that in all his life he had never found Indians so kind and ready with assistance as those in the Island of Trinidad. I repeat this to emphasise the importance of his confession and to show how great was his sin.

'Such things have often been done on the mainland repeatedly, the Indians being taken and enslaved without restriction. Should such things be allowed to continue and should Indians taken in this way be sold as slaves?'

The best commentary on the strictures of Las Casas is provided by the story of the Amerindian uprising in Trinidad nearly a century and a half later. Trinidad, it is true, had no such outstanding Amerindian rebel chieftain as Hatuey in Cuba, who went philosophically to the stake refusing to become a Christian because, if he went to Heaven, he might find Spaniards there. Trinidad had no such nationalist leader as Enrique who kept Spanish Hispaniola in a state of permanent revolution, and whose exploits have been transmitted to posterity by the Dominican historical novel, *Enriquillo*, by Manuel de J. Galvan. There was no ancient established dynasty in Trinidad to serve as the focus of a nationalist revolt against the conquerors which would have caused the Spaniards to decapitate it as the Viceroy Toledo deliberately decided in respect of the execution of the last recognised Inca prince of Peru, Tupac Amaru.

On December 1, 1699, the Amerindians concentrated in one of several Missions that Spanish priests had set up over the island, the Mission of San Francisco de los Arenales, rose in revolt against Church and State. This is what is known as the Arena Massacre in Trinidad. They killed Capuchin Friars in charge of the Mission where they were building a new Church, one of them at the altar itself, desecrated the statues and the ornaments of the Church, and burnt the entire Mission to the ground. They then proceeded to set an ambush for the Governor and his retinue who were at the time expected on an official visit to the Mission. All but one of the Governor's party died in the ambush, and he himself died from arrow wounds three days later. The Amerindian rebels buried the bodies of the priests hurriedly, threw the Governor's body into the river, and immediately headed for the sea coast in anticipation of retaliation. The Spaniards caught up with them in the Cocal, whence they drove them to Point Galera. Surrounded by water and by their enemies on land, caught as it were between the devil and the deep blue sea, many of them preferred to die rather than to submit to capture. Women pulled their children from their breasts, threw them and their older children into the sea, and then themselves followed with many of the menfolk.

Several were taken prisoner and brought to St Joseph where they were tortured Many ringleaders were hanged and 61 others shot. Here is the sentence imposed by one of the tribunals:

'That these twenty-two above indicated criminals and all the others of the said mission who might be caught be dragged along the public streets of this town, with a crier before them, publishing

their crimes, and after that be hung, until they necessarily die, and
after their hands and heads shall be cut off and exposed and nailed
in the places where they committed and executed their crime, and
their bodies shall be cut in pieces and put along the roads for their
punishment, and good example for the public vengeance, because
so orders the King our Lord by his royal laws '

It was not until April 15, 1701, with the appointment of a new
Governor, that the Spaniards set out to recover the bodies of the
murdered priests. On that day the Governor, the clergy, and many
of the principal inhabitants met at San Francisco de los Arenales
carrying coffins with them. The story of this episode is quoted from
the account written by the official historian of the Capuchins, Fr.
Mateo de Anguiano, in 1704:

'They arrived at the place and found it all deserted and waste.
They went all over the ground finding signs of all that had
happened and with the assistance of witnesses established the sites
where each had been killed They found with surprise and astonish-
ment that the blood shed had remained fresh and red after so long
a time just as if it had recently been shed

'This was a wonderful occurrence but they found an even greater
when they arrived at the foundations of the Church. They had expected to find only the bones but they found the whole bodies without a single sign of corruption or any odour, as though they had
just been killed. More miraculous still when they began to move
the bodies, fresh blood began to ooze from all the wounds.
Astonished at these marvels, they all gave thanks to God, placed
the bodies in the coffins and with joy and satisfaction returned to
the town.

'The bodies were taken to the principal Church and for nine days
remained lying there in state where they provided to the Christian
Piety of the faithful of this Island an exceptional opportunity of
praising God. During this Novena various addresses on their virtues
and martyrdom were delivered in which the fervour of the orators
moved their hearers to tears now of joy and now of compassion.
During all this time there was no change of any kind in the bodies
which retained all their freshness as before.'

There is an interesting sequel to the Massacre. In 1885 a Dominican Missionary, Fr. Cothonay, claimed to have discovered, somewhere in the neighbourhood of Tamana, the site on which had stood
the Mission of San Francisco de los Arenales. After a long journey
through the forest leading out of Tumpuna with their giant hard-
wood trees and what he described as their 'incomparable fields of
green with festoons of blossoming vines (which) linked them one to
another', he was brought to a site where, he claimed, 'bits of bottles
and broken glass afforded living witnesses of civilisation in the heart
of so great a forest . . sufficient proof that I was indeed on the spot

hallowed by the blood of martyrs'. Fr. Cothonay took away a few
pieces of the perfumed resin from the aromatic trees which surrounded
the place to keep them as relics and as substitutes for the bones of
the martyrs, while on the site of the old Church pointed out by the
Amerindian guide, he gathered three species of orchids which he
planted near his cell in Port-of-Spain in memory of the massacre of
San Francisco de los Arenales. Fr. Cothonay claimed that the final
proof that he had indeed found the site of the massacre was the
various reports of traditions among the Amerindians that each year
on Holy Thursday and Good Friday remarkable things happened
in the deserted spot and that more than one person claimed to have
heard voices talking and singing including the accents of a priest saying Mass and the murmur of people praying aloud.

One result of the Arena Massacre was the Royal Decree sent to
the governor of Trinidad in 1716 regarding the treatment of the
Amerindians. Emphasising an earlier decision to take away all
Amerindian workers from the settlers and concentrate them in his
Royal estate in the interests of their spiritual welfare, the King commanded that any settler who ill-treated his Amerindian workers, who
had in any way tolerated or committed excessive wrongs against these
workers, should be deprived of them. Any Amerindian who was converted to Roman Catholicism should be exempted from paying tribute
of any kind for twenty years from the day he was baptised, and under
no circumstances was he to be required to labour on estates if he did
not wish to do so.

What then? No ships, no soldiers, no tobacco, no white settlers –
no labour as well? Faced with a similar situation the Royal officials
and planters and clergy in Hispaniola and other West Indian islands
called for the substitution of African slaves for Amerindian labour.
Even Las Casas himself fell for the trap, though, unlike the others,
he later repented openly and acknowledged his error.

The first signs of a similar policy in Trinidad came with the report
from de Berrio to the Council of the Indies on January 15, 1593. Re-
minding the Council that he had a licence to introduce 500 African
slaves into Trinidad free from all duties, he indicated his desire to
associate with a trader who was not a buccaneer to bring in for barter
hatchets, billhooks, knives, amber and glass beads, needles, cloaks,
mirrors large and small – precisely the type of cargo which dominated
the African slave trade in later years and which came to be lumped
together under the general French term *pacotille*, a word still used
in Trinidad to denote baubles and objects of no value surrendered
in exchange for something very valuable.

In 1618, with the first report of the discovery of cocoa, the warning note was sounded that Trinidad would go the way of other West
Indian islands. It was suggested that in order to develop the cocoa
industry, 300 'pieces of slaves' should be sent to Trinidad, of whom
two-thirds should be men and one-third women.

This until 1777, was Trinidad under Spanish colonialism – poor,

undeveloped, a showpiece of metropolitan incompetence and indifference. The Spanish capital, St Joseph, was the symbol of this
neglect and apathy. It boasted in 1772 of a population of 326
Spaniards and 417 Amerindians. Its houses were mud huts with
thatched roofs. Its Governor, part of the metropolitan rubbish exported to the colonies, was thus described in 1609, possibly by an
enemy:

'He acts without any idea of Christianity or consideration that
he is a servant of our Majesty but as an absolute King and Lord
of that country. Neither the law of God nor the law of man
is regarded in that country, but only that of his own will and
pleasure, which he does not exercise in anything which tends to
Christian virtue, just like an infidel and a savage.'

The Governor was associated in the government of the island with
a Cabildo which had no real powers. The Spanish Government in
Trinidad, including Governor and Cabildo, and with the metropolitan
country in the background, is immortalised in the following extract
from the Archives of the Cabildo for April 28, 1757:

'Read a letter from His Excellency the Governor, directing the
Board to proceed immediately to arrange and put in proper order
the papers of the Cabildo which are in a very confused state; to
take an inventory of the same and to order a press to be made with
two keys to keep the papers in safety; to buy a decent book,
properly bound, to enter the Minutes of the Board; to proceed
without delay to build a Town Hall which had been begun and
abandoned; to cause the vacant lots and streets of St Joseph to be
cleared of the bush which covers them and to have the holes and
ditches in the streets filled up; to give proper orders to have the
roads and principally the avenues of the town cleared of woods and
thickets; to regulate the pieces of articles of provisions which are
produced in the Island by making a proper tariff . . . etc.
'The Cabildo in their reply to the Governor represented the
impossibility of carrying these orders into execution considering
the very small number of inhabitants and their extreme poverty;
the total want of money; the want of cattle and of all sorts
of provisions; that the inhabitants feed themselves and their families
with what little they can get personally in the woods and the sea
and that many days they return to their homes without anything
to eat which has induced many to leave the Island; that their occupation of weeding their little plantations takes up all their time;
that they are constantly employed in mounting guard at the mouth
of the Caroni (there being ten soldiers in the Island) and doing other
public services to the detriment and often to the total loss of their
gardens; that if forced to perform other works they would leave
the Island and that if all the inhabitants together were put to work
at repairing the holes and ditches of the town they could not finish

the work in one year; and lastly that they have no tools nor are there any to be had in the Island, and that even if there were, they have not the means to purchase them.

'Notwithstanding all these obstacles, orders will be given to oblige Pedro Bontur, the only carpenter in the island, to make the press for the Archives and to receive payment in provisions as they can be collected from the inhabitants on whom a contribution will be laid to that effect; but His Excellency the Governor must provide the boards (the Cabildo knowing no one in the Island who has them or can make them) and procure from the Main when an opportunity offers, the locks and hinges for the same, nothing of the kind being to be found here; that orders will be given to arrange the papers of the Cabildo in proper order and that the book will be made when they can get the paper, there not being a single sheet amongst all the members of the Cabildo, &c.'

This was the unrelieved dismalness of the Trinidad scene from 1498. By itself Spain was impotent Africa and France came to the rescue and changed the whole course of the history of Trinidad.

CHAPTER 4

Africa to the Rescue

Who were these Africans? They were dragged by the millions from their native land in Africa to the Western Hemisphere. What began as a mere trickle in 1441, with twelve African slaves captured by the Portuguese and taken to Portugal, became a roaring torrent in the 18th and 19th centuries, and one estimate, almost certainly on the conservative side, is that the slave trade cost Africa at least 50,000,000 souls. Africans became important elements in the population in all the Caribbean countries, in Brazil, and in the United States of America. They constituted also an important element in the population of Trinidad and Tobago, and were automatically resorted to, as in other parts of the Spanish dominions, as soon as the decimation of the Amerindians by the Spanish conquest was recognised. It would therefore be in any case important to identify this new addition to the population of Trinidad and Tobago. It is all the more important today because of the historical lie of African inferiority.

The first and one of the most important of the strictures on the inferiority of African Negroes was expressed by the celebrated British philosopher, David Hume, in his essay 'Of National Characters' written in 1753. This reads as follows:

'I am apt to suspect the Negroes to be naturally inferior to the Whites There scarcely ever was a civilised nation of that complexion, nor ever any individual, eminent either in action or speculation. No ingenious manufactures among them, no arts, no sciences. On the other hand, the most rude and barbarous of the Whites, such as the ancient Germans, the present Tartars, have still something eminent about them in their valour, form of government, or some other particular. Such a uniform and constant difference could not happen, in so many countries and ages, if nature had not made an original distribution between these breeds of men. Not to mention our colonies, there are Negro slaves dispersed all over Europe, of whom none ever discovered any symptoms of ingenuity; though low people, without education, will start up amongst us, and distinguish themselves in every profession. In Jamaica, indeed, they talk of one Negro (Francis Williams) as a man of parts and learning; but it is likely he is admired for slender accomplishments, like a parrot who speaks a few words plainly.'

Hume was writing from England, and he knew nothing of the plantation system in the West Indies. But if this could have been said by a British philosopher, the father of scepticism, one could imagine what would be said by British planters on the slave plantations, surrounded by hundreds of Negro slaves of whom they lived in mortal dread. A Jamaican planter, Edward Long, who wrote a history of Jamaica in 1774, concluded that Negroes are 'a different species of the same genus', equal in intellectual faculties to the orang-outang, which, he claimed, has in form a much nearer resemblance to the Negro than the Negro bears to the white man.

Thomas Jefferson, the second President of the United States of America, was in a little difficulty to reconcile his views of a statesman on the natural rights of man with his interest as a Virginian planter. The contradiction reflected itself in the following views on the inferiority of Negroes:

'The opinion that they are inferior in the faculties of reason and imagination must be hazarded with great diffidence. To justify a general conclusion requires many observations, even where the subject may be submitted to the anatomical knife, to optical glasses, to analysis by fire or by solvents. How much more then where it is a faculty, not a substance, we are examining; where it eludes the research of all the senses; where the conditions of its existence are various and variously combined; where the effects of those which are present or absent bid defiance to calculation; let me add too, as a circumstance of great tenderness, where our conclusion would degrade a whole race of men from the rank in the scale of beings which their Creator may perhaps have given them. To our reproach it must be said, that though for a century and a half we have had under our eyes the races of black and of red men, they have never yet been viewed by us as subjects of natural history. I advance it, therefore, as a suspicion only, that the blacks, whether originally a distinct race, or made distinct by time and circumstances, are inferior to the whites in the endowments both of body and mind.'

The depreciation and disparagement passed on into the period after emancipation. A quarter of a century after emancipation by Britain, Anthony Trollope, the distinguished English novelist, of whom we shall have more to say later, paid a visit to the West Indies, as a result of which he wrote of the emancipated Negro of Jamaica:

'But yet he has made no approach to the civilisation of his white fellow creatures, whom he imitates as a monkey does a man . . . he is idle, unambitious as to worldly position, sensual, and content with little. Intellectually, he is apparently capable of but little sustained effort; but, singularly enough, here he is ambitious. He burns to be regarded as a scholar, puzzles himself with fine words, addicts himself to religion for the sake of appearance, and delights in aping the little graces of civilisation. He despises himself thoroughly, and would probably be content to starve for a month if he could appear as a white man for a day; but yet he delights in the signs of respect paid to him, black man as he is, and is always thinking of his own dignity. If you want to win his heart for an hour, call him a gentleman; but if you want to reduce him to a despairing obedience, tell him that he is a filthy nigger, assure him that his father and mother had tails like monkeys, and forbid him to think that he can have a soul like a white man . . . I do not think that education has as yet done much for the black man in the Western world He can always observe, and often read; but he can seldom reason. I do not mean to assert that he is absolutely without mental power, as the calf is. He does draw conclusions, but he carries them only a short way . . .'

A little more than a quarter of a century later another distinguished English intellectual, this time the Professor of Modern History at Oxford, James Anthony Froude, of whom we shall have very much to say later, visited the West Indies. By this time, half a century after emancipation, one would have imagined that the metropolitan government would have had ample time to remedy the 'defects of character' of the emancipated African. Addressing himself also to this question which for over three centuries had been bothering the minds of Europeans, the question of Negro inferiority, Froude offered this contribution to the discussion:

'The West Indian Negro is conscious of his own defects, and responds more willingly than most to a guiding hand He is faithful and affectionate to those who are just and kind to him, and with a century or two of wise administration he might prove that his inferiority is not inherent, and that with the same chances as the white he may rise to the same level . . . The poor black was a faithful servant as long as he was a slave. As a free man he is conscious of his inferiority at the bottom of his heart, and would attach himself to a rational white employer with at least as much fidelity as a spaniel. Like the spaniel, too, if he is denied the chance of developing under guidance the better qualities which are in him, he will drift back into a mangy cur.'

So there we were. In Trinidad, and in the other parts of the Spanish West Indies, the conquest had decimated the Amerindian population, whom the jurist Sepulveda had contemptuously dismissed as being closer to the monkey than to man. So the Spaniards and other Europeans after them, promptly proceeded to introduce, as a substitute for Amerindian labour, the labour of slaves from Africa whom they regarded as closer to the monkey than to man, so much closer in fact that fifty years after the abolition of slavery they were still closer to the monkey than to man.

This was obviously an extravaganza. But the more fundamental question arises, why the absurdity?

The explanation is, not that the Africans had no civilisation and knew nothing of manufactures, arts and sciences, even if this could properly constitute the justification of their enslavement. It was precisely the opposite, that the Africans *were* civilised, as the standard of medieval civilisation went, but that, since they, like the less developed Amerindians in the West Indies, could not withstand the onslaught of superior weapons and superior technology, one could only justify the enslavement of civilised men by the alibi that they were not men at all but were at the level of brutes in the order of creation.

Within the last two or three years a most remarkable condensation and collation, in an easy popular style, of the vast mass of archaeological and historical research on the Continent of Africa has been made available through the pen of Mr Basil Davidson. His two books, *Old Africa Rediscovered* and *Black Mother*, are sufficient refutation of the indictment drawn up against the whole people of Africa for some four centuries.

Archaeological research in Ethiopia, Egypt, Kenya, Rhodesia, the Sudan and West Africa has brought to light a most astonishing civilisation in Africa going right down from the ancient world to the 16th century We know today, what possibly David Hume and Thomas Jefferson and Anthony Trollope and James Anthony Froude did not know, safely ensconced as they were in the superiority of imperialism, that metallurgy was highly developed and spread all over Africa to the point where the blacksmiths were often treated as a social privileged caste; Davidson describes the ruins of the ancient city of Meroe in Egypt, the Birmingham of Ancient Africa, as among the great monuments of the ancient world, their history being an important part of the history of man. We know today, from the great number of specimens of the Nok Figurine Cult, that more than 2,000 years ago people on the Nigerian plateau were making fine heads in terracotta in great abundance We know today from the ruins at Engaruka in Kenya discovered in 1935 that the people of Kenya had been able to develop, some three hundred years ago, a city of some 7,000 well-built houses, with a population estimated at between 30,000 to 40,000 with well-made stone walls, terraces, and other works associated with cultivation and irrigation.

And we know today, from the archaeological researches of Dr Gertrude Caton-Thompson among the enormous ruins of Zimbabwe in what is now Rhodesia, whose competence for self-government is being questioned, that African architects were able to build huge military and religious structures that compare with the best in ancient Athens. So explosive were the political and racialist implications of this discovery that it was for long concealed; when it was eventually reported, it was attributed to the influence of the Orient or Europe or Phoenicia.

The best indication of the unwillingness of Europeans to accept as African the work of Africa because this would have contradicted the conventional rationalisation expressed in Hume's dictum that Africans had no arts and no sciences, was the enormous discovery of the masterpieces of Benin brought back from an expedition in 1897. These famous Benin Bronzes, from what is today Southern

Nigeria, are now accepted as entirely African, indicative of the maturity of the iron age in Africa. They were at first regarded, however, as of Greek origin or even as products of the European Renaissance, and one well-known British imperialist attributed them to the inspiration of the Portuguese. They stand in the British Museum in London, together with the famous Golden Death Mask of an Ashanti King in the Wallace collection, as living proof of the capacity of these Africans defamed by Hume and Jefferson and Trollope and Froude and degraded by centuries of plantation slavery.

In addition to the archaeological evidence, there is the historical data which has become available in increasing quantities in recent years and which modern progressive thinking has been more and more willing to bring into the open. We have available today a number of Arabic manuscripts and records of Africa. There is an account of East Africa in 947 by El Mas'Udi and Edrisi's geography in 1154 We have El Bekri's account of Ghana contemporary with the Norman Conquest of England. We have the accounts of that inveterate traveller in Asia and in Africa, Ibn Battuta. We have the Tarikh es Sudan of Abderrahman es Sadi, a chronicle and description of Timbuktu around 1655. We have another work, written also in Arabic, largely on account of the ancient kingdom of Songhay, the Tarikh el Fettach of Mahmoud Kati, a learned Negro citizen of Timbuktu. We have also the well-known description of Africa in 1526 by a converted Moor, Leo Africanus, the protégé of Pope Leo X. There are also the works of the more modern writers, like the traveller Mungo Park, Heinrich Barth in the middle of the 19th century who drew on the Muslim records, and in the early 20th century the greatest of all students of African civilisation, Leo Frobenius.

The archaeological evidence and the historical data combine to give us an astonishing picture of these ancient African cultures, which is only confirmed by observations and accounts of the early Portuguese conquerors in West Africa, especially in the Congo.

We know today of the great West African Empires, first the Kingdom of Ghana, secondly, the Empire of Mali, the Mandingo State that followed Ghana, thirdly the Songhay Empire which succeeded Mali. The King of Ghana in 1067, Tenkamenin, was described as master of a great Empire and of a power just as formidable, who could put 200,000 warriors in the field, more than 40,000 of them armed with bows and arrows Ibn Battuta was able to write of the Mandingo State of Mali: 'One has the impression that Mandingo was a real state whose organisation and civilisation could be compared with those of the Musselman kingdoms or indeed the Christian kingdoms of the same epoch' Timbuktu, for so long a name of reproach, was one of the great cities of learning in the world in the 14th century, famous for its scholars and its books and its Sankure mosque. 'Let them go and do business with the King of Timbuktu and Mali', was the advice of Ramusio, Secretary to the Doge of Venice, to the merchants of Italy in 1563. Askia the Great ascended the Songhay throne in 1493, shortly after Columbus discovered the West Indies. He reigned for 19 years, ruler of a vast central state in which the city of Gao was, for learning, for trade and government, what Timbuktu was to Mali. As Leo Africanus wrote of the city, 'It is a wonder to see what plenty of merchandise is daily brought hither, and how costly and sumptuous all things be.'

These accounts, contemporary with the great age of African civilisation, were confirmed by early Portuguese invaders. An Italian priest in 1687, Father Cavazzi, had this complaint to make of the states of the Congo:

> 'With nauseating presumption, these nations think themselves the foremost men in the world, and nothing will persuade them to the contrary. Never having been outside of Africa they imagine that Africa is not only the greatest part of the world, but also the happiest and most agreeable. Similar opinions are held by the king himself but in a manner still more remarkable. For he is persuaded that there is no other monarch in the world who is his equal, or exceeds him in power or the abundance of wealth '

What destroyed this civilisation was the European slave trade. The Europeans came for gold and ivory and found that it was more profitable to take Negroes On arrival in the Congo, the Portuguese were welcomed and treated as equals, and a remarkable correspondence developed between the King of Portugal and the King of the Congo, each addressing the other as my 'Royal Brother.' One of the sons of the King of the Congo was elevated by the Pope to the rank of Bishop on May 5, 1518, on the formal proposal of four Cardinals, as the first African Bishop, and a Congolese Embassy appeared in Rome in 1513. But the Congo had the first colonial experience of requests for technical assistance from a metropolitan country. The King of Portugal repeatedly refused to agree to the request of the King of the Congo to give him a ship or the means of building one, and the pitiful letter of the King of the Congo in 1526 requesting the King of Portugal to send him drugs, two physicians, two druggists, and one surgeon would readily evoke the sympathy of colonials

Equality was superseded by slavery. One million slaves were taken from Angola in the first century of European contact, as we read in a *Description of the Kingdom of Congo* published in 1680 by Oliviera Cadornega: other reports indicate the extraction of a further half a million slaves from the neighbouring land of the Congo.

No society could hope to withstand such a pressure. As the demand for slaves grew in voracity, the supply had to be sought further and further inland. Africans enslaved other Africans; the best means of defence was attack, and one enslaved in order not to be enslaved oneself. European guns intensified the tribal warfare fomented by the slave trade. African cupidity was nourished on European greed. A pitiful letter from the King of the Congo in 1526 to King John III of Portugal reads as follows:

'We cannot reckon how great the damage is, since the above-mentioned merchants daily seize our subjects, sons of the land and sons of our noblemen and vassals and our relatives . . . Thieves and men of evil conscience take them because they wish to possess the things and wares of this Kingdom . . . They grab them and cause them to be sold: and so great, Sir, is their corruption and licentiousness that our country is being utterly depopulated. And to avoid [them], we need from [your] Kingdoms no other than priests and people to teach in schools, and no other goods but wine and flour for the holy sacrament, that is why we beg of Your Highness to help and assist us in this matter, commanding your factors that they should send here neither merchants nor wares, because it is *our will that in these kingdoms* [of Congo] *there should not be any trade in slaves nor market for slaves.'*

The King of the Congo might as well have appealed to the wolves. More than two and a half centuries later, an African King of Senegal enacted a law that no slaves whatever should be marched through his territories. The law remained a dead letter. African was set against African in order to provide slaves for European traders to be transported to the European sugar plantations in Trinidad and the West Indies.

Leo Frobenius, has passed judgment on this medieval African civilisation and on this great lie of the European slave traders, their governmental promoters and their intellectual defenders, that Africa had no history before the arrival of the Europeans. Frobenius has written in his history of African Civilisation, originally published in German, and, perhaps not surprisingly, never translated into English:

'When they [the first European navigators of the end of the Middle Ages] arrived in the Gulf of Guinea and landed at Vaida, the captains were astonished to find streets well cared for, bordered for several leagues in length by two rows of trees; for many days they passed through a country of magnificent fields, a country inhabited by men clad in brilliant costumes, the stuff of which they had woven themselves! More to the South in the kingdom of the Congo, a swarming crowd dressed in silk and velvet; great states well ordered, and even to the smallest details, powerful sovereigns, rich industries – civilized to the marrow of their bones. And the condition of the countries on the eastern coast – Mozambique, for example – was quite the same.

'What was revealed by the navigators of the fifteenth to the seventeenth centuries furnishes an absolute proof that Negro Africa, which extended south of the desert zone of the Sahara, was in full efflorescence, in all the splendour of harmonious and well-informed civilisations, an efflorescence which the European conquistadors annihilated as far as they progressed. For the new country of America needed slaves, and Africa had them to offer, hundreds, thousands, whole cargoes of slaves. However, the slave trade was never an affair which meant a perfectly easy conscience, and it exacted a justification; hence one made of the Negro a half-animal, an article of merchandise And in the same way the notion of fetish was invented as a symbol of African religion As for me, I have seen in no part of Africa the Negroes worship a fetish The idea of "barbarous Negro" is a European invention which has consequently prevailed in Europe until the beginning of this century.'

These were the people who were brought to Trinidad and the West Indies to take the place of the Amerindian inhabitants, and to become, as the Brazilian sociologist, Gilberto Freyre, has written, 'the white man's greatest and most plastic collaborator in the task of agrarian colonisation' in the Western Hemisphere. Slavery on the West Indian sugar plantation allowed them neither time nor scope nor encouragement to develop their native capacity and to reproduce their native arts and crafts. Deliberately divided to break up not only families but also tribes in order that they might more easily be ruled, the absence of a common language and the mixing up of different customs and cultural traits were further obstacles in their way. Once freed, however, of the incubus of slavery and the restraints on their native talent, they were able to develop in a surprising manner, as the Bush Negroes of Surinam have demonstrated.

The Bush Negroes of Surinam were runaway slaves who fled the plantations, like the Maroons in Jamaica, and lived in the impenetrable jungle, isolated from the slave society, in communities organised on the African pattern. The Bush Negroes, like the Maroons, fought for decades against superior European soldiers, so successfully that they anticipated the later slave revolution in Saint Domingue and established independent African states thirty or forty years before the Independence of Haiti was achieved. The Dutch signed a treaty with the Bush Negroes, as the British did with the Maroons, guaranteeing them their independence. Safe from the Dutch above the waterfalls, expert oarsmen and builders of boats, the Bush Negroes have been able to maintain their independence, and it is only today that they are being brought into the stream of the national community in Surinam with the emergence of the nationalist movement and its penetration of the hitherto impenetrable jungle with a huge road to the Brokopondo region where American investors mining bauxite are collaborating with the Surinam Government in the construction of a vast hydro-electric project.

The African arts and capacity for civilisation which Hume depreciated and denied are very much in evidence in Surinam today and are the theme of a remarkable little volume published in 1954 by P. J. C. Dark, entitled *Bush Negro Art: An African Art in the Americas*. Evidence of their art, using wood, principally in the form of panellings, trays, vessels and paddles as well as canoes, is being brought more and more to public notice by the deliberate decision of the Government of Surinam to decorate and embellish public buildings with representations of Bush Negro art. One can find in any curio shop in Surinam folding chairs made by the Bush Negroes, all in one piece, of intricate workmanship and elegant design. One finds massive and neatly decorated combs used by the women for dressing their hair. One finds beautiful trays, all round, always carved from one piece of wood, of varying sizes ranging in diameter from 15 to 30 inches, decorated in some cases with most elaborate designs. Most of the carvings have symbolic associations with sex; many, although of utilitarian value, are also carved as love tokens.

Whilst it is not unlikely that the Bush Negroes, through their slavery on the Surinam sugar plantations, had become familiar with European art, particularly that of cabinet and furniture making, the emphasis in Bush Negro art is emphatically African. Mr Dark writes:

'Apart from the facets of African culture which have contributed to the formation of Bush Negro society, many of which have retained their African forms today, there are many specific items of Bush Negro art which can be identified as African in origin. Most striking of these are drums, not only in form but in construction, and in the form of pegging for tuning the skin stretched over the drum head. Some seats are similar to those found in West Africa. Carved wooden locks like those of the Bush Negro are found in West Africa and in the Sudan The use of brass tacks and cartridge marks is widespread in Africa. Many other items could be listed and many suggestions of affinities are to be found in the works of such as Linblom, van Panhuys, Kahn and Herskovits. The main problem, however, is the difficulty of assigning a specific trait to a specific provenance in West Africa. Some Bush Negro intertwined eight designs are very similar to those found on Benin bronze work. Other designs are similar to those found on Nupe brass trays. A photograph of some contemporary Yoruban ivory combs in the possession of the writer, at first glance looks like a photograph of Bush Negro combs. Perhaps it might be tentatively suggested that the Ashanti, Dahomeans and Yorubans contributed most to Bush Negro art. All in all the contributions made by the various provenances of Africa are not separable. It is clear that many traits were contributed from that continent and much of the subjective feeling engendered by Bush Negro art recalls African work. Further, Bush Negro art owes most to its African origins.'

As far as Trinidad is concerned, we have a study by the well-known American anthropologist, Melville J. Herskovits, of African survivals in his book, *Trinidad Village*. The book is a study of the village of Toco in 1946. Herskovits analysed the cultural integration, the amalgam of Europe and Africa, which was Toco, with the emphasis on the retention and reinterpretation of African customs and beliefs.

For example, he found the diet of the people of Toco marked by certain dishes that came directly from Africa. The most important of these dishes were sweet and salt *pemi* and *sansam*, pounded parched corn mixed with salt or sugar and eaten dry; *cachop*, a special Yoruba dish, made of cornmeal baked in a pot rather than boiled. *Callaloo*, for which Trinidad is famous, is well-known as an African dish over all the New World. *Accra*, boiled salted fish dipped into flour, flavoured liberally with pepper sauce, and fried in deep fat, is another well-known African inheritance.

Herskovits found also that the eating habits in Toco were African, and so was the sexual differentiation of labour. The Gayap, the Trinidad version of the Haitian *coumbite*, is essentially African. So is the 'papa-bois' and the susu, the savings device of the people taken over without change of name from their Yoruba ancestors.

The high economic status of the women in Toco corresponded with the position of women in West African society. The well-known Trinidad custom of the legal marriage subsisting side by side with the informal union termed 'keepers', or, as the Trinidad wits would put it, the combination of *de jure* wife and *de facto* wife, which has provided the basis for extensive moralising both at home and abroad on the illegitimacy statistics, is seen by Herskovits as the 'translation, in terms of the monogamic pattern of European mating, of basic West African forms that operate within a polygynous frame.'

The shouters and the shango, the latter the God of Thunder of the Yoruba people, have come to Trinidad straight from Africa. So have the traditions of burials, especially in respect of wakes, with which the Bongo is traditionally associated – as it is in the well-known calypso, 'Tonight is the bongo night'. The prevalence of and the concern with obeah, magic and divination also have an African inspiration: the use of the frizzle fowl to detect any charm set against its owner, placing a broom upside down near the door, putting in front of a doorway grains of cereal to be counted, leaving a needle with a broken eye to be threaded – all techniques for protection against the evil eye, a combination of the French *loupgarou* and the West African vampire.

Finally, most important of all, the calypso for which Trinidad has become famous, the use of song to comment on current happenings, to phrase social criticism, to convey innuendo, is in the African tradition. As Herskovits writes ·

'Even though some of the music is cast in the mould of European folk tunes, and the words are in English, nothing of African purport or intent has been erased For despite its non-African form, this musical complex can be regarded as nothing less than a retention of the purest type.'

These were the people who came in their thousands to the West Indies, though in relatively limited numbers to Trinidad during the slave period, to develop for the colonies of all the European metropolitan countries what a British writer in the middle of the 18th century described as 'a magnificent superstructure of American commerce on an African foundation.'

Spain Reigns but France Governs

Africa had been brought in by Spain into Trinidad and the West Indies as the solution of the labour problem. France was now brought into Trinidad as the solution of the problem of white management A French planter from Grenada, Roume de St Laurent, visited Trinidad and submitted a memorandum to the King of France on March 20, 1777. The result of this memorandum was to transform a backward Amerindian colony governed by Spain into a Spanish colony run by Frenchmen and worked by African slaves.

The proposals of Roume de St Laurent were designed to facilitate the immigration of French planters into Trinidad. In effect they amounted to the setting up of a French State within a Spanish State. There was nothing singular in such a condominium in a single island, either in fact or in law. In 1685 Brandenburg, one of the States in the German confederation, had agreed with the Danes in St Thomas in the Virgin Islands for the lease of an area in St Thomas for the employment of 200 slaves. For some 70 years before the Treaty of Utrecht in 1713, English and French jointly occupied the island of St Kitts. Even today the tiny island of St Martin is shared between France and Holland.

The essence of the plan of Roume de St Laurent was the transfer of as many planters as possible and their African slaves from the French islands of Martinique, Guadeloupe, Dominica, St Lucia, St Vincent and Grenada. He emphasised that all of them suffered more or less from a variety of hardships: hurricanes, ants which destroyed the sugar crop, bankruptcy, debts, the low price of coffee, and soil exhaustion. He was afraid that the British mainland colonies of North America would offer such incentives to these planters that they would migrate to populate the States of Georgia, Carolina and Florida. In his opinion they should be, as far as possible, encouraged to remain in the West Indies, preferably in Trinidad, where he argued that the interest of both France and Spain would be strengthened as against Great Britain.

St Laurent estimated that some 383 white families would be interested in these proposals. Of these 286 were from Martinique, 40 from Dominica and 57 from Grenada. Allowing four persons to a family, this meant a possible addition to the white population of Trinidad of 1,532 persons. These would bring with them a total of 33,322 African slaves of whom 24,710 were in Martinique, 3,647 in Dominica and 4,965 in Grenada

The very first glimpse of the possible development of Trinidad involved, in other words, migration from the neighbouring small islands.

The Spanish Government accepted the proposals of Roume de St

Laurent. On November 20, 1783, the King of Spain issued the famous cedula of population opening Trinidad's doors under certain conditions to foreign immigrants. The terms of the cedula, summarised, were as follows:

1. The foreigners must be Roman Catholics and subjects of nations in alliance with Spain.
2. They must take an oath of allegiance to Spain and agree to abide by the Spanish laws.
3. Every white immigrant, male or female, would receive 4 fanegas and 2/7ths of land and in addition half of that quantity for each slave introduced by him.
4. Free Negroes and people of colour would receive half the quantity of land assigned to whites, with an additional half for each slave introduced by them.
5. After five years residence in Trinidad the settlers and their children would have all the rights and privileges of naturalisation, including eligibility for public office and posts in the militia.
6. No head tax or personal tribute would be imposed upon the settlers at any time, except that after ten years they would each pay an annual sum of $1.00 for each Negro or coloured slave with the guarantee that this sum would never be augmented.
7. During the first five years the settlers would be free to return to their countries or former place of abode and to take with them all goods and property introduced by them into Trinidad without any export duty.
8. The settlers would be free from the payment of tithes on the produce of their lands for ten years beginning January 1, 1785, after which they would pay only one-half tithe, that is to say, 5 per cent.
9. For the first ten years the settlers would be free from the payment of the royal duty on the sales of their produce and merchantable effects, after which they would pay only 5 per cent; but all their exports shipped to Spain in Spanish vessels would be for ever exempt from any duty on exportation.
10. All vessels belonging to the settlers, whatever their tonnage or make, would be registered in Trinidad and accounted Spanish vessels, as well as vessels acquired from foreigners by purchase or legal title before the end of the year 1786.
11. The Negro slave trade would be totally free of duties for a period of ten years reckoned from the beginning of the year 1785, after which the settlers would pay only 5 per cent on the current value of slaves at the time of their importation.
12. The settlers would be permitted, under Government licence, to go to the West Indian islands in alliance with Spain, or to neutral islands, to procure slaves, on the understanding that only Spanish ships would be used.
13. For ten years computed from the beginning of the year 1785,

Spanish subjects would be free to make voyages to Trinidad with their cargoes direct from ports of France in which Spanish Consuls were resident and to return direct to those ports with the products of Trinidad, except money, the exportation of which was absolutely prohibited by that route.

14 The royal officials in Caracas were instructed to purchase on the King's account and transport to Trinidad black cattle, mules and horses, and to sell them to the settlers at prime cost until such time as they had sufficient stock to supply themselves.

15. Similar instructions were issued with respect to the supply of flour and meal to Trinidad for a period of ten years.

16. All Spanish manufactures needed by the settlers for their agriculture were to be imported into Trinidad and sold to the settlers at prime cost during a period of ten years.

17. Two priests of known erudition and exemplary virtue and expert in foreign languages were to be appointed to Trinidad to act as parish priests to the new settlers.

18. The settlers were permitted to propose to the King, through the Governor, such Ordinances as were necessary for regulating the treatment of their slaves and preventing their flight

19. The Governor was to take the utmost care to prevent the introduction of ants into Trinidad.

20. When the cultivation of sugar had become fully expanded in Trinidad, the settlers were to be allowed to establish refineries in Spain with all the privileges and freedom from duties previously extended to Spaniards or foreigners.

21. The settlers would enjoy the privilege of directing representations to the King through the medium of the Governor and the General Secretary of State for the Indies.

This, in modern parlance, was the first set of incentives offered in Trinidad to attract foreign capital. It constituted a confession of the total failure of Spanish colonialism. The Spanish Exclusive could be maintained only inclusive of France.

Not content, the Spanish government went further a little more than two years later. On January 30, 1786, another decree amended the cedula of colonisation and liberalised the incentives. The 5 per cent in lieu of tithes and the 5 per cent royal duty on the sales of their products, which the settlers were to pay after ten years, were reduced to 2½ per cent The time for naturalising foreign built merchant vessels was extended from 1786 to 1788. The exemption from duty on the importation of Negro slaves was extended from ten years and made perpetual, and the duty of 5 per cent which the settlers were to pay after ten years was for ever abolished. Instead of paying 5 per cent on all produce exported to foreign countries for the purpose of purchasing slaves, they were to pay only 3 per cent The duty on the export of produce to France was similarly reduced from 5 per cent to 3 per cent, and a similar reduction was made on all produce exported for the purpose of purchasing flour whenever there was a scarcity in the islands.

This liberal policy was followed by permission of the King of Spain to the Governor of Trinidad, on April 20, 1790, to raise from any European nation whatsoever a loan in the sum of $1 million on condition that it would be repaid from the value of the crops in their plantations. This, Trinidad's first loan on the world market, was proof that colonial development could not be achieved under the umbrella of any one country and was in fact a condemnation of the very foundation on which European colonialism had rested up to that date. It compares favourably with the uproar raised in the House of Commons in 1772 when a proposal was first mooted to permit foreign investment in the West Indian territories acquired by Britain from France at the Peace of Paris in 1763.

The cedula of colonisation, virtually coinciding with the arrival in Trinidad of its most distinguished Governor, Don Jose Maria Chacon, was the signal for an unprecedented development of the Trinidadian economy, as well as an unprecedented initiative on the part of the Governor of Trinidad. Chacon himself, a man of no mean intellectual gifts and administrative ability, proceeded to reorganise the ineffective government which he had inherited. One of his first and most important measures was his reorganisation in 1787 of the administrative divisions of the colony which he divided into three parts with a Commissioner of Population in charge of each. The three divisions were as follows: the first, Las Cuevas, Salybia, Guanapo, Tacarigua, Laventille, St Ann's, Tragarete, Maraval, Diego Martin, Carenage (virtually the limits of the present County of St George); the second, Naparima, Galeota, Cocal and Guatero; the third, Guapo, Los Gallos and Guayaguayare

These comprehensive regulations, as expanded in 1788, are a good example of Spanish paternalism.

The first responsibility of the Commissioners of Population was a census of population, distinguishing free men from slaves, identifying class and national origin. Anyone changing his estate or plantation was required to notify the Commissioners, who had to submit a statement of the population to the Governor in December of each year, noting the births and deaths in that year.

The second responsibility of the Commissioners related to agriculture. They were to ascertain the area of land cleared, the area cultivated, the crops grown, the yield of those crops, the labour and machinery employed on plantations They were to measure and survey each plantation and to verify all litigation, past and pending; no land was to be alienated or sold without notice to the Commissioners.

The third responsibility of the Commissioners related to the roads. The Commissioners were to prepare plans for the course of Royal roads, to estimate their cost, and to recommend the means to be employed. They were to ensure that planters planted lime trees, trees of campeachy wood or other useful trees, interspersed with orange and other fruit trees, on the part of their estate bordering a public road, 'so as to delight the eye and temper the heat of the sun for the relief of travellers'. Twice a year the Commissioners were to arrange for the clearing and repairs of roads, distributing the work among the planters according to the number of slaves belonging to each, the quantity of land owned, and the frontage on each public road.

The policing of the island was the Commissioners fourth responsibility They were to take cognisance of all robberies, quarrels and disorders.

The Commissioners, in the fifth place, were to pay special attention to the government of the slaves. They were to prevent inhumanity to and ill-treatment of the slaves, to ensure that each plantation grew an adequate quantity of provisions for the maintenance of the slaves, and to note particularly all offences involving slave and master or slave and freeman.

One can well understand what Chacon meant when he decreed that the Commissioners were to know 'with the greatest exactitude' the lands in their respective divisions.

Chacon's second major reform was, in a proclamation of July 27, 1785, the removal of some of the confusion relating to land grants and land titles. All lands which had not been alienated by a formal concession were declared Crown lands. Immemorial possession ceased to be admitted as a sufficient title Inhabitants who from a distant period of time held ungranted land, on condition that such land was cultivated, were given priority over other claimants in respect of free grants, provided that they presented themselves within three months to the Government to obtain their title of concession. All the ancient Spanish inhabitants who, without title of property and concession, claimed lands in different parts covered with wood, because they had not the means to clear them, were within three months to select the situation in which they wished to establish themselves and present themselves in order to obtain a grant thereof. A stop was put to the excessive ambition of many Spaniards who wished to be proprietors of considerable areas of lands in different localities though they were unable to put a single acre into cultivation, and who, quitting these, passed over to Crown lands on which they employed the little labour of which they were capable. The Proclamation required these persons to select within three months the site most suitable for their establishment, whether on their pretended property or on Crown lands All the surplus land would revert to the King, to be distributed to others who would acquire and cultivate them.

The spirit of the Proclamation was clearly stated as being to remove every impediment whatever to the cultivation of land. It was made clear that, should the legitimate possessor not have the means to work his lands, they would be granted to others who had the means of cultivating them on condition that these others paid to the possessor the sum or value for which they were obtained leaving the original owners such portion of land as they might be capable of cultivating.

This Proclamation of Chacon in 1785 represented one of the most decisive and constructive efforts ever made in the West Indies to deal with the problem of latifundia or plantations which had, throughout the 17th and 18th centuries, impeded the full development of other colonies, particularly Jamaica. It was intended also to take care of the situation which had arisen in such colonies like Barbados and the Leeward Islands where the large plantation had made it difficult for the small white settler even to obtain a couple of acres of land for a small farm

The third major achievement of Chacon was the cedula of 1789 for the protection of slaves. This is in the tradition of the more liberal Spanish legislation which prevailed in such colonies like Cuba and which compared favourably with the much harsher legislation of the British colonies. In this, perhaps, there was no necessary superiority of the Latin temperament over the Anglo-Saxon in respect of its dealings with subjugated races. Nowhere in the West Indies in 1789 was there a greater hell on earth than the French colony of Saint Domingue (later known as Haiti) from which some of the very planters who later found refuge in Trinidad with their slaves were to migrate. If the Cuban law in 1789 was superior to or less harsh than the slave code in Saint Domingue or in Jamaica or in Barbados, it was because Saint Domingue, Jamaica and Barbados were plantation colonies producing enormous quantities of sugar for the world market.

Cuba in 1789, like Trinidad in 1789, was relatively less developed economically, the large plantation was the exception rather than the rule, and it was possible for the slaves to live in that closer contact with their masters on which legislation like the Code Noir was predicated. When Cuba in 1860 became a typical plantation colony, like the Saint Domingue or Jamaica of 1789, there was very little evidence in practice of the Spanish temperament, and Cuba became as much a hell on earth as Saint Domingue had ever been, in which the Cuban planter could reply contemptuously to remonstrations about inhuman treatment of the slaves: 'the Negroes come here ready made, the bags of sugar have yet to be made'.

Chacon's Code Noir, summarised, is as follows:

1. All owners of slaves were obliged to instruct them in the principles of the Roman Catholic religion, were not to allow them to work on holy days, and were to provide at their expense a priest to say Mass for them and to administer the Holy Sacraments to them. At the end of every day's work the slaves were to say the Rosary in the presence of their master and his steward.
2. The Justices of the districts in which the estates were situated were to determine the quality and quantity of the food and clothes to be given daily to the slaves.
3 The first and principal occupation of slaves was to be agricultural and not labour that required a sedentary life. To this end the Justices of the towns and villages were to regulate the work

to be done by the slaves in the course of the day, two hours daily being allowed to the slaves for labour on their own account. No slave was to work over the age of 60 or below the age of 17, and the women slaves were to be employed in work appropriate to their sex.

4. After Mass on holy days, slaves were to be free to divert themselves innocently in the presence of masters and stewards, care being taken to prevent the mixing of slaves on different estates or male slaves with the female or very excessive drinking These diversions were to be ended before the time for prayers

5. The slave owners were to provide commodious habitations for the slaves sufficient to protect them from the inclemencies of the weather with beds, blankets and other necessaries. Each slave was to have his own bed and there were to be no more than two slaves to a room. A separate habitation, warm and commodious, was to be provided as an infirmary for sick slaves. The slave owner was to pay the charges of a slave funeral.

6. Slaves who, on account of old age or illness, were unable to work, as well as children, were to be maintained by their masters who were not to give them their liberty in order to get rid of them.

7. Masters of slaves were to encourage matrimony among slaves.

8. Slaves were not to be punished by more than 25 lashes, inflicted only by their masters or their stewards, in such a manner as not to cause contusion or effusion of blood.

9. For more serious offences, the slaves were to be reported by their masters or stewards to the Justice.

10. Masters or stewards who failed in the obligations imposed on them by the Cedula were to be fined $50 for the first offence, $100 for the second, and $200 for the third.

11. Masters of slaves were to deliver annually to the Justice of the town or village in the district in which their estates were situated, a list signed and sworn to by them of all the slaves in their possession distinguishing sex and age.

Two other points of general interest during Chacon's administration may be noted. The first concerned the Cabildo. Chacon limited its powers to Port-of-Spain only and forced it to remove from St Joseph. The Cabildo received title to all municipal lands, and Chacon turned over to it also the islands of Monos, Huevos and Patos.

And Chacon himself concentrated on the development and improvement of Port-of-Spain, which was then limited to an area embracing from Charlotte Street to Frederick Street as far north as Prince Street. All the surrounding areas, Laventille, Woodbrook, St Clair, St Ann's, Belmont, Maraval, Diego Martin, Chaguaramas, were under sugar cultivation. A major achievement of Chacon was the diversion of the St Ann's River (the Dry River) in 1787, the Spanish

Government providing the necessary funds for the employment on the job of 638 slaves and 405 free people of colour.

The effects of metropolitan liberalism and governmental efficiency in Trinidad were soon apparent. The Population of Trinidad in 1797 was 17,643. Of these whites numbered 2,086; free people of colour 4,466; Amerindians 1,082; Negro slaves 10,009. Of the total population there were 6,594 men of whom 929 were white, 1,196 free people of colour, 305 Amerindians and 4,164 slaves. Trinidad's production in 1797 amounted to 7,800 hogsheads of sugar from 159 sugar estates; 330,000 pounds of coffee from 130 coffee estates; 96,000 pounds of cocoa from 60 cocoa estates; and 224,000 pounds of cotton from 103 cotton estates.

But the foundations of the colony, Spanish in name, French in fact, African at its base, were hopelessly insecure None knew this better than Chacon himself. He knew that he could not defend Trinidad against any serious invasion. On May 6, 1796, in a letter to the Prince de la Paz, he warned the Spanish Government of impending disaster. He wrote as follows:

'Our garrison is weak, we have no fortification and the lack of buildings of lime and stone leaves me without a prison, barracks, magazine or store house; in a word I am dependent on the good-will of a public composed of people of other nations with but a few of our own In consequence they are disunited by race, they are in discord because of their habits, rivals by custom and enemies amongst themselves by the traditions of their nations and by the development of actual circumstances.

'It was my duty to convince you and to warn you that frequent disputes between the English and the French on land here would involve the greater part of the population and the consequences could only be ruinous to all.'

The danger foreseen by Chacon almost came to a head on one occasion in 1796 when a British warship followed a French ship into the harbour and landed in Port-of-Spain. French and English were drawn up in battle array, the English on what is now Frederick Street, and the French in Chacon Street. The Spanish Governor, with relatively few troops, placed himself between both lines of troops, and expostulated with them for violation of Spanish neutrality. A serious incident was averted, but the entire population of Port-of-Spain and many of the country slaves who found themselves in town were a witness to it. The French Revolution was at its height throughout all the West Indies and Chacon warned the Prince de la Paz of the possible consequences:

'The tricolour cockade which they worship as a symbol of liberty was displayed by many of these slaves and they persuaded their comrades to follow their example.

'This caused me to despatch several parties to the country to suppress right at the beginning such disorder, which is one of the most terrible in these Colonies where slavery is the basis of agriculture . . .

'The contact which our people of colour and our Negro slaves have had with the French and Republicans have made them think of liberty and equality and the first spark will light the whole Colony into a blaze.

'The English are attacking the French islands and as many of the Republicans as can escape fly to the shores of Trinidad where there is no force to prevent them settling. The greater part are Mulattoes and Negroes which increases in consequence our numbers, and infuses them with the same ideas and desires and make the danger of a rising more imminent each day.'

Chacon was on the horns of a dilemma He too had understood, as other West Indian Governors and officials had understood before him, that no Negroes, no sugar. The tremendous spurt which Trinidad's economy had made was the result of slave labour. The continuation and acceleration of economic development depended on the availability of more slaves, which only increased the internal danger and therefore aggravated the external danger In his letter to the Prince de la Paz Chacon called therefore for military assistance, penning in the process one of the most subtle indictments of metropolitan apathy to be found in all the records of the history of West Indian colonies:

'The rapidity with which this Colony has been peopled and extended is such that 4,000–5,000 Negroes are required each year and in two or three years many more will be required. The produce is abundant and of good quality.

'All this brings in riches not only to pay the actual cost of the Government of the Island but also to provide other facilities which are necessary and result in an active commercial community which is the pride of our metropolis, in industrial progress, in increased merchant shipping . . .

'The previous establishments of the King in this Island were developed slowly, their requirements came little by little to the notice of the Ministry which had time to consider carefully all the difficulties, to discuss, compare and finally to select the best remedies.

'In this development it is just the reverse. Special efforts were made to populate and to cultivate the land and in a few years much more produce was being raised than in other colonies of two centuries duration.

'This prosperity is such as to require much prompter decisions, and the difficulties must be met by executive action. It is not possible to proceed with that leisurely manner and considered thought that is convenient in other places

'I have to insist on this difference, this necessity, this urgency and desire to fulfil my obligations and beseech in the name of this community their Sovereign's protection. May His Majesty be pleased to send with the quickest possible dispatch a division of two ships, two frigates and two small vessels such as brigantines . . . with 800 to 1,000 men to remain here at least during the war between the neighbouring nations, and to preserve the peace in this Colony.'

It was in these circumstances that the British captured Trinidad from the Spaniards in 1797 when Britain and Spain were at war. The military forces at the disposal of Chacon, both on land and at sea in the Spanish naval base of Chaguaramas under Admiral Apodaca, were unequal to the forces at the disposal of the British Commander, Sir Ralph Abercromby. Chacon had four ships – one of 84 guns, two of 74 guns, and one of 36 guns Abercromby had 18 ships – one of 98 guns, four of 74 guns, two of 64 guns, one of 44 guns, one of 33 guns, one of 32 guns, five of 16 guns, one of fourteen and one of twelve. The force at Chacon's disposal included 700 rank and file in the warships, chiefly recruits intended for the garrison at Cartagena, whose number was reduced to 500 by death and sickness. The local militia, strong on paper, was indisciplined and untrustworthy. Abercromby's land forces consisted of 7,650 men.

Chacon had the slaves to contend with, and he was very doubtful of the loyalty of the free people of colour most of whom were French in origin and republican in politics. So Apodaca set fire to his ships in Chaguaramas Bay without a fight and Abercromby, landing at Mucurapo which was then a sugar estate, marched unmolested to the hills of Belmont to receive the capitulation of Chacon, whose forces were stationed on the Laventille hills. After 300 years of Spanish rule, Trinidad passed without a shot being fired into British hands.

Chacon and Apodaca were subsequently tried before a Council of War in Cadiz appointed by the King After hearing the evidence of the accused and the submissions of their lawyers, and having carefully examined the evidence, after full discussion, the Council of War unanimously agreed that both Chacon and Apodaca had fully justified their actions and that they should forthwith be liberated. The Council recommended to the King to direct that their innocence should be proclaimed in all the Spanish dominions in both Europe and America and especially in the Province of Caracas and in the West Indies.

The King of Spain was furious. His house of cards had come tumbling down on his head, so he had to find a scapegoat. He considered that Chacon and Apodaca had failed to comply with their obligations in a position which was highly important to the King's service and criticised the decision of the Council of War as contrary to justice and to the public interest. The King's instructions as conveyed to the Director General of the Royal Navy of Spain on March 20, 1801, read as follows:

'Having consulted his Council of Ministers His Majesty has been able to find sufficient extenuating circumstances, such as influenced the proceedings of the Council of War, to mitigate the necessity of providing a punishment which, notwithstanding all this, would have corresponded to their offences and would have served as an encouragement to those who find themselves in a similar position, to comply with all that their honour and their obligations to the Service require.

'In consequence His Majesty has been pleased to decide that Don Jose Maria Chacon had not defended the Island of Trinidad as far as his circumstances allowed and that Don Sebastian Ruiz de Apodaca had decided prematurely to burn the ships under his command and without strict observance of the orders provided for such circumstances.

'And therefore His Majesty has condemned the one and the other to deprivation of their respective posts from which they shall be forthwith recalled and also the first to perpetual banishment from all Royal Dominions . . .

'It is further ordered that in no case, neither to Chacon nor to Apodaca . . . is any appeal allowed and to this end His Majesty enjoins perpetual silence on these offenders.'*

Thus ended three centuries of Spanish colonialism – in the injustice meted out to, and in the unnecessary humiliation inflicted on, the only Governor who could not be regarded as part of the metropolitan rubbish exported by Spain to the colonies.

*On July 7, 1809, Apodaca was rehabilitated and restored to his former rank and place on active service.

CHAPTER 5

Tobago in a State of Betweenity

If there was one West Indian colony with a sadder history than that of Trinidad in the first 300 years after its discovery by the Spaniards, that colony was Tobago.

Trinidad suffered from the ineptitude and inefficiency of Spanish colonialism. Tobago suffered rather from the competition of rival colonialisms. In Trinidad the Spanish metropolitan government saw to it that nothing was done. In Tobago the conflict of the rival metropolitan governments made it impossible for anything to be done. If Trinidad remained a Spanish colony subject to occasional attacks by Spain's enemies, Tobago was no man's land Whilst the Spanish flag, however tattered, continued to fly over Trinidad, Tobago changed flags almost as regularly as it changed seasons, and the people of Tobago lived, in a phrase made popular by wags in British Guiana who, similarly circumstanced, did not know where they were going from day to day, in a state of betweenity.

It was a never-ending free-for-all in Tobago Britain claimed the Island on the ground that it formed part of the acquisition of Sir Thomas Warner in 1626. France claimed it as part of the grant made by Cardinal Richelieu to the French West Indian Company some twenty years later. Holland, grant or no grant, asserted its own claim to the Island. Spain lived in constant apprehension of an attack from Tobago on Trinidad. The Duke of Courland, ruler of a principality in the area which is now Latvia, claimed it on the basis of a grant from the King of England in 1664. And even the buccaneers, operating on a commission issued by the Governor of Jamaica, manifested an interest in the Island which reads curiously today in the light of Jamaica's notorious indifference to its Eastern Caribbean neighbours.

This is how Tobago lived up the end of the 18th century – between Britain and France, or between France and Holland, or between Holland and Britain, now invaded by the buccaneers, now attacked by Spain, now settled by Courlanders. Holland changed the island's name and called it New Walcheren The French changed the name of Scarborough and called it Port Louis. Betwixt and between, betwixt changes of ownership and between national flags – that was colonialism in Tobago.

This metropolitan interest and these national flags more often than not were mere euphemisms for individual beneficiaries of the European governments Tobago was given away to individuals as if it was no more than an area of Crown land in another island Take for example a letter from Lord Willoughby, Governor of Barbados, to the King of England on January 29, 1666, requesting a lease of Tobago for thirty-one years and all the profits that might arise from it, with

51

the privilege of free trade. Willoughby undertook to surrender the island on the expiration of his lease well settled and improved.

As another example, take the grant of Tobago made by the King of England to the Duke of Courland on November 17, 1664. The King of England granted Tobago to the Duke together with all the land, houses, creeks, rivers and profits belonging to the same. The conditions of the grant were that only subjects of the King of England or the Duke of Courland were to be permitted to settle in Tobago or build houses; English subjects were to enjoy all the privileges, liberties, immunities and benefits extended to the subjects of Courland, and to pay no taxes, contributions or impositions except those necessarily required for defence, and then equally in the same proportion paid by the subjects of the Duke. No products were to be exported out of Tobago or imported into Tobago except to or from English ports or Courland ports, or the City of Danzig. If England was at war the Duke of Courland undertook to provide one good ship of war with 40 guns, to send the ship to such place as England decided, to man the ship with seamen and supply them with food and wages for their service which was not to exceed one year at any one time.

Yet another example of a policy that was not far removed from the Spanish policy to the conquistadors, one Captain Poyntz signed an agreement with the Duke of Courland in 1680 whereby the Duke granted the Captain an area of 120,000 acres in Tobago and in return the Captain undertook to take to Tobago 1,200 persons within a period of three years, and another 1,200 persons within the next five years and to settle them on the land in Tobago It was almost like taking chickens to Tobago, or rather it was almost like giving away Tobago as if it was a chicken itself.

The final example of this English conquistador attitude to Tobago is the petition of one Moses Stringer, a physician, to the Queen of England in 1704. The petitioner requested a charter and letters patent for settling and fortifying the lands of Tobago and Trinidad, and, among other things, for building and endowing a college in Tobago. Because of the constant threat to Tobago from the Caribs in Trinidad, whose emperor, Dr Stringer asserted, went once a year to Tobago in his pirogues in procession around the island which he claimed as his own, Dr Stringer undertook, with Her Majesty's permission, to go at his own expense as Her Majesty's ambassador to the Emperor of the Carib nation and make a perpetual peace with him.

In this free for all between the European nations, there was one policy common to all of them: that was that nobody should have Tobago None of them could spare either the manpower or the ships really to develop the island and defend it, but none of them really wanted any of its rivals to be in a position to do this So colonialism in Tobago became a question of wanton destruction If Tobago could not be a colony of any one of the particular powers, then Tobago was to be a waste land. If one country could not have it, nobody else was to have it. The bankruptcy of colonialism reached its nadir in Tobago.

First, England England's policy was stated quite bluntly: Tobago was to be a waste land, the property of the King of England, for the use of his subjects. The President and Council of Barbados so recommended in a communication to the Secretary of the Council of Trade and Plantations on August 14, 1673 as follows:

'We presume that Island is so laid waste as will hinder all settlement there during this time of war, and if any nation shall presume there to make any small beginnings without His Majesty's commission we shall use our endeavours to destroy such beginning and thereby preserve it for His Majesty In any other manner we are unable to keep it, for to leave a small garrison there had been to render them a prey to the Dutch and therewith lose His Majesty's title, and to place there such a garrison as should be able to hold it against the Dutch is more than we are able to maintain to keep it. Therefore as a waste belonging to His Majesty for the use of his subjects, we deem it the only way to have to preserve His Majesty's right thereto.'

The French Government, quite naturally, refused to accept this statement of English policy. A great argument ensued at the end of the 17th century between Britain and France as to the ownership of Tobago. Britain refused to abandon its claim. But what was Britain claiming Tobago for? The Commissioners of Trade and Plantations wrote to the King on January 4, 1700:

'. . . the continuance of possession by Your Majesty is much more easily proved by the constant frequenting of that Island by Your Majesty's men of war and other ships of Your Majesty's subjects which resort there daily from Barbados and stay there 2 or 3 months at a time or more to furnish themselves with wood and water and other necessaries in the said Island which depends absolutely on Your Majesty's government of Barbados as other Islands lying to the windward of Guadeloupe.

'And in order to the further asserting of Your Majesty's right to Tobago exclusive of all others and to hinder the settlement of any colony there, pursuant to Your Majesty's intentions signified on that behalf, we are most humbly of the opinion that the Governor of Barbados for the time being should take care by Your Majesty's frigates or otherwise to hinder any settlement to be made upon that Island by any foreign nation whatsoever or even by Your Majesty's subjects otherwise than such Governor with the advice of Your Majesty's Council shall judge necessary for maintaining Your Majesty's sole rights to the said Island and in such manner as may be for the use and benefit to Your Majesty's subjects inhabiting Your Majesty's Island of Barbados.'

The French put up counter arguments, based on their capture in 676 from Holland. And what did France claim Tobago for? As a vaste which no other nation was to be permitted to be developed. If

Tobago was to be a waste land, the waste must be French The French Ambassador in London wrote to the English Secretary of State on November 3, 1699, as follows:

'When His Most Christian Majesty had decided to destroy the fortifications no one was left there to preserve his rights and his vessels had orders to go there twice yearly to prevent any other nation from taking possession contrary to his rights therein.'

Spain, too, wanted to see Tobago as a waste land Spain was particularly apprehensive about an Amerindian coalition between the Amerindians of Trinidad and the Amerindians of Tobago sponsored by the Dutch with designs on Spanish Trinidad The Spanish Governor in Trinidad considered Trinidad most vulnerable to such attacks, especially on the northern coast, and particularly at Maracas Thus, apart from concentrating on the destruction of the Amerindian settlements on the north coast of Trinidad around Point Galera, the Governor of Trinidad decided to attack Tobago. Trinidad and Tobago went to war.

The Spanish Governor of Trinidad, showing an energy and a determination seldom equalled by his predecessors or his successors, took the field in person. The expedition left Trinidad in November, 1636, and was able successfully to negotiate the difficult crossing from Trinidad to Tobago. The surprise attack on Tobago was successful. The Spaniards found in the fort a real international force – Englishmen, Dutchmen, Frenchmen, Flemings and African Negroes. The Dutch surrendered, and the Spaniards took away all ammunition and arms and set fire to all buildings and forts Thus laden with their spoils and prisoners, with vessels designed to carry 25 men carrying more than 60, they encountered typical weather to the extent that their ships were nearly swamped. It is not difficult to appreciate today, when reading the Governor's account of the expedition, the joy with which he anchored at Monos on his return to Trinidad.

The policy of the buccaneers from Jamaica was equally a policy of destruction. The Governor of Barbados, Lord Willoughby, encountered them in Tobago in 1666. He described them in a letter to the British Secretary of State on January 29, 1666, as follows:

'They are all masters and betake themselves to what course and which way they please, reckoning what they take, as well the Island as anything upon it, to be all their own and themselves free princes to dispose of it as they please . . . The Island was pretty well settled, having many good plantations upon it, well stocked with negroes and cattle and pretty good horses, but because my purse could not reach to purchase these of them, they did break up all things that were portable and untiled the houses; whereby they have left the Island in as bad a condition almost as it was at first settling, for hands being wanting, all the plantations must run to ruin, for indeed they have eaten up and destroyed all that they could not carry away, which hath been their custom in all places wherever they come.'

The story became even more fantastic in 1749 when Britain and France, unable to agree on the ownership or disposition of Tobago, solemnly agreed that Tobago, together with St Lucia, St Vincent and Dominica, should be neutral islands and should be evacuated by the nationals of both countries. Tobago's neutrality, however, was of short duration as it again got caught up in the European struggles which only ended with the Battle of Waterloo in 1815 So Tobago continued to change hands and to change flags, and to live between England and Holland and France

No economic development of Tobago could be expected under such conditions. Tobago had no gold, and no one took seriously the report of Captain Pyntz in 1702 that he had secretly discovered rich mines and lapis lazuli as well as pearls and ambergris Occasional efforts were made to recruit settlers, as for example, the prospectus for settlers in Tobago issued in England in 1686. Prospects were held out to the small man who had no more than a capital of £100 sterling. With a family, estimated at eleven all told, he could get a passage to Tobago for £50. Tools and implements and supplies for the first year would cost him £47 10s. With the remaining £2 10s. he could get a lease of 50 acres of land for 1,000 years, a shilling an acre a year. Within 12 months he could cultivate sufficient ground provisions and get two crops of tobacco. Assuming even a low yield of 8,000 pounds, this, allowing merely one-eighth part of the price at which the Spaniards sold tobacco in Trinidad, would bring him £100 sterling; so that he would recover his outlay in the first year and proceed to buy slaves with which he could keep on doubling his income year after year, until at the end of the seventh year's crop he could expect by a modest computation to clear from the 50 acres of land at least £5,000 sterling This was too good to be true, and of course no one took it seriously.

In so far as the British Government envisaged any economic policy for Tobago, that policy emphasises one of the principal considerations which faced all the European countries. The West Indian scene was a scene of rivalry not only among the European metropolitan countries, but also among the planters of the various islands Each one was jealous of the other, and the British policy to Tobago of leaving it a waste was due very largely to the fact that the planters of Barbados saw in Tobago a possible rival. When in 1721 the British Government did work out some sort of a policy to Tobago, that policy, as stated in royal instructions to the Governor of Barbados, emphatically stipulated that Tobago was not to rival Barbados

It was the same old story of one colony seeking to profit at the expense of others, sometimes within the same national jurisdiction, and it is to this long tradition more than anything else that is to be attributed this jealousy of West Indian islands one for the other even today which has astonished foreign observers and exasperates West Indian planters

The principle explicitly laid down for new settlers was that they

C

should not plant sugar. They were to grow instead cocoa, annato and indigo. Large scale enterprise was restricted; no grant was to exceed 300 acres and none was to be less than 15 acres. Every person who received a grant of land was to be obliged to cultivate one acre out of every 50, that is to say, 2 per cent of the acreage, every year from the date of the grant. Such person was further obliged to maintain for every forty acres one white man or two white women within a year after the date of his grant, and one white man and two white women for every twenty acres three years after the date of his grant. Finally, no grants were to be made to any planter who had land in Barbados or in any other of the British islands in the West Indies.

As in Trinidad, so in Tobago, the first real stimulus to economic development came from the French. But whereas in Trinidad this took place through French immigration under the Spanish flag, in Tobago it was the result of the French capture of the island from the British in 1781

The French, it is true, were determined to maintain the Exclusive just as much as the Spaniards. In 1783 the Council and Assembly of Tobago petitioned the King of France to declare the island of Tobago a free port, unlimited and unrestrained in its import and export trade for such period as the King might approve. The Minister of Colonies in France, Marshal de Castries, curtly advised the Administrators of Tobago in 1785 that the policy of the French Government in respect of commerce must be maintained in Tobago

It is true also that the French seem to have impressed on the inhabitants of Tobago for the first time the importance of local taxes in economic development. A new note was struck in colonial history when the Minister of the Colonies informed the Governor of Tobago as follows:

'As regards the finances of Tobago, a balanced budget is necessary and revenue and expenditure must be made to equate. The large deficits of the past few years must cease.'

As a result the Assembly found itself faced with raising the sum of 200,000 livres. It imposed a poll tax of 22 livres 10 sols on every slave between the ages of 14 and 60, and in order to obtain an equitable contribution from merchants, artisans and others, and not allow the planters to bear the entire burden of taxation, an additional tax of 8 per cent on the capital value was levied on all buildings in Scarborough, Plymouth and Georgetown. This was in 1786 and was followed in 1788 by another tax bill to raise 240,000 livres. This was organised as follows:

12 livres per Quintal of cotton	=	177,237 livres
2 livres 10 sols per Quintal of clayed sugar	=	6,585 livres
1 livre 13 sols per Quintal of muscovado sugar	=	40,021 livres

15 livres per Boucaud of rum	=	26,055 livres
10 sols per Pound of indigo	=	2,500 livres
6% on the profits from jobbing Negroes	=	4,500 livres
50 livres a head on Town Negroes	=	25,000 livres
6% on the rent of houses	=	10,800 livres

While the Spanish Government in Trinidad was offering liberal incentives for the economic development of Trinidad, the French Government in Tobago was holding out parallel incentives for the economic development of Tobago. The Tobago Legislature passed an Act to the effect that, from January 1, 1787, any person who established in uncultivated lands a plantation of sugar or cotton or indigo or coffee or cocoa would be exempt from all taxes on lands, slaves or produce, for six years from the beginning of the cultivation in the case of sugar or coffee, for three years in the case of cotton and indigo, and for eight years in the case of cocoa.

The Governor of Tobago went further and recommended to the Minister of Colonies in France that 'money bribes' should be offered to persuade 4,000 French artisans, free people of colour, to leave Trinidad and migrate to Tobago. Poor Trinidad. It was able to take the first halting steps to development by offering encouragement to French people to migrate to Trinidad, many of them people of colour. Now the French territory of Tobago was advancing the view that French settlers should be bribed to migrate to a French territory and not to a Spanish territory This was merely another variation of the old West Indian story of robbing Peter to pay Paul.

The Assembly of Tobago crowned the list of incentives during the French régime by passing in 1788 a bill to give every father of a family a tax allowance of 5 per cent for each living child under the age of 14.

The metropolitan country itself offered incentives to development. The Governor was advised by the Minister of Colonies in 1786 that 'it is the desire of the Government to do all that is possible to help the people and to assist the agriculture and commerce of Tobago.' In accordance with this pledge the French Government in 1786 reduced the duty on imported slaves from 100 livres a head to 6 livres. The French Government was so impressed with the potential of Tobago that it endeavoured to encourage migration from other West Indian territories, principally Grenada, in much the same way as Roume de Saint Laurent had urged the Spanish Government in Trinidad to attract French settlers from Grenada and other West Indian Islands. And as a further concession to colonial interests, the French Government in 1788 was pleased to decree that a colonial assembly, similar to that in other French West Indian islands, should be established in Tobago. The Assembly was to consist of the Governor, the Treasurer, the Commandant, two elected deputies from each parish except the sparsely populated parishes of St John and St Louis which were to have one each, and two elected deputies from the town of

Scarborough which, as indicated above, the French had renamed
Port Louis.

Under these incentives Tobago, in French hands, was able to make
the first tentative steps forward Whilst in British hands after 1763,
no one apparently had wanted to leave Grenada and migrate to
Tobago. The Governor of Barbados reported in 1764 the universal
determination of both rich and poor in Grenada against settling
Tobago. This reads curiously today, not only because it must be the
first and only time that people did not want to leave Grenada to come
to Trinidad and Tobago, but also because the alleged reason was that
Tobago, today well known as a healthy resort, was then regarded as
being particularly unhealthy. The British hope that the lower orders
of people in Barbados, who were numerous and for the most part unemployed, would find settlement in Tobago attractive seemed to have
had no greater success, despite the action of the Governor of Barbados
in changing the name of the Bay formerly called Gros Cochon to Barbados Bay. In 1768, under British rule, the majority of landowners
in Tobago were absentees. Out of a total of 77, twenty were residents
of Tobago. The distribution by other countries was as follows:
Grenada, 28; St Vincent, 5; Dominica, 3; Barbados, 9; Antigua, 2;
St Kitts, 3; Great Britain, 6; and Surinam, 1.

The effects of France's policy are reflected in various statistics of
population and production available for Tobago in the twenty years
between 1771 and 1790. In 1771 the population was 5,084. In 1791 it
was 15,020. The number of white men in 1771 was 243; no figures are
given for white women, and one is free to draw any conclusion from
that. The number of whites had increased by 1790 to 541, of whom
434 were men, and thereby hangs a tale, the tale of West Indian social
development The 1771 census gives no indication of free people of
colour. By 1790, 303 were identified, of whom 198 were women, the
other part of the tale of West Indian social development.

The slave population in 1771 numbered 4,716, and in addition 125
were listed as runaways. By 1790 the slave population had increased
to 14,170. For every slave in 1771 there were three in 1790. Between
1773 and 1780 the slave population increased by nearly one-half.
Between 1782 and 1785 the increase was nearly 10 per cent; between
1785 and 1787, about 15 per cent; between 1787 and 1790, about 12
per cent. The slave population in Tobago tended to show a smaller
disproportion between the sexes than many other slave colonies. In
1790 there were 7,548 male slaves and 6,522 female slaves. But the
unwritten law of slavery was very much at work. Slave births
amounted to 318 and slave deaths to 645. The excess of deaths over
births was just over 2 per cent of the slave population in that year.

Thus Tobago in 1790 was essentially an African population and
fundamentally a slave society. Out of every 100 people in the community, 94 were African slaves. A further two had a large admixture
of African blood, though they were free. In Tobago, the former
Amerindian island, the Amerindian had become a rarity. The 1786

census identified 24 people who were listed as Caribs at Man of War Bay. The 1790 census identified five Caribs in Little Tobago, from which apparently they were soon to be excluded by the Birds of Paradise imported from New Guinea.

In this development of Tobago under the French, sugar was king The very island whose sugar development Britain had sought to restrain in 1720 as a potential sugar rival of Barbados, became in 1770, when the first shipment of sugar was made from the island, a country which, it was predicted, would in a few years make at least as much sugar as any of the Leeward Islands The nutmeg was discovered in abundance in 1768 and 40 plantations were immediately started. Cotton and indigo and ginger also received attention. But sugar became, as it had become or was to become in one West Indian island after another, the principal object of attention. The British Governor wrote to the Secretary of State in 1796 when Tobago had again changed hands:

'With respect to the cultivation of the arrowroot which Your Grace desires may be recommended to the Legislature, I have the honour to inform you that the curing of a piece of land, not particularly fertile but planted in Bourbon canes, sold here a short while ago for £70 sterling an acre (near double the worth of the land).

'This circumstance will enable Your Grace to judge how impossible it will be to turn the attention of the planters from so profitable a production as that of the Bourbon or Otaheite cane.'

In 1790 Tobago produced 2,401,639 pounds of sugar, just under 1,100 tons, a little less than double the production of 1786, but apparently just over 60 per cent of the 1780 production of 3,934,830 pounds. Cotton production in 1790 amounted to 1,374,336 pounds, approximately the average of the years 1780 to 1788. Indigo and ginger disappeared from the statistics after attaining a production of 20,580 pounds in 1780 and 10,300 pounds in 1782, respectively. In 1790 of the land in cultivation 4,878 acres were in sugar, 14,436 in cotton, 134 in coffee, 2 in cocoa, 4,842 in ground provisions, and 5,356 in pastures. Tobago had 37 sugar factories in operation (the 1787 census indicated an additional 38 in ruins), 99 cotton factories (as against 114 in 1787) and 4 coffee factories (as against one in 1787). Indigo, of which there were 55 acres in cultivation in 1787 with 8 factories, had disappeared. Tobago's reputation for the rearing of pigs and sheep and goats seems already to have been well established. In 1790 there were 3,030 sheep and goats and 441 pigs, as well as 291 horses and 524 mules.

The basis of this economic development was slave labour. A slave society lived on a volcano; or to use Chacon's words in Trinidad disorder was one of the most terrible features in colonies where slavery was the basis of agriculture. So it was in Tobago, as the slave uprising in 1770 and the disturbances in 1798 demonstrated. As a result of the latter, the Council of Tobago called on the Governor to have all the houses not inhabited by whites, and particularly houses in Scarborough inhabited by French people of colour, searched for firearms and offensive weapons, and also to prevent all drumming or illegal meetings of Negroes in Scarborough.

This, however, must not detract from the importance of one feature of slavery in Tobago which deserves special mention. The history of West Indian slavery in general demonstrates that reforms such as they were, came from outside of the islands, from the metropolitan countries, or from metropolitan clergymen stationed in the island. This was true of almost every West Indian territory, except the Spanish colonies of Cuba and Puerto Rico where a really large Spanish population had settled and become acclimatized For the most part small farmers, growing food crops in Puerto Rico or tobacco in Cuba, they were opposed to slavery. Puerto Rico and Cuba were unique in this demand for emancipation from the colonies themselves, by Puerto Rican spokesmen in Spain and revolutionaries in Cuba, in both cases in the face of the pronounced hostility of the metropolitan government.

A report in 1798 of a Committee of both Houses of the Legislature in Tobago appointed to consider the state of the slaves in Tobago and possible measures of ameliorating their condition, stands out as a landmark in the history of all the slave colonies that ultimately formed part of the British West Indies.

The first question to which the Committee of the Tobago Legislature addressed itself was the causes which had retarded the natural increase of the slaves. In their proposals the Committee recommended the fixing by law of the commodities and quantities which should be provided for the slaves: 3 lbs of salted pork or 4 lbs of salted beef or 4 lbs of salted fish or 14 good herrings per week for each working slave and pro rata for children of different ages; 7 quarts weekly of wheat flour or oatmeal or ground provisions such as Indian corn, peas, plantains, yams, potatoes, eddoes for each working slave and pro rata for children of different ages; for men a cloth jacket, hat, frock and a pair of trousers in June and another frock and pair of trousers in December; for women a cloth jacket, hat and coarse handkerchief, a petticoat and a wrapper in June and another petticoat and wrapper in December.

The Committee further proposed – a revolutionary proposal for islands which crudely and contemptuously took the view that it was cheaper to buy slaves than to breed them – a duty on all imported slaves above 25 years of age together with a premium on all female Negroes imported between the ages of 8 and 20, in order to encourage the development of a creole population. The Committee was fully aware of the revolutionary nature of this proposal, for it reported:

'This measure appears to Your Committee of the highest importance at this moment when Legislatures in the West Indies seem

determined to attempt the instruction and civilisation of the
Negroes. Young Africans may be civilised, but old men and women
cannot be expected to forget their country or language, and with
them are likely to retain their barbarous habits and customs.'

The Committe further proposed, in its consideration of this question of slave mortality, the erection of a comfortable house on each
estate with a boarded platform for the accommodation of slaves, and
the appointment of a proper person to inspect their clothing daily and
to prevent them from disposing of it for rum or tobacco.

The Committee attributed the principal reason for the failure of
the slave population to increase by natural means to the incidence of
absenteeism among proprietors in the island. They recognised that
this was a familiar phenomenon all over the West Indies. But they
could do no better than to propose for Tobago a pale imitation of the
so-called deficiency laws which had been tried in other islands in the
West Indies and particularly in Jamaica for a hundred years before
the Tobago proposal. That was the imposition of a tax on all
absentee landowners the proceeds of which were to be utilised
for the encouragement of humanity and the care of the Negro
slaves.

Turning its attention to the question of Negro children when born,
the Committee of the Tobago Legislature recommended that slave
mothers should be prevented by law from carrying their young children into the fields, and to implement this, the law should oblige every
estate to establish a nursery for the care of young children.

Concentrating on its main objective, that of establishing a settled
and contented creole slave population, the Committee recommended,
as a measure designed to instil in the slaves habits of industry and to
inspire them with a desire for property, the distribution of a sufficient
quantity of good land to the slaves and the provision by law of a sufficient period of time to them for the cultivation of this land.

A second important question to which the Committee turned its
attention after its consideration of the causes retarding the natural
increase of the slave population, was that of family planning, the
emphasis now being on increase and not decrease of the size of families. The Committee recommended, as an incentive to matrimony
among the slaves, the erection of a comfortable house at the expense
of the slave owner for a young woman upon her marriage, a gift of
livestock the value of some $16 or $20, and clothing of superior
quality Over and above the Tobago custom of slave owners giving
presents to young children and to midwives at Christmas time, the
Committee recommended that a law should be passed entitling a mid-
wife to a fee of one dollar from the proprietor for every child that she
should bring into the world And to protect the health of mothers the
Committee recommended that it should be prescribed by law that no
woman should be required to work for at least five weeks after the
birth of her child, and even then work was to be permitted only on the

basis of a certificate from the surgeon that mother and child were progressing

To encourage and promote further the breeding and rearing of children, the Committee expressed the view that it might be advisable to grant total exemption from labour to all mothers of six children and upwards, of whom six were alive, and that to the six persons in charge of the plantations which registered the greatest natural increase in their population for the preceding year, premiums should be paid from the Public Treasury, varying from £100 for the highest numbers to £50 for the overseer on the plantation which was sixth in order of merit.

Turning its attention to another question, the Committee of the Tobago Legislature recommended immediate measures to provide for such number of missionaries as the Legislature might judge necessary for instilling into the minds of the slaves the principles of religion and morality.

The Committee finally recommended the appointment of two or three Guardians of the Rights of Negroes in every parish of the island to take cognisance of all complaints and ill-treatment made to them by the slaves, and with authority to summon such slaves before them for the elucidation of the complaint as well as such white men as they might consider necessary, in order either to redress the real grievances of the Negroes or to order that they be punished for making groundless complaints. Not many West Indian territories could have boasted at this time of their readiness to recognise the right of the slave against his owner or to receive complaints from him, or to admit that in certain cases the testimony of slaves might be received against white people.

Few of the slave codes of the West Indian territories at the end of the 18th century could claim to be superior to the ideas recommended by the Committee of the Tobago Legislature. It is not at all unlikely that we must see in this attitude of the Tobago plantocracy, as in the regulations of Chacon in Trinidad already referred to (not forgetting the limited number of slaves in both islands), one of the principle reasons for the comparative harmony or lack of serious revolts in the history of Negro slavery in Trinidad and in Tobago as compared with the history of other West Indian territories – for example, the great slave revolt in Haiti in 1793, the slave revolt in 1823 in British Guiana, the state of permanent slave revolution in which Barbados found itself in the two decades before emancipation and so on.

This, then, was Tobago under French rule before its final acquisition by Great Britain in 1802, confirmed and ratified in 1814, put an end to the changing of flags in Tobago. The changes of flags did not bother the planters to any great extent; they became a part of the routine of existence. When Great Britain captured the island in 1793, the Assembly of Tobago passed a resolution typical of West Indian society of the day, thanking Major General Cuyler for the service rendered to his country and to Tobago, and voted him a sword to the value of 100 guineas. This was on February 19, 1794 and was inspired no doubt by the British element in the island. But before this, on April 16, 1791, the members of the Assembly of Tobago, some of them emphatically British, and no doubt inspired by the French Revolution, sent an address to the Governor-General of Martinique praising him in the highest terms for his energy and persistence against the enemy and expressing the hope that in preserving Martinique as a French possession, he would receive from the representatives of the Nation and from the King of France those evidences of satisfaction which his conduct and qualities merited.

Thus it was that Tobago's history in this period of changing flags and varying allegiances could be brought to an end with the strangest episode of all, Tobago's tribute to the dictator of France, Napoleon Bonaparte, and its endorsement of his action in making himself First Consul for life. The whole history of the West Indies reveals the curious ability of the West Indian planter to accommodate himself to another flag and to switch loyalties as well. The French planters in Saint Domingue in 1791 negotiated treacherously with Britain against France on condition that slavery was maintained. The Jamaican planters in 1832 negotiated treacherously with slave owners in the United States of America with a view to becoming an American satellite on condition that slavery was maintained. The Barbadian planters in 1885 long after the abolition of slavery, negotiated with Canada for entry into the Canadian Confederation as a counter attack against British designs to establish some sort of federation in the West Indies. The address by the Legislative Council of Tobago to Bonaparte on November 25, 1802 is the most curious illustration of this facility. This important document in the history of the people of Tobago reads as follows:

'First Consul.

'The members of the Council and Assembly of the Island of Tobago beg leave to express these sentiments of loyalty and fidelity to the French Republic and of gratitude to you for the many marks of paternal solicitude you have condescended to show for the welfare of this Colony, and that at a time when your thoughts must have been employed in deciding the fate of Europe and arranging the weighty concerns of nations.

'On this occasion, words fail us to convey an adequate idea of our sentiments. To no man recorded in ancient or modern history is the character of being an accomplished Hero and consummate Statesman so appropriate and so justly applicable as to you; we therefore see with joy and satisfaction that you have justified the wish of the French Nation in consenting to be First Consul for life.

'The inhabitants of this Colony had it not in their power to give their suffrages on this occasion, but they unanimously concur therein as being a measure necessary to give the Government their stability, which must discourage its enemies, establish credit within and confidence without, and which cannot fail to raise the nation to the highest pitch of happiness and glory . . . in which they, being now firmly united to France, expect to participate.

'First Consul, we entreat you to believe that the minds of the inhabitants of this Colony are, in a particular manner, impressed with sentiments of gratitude for the intentions you have shown to their known interests and means of promoting the prosperity of the Colony by granting to them the enjoyment of their laws and internal legislation, for which the inhabitants of Tobago may, from education and habit, be pardoned for having a partiality and which may, on that account, be better suited to their character and circumstances.

'And we do humbly hope that our loyalty and fidelity to the Republic and our obedient and respectful attachment to you may induce you to continue to these people whom you have reunited to the Empire . . . an institution which they feel essential to their happiness.

'Could anything add to the sentiments which we have faintly expressed, it would be the proof you have lately afforded of the interest you have in our gratification by extending the benefits of your protection and patronage to our posterity, in the way in which you have honoured our children in the National Printannee where they will be taught to realise the virtues of the regeneration of France, to comprehend the value of such a Benefactor, and to perpetuate the sentiments of their Fathers by their gratitude and by their emulation to render themselves worthy of such a Protector.

'We salute you with respect.'

Thus in 1802, as Bonaparte stood poised, ready to launch his attack for world domination which was to plunge the whole world into a further twelve years of war that ended only with the Battle of Waterloo, Bonaparte could proceed with absolute confidence. Tobago had advised him, if we may parody a famous West Indian joke at the expense of Barbados, 'go ahead, Bonaparte, Tobago is behind you.'

CHAPTER 7

Trinidad as a Model British
· Slave Colony

Having annexed Trinidad from Spain, Britain had now to decide what to do with the island.

Trinidad, as we have seen, had a total population in 1797 of 17,643 of which 10,009 were Negro slaves. Had Britain annexed Trinidad fifty years or twenty-five years or even ten years before 1797, there would have been no decision to make. Britain and France had been competing for a hundred years for supremacy in the world sugar market The struggle had steadily shifted in favour of France until by 1789, when the Privy Council of England appointed a special committee to study the whole question of the British colonies in relation to their rivals, the French colony of Saint Domingue was generally regarded as superior in value to all the British West Indian colonies combined French costs of production were lower than British costs of production, and the French were steadily driving the British out of the world sugar market. The acquisition of so valuable a territory as Trinidad, with its sugar potential, would have been followed, even in 1787, by an enormous influx of African slaves for the increase of sugar production.

In 1797 it was a different story. The British Parliament and people had been aroused by Clarkson outside of Parliament and Wilberforce inside to the unprofitability of slavery, to the injustice and inhumanity of the slave system, and to the impolicy of the slave trade. Parliament had committed itself in principle to gradual abolition of the slave trade; British capitalism, getting ready for the enormous leap forward it would make early in the 19th century, had begun to realise that apart from certain special vested interests the main centre of which was Liverpool, the slave trade and slavery had served their purpose, were no longer essential to the accumulation of capital, and no longer provided a most important and lucrative market to British industry which at that time had no equal anywhere in the world.

These general considerations – the acceptance in principle of gradual abolition of the slave trade, the mass crusade against slavery, and the capitalist independence of the slave market – were reinforced by two other considerations of great importance The first was the lesson of the slave revolution in Haiti and the growing recognition of the danger of servile revolt. The second was the recognition by the British West Indian planters themselves, in the older islands of Jamaica, Barbados Antigua, St Kitts and others, that they could not possibly compete in the British market against the-virgin soils of Trinidad. In their own self-interest, therefore, they were prepared to demand that, whilst the slave trade should be allowed to continue to the older islands, it should be decisively prohibited in Trinidad and in their other rival, British Guiana.

The West Indian planters of the older islands concentrated upon this argument It was only a part of their general philosophy that was almost a hundred years old. It will be recalled how Barbadian planters had effectively stepped in to restrain the development of sugar cultivation in Tobago. The established British West Indian planters in Barbados and Jamaica had constantly opposed throughout the 18th century British annexations in the West Indies. It was pressure from them that led the British Government in 1763 to return Cuba to the Spaniards and take Florida instead. It was pressure from them that led the British Government in the same year 1763 to restore Guadeloupe to France and annex Canada instead. It was this same West Indian pressure which explained the restoration in time of peace of sugar islands like Tobago or Grenada or St Lucia captured by the British in time of war.

Whether the self-interest of the older West Indian planters would have prevailed even in 1797 if it had not been for the general recognition by capitalists and humanitarians in Britain that slavery was on its last legs is a point on which one can only speculate It is certain that, West Indian vested interests apart, there was a general refusal in Britain, in the light of the decision in principle to work towards the gradual abolition of the slave trade, to accept any plan for the economic development of Trinidad which, if its basis was to be Negro slavery, would necessarily involve, as the British spokesman said in the House of Lords in 1807 in sponsoring the Bill for the abolition of the slave trade, the continuation of the slave trade for two or three centuries longer in order to bring the whole of Trinidad under cultivation. This argument was the principal submission of George Canning, the future Prime Minister, in the House of Commons debate on his motion respecting Trinidad in 1802 Canning said:

'If the whole Island was to be, at once, brought into cultivation by newly imported Negroes, it would produce an extension of the Slave Trade, to a degree which must appal the feelings of every Member of that House.

'Only one twenty-fifth of the Island was now in cultivation and 10,000 Negroes were there already; to cultivate the whole would require 250,000 at a moderate calculation. Jamaica contained as many in 1791 and yet the number of acres fit for sugar were less than in Trinidad Jamaica had been nearly a century and a half arriving at its present state of cultivation, and was in 1763 in nearly the same state as Trinidad at present. Above 800,000 Negroes had been imported into Jamaica during that time; and if there was a question of suddenly cultivating such an Island as Trinidad, we must make up our minds to the destruction of about a million of the human species.'

Britain therefore had given its first answer to the question of what to do with Trinidad. Trinidad's population was not to be supplemented by Negro slaves from Africa

The general question raised a further consideration: What sort of government was Trinidad under British rule to enjoy?

Fifty years before 1797 there would have been no difficulty either in answering the question. Britain could quite easily have decided to follow the traditional pattern in the West Indies and establish, as in Jamaica and Barbados, the system which, in a sort of a way imitating the British Constitution, would have produced a Legislature of two Houses, the lower one elected, with a Governor, representing the Sovereign, working more or less in harmony with the elected representatives of the people.

In 1797, however, the British rejected this solution for two reasons

The first related to the general question of slavery and the position of the slave population in a territory governed by an Assembly controlled by white planters and white slave owners. As was to be stated in later years by the Principal Under Secretary in the Colonial Office, James Stephen, himself an abolitionist and a man of pronounced liberal views, 'popular franchises in the hands of the Masters of a great body of Slaves were the worst instruments of tyranny which were ever yet forged for the oppression of mankind.' The point of view of the British Government was that later expressed on January 30, 1832, in a despatch from Lord Goderich to the Governor of Trinidad:

'Theirs is a society in which the great mass of the people to be governed are slaves, and their proposal is that the laws should be made by a body composed of and elected by slave proprietors. Bringing this plan to the test of those general principles . . . it is to be inquired how such a scheme would provide for that identity of interest which they rightly think ought to subsist between the legislator and the subject . . . Society in Trinidad is divided into castes as strongly marked as those of Hindustan, nor can any man who has but an ordinary knowledge of the history and general character of mankind doubt what must be the effect of such distinctions when, in addition to their other privileges, the superior race are entrusted with a legislative authority over the inferior.'

There was a further consideration which was uppermost in the minds of the British authorities That was the nature of the Trinidad population inherited with annexation of the island. Chacon, with Spanish colonialism on its death bed, had emphasised in 1796 the disunity in the country which he attributed to the mixture of nationalities and races and colours. The census of 1808 illustrates the mixture. In a total of 31,478 persons, there were 2,476 whites, of whom less than half were British, nearly one-third French, and nearly one-fifth Spaniards. The figures were: British, 1147; French, 781; Spanish, 459; Corsican, 36; German, 29; and others, 24. The free people of colour, in Chacon's day overwhelmingly French in sympathy and in politics, numbered 5,450, more than double the whites. These were divided almost equally between British, French and Spanish. The population included 22 Chinese, 1,635 Amerindians, and 21,895 slaves.

Thus the representative principle of self-government in Trinidad would have meant not only entrusting a local legislature with jurisdiction over the slaves, but the domination of the local legislature itself by non-British elements, and would have raised what was in the West Indies at the time the grave question of the position of the free people of colour, some of whom were themselves proprietors.

This, then, is how the British Government saw the political problem of Trinidad, and how it reacted to the first attempt for constitution reform in Trinidad. On the one hand, slave owners would seek, in Trinidad as elsewhere, to nullify and oppose any British measures relating to slavery. On the other hand, a self-governing legislature would be dominated by Frenchmen and Spaniards, and the British element would be in the minority.

The planters naturally thought otherwise. A petition was sent by the Cabildo of Trinidad to the King of England on December 14, 1801. It carried the following signatures: Begorrat, Farfan, de Gourville, Langton, Portel, de Castro, Indave, Bontur, Alcala.

Claiming as its precedents the continuation of existing laws when Tobago was ceded to France in 1783 and Canada to Britain in 1763, the Cabildo requested the provisional continuation of Spanish laws and the Spanish religion in Trinidad until an Assembly could be selected by representatives chosen by the free suffrage of the 23 parishes in the island and the eight districts of the town of Port-of-Spain.

The Cabildo's petition was followed in the next year by an address to the King of England by the principal inhabitants of the island, in which they petitioned for a free representation in the House of Assembly and trial by jury. Eight years later, on August 10, 1810, the planters who had been living in the island at the time of its annexation in 1797 again requested some form of elective system, proposing, as a qualification for electors, habitual residence in their district for at least two years and ownership of a property cultivated by at least ten slaves, and for representatives, ownership for over two years of an estate cultivated by at least thirty slaves on which they had habitually resided.

The British abolitionists viewed these demands from the planters in Trinidad with considerable apprehension. A debate took place in the House of Commons in 1811 on the administration of justice in Trinidad. Lord Brougham condemned the planters' demand for trial by jury as calculated to involve a mockery of justice, by placing its British principle 'into the hands of men who had left every humane principle of Englishmen behind them'. Supporting his arguments by precedents taken from Barbados, Brougham concluded:

'The Trial by Jury was only good where there was such a population that a fair jury could be selected from it; but to give the 500 whites of Trinidad the complete dominion over all the lives and properties in the Island, would be highly detrimental to the course of Justice'

The first Governor of Trinidad, Colonel Thomas Picton, opposed all these demands from the planters. In a letter to the Secretary of State on June 28, 1802, he advised against any concessions in respect of elections and recommended a solution to the British Government. Picton wrote:

'Popular Elective Assemblies have been productive of much ruinous consequences in some of the neighbouring Islands where the elements of society are too different to admit a similar composition to those of the Mother Country.

'An Elective Assembly will unavoidably introduce a question which cannot fail to generate the seeds of lasting fermentation, in a country composed of such combustible material.

'One of the objects, first and most important to determine, will be the right of voting, and it may be thought expedient, as in the old Islands, to exclude the Free People of Colour; here by far the most numerous class in the Colony and of whom many possess considerable property.

'This distinction will render them at all times dissatisfied with the situation and liable to be affected in their loyalty by every prospect of change or amelioration. Of two things one will necessarily happen, they must be either formally rejected, or openly acknowledged. Disaffection is the natural consequence of the former; the latter may have an ill effect in its consequences on the same class in the neighbouring islands.

'Leaving a Popular Elective Assembly out of the question, the difficulty disappears. There will be no necessity of any legal humiliating distinction. Equal laws and severe police will secure good order and a permanent foundation.'

The British Government decided that Trinidad was not to have a self-governing constitution like Jamaica or Barbados. Instead it was to be a Crown Colony, with all essential powers reserved to the British Government through the Governor. As the policy decided on by the British Government was to remain, with some modification in 1831 in respect of the establishment of a Legislature, substantially unchanged until 1925, the British Government's decision, in the form of a despatch from the Secretary of State, Lord Liverpool, to the Governor of Trinidad on November 27, 1810, is reproduced almost in its entirety:

'The application of the proprietors, white inhabitants of Trinidad, may be divided into two; the British Constitution as it is understood and supposed to be enjoyed by the other West India islands –

the British laws under whatever frame of Government His Majesty may be pleased to establish in that Colony.

'With respect to the first of these points, it has undergone the most deliberate consideration in all its different bearings. The question proposed for discussion has no necessary reference to that state of things which has existed for so many years in the old West India Islands but may be stated to amount to this:— whether in a new colony in which the rights of the Crown and Parliament must be admitted on all hands to be entire, it would be advisable to surrender these rights in whole or in part and to establish a system of government analogous to that of the other West India Islands.

'Even if the circumstances of Trinidad were in all respects much more nearly the same as those of the other West India Colonies than they unquestionably are, the determination of Government would probably be to negative such a proposition. But it so happens that the circumstances of the Island of Trinidad are in many respects so materially different from those of all the West India Colonies that supposing the system of Government established in those Islands to be the best could be afforded them in their situation, it would not follow that the same system could be rendered applicable either in justice or in policy to the Island of Trinidad.

'In all the other West India Islands (with the exception of Dominica, an exception which arises out of recent circumstances) the white inhabitants form the great majority of the free people of the Colony and the political rights and privileges of all descriptions have been enjoyed exclusively by them.

'The class of free people of colour in these Colonies, as far as even their numbers extend, has grown up gradually. They have thereby in some degree been reconciled to the middle situation which they occupy between the whites and the slaves. But in the Island of Trinidad the free people of colour at this time form a very great majority of the free inhabitants of the Island and the question would arise according to the proposed system whether in establishing, for the first time, a popular government in that Colony, we shall exclude that class of people from all political rights and privileges. Such an exclusion we know would be regarded by them as a grievance and it may be doubted how far it would be consistent with the spirit of the capitulation by which their privileges were to be secured and their situation certainly not deteriorated from that which they enjoyed under the Spanish Government

'In the second place in most of the West India Islands, the great body of the proprietors and white inhabitants are British or descendants of British families to whom the British Constitution and the Laws have become familiar; they have been educated or supposed themselves to be educated in the knowledge of them and though the resemblance is certainly not great between the Constitution as it is supposed to exist in our West India Islands and as it is enjoyed in Great Britain, the circumstances above referred to would in some degree account for the attachment of the inhabitants of the old West India Islands to a system of government in which popular assembly forms a material part.

'But in the Island of Trinidad, the white population consist of a mixture of people of all nations. The greater part of them must be wholly ignorant of the British Constitution and unaccustomed to any frame of government which bears any analogy to it In the case of Trinidad therefore, amongst the most numerous class of white inhabitants, there can be no material prejudice either of habit or education in favour of such a system and the partial and exclusive principle on which it is proposed by the white inhabitants to be founded, whereby the largest proportion of the free inhabitants of the Island would be excluded from all participation in its privileges, appears to defeat the object of it and to constitute in point of justice and upon the very principles of the system itself, a decided and insuperable objection against it

'The question has hitherto been considered as far as it may affect the internal state of the Colony itself. But in addition to these considerations it is material to add that the abolition of the Slave Trade by Parliament imposes upon Government the necessity of keeping within themselves any power which may be material for rendering this measure effectual.

'It is essential for this purpose that in a new Colony the Crown should not divest itself of its power of legislation and that neither the Crown nor the Parliament should be subject to the embarrassments which on such an occasion might perhaps arise from the conflicting views of the Imperial Parliament and of a subordinate Legislature.

'Under these considerations you may consider it a point determined that it is not advisable to establish within the Island of Trinidad any independent Legislature.

'In reserving to himself the power of legislation, His Majesty will delegate in some degree that power as far as local considerations may render necessary or expedient to the Governor as His Representative whose acts will be always subject to be reviewed, altered or revoked by His Majesty himself.

'In exercising this power for local purposes His Majesty feels the advantage which may arise in a Council selected by the Governor from the most respectable of the inhabitants of the Island, but such a Council must be considered as a Council of advice and not of control. The determination of the Governor, even if it should be contrary to the opinion of such a Council, must be considered as obligatory till such time as His Majesty's pleasure shall be known; the members of the Council may, however, in such cases be allowed to transmit their opinion together with their reasons for His Majesty's consideration

'The advantages of a government of this description in Colonies and remote settlements have been experienced in other instances and furnish the strongest possible inducements for acting upon this principle upon the present occasion

'Upon the second point – the introduction of British laws into the Island of Trinidad – I am not as yet enabled to give you a decided opinion. The subject is necessarily extensive and complicated. It is at the time under the serious consideration of His Majesty's Government and I hope to be able soon to communicate to you at large their sentiments upon it But I thought it of importance that no time should be lost in conveying to you the determination of His Majesty's Government for the information of the inhabitants of the Colony upon the important subject of an internal legislature.'

Trinidad therefore began its association with the British Empire as a type of colony unknown at that time, a Crown Colony in which the British Government retained complete control, and which the British Government hoped to establish as a model for the self-governing colonies in the West Indies, in respect of legislation governing the treatment of the slaves Let it be understood, however, that the principal reason for this decision was to deny the vote to people of colour who were otherwise qualified. This decision must be seen also in the context of the colour discrimination practised in Trinidad at the time

The free people of colour had to pay a special tax for dances and public entertainments. They had to be off the streets at the ringing of the jail bell at 9 30 p m. They were charged half price for passports and charged less than the whites for medical attendance A broken leg was set for a white person for $86.40, for a free person of colour for $68 12. But the price for a thigh bone was the same, whatever its colour. In 1822 Governor Woodford sought a ruling from the Secretary of State as to whether he ought to permit a young coloured doctor trained in England to practise in Trinidad.

How seriously Britain took its decision to introduce the Crown Colony system is seen in a despatch of the Secretary of State on February 4, 1808, in which he rapped the Governor of Trinidad on the knuckles for falling into some misapprehension with respect to his prerogatives and to the power of the Cabildo over colonial revenues and officers in Trinidad. Lord Castlereagh wrote as follows to Governor Hislop:

> 'There is at present at Trinidad no regular Colonial form of Government, analogous to the old Governments of the other West India Islands, but the Island is governed by His Majesty's Prerogative in consequence of the Capitulation; as you have repeatedly been informed
>
> 'The Colonial Revenue, therefore, and the appointment to all Offices in the Colony, are entirely subject to His Majesty's Pleasure and there is no authority in the Colony that is known or recognised here which can order the expenditure of any sums of money except the Governor under His Majesty's authority.

'Neither is there any authority in the island which can create a new office or appoint a new officer or remove an officer appointed, except the Governor under the authority of His Majesty; and you are restricted merely to the power of suspending officers who misconduct themselves, until His Majesty's Pleasure be known.

'It is therefore wished you would not, upon any account, permit His Majesty's Authority and Prerogatives which are entirely entrusted to your care to be entrenched upon by any other Body, and that you would guard them from every intrusion whatever.'

The Trinidad planters continued to agitate for self-government. A Royal Commission of Legal Enquiry, which in 1823 enquired into the administration of civil and criminal justice in Trinidad, noted that it was the unanimous feeling of the planters 'that no change which did not at the same time confer on them the benefit of a reasonable control over the taxation and expenditure of the colony' would satisfy them. The result was the British decision in 1831 to replace the Governor's Council of advice by the Colony's first Legislature, the Council of Government

The Council consisted of the Governor as President, six official members – the Chief Justice, the Colonial Secretary, the Attorney General, the Colonial Treasurer, the Protector of Slaves and the Collector of Customs–, and six unofficial members selected by the Governor from among the principal proprietors of the Colony The Governor was given both an original and a casting vote. At the same time an Executive Council with advisory powers was established, comprising the Governor as President, the Colonial Secretary, the Attorney General, and the Colonial Treasurer. In a despatch on May 25, 1831, to the Governor of Trinidad, Lord Goderich, the Secretary of State for the Colonies, explained one of the reasons for the refusal to grant Trinidad a self-governing Assembly instead of the Crown Colony Legislature, the final vestiges of which were not removed until the Constitution of December 1961, by which Trinidad achieved its aspirations to full internal self-government. Lord Goderich wrote as follows: —

'The benefits resulting from the election by the proprietary body, in every country, of the popular branch of the legislature are too familiar to require notice, and are so universally admitted as to preclude all controversy on the abstract principle. That principle is however wholly inapplicable to a state of society in which a very large majority of the people are in a state of domestic slavery, and in which those persons who are of free condition are separated from each other by the indelible distinction of European and African birth or parentage . . As society is at present constituted in the island His Majesty's Ministers will abstain from advising the introduction of a representative assembly and popular elections.'

The crucial issue involved in this British decision not to introduce into Trinidad an elected assembly was the labour question. Sugar in particular required a great deal of labour, and no one thought of anything but sugar. For example Picton wrote to the Secretary of State on July 30, 1799:

'Trinidad should be regarded as a sugar Colony, the lands being generally more favourable to the production of Cane, than of Coffee or Cotton. The quantity of land to be granted should certainly depend upon the means of cultivation, but everything considered the smallest class of sugar plantation cannot consist of less than 200 acres of good land, of which 100 acres for cane, 50 for pasture, and 50 for Negro grounds, establishments and Casualties A plantation of this class carried on with the greatest economy will require a capital of about £8,000 sterling.'

Everybody agreed that Trinidad needed labour. The difficulty was, if Negro slaves were not to be imported from Africa, where then was the labour to come from? This raised two separate issues: (1) the recruitment of labour from outside of Trinidad; (2) the treatment of the slaves in Trinidad

First, the efforts to recruit labour from other countries. In this matter Trinidad was international in outlook and catholic in taste. Everybody was welcome.

Attention was concentrated on the possibility of attracting additional white settlers. The British Government in Trinidad behaved as if the West Indian slate in this matter was entirely clean, and ignored all the precedents for 300 years which indicated that labour could not be provided from those sources. In December, 1802, the Secretary of State for the Colonies urged the Governor of Trinidad to give attention to attracting industrious Protestant dissenters from Ireland and Scotland on a three-year indenture at 60 cents a day for labourers and $1 20 a day for artisans and with the grant of three acres of land for an adult and two for a child. All the Secretary of State had to do was to read up British records on similar 17th century efforts in Jamaica and Barbados or to ask the French Government for advice based on their 17th century experience. The Secretary of State also proposed efforts to attract men from the Army and Navy who were no longer on active service, on the basis of land grants varying from 150 acres to Field Officers and 10 acres to Corporals. As the Secretary of State put it: 'The advantages which might be expected to accrue from the introduction of a European yeomanry in Trinidad are so great that I cannot too strongly recommend that subject to your most serious consideration.'

The great problem where the European settlers were concerned was climate. Picton issued a stern warning about this and suggested that Europeans should be located on the higher parts of the river Caroni. The first Germans who arrived appeared to have been placed on the borders of the Arouca Savannah, and were regarded as a very valuable acquisition. The Trinidad Government was of the opinion that success in respect of European immigration depended very largely on the provision of houses for them in or near Port-of-Spain which they might rent until accommodation was available in the area to which they might be assigned.

Particular emphasis was placed on the other West Indian Islands as a source of labour for Trinidad. Governor Picton anticipated a large influx from the Bahamas, Barbados and all the Windward and Leeward Islands. One William Tucker of Bermuda petitioned in 1804 for permission to settle Guayaguayare with mechanics and seamen from Bermuda; at the time the population of Guayaguayare was 66 planters, mostly French, with 400 slaves, whilst at Mayaro, which was virtually covered with sugar plantations, there were 120 French settlers with 380 slaves.

This was the basis of the considerable intercolonial slave trade which developed after the abolition of the slave trade in 1807, under the guise of domestic servants attending on their master. What was really involved was the transfer of slaves from the less productive and less profitable older islands to the newer and virgin soils of Trinidad and British Guiana. Between 1813 and 1821 Trinidad received over 3,800 such slaves, of whom nearly 1,100 came from Dominica and nearly 1,200 from Grenada.

The trade was a fraud and was not really an immigration of domestic servants For example, an indigent planter in Barbados came to Trinidad with his family attended by 14 slaves, one of whom was a carpenter Of 266 domestics imported into Trinidad from Barbados during the year 1827, 204 had changed owners by the end of the year and 81 had ceased to be domestics. People who used to travel before with no servant at all suddenly began to travel to Trinidad or Guiana accompanied by two domestic slaves for each member of the family, however numerous.

It was the superior value of slaves and the greater fertility of the soil of Trinidad and Guiana which formed the background to this intercolonial slave trade. The cost of a slave in Barbados or Antigua was only £35 or £40, in Guiana and Trinidad it was from £80 to £90. The relative fertility of Demerara and Barbados, as judged by exports, was in the proportion of four to one. In Demerara it took 200 days' labour to produce 5,000 lbs. of sugar, in Barbados 400. In the former the sugar was produced without any outlay of capital for manure, in the latter it required twenty-five per cent of the labour of the plantation. The canes in Trinidad produced saccharine matter in the proportion of 5 to 2 as compared with the older islands; the average output of sugar was three hogsheads per slave as compared with one in the older islands.

This trade continued and developed with the connivance and the full protection of the authorities in Trinidad. The Governor of Trinidad, for example, Sir Ralph Woodford, wrote touchingly contrasting conditions in Tortola and in Trinidad; in Tortola, he said, the poor slaves had only six pints of cornmeal per week, whilst in Trinidad no one starved and the Negro had not only his pig but half a dozen goats as well and the fertility and extent of the soil permitted the planters to give the slaves more land for the cultivation of their provisions. And as Trinidad was maintained by the British as a model slave colony, where, unlike the self-governing islands, British legislation by order in council was in effect and in force, the Trinidad planters, with the Attorney General as their mouthpiece, speciously urged that 'if the order in council cannot go to the slaves, the slaves might be permitted to come to the order in council in Trinidad.'

The third possible source of labour for Trinidad was China, and the early documents of Trinidad under British rule are full of the Chinese prospects It was proposed to the British Government by Governor Picton as early as 1802. High hopes were placed on the Chinese, one lobbyist going so far, in advancing the superiority of free labour over slave, as to estimate that two Chinese labourers with a light plough and buffalo would do as much work as 40 stout Negroes. In 1806, 147 Chinese workers arrived in Trinidad, followed by a further 192 in the same year But the following year thirty or forty applied for permission to return to China and the first criticism was voiced by the Council of Trinidad of this emigration, on the ground that it would prove 'an external expense to the Government'.

One of the difficulties was that Chinese women did not accompany the workers, and the free women of colour in Trinidad, it was alleged, considered themselves superior to the Chinese who, though free in name, were performing the work of slaves. So the Governor reported in 1807. Anyone familiar with the complex nature of the Trinidad population of today will readily recognise that, if this were true in 1807, the women of Trinidad soon changed their minds. By 1814 the hopes placed on China had failed. Those who remained, about thirty in number, were regarded as useful fishermen and butchers. Had they, in the Governor's opinion, brought with them wives and families and priests, they would have been a very valuable addition to the Trinidad population. But those who were brought to Trinidad seemed incapable of and disinclined to the fatigues of agricultural labour in the tropical sun.

The planters, in their desperate search for labour, thought of Africans, Amerindians, and even convicts. In 1825 the Governor recommended that African women should be brought in from Sierra Leone. Almost incredibly, the British Government, in 1802, suggested the use of Amerindians from the South American continent. And as if the whole previous history of European colonialism in the West Indies did not cry out aloud against the use of convict labour the Secretary of State suggested that consideration should be given to a selection from the least undeserving of convicts who should be assigned to various employers to be clothed and fed by them until they had served their sentence.

There was only one country, India, that really remained to which consideration might be given, and the Governor, Sir Ralph Woodford, recommended it in a despatch to Earl Bathurst, Secretary of

State for the Colonies, on October 3, 1814. His recommendation read
as follows: —

'The cultivators of Hindostan are known to be peaceful and
industrious. An extensive introduction of that class of people accustomed to live on the produce of their own labour only, and totally
withdrawn from African connections or feelings, would probably
be the best experiment for the population of this Island where the
King has the power of enacting the laws and regulations he may
think fit for their protection and support and where the soil is grateful and probably corresponds much with that of their own country.
But without their priests, their chiefs (one of whom it would
be desirable should be acquainted with some one of the European
languages), their families, their artisans, their plants and seeds, the
success of such a plan could not be expected.

'They might easily select a favourable spot for their residences,
and if after some time they should find an inclination to work on
the sugar estates, the Planter would have the best means of satisfy-
ing himself of the advantages of free labourers over slaves If sugar
can be raised in the East Indies at so much less an expense than in
the West, the best means would soon be in the power of the specula-
tive planter to commence an establishment by which from the
reduced capital that only would be necessary and the avoiding the
purchase of foreign provisions, he would be able to undersell every
competitor whose produce might be raised by slaves.'

The first suggestion that India might replace Africa as the source
of labour in Trinidad involved the use of Indians not in a state of
semi-servitude, working on the plantation for wages, but as small
farmers cultivating their own land.

Whilst all these efforts were being made to recruit labour from all
parts of the globe, slave labour was becoming increasingly difficult,
at least on the old terms. As Trinidad was a model British slave
colony, the British Government experimented with it for the introduction of ameliorating measures designed to satisfy the criticisms
of the abolitionists in England. The most important of these was the
Order in Council of 1823 which the British Government hoped, after
its introduction in Trinidad, would be adopted in the self-governing
colonies. The principal features of the Order in Council were as
follows·

(1) A Protector of Slaves whose duties were regulated was to be
    appointed.
(2) Sunday markets were abolished.
(3) The performance of any labour by slaves between sunset on
    Saturday and sunrise on Monday was prohibited.
(4) The carrying of any whip for the purpose of coercing slaves
    to perform labour was declared illegal.
(5) No slave was to be punished until 24 hours after the offence,

and then only in the presence of at least one free person in addition to the person ordering the punishment.

(6) The use of the whip on female slaves for any offence was prohibited.

(7) Books and records, including one for punishments, were to be maintained.

(8) The onus was placed on the slave owner to prove that no punishment was inflicted, should a slave prosecute the owner for improper punishment.

(9) Marriages among slaves were to be encouraged.

(10) The division of families when slaves were sold was prohibited

(11) The slave was permitted to possess and bequeath property.

(12) The slave was permitted to manumit himself without the owner's consent.

(13) The fee for manumission was fixed at not more than 20 shillings.

(14) Appraisement of his value when a slave was affected in a mortgage or a law settlement was regulated.

(15) When a slave under six years or over fifty was manumitted, the owner was required to provide gratuitously a bond of £200 so as to provide for his sustenance.

(16) Clergymen were authorized to certify that slaves had sufficient religious instruction to understand the nature of an oath and to be competent witnesses in a Court of Law.

The second British measure for the control and amelioration of slavery was the Slave Registration Bill of 1816. This Bill, as applied to Trinidad by an Order in Council of March 26, 1812, was designed specifically, by establishment of a Public Registry for the registration of the names, description, births and death of all slaves, to prevent illegal and clandestine importation of slaves into Trinidad in violation of the Bill for the Abolition of the Slave Trade in 1807. The registration, as of January 1814, produced a total of 25,717 slaves, of whom 8,633 were domestic slaves and 17,084 plantation slaves.

It was against this background of an acute shortage of labour that Trinidad's economic development proceeded in the period between its annexation by Britain and the emancipation of the slaves in 1833. The island's sugar exports to Britain increased from 5,920 tons in 1812 to 10,334 tons in 1833. Trinidad's rum exports to Britain declined in the same period from 39,126 gallons to 223 gallons. Its cotton exports to Britain stood at 745,049 lbs. in 1812 and 11,951 lbs in 1833. Coffee exports increased from 75,500 lbs. to 154,901 lbs. during the same period. Exports of cocoa increased from 204,400 lbs. to 1,755,144 lbs.

Cocoa was king, and in 1818 the Governor emphasised that it was only by encouraging the growth of cocoa that Trinidad could be settled. The island's total exports of cocoa increased from 96,000 lbs in 1797 to 3,090,526 lbs. in 1833. One enthusiast, in a communication to the Governor, recommended that Trinidad should be made a cocoa island and all the slaves who were employed in distilling poisonous rum and making bad sugar should be made to plant cocoa.

The only other important feature of Trinidad's economy in the period under British rule before emancipation was its trade relations with Venezuela. From the very outset Trinidad's importance to Britain was seen in the context of the advantage which its strategic position afforded of shipping British manufactures into South America in contravention of the Spanish Exclusive. Trinidad, which was of no use to Spain at all, found its principal advantage to Britain in its goegraphical location in respect of Spanish South America. Thus one of the principal objectives of the Trinidad Government was to maintain good relations with Venezuela. It protested sharply when in 1816 Simon Bolivar decreed the emancipation of slaves, partly because this would inspire the slaves of Trinidad, and partly because the resulting disturbances would disrupt commercial relations with Trinidad. It went almost frantic when Trinidad conspirators congregated on Chacachacare in 1813 to plot an attack on Venezuela; the Governor immediately ordered a detachment of the first West India Regiment to proceed to Chacachacare to disperse them, and followed this up by a Proclamation of neutrality in 1815 threatening with deportation and banishment all inhabitants of Trinidad detected in conveying to the Spanish province of the Continent of South America either arms, ammunition or warlike stores The value of Trinidad's trade with the Spanish Main, which brought mules, cattle, hogs, and cotton to Trinidad and took out British manufactures for Venezuela, was estimated in 1805 at $859,000 in imports and $1,112,000 in exports.

This was Trinidad in the first 36 years of British colonialism, in its economic and political aspects.

In its social aspect this community, whose population increased from 30,742 in 1811 to 42,874 in 1828, presented a powerful contrast with the Trinidad which became Independent in 1962.

The Capital of the island had been shifted from St Joseph to Port-of-Spain. But Port-of-Spain in this period included little more than what are today Duncan, Nelson and George Streets, going as far north as Duke Street and as far west as Frederick Street. The city of wooden structures was reduced on the night of March 24, 1808, for the most part to ashes, as a result of a fire which broke out sometime after 10 o'clock in the house of a druggist. 412 houses and 337 stores were completely burnt out, and the number of people rendered homeless was 3,647, of whom 615 were whites, 1,004 free people of colour and 2,028 slaves. The estimated loss in houses amounted to between three and four million dollars, and that in merchandise and produce equalled half a million sterling. Public buildings destroyed included a Protestant Church, Government House, the jail, the hospital and the Town Hall.

A Committee of the Council appointed to report upon the fire advised that it would be necessary on an average to lend about $500 each to a number of persons to enable them to rebuild their houses and emphasised that the calamity made it impossible to continue public works then in progress for the completion of the wharf, for bringing water from St Ann's to Port-of-Spain, and for improving the main road leading from Port-of-Spain to St Joseph. The Committee therefore recommended an immediate application to the British Government for assistance in the sum of £110,000 sterling, such portion as was required for the benefit of individual sufferers being regarded as a free gift, and the remainder to be advanced as an interest-free loan to be repaid in due course from the funds of the Colony

This disaster was followed ten years later by a similar fire in San Fernando which broke out at one o'clock in the day and which in a short time destroyed 60 houses, 200 hogsheads of sugar, a considerable quantity of rum and several stores of merchandise. The Governor, Sir Ralph Woodford, turned to the British Government In a despatch of May 5, 1818, he wrote:

'Might I hope that this calamity will induce His Majesty's Government to grant us some assistance? The total stagnation of trade from the affairs of the Main renders that assistance more necessary as our wants are daily becoming more urgent. It will be likewise necessary to give shelter to the poor, free people who have lost their houses Is it hopeless to expect a sum by way of a loan for which the Colony might pay the interest which might be secured by an order to the Colonial treasurer to make the half yearly payment to the Collector of Customs?'

Trinidad, in the first three decades of the 19th century, suffered partly from five major problems: bad bread, medical quacks, small pox, illegal immigrants, and bad roads. A Proclamation of July 16, 1814, imposed severe penalties for bad bread and adulteration of flour and established a rigorous system of inspection, under which the Chief of Police was required to visit on one day of the first week in every month all bakeries to inspect the flour and bread in their possession.

The Medical Board was constituted in 1815 in order to protect the population against imposition by so-called doctors of foreign nationality; one such, when asked to show his alleged diploma from the College of Surgeons in London for registration, replied that he was forbidden to do so by the Act of Parliament incorporating the College of Surgeons, and that it was derogatory to him to show the degree which the College had conferred upon him. The Governor issued a Proclamation prohibiting all persons from the practice of medicine or surgery without publication of their names in the Gazette, and prohibiting the sale of medicines or drugs of any kind to any slave without an order in writing from the owner or manager of the estate to which the slave belonged.

In 1819, a Proclamation was issued requiring all the inhabitants to be vaccinated against smallpox.

A Proclamation of 1804 enjoined specific precautions against illegal immigrants and required the frequent search of all houses both by day and by night for the apprehension of suspected illegal immigrants. All houses in Port-of-Spain were to be numbered and each housekeeper, white or coloured, was required to affix to the street door on a card or sheet of paper the names of the persons living in the house, all inmates and lodgers, and all servants and slaves employed therein A Board of Superintendence and Control was set up to investigate all visitors to the colony.

The notorious condition of the roads in Trinidad, especially in Mayaro, was demonstrated by a petition from the inhabitants and planters of Mayaro and Guayaguayare to be allowed to send their produce to Tobago instead of Port-of-Spain

Woodford Square, then known as Brunswick Square, was the subject of a powerful protest from the adjoining proprietors against a proposal to erect a new Protestant Church in the centre of the Square. The proprietors emphasized that the Square was necessary for air, pleasure and amusement and was also the parade ground of the Town Militia. The proprietors appealed to His Majesty's Council to prevent this breach of their privileges and their rights.

In 1825 there were only six schools in the island – one English female boarding school and three French day schools in Port-of-Spain with 175 students, a school kept by the Cabildo for teaching the English language with 60 boys; and a small day school at an Indian village where only Spanish was taught.

In 1810 a number of planters, in a petition to the King begged for the establishment of a Chamber of Agriculture and also a Botanic garden with a view to improving the standard of agriculture and introducing better varieties of plants and new crops.

This was the colony which Britain had developed as a model colony for the self-governing West Indian islands. There was nothing particularly model about its Government in the first few years after its annexation, which saw a fantastic innovation by the British Government to substitute three Commissioners for the former military governor, Picton. This immediately led to a struggle between Picton and the first of the three Commissioners, Fullarton. Even against the background of the well-known jealousy and individualism of Trinidadians, the documents of this unseemly squabble between two of the Governors of the island make unpleasant reading The squabble ended in Fullarton charging Picton with a variety of crimes including torture. The case went to the British courts where Picton was first found guilty, and then, after a retrial, was found not guilty. Rehabilitated, he died fighting for his country at the Battle of Waterloo.

Sir Ralph Woodford, a very young man who was the Governor of the territory for some 14 or 15 years, was superior to much with which the island was afflicted in the next hundred years. The illus-

trious Cabildo inherited from Spain became anything but illustrious
Its annual revenue in 1809 was $21,656 and its expenditure $6,517.
The Cabildo derived its revenue from liquor licences – in 1804 there
were 50 such establishments in Port-of-Spain; licences for billiard
tables; dues in the meat and fish markets; rents from the Five Islands
rented out to cotton planters; rents of land on Marine Square, at the
western extremity of the town, and from the Coconut Walk; the grant
of one-quarter of one per cent of the island's revenue which had been
made by the Spanish Government; payments for the use of the public
well, pump and aqueduct for the convenience of shipping; fines imposed on delinquents in the administration of justice; a tax on carts
of $2 a month each; and a duty on foreign liquor, rum, brandy and
gin.

The Cabildo spent its money on repairs of the public wharf; slave
labour on works of public utility, maintenance of prisoners without
means of subsistence; rent of a Town Hall; repairs to streets; printing; rent of a public jail; expenses of a Police Force and the overseers of public works; and the expenses of such religious festivals as
the Feast of St Joseph and Corpus Christi.

As far as the defence of the island was concerned, it was the general
opinion that Chaguaramas was the best spot for a military base,
though some argued in favour of Chacachacare.

In those days when sugar was cultivated at Laventille and what it
is today the Lapeyrouse Cemetery was a sugar plantation, Chaguaramas was an important part of Trinidad's sugar economy. This was
reflected in the revolt of the slaves in Chaguaramas in 1805. It was
alleged that the intention was a general massacre on Christmas Day of
all whites and people of colour. The plot seemed to have been limited
to slaves who had migrated from the French colonies Two of them
who styled themselves King and one who called himself General-in-
Chief were condemned to hang on December 19; their heads were
to be exposed after death on poles erected for the purpose and their
bodies were to be hung in chains on the estate near the district where
they resided. Subsequently, judgment was passed on six more of the
ringleaders. The most culpable were sentenced to lose their ears, to
be flogged on the gallows and to be banished from the colony fore-
ever. Those less culpable were sentenced to corporal punishment and
to work in chains for a specific period. The general alarm in the colony
was aggravated by reports of slave disturbances in Tobago. Apprehensive of a growing insubordination among the slaves, the Cabildo passed
orders in 1810 forbidding Negroes to carry cudgels or canes.

Slavery was brought to an end with the Emancipation Bill of 1833.
By this Bill the slave planter, and not the slaves, were paid by
the British Government the sum of £20 million compensation. A comparison of Trinidad with the other West Indian territories in this
matter is of considerable importance not only for a study of the
economic development of Trinidad up to 1833 but also for the future
of race relations in Trinidad

The slaves were divided into three broad categories: predial attached, the field slaves; predial unattached; and non-predial slaves, employed in service, such as on the wharves, and domestic servants. There were also the children under six years of age on August 1, 1834, and the aged, diseased, or otherwise non-effective slaves.

In the first three categories the total number of slaves emancipated in the West Indies amounted to 512,823, and the compensation paid for them amounted to £15,524,360. Of these totals the number of slaves in the third class in Trinidad amounted to 17,439 and the compensation to £973,443. The number of slaves in Tobago amounted to 9,078 and the compensation to £226,746. This compares with 254,310 slaves in Jamaica, the compensation for whom totalled £5,853,978; with 66,638 slaves in Barbados, the compensation for whom amounted to £1,659,316; and with 69,579 in British Guiana, whose compensation totalled £4,068,809.

Trinidad had fewer slaves than Grenada (19,009), than St Vincent (18,114), or Antigua (23,350). Trinidad and Tobago combined had fewer slaves (26,517) than Dominica and St Kitts combined (27,331), or than St Lucia and St Vincent combined (28,442).

Not only therefore was Trinidad less significant as a slave colony than the vast majority of West Indian colonies, but Trinidad's economic potential in comparison with that of the exhausted soil of the older islands made the slave in Trinidad an infinitely more valuable piece of property than the slave in any other West Indian colony except British Guiana The average of the compensation paid per slave was £58½ in British Guiana and just under £56 in Trinidad. This compares with an average of £25 in Barbados and £23 in Jamaica. Tobago's average was as high as Barbados. The slave in Grenada or St Lucia or St Vincent averaged £30 in respect of compensation money. The figure for St Kitts, Nevis and Montserrat was £20. The figure for Antigua was a mere £17.

In addition to the adult and working slaves, a further 117,000 slaves were emancipated for whom compensation amounting to £892,000 was paid. These were 88,306 children under six, on whom some £647,000 was paid – a little over £7 each – and 28,701 aged and infirm slaves, for whom £144,000 was paid – a little over £5 each. Trinidad had 2,246 children and 872 aged and infirm slaves. The compensation for the former averaged over £22 per head, for the latter over £12 per head. A child under six in Trinidad fetched a higher compensation than an adult slave in St Kitts, Nevis, Montserrat and Antigua, and as high a compensation as an adult slave in Jamaica. The average compensation paid per child in British Guiana was less than £20, as compared with £11 in St Vincent, £8 in Grenada, a little over £5 in Jamaica, and £4 in Barbados. The average compensation paid per aged slave in British Guiana was a little under £12, as compared with over £8 in Grenada, £8 in St Lucia, £4 in Jamaica, and £2 in Barbados.

There were few slaves in Trinidad in relation to the available land.

A slave, therefore, young or old, field or domestic, effective or ineffective, fetched a high price. But Trinidad in 1833 was not a plantation society. Rather it was a society of small estates operated by a few slaves. Comparing the number of slaves for whom compensation was paid with the number of claims for compensation, the figure in Trinidad was seven slaves per claim, as compared with 23 in British Guiana. The average slave owner in Trinidad, in other words, had seven slaves It is curious to see the classic islands of small farmers today as they emerged in 1833. In Tobago, an island of larger planters and larger plantations, the average was twenty-four slaves per claim Grenada, Montserrat, Nevis, strongholds of the peasantry today, were plantation economies compared with Trinidad in 1833. The average number of slaves per claim was twenty-one in Antigua, twenty in St Vincent, eighteen in Grenada and Nevis, seventeen in Montserrat, fifteen in Jamaica, thirteen in St Kitts, eleven in St Lucia and Dominica and nine in Barbados.

Even this average of seven slaves per claim in Trinidad may create a false picture. An analysis of 1,862 claims, 83% of the total claims, reveals that 30% were claims for ownership of one slave only, 16% were claims for two slaves, 22% claims for three to five slaves, and 12% claims for six to ten slaves. Eighty per cent of the slave owners in Trinidad in 1833 owned less than ten slaves each. One per cent owned more than 100 slaves. By comparison, owners of less than ten slaves constituted 60% of the slave owners in Tobago, St Vincent and Dominica, 50% in Nevis and Montserrat. Persons owning more than 100 slaves constituted 12% of the slave owners in Tobago, 10% in Grenada and Nevis, 8% in Montserrat and St Vincent.

A further point of great significance is indicated in this analysis of the slave compensation claims. The slave society wasted a great deal of labour in purely domestic servants, and the history of slavery in the Western Hemisphere is full of stories of Jamaican big houses with 40 servants, of the Surinam slave planter going to Church on Sundays accompanied by a slave girl carrying the cushion for him to kneel on, and the Brazilian slave planter being shaved by a barber with a slave girl standing by whose duty was at appropriate times to put the lighted cigar into his mouth and to take it out.

The other side of this picture of a gross waste of labour in unproductive occupations was that the domestic slaves were relatively better and more leniently treated than the field slaves. The underdevelopment of Trinidad's economy and the relatively peaceful relations between slaves and masters was illustrated by the fact that there were three domestic slaves for every ten field slaves as compared with a ratio of under two to ten in Jamaica and one to ten in British Guiana.

A further illustration of this point, which had important consequences for the relative ease of race relations after emancipation, as compared with the 1865 rebellion in Jamaica and the Barbados disturbances over federation in 1876, is the fact that the compensation paid for the third category of slaves, in service occupations and as domestic slaves, was higher in Trinidad than elsewhere and indeed was high even in Tobago. The compensation value of a domestic slave in Trinidad was over £55½ as compared with £53½ in British Guiana, £24 in Jamaica, and £23 in Barbados The value attached to a domestic slave in Tobago was over £35.

The presence of a mere 17,439 slaves in Trinidad and a mere 69,579 in British Guiana changed the whole course of history of these two colonies after emancipation. The labour problem led to the introduction of an entirely new population in Trinidad, which converted the island from a society of small farmers into a typical plantation economy. The Crown Colony system made Trinidad safe for the sugar plantation.

CHAPTER 8

Trinidad's Labour Problem after Emancipation

The fundamental question facing Trinidad, and indeed all the West Indian colonies after emancipation, was the question of labour. This meant simply this: would sugar continue to be the principal product? If so, would it continue on the basis of the plantation system? And if the plantation was to be perpetuated, how was a regular and continuous supply of disciplined labour to be guaranteed?

Put in its simplest form, the fundamental question boiled down to this: would the former slaves be prepared to continue, or could they be compelled to continue, to work on the same plantation for their former masters, for wages instead of for lashes?

This problem dominated the discussions on the future of the sugar colonies both in England and in the colonies themselves. There was a division of opinion in both England and in Trinidad, but the opinion that favoured the perpetuation of the plantation system and the necessary measures to ensure a continued supply of labour for the plantations preponderated.

Let us first consider the problem as posed in the metropolitan discussions. Trinidad being a Crown Colony, the metropolitan voice was decisive. In December 1832, on the very eve of emancipation, Lord Howick, Under Secretary of State for the Colonies, outlined the official policy of the British Government in a memorandum which stated the theory as follows:

'The great problem to be solved in drawing up any plan for the emancipation of the Slaves in our Colonies, is to devise some mode of inducing them when relieved from the fear of the Driver and his whip, to undergo the regular and continuous labour which is indispensable in carrying on the production of Sugar . . . Their (the planters') inability . . to pay liberal wages seems beyond all question; but even if this were otherwise, the experience of other countries warrants the belief, that while land is so easily obtainable as it is at this moment, even liberal wages would fail to purchase the sort of labour which is required for the cultivation and manufacture of Sugar . . . The examples of the western States of America, of Canada, of the Cape of Good Hope, and of the Australian Colonies, may all be cited in order to shew that even amongst a population in a much higher state of civilisation than that to which the slaves in the West Indies have attained, the facility of obtaining land effectually prevents the prosecution by voluntary labour of any enterprise requiring the co-operation of many hands.

It is impossible therefore to suppose that the slaves (who, though as I believe not more given to idleness than other men are certainly not less so) would if freed from control be induced even by high wages to continue to submit to a drudgery which they detest, while without doing so they could obtain land sufficient for their support . . . I think that it would be greatly for the real happiness of the Negroes themselves, if the facility of acquiring land could be so far restrained as to prevent them, on the abolition of slavery, from abandoning their habits of regular industry . . Accordingly, it is to the imposition of a considerable tax upon land that I chiefly look for the means of enabling the planter to continue his business when emancipation shall have taken place . . .'

The essence of the Crown Colony system is that it disregards the opinions of the governed. We do not know therefore what the emancipated Negroes thought of the principles and proposals quite unambiguously stated by Lord Howick. If Trinidad was to be settled and developed, it was to be done on the basis of the plantation and not of the small farmer. The Crown Colony system so ruled. To put the matter as crudely as possible, land ownership was to be retained in white hands and it was to be made as difficult as possible for black people to own land.

It has to be borne in mind in all this glib talk that has been prevalent in Trinidad for over a century that the former slaves did not desert agriculture. They deserted plantation agriculture on the terms and conditions prescribed by the Trinidad planters in alliance with the British Government. Everything was done to discourage them from remaining in agriculture after emancipation. Thus it was that in 1841 the Trinidad planters objected to a proposal from the Secretary of State that 40 acres should be the smallest area of Crown land granted to any person, and stated emphatically that it would be most injurious to the interest of the colony to dispose of any area smaller than 320 acres The Trinidad Council of Government went on to point out that the optimum size of a sugar plantation was 640 acres. The Trinidad planters therefore made it quite clear that in their opinion the development of Trinidad's economy was to be based on sugar and on the large sugar plantations.

Acting in accordance with the philosophy outlined by Lord Howick, the British Government did not decree full and unqualified emancipation as from August 1, 1833 This was deferred until 1840 – the period was subsequently shortened to August 1, 1838 In the intervening period the slaves were to be apprentices, required to work under specified conditions and for stipulated wages for their former masters.

The Negroes in Trinidad, and indeed in the West Indies, objected violently. Even today, the long diatribe of the *Port-of-Spain Gazette,* the organ of the planters, on August 5, 1834, against the behaviour of the freed slaves makes amusing reading. The slaves, accustomed for two decades to the hostility of their masters to all the measures

D

proposed by Britain in their behalf, refused to believe that they had not been freed outright They regarded the apprenticeship system as a put-up job between their masters and the Governor. They called their masters 'dam tief' and the Governor an 'old rogue,' and were convinced that the King was not such a fool as to buy them half free when he was rich enough to pay for them altogether.

Thus August 1, 1834, faced the colony of Trinidad with its greatest social crisis until June 19, 1937. The half-emancipated slaves marched into Port-of-Spain from all parts of the island, wending their way to Government House to inform the Governor that they had resolved to strike. The Governor sought to remonstrate with them. They abused him, laughed at him, hooted him, and behaved in what the *Gazette* recorded as a most outrageous manner. Many of them were arrested, and seventeen of the most prominent ringleaders were condemned to stripes and hard labour.

The expectation that this would intimidate the others was hopelessly misplaced. The apprentices in a large number followed the sentenced men to jail encouraging them not to mind their punishment, and vowing their determination to submit not only to punishment but to death itself rather than to return to work. The Riot Act was read without making the slightest impression on the multitude. The troops were thereupon ordered to clear the streets, which they did without accident, but the apprentices promptly congregated in small groups, particularly the women, resolutely expressing their determination not to submit. Their demeanour, whilst determined, was absolutely peaceful. Even the *Port-of-Spain Gazette* had to admit that not one cutlass or stick was to be seen amongst them, not a single individual was intoxicated, nor was one single act of personal violence or robbery reported. Not a single person convicted expressed contrition or even asked for pardon It was quite clear that the former slaves in Trinidad were not prepared to accept conditions in which they were half slave, half free

A similar policy of apprenticeship was adopted in the Danish Virgin Islands after emancipation but there the anger of the Negroes was so pronounced that the system of apprenticeship was brought to an end after violent disturbances in 1878 The French Commission of Enquiry which preceded emancipation in the French islands, headed by the great radical democrat, Victor Schoelcher, totally repudiated the intervening stage of apprenticeship which it described as forced labour and a form of slavery. Schoelcher's Commission reported as follows:

'The Negroes would find it difficult to understand how they could be free and constrained at one and the same time The Republic would not wish to take away from them with one hand what it has given with the other; in the colonies as in the metropolis, the day of fictions is over.'

It was the attempt to maintain the fictions in the British West Indies to prevent Negro land ownership, and to perpetuate the plantation

economy by governmental action, the attempt in other words to interfere with the normal laws of supply and demand in the labour market
and to prescribe the status of men who were in the same breath being
called free, that gave rise to all the social troubles of the 19th century
in the West Indies.

The metropolitan climate was positively hostile to small ownership.
In 1849, Thomas Carlyle, the great essayist and historian, wrote one of
the bitterest denunciations of the West Indian workers in his offensive essay entitled *Occasional Discourse on the Nigger Question*. He
condemned emancipation as ruining the West Indies and as encouraging the former slaves to idleness, to lie in the sun and to eat pumpkins
and yams. Carlyle advocated that the Negroes should be whipped back
into slavery and kept there Less offensive in language but equally
hostile in outlook was Anthony Trollope whom we have encountered
before in his discussion of Negro inferiority. Basing his arguments
principally on Jamaica, Trollope too was of the opinion that emancipation had ruined the West Indies, and he was convinced, as so much
of British policy in the 19th century was designed to achieve, that the
big house of the European plantocracy was the centre of culture and
refinement in the West Indies and the only avenue to civilisation.

Thus it was that when the freed workers of Jamaica petitioned
Queen Victoria in 1865 for land which they could cultivate themselves,
Queen Victoria, through the Secretary of State for the Colonies, made
the famous reply which threw Jamaica right into the sanguinary revolution of 1865 which British troops suppressed with a brutality that
is unparalleled in the sordid annals of West Indian history. Queen
Victoria's reply was as follows:

'That the prosperity of the labouring classes, as well as of all other
classes, depends, in Jamaica, and in other countries, upon their
working for wages, not uncertainly, or capriciously, but steadily
and continuously, at the times when their labour is wanted, and
for so long as it is wanted: and that if they would thus use their
industry, and thereby render the plantations productive, they would
enable the planters to pay them higher wages for the same hours
of work than are received by the best field labourers in this
country; and, as the cost of the necessaries of life is much less in
Jamaica than it is here, they would be enabled, by adding prudence
to industry, to lay by an ample provision for seasons of drought
and dearth; and they may be assured, that it is from their own
industry and prudence, in availing themselves of the means of pros-
pering that are before them, and not from any such schemes as have
been suggested to them, that they must look for an improvement
in their conditions.'

The British defence of the plantation system as a centre of culture
is something that students of West Indian history and society have
never been able to understand It lacked absolutely any basis in fact.
Long ago, as far back as 1787, the well-known traveller, Baron de

Wimpffen, had condemned planter society in Saint Domingue, the principal slave colony of the time, in memorable words. Describing the conversations among the planters, he wrote as follows: 'Each speaks of what interests him, so that one had hardly stopped speaking of one's slaves, one's cotton, one's sugar, one's coffee, before the discussion begins again on cotton, sugar, coffee, slaves. All conversations begin, continue, end and begin again with those subjects.'

Thus it was also that the prominent British abolitionist, James Stephen, of the Colonial Office, could write of the planters in a famous memorandum in October 1831, these very same planters whom Trollope sought to eulogise thirty years later as the defenders and symbols of West Indian culture and civilisation: 'Their lives are passed in a contracted circle amidst petty feuds and pecuniary embarrassments. There is no civilised society on earth so entirely destitute of learned leisure, of literary and scientific intercourse, and even of liberal recreations.'

Thus it was, finally, that an independent American observer, William Sewell, of the *New York Herald Tribune*, who visited the West Indies in 1859 in order to appraise the success of the emancipation legislation, was able to write one of the most devastating indictments of British and colonial policy in the history of the West Indies. Everywhere that Sewell went, in Barbados, in St Vincent, in Jamaica, in Trinidad, he found that production had increased, the Negroes were industrious, the standard of living had risen, the standard of housing had improved, and that emancipation was a success not only socially but also economically. His conclusions represented, in the light of Carlyle's defamation and Trollope's denunciation, one of the most passionate defences of the emancipated slaves ever written for any slave colony. In his well-known book, *The Ordeal of Free Labour in the British West Indies*, one of the most powerful documents in British West Indian history, Sewell summed up the conclusions of his observations as follows:

'I have endeavoured to point out the two paths that lay open to the West Indian Creole after the abolition of slavery. The one was to remain an estate serf and make sugar for the planter; the other was to rent or purchase land, and work for estates, if he pleased, but be socially independent of a master's control. I endeavoured to follow these two classes of people in the paths they pursued – the majority, who have become independent, and the minority, who have remained estate labourers – and I have shown that the condition of the former is infinitely above the condition of the latter. Is this anywhere denied? Can anyone say that it was not the lawful right of these people thus to seek, and, having found, to cherish their independence? Can anyone say that, by doing so, they wronged themselves, the planters, or the government under which they lived. Can anyone say that they are to blame if, by their successful attempts to elevate themselves above the necessitous and precarious career of labour for daily hire, the agricultural field force was weakened, and the production of sugar diminished?

'Is it any argument against the industry of the labouring classes of America that a large proportion annually become proprietors, and withdraw from service for daily hire? Yet this is precisely what the West India Creole has done; this is the charge on which he has been arraigned – this is the crime for which he has been condemned.

'Divested of such foreign incumbrances as defects of African character, and other similar stuff and nonsense, it is simply a land question, with which race and colour have nothing whatever to do. The same process goes on in the United States, in Canada, in Australia, and in all new countries where land is cheap and plentiful and the population sparse. The labourer soon becomes a proprietor; the ranks of the labouring force are rapidly thinned; and the capitalist is compelled to pay high, it may be extravagant wages. In the West Indies the capitalist refuses to pay high wages; he thinks that the control of the labour market is one of his rights He imagines, and upon what ground I cannot comprehend, that farming in these colonies should yield much larger profits than farming anywhere else. He calls it planting, and fancies that there ought to be a wide social distinction between the man who grows cane or cotton and the man who grows potatoes and parsnips. God save the mark! Does anyone dream that if West India planters stuck to their business like English farmers, and possessed one half of their practical ability and industry, the agricultural and commercial interests of the islands would have ever suffered from emancipation? The profits of sugar-cultivation, according to the planter's creed, must be large enough to yield the proprietor, though an absentee, a comfortable income, and pay large salaries besides to overseers and attorneys; otherwise estates are abandoned, and the sugar interest is ruined. These expectations might have been realized in the days of the old monopoly; they certainly are not realized now, and never can be realized again, unless the British people recede from their principles of free trade and free labour If labour in the West Indies is high – so high that sometimes the planter cannot afford to pay the price demanded – he is not worse off than the capitalist in all new countries.'

It was not easy, however, to stem the tide of the metropolitan current fed by its colonial tributaries. Secretaries of State and Colonial Governors combined to condemn the small land owner and to advocate the large plantation. A group of Mandingos in Trinidad petitioned the Secretary of State to be allowed to go back to Africa. War veterans of the West Indies Regiment settled in Manzanilla and Turure, without roads, without bridges, they pleaded either for the amenities which they had been promised on disbandment or for permission to leave the settlement and go elsewhere. Their petition went unheeded. Occasionally a Secretary of State for the Colonies came to the defence of the small man, as was the case with Lord John Russell in a despatch to the Governor of British Guiana, another Crown colony, in 1840. Russell wrote as follows:

'It is not to be expected, that men who can subsist in comfort without hard labour, will continue to devote themselves to it. The state of planter and slave left the West India colonies without a middle class; the more careful and intelligent of the emancipated negroes became petty traders. A few acres of ground will produce provisions for a family, with some surplus to sell at market, and bring home manufactured goods; the negroes who earn high wages, buy or hire plots of land, and refuse to let their daily labour for hire. There is nothing in this singular or culpable. No man in this country, who has capital sufficient to keep a shop, or rent a farm, will follow the plough as a day-labourer, or work from morning till night as a hand-loom weaver.

'Nor, let me observe, were the damage to end here, would the British Government have any cause to feel disappointment. Carrying into effect the religious and benevolent views of the nation at large, it was their object to convert slaves into free men; to rescue their brethren of Africa from the lash of compulsory toil, and establish them as Christian men on the soil where they had been transported as chattels, or beasts of burden On this, the principal question of all, there is, I am happy to say, no room for doubt. None of the most inveterate opponents of our recent measures of emancipation allege that the negroes have turned robbers, or plunderers, or bloodthirsty insurgents. What appears from their statement is, that they have become shopkeepers, and petty traders, and hucksters, and small freeholders; a blessed change, which Providence has enabled us to accomplish.

'But, supposing everything to be done, which, by bounties on emigration, locating captured negroes and natural increase of population can be expected, it will still remain a problem, whether it would be possible to maintain sugar cultivation to its former extent, for this is what is meant by the term "prosperity" while, on the other hand, the term "ruin" is used to designate not the poverty of the people, not the want of food or raiment, not even the absence of riches or luxury, but simply the decrease of sugar cultivation

'Let me, then, look at this question largely. It is stated (I take it only from illustration), that the wages of a day labourer are, in Guiana, 1s. 6d. per day, and in Hindostan not more than 2d. When you should have removed to Guiana a large number of labourers, they are still to be free labourers; the soil is fertile, the climate invites to indolence: the African race love ease and enjoyment, at least as much as any other; you have still no certainty for your sugar crop. In the meantime it is a mere matter of calculation to the capitalist what sugar will cost him to raise in Hindostan, to bring to England, and to clear of duty; and whether, all this done, he can compete successfully with the Demerara planter. If he can, the sugar business will rise in Bengal, and the Coolie remain at home; the plantation will be found for the labourer, and not the labourer go to the plantation. Changes in commerce as great as this took place when woollen manufacturers came from Tuscany to England, and fabrics of silk went from the East to France

'Having made these observations, I have to add, that I have no indisposition to allow the attempt to be made to recruit extensively the population of Guiana . .

'But in whatever degree I might be disposed to yield to the representations of the merchants and proprietors, whether in this country or in the colonies, I must enjoin upon you to bear in mind, that the happiness of the inhabitants of the colony you are appointed to govern is the chief object. Encourage religious instruction, let them partake of the blessings of Christianity, preserve order and internal peace, induce the African race to feel that wherever the British flag flies they have a friend and a protector, check all oppression, and watch over the impartial administration of the law. By such means our colonies in the West Indies will be made to flourish, though in a different form and a different sense from that in which the term has been hitherto used. The Queen, whose commands I now convey to you, looks for Her reward in the faithful attachment of a million of Her people, whom it has been Her care to render worthy of the boon which it was the happiness of Her predecessor to be enabled to grant, by the liberal assistance of His Parliament, and amid the joy of His subjects.'

The Parliament, itself full of members who owned estates in the West Indies and had drawn on the compensation paid for the slaves, was unambiguously on the side of the planters and against the farmers. A Committee of the House of Commons on the West Indian colonies arrived at the following resolutions on July 25, 1842:

'1. THAT the great act emancipating the Slaves in the West Indian Colonies has been productive, as regards the character and condition of the Negro Population, of the most favourable and gratifying results

'2 THAT the improvement in the character of the Negro in every Colony into the state of which this Committee has had time to extend inquiry, is proved by abundant testimony of an increased and increasing desire for religious and general instruction; a growing disposition to take upon themselves the obligations of marriage, and to fulfil the duties of domestic life; improved morals; rapid advance in civilisation, and increased sense of the value of property and independent station.

'3 THAT, unhappily, there has occurred, simultaneously with this amendment in the condition of the Negroes, a very great diminution in the staple productions of the West Indies, to such an extent as to have caused serious, and, in some cases, ruinous injury to the proprietors of estates in those Colonies.

'4. THAT while this distress has been felt to a much less extent in some of the smaller and more populous Islands, it has been so great in the larger Colonies of Jamaica, British Guiana, and Trinidad, as to have caused many estates, hitherto prosperous and productive, to be cultivated for the last two or three years at considerable loss, and others to be abandoned

'5 THAT the principal causes of this diminished production and consequent distress are, the great difficulty which has been experienced by the Planters in obtaining steady and continuous labour, and the high rate of remuneration which they give for the broken and indifferent work which they are able to procure.

'6 THAT the diminished supply of labour is caused partly by the fact that some of the former Slaves have betaken themselves to other occupations more profitable than field labour; but the more general cause is, that the labourers are enabled to live in comfort and to acquire wealth without, for the most part, labouring on the estates of the planters for more than three or four days in a week, and from five to seven hours in a day; so that they have no sufficient stimulus to perform an adequate amount of work.

'7. THAT this state of things arises partly from the high wages which the insufficiency of the supply of labour, and their competition with each other, naturally compel the Planters to pay; but is principally to be attributed to the easy terms upon which the use of land has been obtainable by Negroes.

'8 THAT many of the former Slaves have been enabled to purchase land, and the labourers generally are allowed to occupy provision grounds subject to no rent, or to a very low one; and in these fertile countries, the land they thus hold as owners or occupiers not only yields them an ample supply of food, but in many cases a considerable overplus in money, altogether independent of, and in addition to, the high money wages which they receive.

'9. THAT the cheapness of land has thus been the main cause of the difficulties which have been experienced; and that this cheapness is the natural result of the excess of fertile land beyond the wants of the existing population.

'10. THAT in considering the anxious question of what practical remedies are best calculated to check the increasing depreciation of West Indian property, it therefore appears that much might be effected by judicious arrangements on the part of Planters themselves, for their own general advantage, and by moderate and prudent changes in the system which they have hitherto adopted.

'11. THAT one obvious and most desirable mode of endeavouring to compensate for this diminished supply of labour, is to promote the immigration of a fresh labouring population, to such an extent as to create competition for employment.

'12 THAT for the better attainment of that object, as well as to secure the full rights and comforts of the immigrants as freemen, it is desirable that such immigration should be conducted under the authority, inspection, and control of responsible public officers.

'13. THAT it is also a serious question, whether it is not required by a due regard for the just rights and interests of the West Indian Proprietors, and the ultimate welfare of the Negroes themselves, more especially in consideration of the large addition to the labouring population which it is hoped may soon be effected by immigration, that the laws which regulate the relations between employers and labourers in the different Colonies, should undergo early and careful revision by their respective Legislatures.'

If the emancipated slaves would not work on the plantations on terms which the planters and the British Government considered essential to the maintenance of plantation profits, then a totally new population was to be brought in to compete with the emancipated slaves and to reduce wages. The point of view was stated even more brutally in the French colonies, of which Jules Duval, a well informed writer on colonial questions, wrote on December, 1, 1859:

'The important matter of immigration is beginning to be settled. The solution seems to have been found, on condition that no account is taken of the former slaves and their descendants, who, left to themselves, without the paternal solicitude of their former masters, are relapsing into barbarism.'

No account was to be taken of the former slaves. *The metropolitan Governments had emancipated them and paid compensation not to them but to their owners.* Only one voice was raised in favour of compensation to the slaves, the powerful voice of Victor Schoelcher of France. 'If France owes compensation for this social state which it has tolerated and is now suppressing,' wrote his commission, 'it owes it rather to those who have suffered from that state rather than to those who have profited thereby'. Schoelcher wished to compensate the victims of slavery. He was overruled. The metropolitan governments compensated the beneficiaries of slavery It was compensation not for the deprivation of liberty but for the expropriation of property. Much has been written about the magnanimity of the metropolitan governments, but it was magnanimity to the planter and not to the slave. No requirement was imposed that the money should be used to finance the necessary rationalisation of the Caribbean sugar economy. The planter was free to dispose of his money as he pleased; the absentee interests for the most part withdrew from the West Indies altogether

The slaves of Martinique, Jamaica and Barbados and, in their more limited way because of the paucity of their numbers, of British Guiana and Trinidad, unless they agreed, after emancipation, to work in the same economic relationship, notwithstanding the juridical change and the change in social conditions, to their masters as it prevailed before emancipation, then no account was to be taken of them. If they insisted on rising in the scale of civilisation through ownership of property and cultivation of their small farms, then they were to be allowed to vegetate in the island like the Manzanilla veterans, or to relapse into barbarism A new population would be recruited, from somewhere in the world, to accept conditions of employment which the planters considered necessary to the maintenance of their profits and the preservation of the big house which Trollope endowed with a civilising mission

This attitude of mind, exemplified by the resolution of the Committee of the House of Commons, reflected in the philosophy of Duval, and strongly supported by the planters of Trinidad, was sharply denounced by the Governor of Jamaica, Lord Elgin. In a despatch to the Secretary of State for the Colonies, Lord Stanley, on August 5, 1845, Lord Elgin condemned the resort to immigration:

'I have always considered a reliance on Immigration exclusively, as the only practical and available remedy for the material difficulties of the Colony, to be a serious evil, and averse to its best interests. At the time to which I refer it had already led to a reckless expenditure of the Public Funds. It was based on the hypothesis, expressed or understood, that the system of husbandry pursued during slavery was alone suited to tropical cultivation. Its tendency therefore was to discourage agricultural improvement, and to retard the growth of that more intimate sympathy between the enlightened friends of the Planter and the Peasant which I was so desirous to promote.'

But there it was. Sugar was to remain king, and therefore no account was to be taken of those who had been emancipated from the slavery which sugar had imposed upon them. It was a reaffirmation of the fundamental thesis of West Indian society: no slavery, no sugar. Abolish slavery, and immediately reintroduce it in some form or other, whatever its modifications. The die was cast, and the future course of Trinidad's history prescribed.

In 1848, on the eve of the vast new wave of immigration which was to continue until 1917, the Governor of Trinidad, Lord Harris, wrote memorable and prophetic words: 'A race has been freed, but a society has not been formed.' An Oxford Professor, lecturing to his students on Colonisation and Colonies, echoed the Governor's words. Speaking of the decision to bring in by immigration a new supply of labour in the colonies, he stated: 'Such a colony is but a great workshop rather than a miniature state.'

The British decision to maintain the Crown Colony of Trinidad as a plantation economy and to authorise the recruitment of a new supply of labour on contract guaranteed that Trinidad, grossly underpopulated in 1833, would become a great workshop, that no further account would be taken of the race that had been freed, that a new race would be brought in which would subsequently have to be freed, and that the formation of a society as well as a miniature state would have to be deferred for over a century.

Where was this new supply of labour to come from? Some came in from Portugal in 1834 and 1839, others came in from France in 1839, and some additional European immigrants in 1840. The piteous petition of the Portuguese in 1835 to the Governor of Trinidad is the best commentary on this phase of the Trinidad labour policy after emancipation. The petition reads:

'The humble Petition of the undersigned subjects of the Crown of Portugal respectfully sheweth

'That with many others of their countrymen, they were induced by certain evil disposed persons, under false pretences, to quit their native country, Fayal, to become agricultural labourers in this Colony.

'Of the whole number thus cajoled, one third only are still in existence. The rest have fallen victims to the unhealthiness of the climate or to the cruelties of the slavery system to which we, equally with the unfortunate blacks have been subjected. For let speculators in human blood deny it as they will, the awful calamity which has occurred among our countrymen, in so short a period as ten months, must have resulted from one or the other of these fatal causes, or from both combined.

'Men, women and children, have suffered the greatest misery and oppression on the several estates where they have been forced to work far beyond their strength by coercion of the whip, without proper shelter at night or adequate food during the day.

'The consolation of religion has been denied them in the hours of sickness and death; whilst the bodies of the miserable victims of avarice have been thrown into holes and ditches without Christian burial

'The cries of the fatherless children and widows have been loud in the land, but there was no response from Christian Charity to soften their grief, no arm of justice to relieve them from the hands of oppressors.

'Few are they who are left to tell their tale of woe.

'Your Excellency has often been apprised of these truths but our sufferings are unheeded We have been advised that an appeal to the Governor General for the information of His Britannic Majesty's Government, would be attended to; but we hope Your Excellency will obviate the necessity for such an appeal by mercifully acceding to the prayer of your humble petitioners; which is

'That Your Excellency will be pleased to collect together the few Portuguese labourers yet in existence in this Colony.

'That you will humanely relieve their immediate and pressing wants, particularly those of the poor and helpless orphans;

'And that you will cause them to be transported back to their native country.'

*   *   *

African immigration was also inevitably contemplated, principally from Sierra Leone. One important source of African recruits was the slaves captured by British men-of-war from Brazilian and Cuban slave ships which persisted in carrying on the slave trade in contravention of the declaration of the European powers against the slave trade at the Congress of Vienna in 1815 which brought to an end the wars with Bonaparte. For some thirty years Britain's relations with Spain, France and the United States of America were bedevilled and jeopardised by Britain's insistence on the right of search of their vessels and their transportation of the captured slaves to British colonies, particularly Trinidad.

It was hardly to be expected that Britain's rivals would see in Britain's policy anything more than a hypocritical attempt by Britain, under the guise of the suppression of the slave trade, to supply Negro labour to its under-developed colonies like Trinidad, without exposing itself to the charge that it was engaged in the slave trade. The Spanish Government, with Cuba on the threshold of that enormous expansion of sugar production which was to astonish the world in the 19th century, did not see eye to eye with Britain on this matter, and developed the most ingenious methods of agreeing to Britain's demands on paper and contravening them in fact.

Behind it all lay Britains fear's of the intentions of the United States in the Caribbean, and particularly of American designs on Cuba The British Government in 1826, through a letter from Canning to the British minister in Washington, expressed this fear as follows:

'The avowed pretension of the United States to put themselves at the head of the confederacy of all the Americas, and to sway that confederacy against Europe (Great Britain included) is not a pretension identified with our interests, or one that we can countenance or tolerate.'

Members of Parliament were more outspoken. One of the leading spokesmen in the Conservative Party, Lord George Bentinck, who went so far as to suggest that Britain should annex Cuba in order to put down the slave trade and thus protect rising British colonies like Trinidad which were denied the slave trade, issued a warning to Britain in 1848 that the United States was thinking of the Continent, the whole Continent and nothing but the Continent:

'Uncle Sam will not be satisfied until , putting his hat on the British Colonies, resting his right elbow on the paradise of California, with his left hand on the eastern seaboard, he can throw his leg like a freeman over the Southern continent, with his heel in Cape Horn and Cuba for a cabbage-garden.'

But by 1844 it was clear that all these palliatives would not suffice and that an adequate and dependable supply of labour could not be obtained for Trinidad from Europe or from Africa through Britain's efforts to suppress the slave trade to Cuba. It was clear also that other

West Indian colonies like Barbados and Grenada would not readily agree to the migration of their own workers merely in order to develop Trinidad. In 1844 therefore the British Government took the bull by the horns and agreed to an immediate immigration from India to Trinidad of 2,500 Indian workers, the immigration being permitted from two ports, Calcutta and Madras.

Considerable apprehension was expressed with respect to this new immigration James Stephen of the Colonial Office warned that immigration might well, instead of reducing wages, increase them by enhancing the demand for houses, furniture, food, clothing for immigrants, and therefore the demand for builders, tailors, provision growers and so on. Stephen stated:

'In these attempts to recruit a defective labouring population by artificial methods, we are engaged in a struggle against one of the fundamental laws of human society, and that it is only by the natural increase of the species that Trinidad or any other place can ever attain to that balance between capital and manual labour which secures to capital the maximum of profit, which is compatible with the general prosperity of the labourers '

The arguments were taken up by the abolitionists in the House of Commons. One of the most vigorous, George Thompson, said that the Indian immigrants into Mauritius were indolent, mendicants, runaways, vagrants, thieves, vagabonds, filthy, diseased, dissolute, immoral, disgusting, covered with sores; some were priests, jugglers, barbers, wrestlers, cooks, grooms, buffoons, herdsmen, pedlars, scullions, bakers, tailors, confectioners, instead of agricultural labourers. 'It would be found', he added, 'wherever this system was scrutinised, whether in India, Africa or Demerara, that these persons were a deeply demoralised class of human beings . . The system of emigration had been false, and to attempt to carry it out extensively, would only be to create a new slave trade under the false colours, and of a modified description, so as to injure materially the interests of the colonies, as to their social and moral condition.'

But the British Government went its way and permitted Trinidad not only to recruit immigrants from India, but to do so at public expense. One third of the cost of the immigrant's passage to Trinidad, as well as of any return passage that might be involved on the expiration of his contract, was to be borne out of public funds, in addition to which the conditions of immigration required the Colonial Government to spend more money on the Office of Protector of Immigrants, on medical service for the immigrants, and on the Police Force needed to keep the immigrants under control. The Government also stepped in to prescribe the rate of wages, that is to say to keep them down in the interests of the planters. These rates as published by the Trinidad Government in 1844, amounted to $2.40 a month for male Indian labourers and $1.45 for female labourers, $3.35 for a sirdar and $2.90 for a headman.

The planters, like Oliver Twist, were always asking for more. In Trinidad and British Guiana the Public Treasury contributed approximately one-third to the cost of immigration. In Jamaica, in 1876, they asked for one-half. In exasperation the Governor of Jamaica, Sir Anthony Musgrave, wrote to the Secretary of State for the Colonies, Sir Michael Hicks-Beach, on March 8, 1878, as follows:

'By the new scheme, at large sacrifices by the community for this purpose, certain labour, labour secured by indenture for five years, is offered to the sugar plantation, at rates which do not amount to 1s 6d. per day; and under the scheme now proposed, the portion which constitutes the 6d is virtually advanced to the planter by the public, and the repayment divided over five years. It is my deliberate opinion that if sugar cultivation cannot be continued at that rate of wages for labour in Jamaica, . . . the causes of the failure must be sought elsewhere than in the quarters where they are alleged to be found . . . And yet a section of the planting body, though I am glad to believe only a small section, protest clamorously that it will be impossible to carry on the cultivation on such terms as these. And one is led almost to the conclusion that no system for the future will be satisfactory to them which does not provide at the public expense for the payment of the estates weekly wages as well as the whole cost of the introduction of the immigrant to be employed.'

Indian immigration was thus financed to a considerable extent by those with whom it was intended that the Indian immigrant should compete.

Thus it was that the whole population pattern in the West Indies underwent a drastic change. Between 1838 and 1917, no fewer than 238,000 Indians were introduced into British Guiana, 145,000 into Trinidad, 21,500 into Jamaica, 39,000 into Guadeloupe, 34,000 into Surinam, 1,550 into St Lucia, 1,820 into St Vincent, 2,570 into Grenada. In 1859, there were 6,748 Indians in Martinique. These are fragmentary statistics, and do not give the whole picture. Yet they are sufficient to show a total introduction of nearly half a million Indians into the Caribbean.

Some idea of the scope of the immigration is afforded by statistics for various years chosen at random; 1894—10,885; 1873—11,823; 1869—12,805; 1878—14,371. The importations into British Guiana averaged nearly 3,000 a year, into Trinidad about 1,800. Imports into British Guiana were 9,101 in 1878; 7,512 in 1873; 7,258 in 1885; 7,168 in 1869; 7,160 in 1894. Trinidad imported 3,796 in 1905; in 1872, 3,607; in 1869, 3,329; in 1875, 3,274; in 1892, 3,254; in 1910, 3,228; in 1867, 3,267. In the four years 1878–1881, Guadeloupe imported 2,213, 2,141, 2,672 and 2,770, respectively. Surinam's peak was 1,867 in 1909; in 1908, the figure was 1,674; in 1915, 1,567. The year of highest importation in Jamaica was 1847—2,438 immigrants; in 1912 the number was 1,985; and in 1846, 1,651. In 1862, 1,097

Indians were introduced into Grenada.

It only remains now to explain the reason for Britain's new policy to the West Indies and particularly to Trinidad. In 1846 the British Government abandoned its traditional colonial policy of the Exclusive and protection for colonial products in the British market. The industrial revolution in Britain was then in full swing and British goods, cheapest and best in the world at that time, required no protection in the small and limited colonial markets. Britain wanted to buy sugar from anywhere in the world in order to sell British goods to those sugar countries outside of the West Indies. Therefore Britain, as part of its general policy of free trade, abandoned the preferential sugar duties which had protected the British sugar colonies. The equalisation of the duties was to take effect six years later in 1852.

Britain, in other words, abandoned the Empire in 1846. The Empire remained a political association and its economic foundations were destroyed. It was not only a Government decision. The decision had the support of the overwhelming body of people in the country, except for a section of the Conservative Party led by Disraeli, who, whilst sharing in the prevailing mood of disgust with the colonies which he called millstones around Britain's neck, opposed the abandonment by the Conservatives of the traditional policy of protection, and, in a famous phrase, condemned the Conservative Government as nothing but an organised hypocrisy.

Britain had already paid £20 million in compensation to the slave owners, 80 per cent of this to West Indian slave owners. If Britain was to abandon the traditional sugar preferences, then some further concession had to be made to the West Indian planters. That concession was the immigration of a new supply of cheap labour working under some form of coercion, financed not by the planters in its entirety, but in part out of public funds, that is to say by the taxes of the very emancipated slaves with whom the new workers were to compete. Indian immigration in Trinidad and the West Indies was the price that Britain had to pay for abolishing the preferential sugar duties under the umbrella of which the West Indies had been developed.

CHAPTER 9

The Contribution of the Indians

The laws relating to immigration and Indian immigrants in Trinidad were consolidated and amended by an Ordinance of July 17, 1899. The analysis of this comprehensive Ordinance, which consisted of 276 paragraphs and 52 long printed pages, exclusive of the Schedules, provides the best available evidence of the treatment to which the Indian immigrants were subjected in Trinidad.

Part I of the Ordinance deals with the Immigration Department. At the head of this Department was an official styled the Protector of Immigrants, assisted by the Sub-Protector of Immigrants. The Ordinance provided for Inspectors, Assistant Inspectors, Clerks, and Interpreters attached to the Immigration Department, and paid cash salaries and allowances as were approved by the Legislative Council The Medical Officers of the Government, headed by the Surgeon General, were authorised to visit any plantation on which there were immigrants, inspect the dwellings of the immigrants, the yards and grounds surrounding them, the hospital and all books and registers kept in connection with the hospital The Protector of Immigrants was given wide powers to visit all plantations on which there were indentured immigrants, to enquire into all complaints of and by immigrants, to conduct investigations and to institute prosecutions The Ordinance also empowered the Government to appoint Immigration Agents to superintend the immigration of workers from any part or place from which immigrants might be introduced in Trinidad

Part III of the Ordinance deals with the arrival and allotment of indentured Indians On arrival in Port-of-Spain, ship and immigrants were visited by the Protector, assisted by a Medical Officer. The Protector was given power to allot any immigrant under the Ordinance for domestic or other service when all the approved applications for immigrants had been complied with, on the understanding that husbands were not to be separated from wives, nor minors and infants from their parents or natural guardians

Part V of the Ordinance deals with the dwellings of immigrants. No immigrants allotted to a plantation were to be delivered to the employer until the employer had furnished the Protector with any information required by him with regard to the dwellings to be assigned to such immigrants. The employer was required at all times to provide an immigrant under indenture upon his plantation with a suitable dwelling and to keep such dwelling in sufficient repair with its roofs water tight, and to keep the yard and grounds or a sufficient space around well drained, and the drains clean and in good order, and the yard and grounds free from bush, weeds and rubbish of every description. No dwelling which, in the opinion of the Surgeon

102

General, was unfit for habitation, was to be assigned to any indentured immigrant; and except with the special permission of the Surgeon General, no adult was to be allowed less than 50 feet of superficial space, and an apartment of not less than 120 feet of superficial space was not to be assigned to more than three single men or to more than one man and one woman with not more than two children.

Part VI of the Ordinance specified the rations that the employer was required to provide for his immigrants during the first twelve months after they were assigned to him, and prescribed that not more than six cents was to be deducted from the immigrant's wages for each day's earnings

Part VII deals with hospitals, requiring every plantation to which immigrants were assigned to maintain a hospital at the rate of at least four beds for not more than 40 immigrants, 5 beds for from 40 to 70, and 10 beds for from 70 to 100, with an additional 7 per cent for every additional 100 immigrants after the first 100. Completely separate accommodation was to be afforded for male and female immigrants. The Ordinance empowered the Protector and the Surgeon General to make regulations for the management of hospitals and to specify the furniture, medicine, clothes and appliances which were to be kept in each hospital. Any employer who refused or neglected to send to hospital any indentured immigrant who was in need of medical care, or who refused or neglected to provide him with the medicines, medical comforts and diet which were ordered for him, was liable to a penalty not exceeding $24. On the other hand, any indentured immigrant who, having entered the hospital, was found beyond the limits of the hospital before his discharge, or who refused or neglected to go to the hospital when ordered by his employer to do so, or who contravened the hospital regulations, or behaved himself in a disorderly or refractory manner while he was in hospital was liable to a penalty not exceeding $4 80 or to imprisonment for any term not exceeding 14 days.

Part VIII of the Ordinance, the core of the Ordinance, deals with labour and wages. The Ordinance required the employer to provide every indentured immigrant with sufficient work for a full day's labour every day of the week except Sundays and public holidays · any immigrant willing and able to work, who was not provided with work on any working day, was entitled to his full day's wage for every day on which work was not so provided The working day was fixed at 9 hours, with half-hour daily for eating and resting after 4½ hours, this half-hour being included in the 9 hours. The legal daily wage was fixed by the Ordinance at not less than 25 cents for an able-bodied adult immigrant, and not less than 16 cents if he was indentured as other than an able-bodied adult immigrant.

Any indentured immigrant who, without reasonable excuse, refused or neglected to amend any work which was not accepted because it had been improperly done, was liable on the first conviction to a maximum penalty of $4 80 or 14 days imprisonment, and on a second or other subsequent conviction, to a maximum penalty of $9 60 or one month's imprisonment Every indentured immigrant who was found drunk in or about the plantation buildings, or while he was on the job, or during any time on which he was required to be at work, or who was guilty of any fraud or wilful deception in the performance of his work, or who used abusive or insulting words or gestures to his employer or to any person in authority, or who was guilty of wilful disobedience to any lawful or reasonable order, was liable to a maximum penalty of $4.80 or 14 days imprisonment Every indentured immigrant who used threatening words or gestures to his employer or to any person in authority, or who by negligence or carelessness endangered or damaged the property of his employer, or who hindered or molested any other immigrant in the performance of his work, or who persuaded or sought to persuade any other immigrant to refuse or absent himself or to desist from work, was liable to a maximum penalty of $24 or two months imprisonment.

Part IX of the Ordinance deals with leave and desertion. Every indentured immigrant was bound to reside on the plantation to which he was indentured. Any immigrant found on a public highway or on any land or in any house not the property of his employer, or in any ship or boat within the waters of the island, could be stopped without warrant by the Protector of Immigrants or any person authorised in writing by him, or by any Estate Constable attached to the plantation to which the immigrant was indentured, or by the employer of the immigrant or his manager or overseer, and if the immigrant failed to produce a certificate of industrial residence or of exemption from labour or a ticket of leave, he could be arrested and taken to the nearest Police Station and detained there until he appeared before a Justice of the Peace. Every indentured immigrant who absented himself without leave from the plantation either when he was required to be at work or in such manner or in such time as to constitute a breach of the obligation of residence, was liable, if a male, to a maximum fine of $9.60, and if a female, to a maximum fine of $4 80. Every able-bodied indentured immigrant who had earned $1.25 per week during the two consecutive weeks, was entitled to be provided by his employer with a free pass for as many days as he required for leave of absence, provided that such leave of absence was not to exceed seven days at any one time or 26 days in any one year. Any indentured immigrant who absented himself for three days without leave from the plantation was deemed a deserter, and the manager could thereupon apply to the Magistrate for a warrant for his apprehension. Every indentured immigrant who deserted his plantation was liable to a maximum penalty of either $24 or two months imprisonment or to both such penalty and imprisonment. Any indentured male immigrant absent from work without lawful excuse for twelve days in any one month or in any two consecutive months was deemed a habitual idler and was liable to imprisonment for a maximum period of three months.

This was what the colonial authorities and the British Government called free labour. The Crown Colony system, instituted in Trinidad on the plausible ground that it was the best method of protecting the Negro slave from the sugar planters, was converted, long after the abolition of slavery, into a method for protecting the sugar planters from his indentured immigrants. The British Government appointed a Protector of Slaves to protect the slaves from their masters The Protector of Immigrants was in effect the protector against immigrants. The grand discipline of slavery and the principal incentive to labour was the whip. The grand discipline of the system of indenture and the principal incentive to labour was the jail. Indentured labour was, to paraphrase Carlyle, slavery plus a constable.

The system of indenture was one thing where the Ordinance of 1899 was concerned. The reality was a horse of a different colour. The Ordinance spoke learnedly and with legal precision, for example, of the housing to be provided for the immigrants. The type of housing provided in fact was ruthlessly exposed in a memorandum submitted to the Royal Franchise Commission of 1888 by Mr Lechmere Guppy, Mayor of San Fernando, an Englishman who had resided in Trinidad for forty years. This is what Guppy said at the meeting of the Commission on July 14, 1888:

'As first in the list of evils which afflict the Colony, I look upon the system of housing the Indian Immigrants in barracks. It was not introduced until after Major Fagan had been dismissed and the subjugation of the coolie to a five years' indenture to a master imposed upon him by the Government had become complete. At the outset barracks were only built for the Indians who came unaccompanied by women, and free labourers were lodged as before in separate cottages. The first in Naparima was erected at Palmyra Estate, and I think that one was the first in the Island: but as the estates got fully supplied with coolies the cheapness of the barrack caused it to be adopted universally. The barrack is a long wooden building eleven or twelve feet wide, containing perhaps eight or ten small rooms divided from each other by wooden partitions not reaching to the roof. The roof is of galvanised iron, without any ceiling; and the heat of the sun by day and the cold by night take full effect upon the occupants. By standing on a box the occupant of one room can look over the partition into the adjoining one, and can easily climb over. A family has a single room in which to bring up their boys and girls if they have children. All noises and talking and smells pass through the open space from one end of the barrack to the other. There are no places for cooking, no latrines. The men and women, boys and girls, go together into the canes or bush when nature requires Comfort, privacy and decency are impossible under such conditions. A number of these barracks are grouped together close to the dwelling house of the overseers, in order that they may with the least trouble put them out to work before daylight in crop time, which they do by entering their room and, if necessary, pulling them off their beds where they are lying with their wives. If a man is sick he is not allowed to be nursed by his wife, he must perforce go to the hospital far away, leaving his wife, perhaps without the means of subsistence, in such a room as I have described, to her own devices, amid the temptations surrounding her. With all this, can any one wonder at the frequent wife-murders and general demoralisation amongst the Indian immigrants? In fact the barrack life is one approaching to promiscuous intercourse. And the evil is not confined to the coolies No decent black labourer can take his wife to live amongst such surroundings For very long past I have watched the spread of immorality among the lower classes consequent on the barrack system At first the married negro who was employed in crop time on a plantation left his wife in San Fernando or other place where he had a cottage, returning to his home on Saturday night and leaving it again on Monday morning. Thus the husband and wife were parted for a week, and too often formed other relations Mutual support and comfort existed no longer, the moral tie was broken and it was clear that marriage was a useless unmeaning clog which it is no shame to omit. From the estates the curse has spread to the towns. It is a more profitable investment to build barracks and let single rooms in them than to build detached cottages: and unmarried men and unmarried women occupy in this manner whole ranges of rooms. On plantations the demoralization is carried as far as it can go. The absentee proprietor is not there to witness the scandals. The overseers will tell you, as I have often been told by them, that they are put there to make sugar and not to look after the morals of coolies. The owner in England compares notes with other absentees and expects his crop to be made at the lowest rate As to the means, that matters not to him. The overseer holds his situation subject to twenty-four or forty-eight hours' notice and to escape losing his place and consequent beggary he must have but one object in view: that of screwing the most he can out of his bondsman.'

A Commission of Enquiry which was sent out by the Government of India to investigate the conditions of Indian immigrants in Trinidad, three other British colonies and Surinam in 1913, when the indentured system was on its last legs, found the Indian population riddled with hookworm, debilitated by malaria, living frequently in swampy and insanitary surroundings, because the employer, as was to be brought out much later in many parts of the West Indies, would not provide the facilities for protecting the health of the immigrants.

The 1899 Ordinance prescribed and fixed rates of wages and a stipulated amount of work to be provided for each immigrant. The rule adopted in Trinidad was that no plantation could obtain additional indentured immigrants where more than 15 per cent of those in residence had earned less than sixpence per day during the preceding year. The Ordinance was first put into force in 1892, whereupon it was found that so many plantations were affected that immigration would cease. Consequently, a special law was passed authorising the introduction of immigrants despite the ordinance. In 1895, of 69 plantations in Trinidad utilising indentured labour, only on ten did the percentage of indentured immigrants earning less than sixpence a day fall below the 15 per cent required by law; seven of these were cocoa plantations. The percentage on sugar plantations was 43 for Usine Ste Madeleine, 30 for Caroni, 54 for Waterloo, 35 for Woodford Lodge and Brechin Castle.

Trinidad was not unique in this respect. In British Guiana, in 1912, the average weekly earnings of an indentured immigrant was $1.23 in Demerara and Berbice, $1.14 in Essequibo. The percentage of working days worked by each woman immigrant varied from 31 on Providence Plantation to 84 on Farm Plantation, both owned by the Demerara Company; for men from 64 on Providence Plantation to 87 on Farm. In Surinam the Commission of the Government of India stated in 1915 that 'the regulation entitling the employer to require six days' work weekly is certainly not abused. Apparently four labourers are imported to do work which would be light employment for three.' The male immigrants lost one-third of the working days; the average number of days worked in 1811 was 177. Male earnings amounted to 26 cents per day worked; female, 18 cents.

The Indian immigrants lived in the shadow of the jail. In whatever else the Ordinance of 1899 fell short, it certainly did not fall short in respect of prosecutions In the three years 1909 to 1912, there were 7,899 prosecutions of Indian immigrants in Trinidad. First in the list of offences was desertion; the number in the three-year period was 1,668. Then came absence from work without lawful excuse – 1,466 prosecutions in the three-year period. Refusing to begin or finish work was the cause of 1,125 prosecutions. Vagrancy prosecutions numbered 983. There were 603 prosecutions for neglecting to obey a lawful order; 412 for habitual idleness; 355 for using threatening words to those in authority; 346 for breach of hospital regulations; 271 for refusal to obey a lawful order; 255 for absence from the estate without leave; and 187 for malingering. The figures were similar for other offences, but 52 prosecutions were for persuading immigrants to desist from work and 71 for damaging the employer's property.

In the case of 6,777 of these prosecutions, 2,009 immigrants were fined, 1,532 were imprisoned, 1,027 convicted and reprimanded or discharged, and 1,441 discharged for want of prosecution or want of evidence. In other words, one in every four immigrants charged in the three years was fined, and one in every five sent to jail. We have noted the offences for which they were fined or jailed. In these three years, with 7,899 prosecutions, only 9 were for threats to murder and only 7 were for being drunk at work; 34 involved harbouring an immigrant's wife, 13 enticing away an immigrant's wife, and six involved an immigrant threatening his wife.

Thus it is clear that it was the system of labour developed under indenture, it was the labour code itself, which produced a population that was always in the Magistrate's Court. No society with proper industrial relations would ever have tolerated the Ordinance of 1899.

With all this, Indian indentured immigration was notoriously inefficient. It was inefficient in two ways. In the first place, as with the Negro slave before him, the indentured Indian immigrant resorted to the only weapon at his command – passive resistance. He simply malingered, or pretended to be sick, or went into the hospital Some positively alarming statistics of the man-days lost in hospital are available for the West Indies. In French Guiana, in the first six months of 1875, where the indentured immigrants averaged 350 a month, the man-days worked numbered 26,852, and the man-days lost in hospital 26,602; the average number of days worked by each immigrant was twelve per month, while, for every day worked, one day was spent in the hospital. In Trinidad, in 1895, for 10,720 Indian immigrants, there were 23,688 admissions to hospitals. Thus each Indian went at least twice a year to the hospital, at the expense of the planter and the government. This meant, as the Surgeon-General of the Colony stated, a loss of 165,816 man-days of labour, or about £8,000. Whilst the immigrant lost his wages during his hospitalisation, the employer had to maintain him and contribute to the upkeep of the hospital, and he lost also the man's labour during the period. The manager of the Usine Ste Madeleine Sugar Company in Trinidad, on the basis of the records of 1,996 indentured immigrants for the years 1892–1895, estimated that only 63 per cent of the 280 contract days were worked; one day in every three was lost to the plantations. Eleven per cent of the time was lost through sickness

The indentured population was a sick population. Less than 10,000 in number, the number of cases of sickness treated in 1911 was over 24,000. Malaria and ankylostomiasis were the chief scourges. There were 8,400 cases of malaria; a considerable proportion of the nearly 6,000 cases of anaemia, parasites, skin diseases and ground itch needed to be added to the 1,100 cases of ankylostomiasis The situation was at its worst on sugar plantations. The proportion of malaria cases to population was 92 on sugar plantations, 56 on cocoa estates; the combined proportion of ankylostomiasis, anaemia, parasites, and ground itch was 33 on sugar plantations, 28 on cocoa estates; the proportion of skin diseases was 43 on sugar plantations, 17 on cocoa estates The death rate on sugar plantations was half as much higher than the rate on cocoa estates. The venereal disease rate was much higher also on the sugar plantation, but the proportion of dysentery cases lower than on the cocoa estate. Introduced for sugar, the Indians lived and died by sugar.

Much of this disease was directly traceable to the barrack system The barracks in 1911 were provided with an insufficient and unsatisfactory water supply for drinking purposes. They leaked and were not watertight, and were entirely unprovided with latrines, notwithstanding recommendations that future allotments of immigrants should be made contingent upon the provision of sufficient and approved latrine accommodation. Another possible method of dealing with the problem – to reduce the incidence of infection rather than to improve the habits which produced it – the provision of shoes to the immigrants, was rejected by a commission of inquiry because of doubts as to whether the Indians could be persuaded to wear them regularly and of uncertainty as to the extent to which shoes afford protection.

In addition to sickness, much time was lost through desertion and absence without leave. On the Usine Ste Madeleine, the percentage from these causes was 17 – that is, one out of every six working days. In British Guiana, of 105,205 immigrants introduced between 1874 and 1895, there were 13,129 desertions: one out of every eight Indians deserted

In the second place, indentured immigration encouraged inefficiency on the part of the planter. Economic improvements were rejected in favour of cheap manual labour living in a condition of semiservitude. The sugar planters had previously rationalized their archaic preference for the hoe over the plough on the ground that the inability of the Negro to see straight rendered the use of the plough impossible. In 1860 implemental husbandry was unknown in St Vincent, while in 1870 the steam plough was a novelty in the British West Indies. In 1896 Barbados employed 42,000 workers for 65,000 acres under sugar cultivation. In 1848 one of the most enlightened West Indian planters complacently confessed that he could not understand why people should want to have canes which yielded twenty tons to the acre when they had good canes which yielded two, and it was not until 1886 that the first experiments in cane breeding were undertaken in Barbados. Technological progress in the factory was similarly retarded. In 1846 the British West Indies had only 12 miles of railway, while Cuba had 800. In 1870 there was only one factory in the British West Indies which had adopted the process of diffusion. In 1896 the Barbados crop of 40,000 tons of sugar was produced on 430 plantations, each equipped with its own factory The average production per factory was slightly over 90 tons. Three-quarters of the factories were still run by wind power.

One can only wonder today how it was possible for any country that had abolished Negro slavery on the ground that it was inhuman to justify Indian indenture with its 25 cents a day wage and its jails. The Europeans had distorted and maligned African civilisation in order to find an alibi for Negro slavery. In the same way they distorted and maligned Indian civilisation in the 19th century in order to justify Indian indenture.

As the great names in Britain's intellectual history are associated with the distortion of African civilisation and the defamation of the

African character, the great names of Hume, Trollope and Froude, so the great names in Britain's intellectual history are associated with the distortion of Indian civilisation and the defamation of the Indian character, the great names in particular of Lord Macaulay, the historian; and Lord Acton, the Professor of History at Cambridge University.

In 1834 Lord Macaulay wrote his *Minute on Indian Education*, the British classic in the history of the depreciation of Indian cultural achievements. It reads as follows · —

'I have no knowledge of either Sanscrit or Arabic. But I have done what I could to form a correct estimate of their value I have read translations of the most celebrated Arabic and Sanscrit works . . . I am quite ready to take the Oriental learning at the valuation of the Orientalists themselves. I have never found one among them who could deny that a single shelf of a good European library was worth the whole native literature of India and Arabia . . . when we pass from works of imagination to works in which facts are recorded and general principles investigated the superiority of the Europeans becomes absolutely immeasurable. It is, I believe, no exaggeration to say that all the historical information which has been collected from all the books written in the Sanscrit language is less valuable than what may be found in the most paltry abridgments used at preparatory schools in England '

Just as Froude had, in relation to the West Indies, presented his conception of the White Man's Burden in the political and cultural field, so Lord Acton, in the course of a review of a history of Ireland which was also a British Colony, presented his conception of the White Man's Burden insofar as it related to India

'   . The Persians, the Greeks, the Romans, and the Teutons are the only makers of history, the only authors of advancement Other races . . . are a negative element in the world; sometimes the barrier, sometimes the instrument, sometimes the materials of those races to whom it is given to originate and to advance. Their existence is either passive, or reactionary and destructive . . . The Chinese are a people of this kind . . . So the Hindoos; being Pantheists, they have no history of their own but supply objects for commerce and for conquest . . . So the Slavonians, who tell only in the mass . . .

'Subjection to a people of a higher capacity for government is of itself no misfortune; and it is to most countries the condition of their political advancement . .   A nation can obtain political education only by dependence on another . . .'

What could one expect of a Colonial Governor, in the context of the metropolitan rubbish exported to the colonies, when these great British intellectuals exemplified the climate of public opinion in England in relation India? One is therefore not surprised to read the following comment of the Governor of Trinidad, Lord Harris, in the middle of the 19th century in which, very significantly, he lumped together Africans and Indians. This is what Lord Harris wrote: —

'The only independence which they would desire is idleness, according to their different tastes in the enjoyment of it; and the higher motives which actuate the European labourer . . . , that to be industrious is a duty and a virtue; that to be independent in circumstances, whatever his station, raises a man in the moral scale amongst his race; and that his ability to perform his duties as a citizen, and, we may add, as a Christian, is increased by it. These, and such motives as these, are unknown to the fatalist worshippers of Mahomet and Brahma, and to the savages who go by the names of Liberated Africans . . . .

'After having given my best consideration to the subject, it appears to me that, in the first place, the immigrants must pass through an initiatory process; they are not, neither Africans nor Coolies, fit to be placed in a position which the labourers of civilised countries may at once occupy. They must be treated like children – and wayward ones, too – the former, from the utterly savage state in which they arrive; the latter, from their habits and religion.'

This was the Governor of the colony, who played a very large part in the history of indentured Indian immigration, the very man who had said pontifically in 1848 that a race had been freed, but a society had not been formed One could hardly expect the planters, obsessed with purely material considerations, to do better than the Governor.

A Trinidadian, some decades later, in a general account of Trinidad's geography, natural resources, administration, condition and prospects, described the Indians as liars, filthy in their habits, lazy and addicted to pilfering. Compare this with a declamation in 1512 against the Amerindians as being arrogant, thieves, liars stupid asses, cowardly, dirty like pigs, and filthy in their eating habits. Compare the declamation against the Indians in Trinidad with a declamation against the Africans published in Paris in 1790 to the effect that they were by nature unjust, cruel, barbarous, anthropophagous, traitors, liars, thieves, drunkards, proud, lazy, unclean, unchaste, jealous to fury and cowardly.

The West Indies must have been a very curious society which could have produced in 1512 against the Amerindians, in 1790 against the Africans, and in 1869 against the Indians exactly the same defamation of character of races which had no previous connection or intercourse and which were drawn from widely separated parts of the world.

The same contempt for the Indians was brought out in the evidence of Canadian merchants before the Royal Commission on Trade Relations between Canada and the West Indies in 1911. This is the evidence of Mr J. D. Allan, member of the firm of A. A. Allan & Company in Toronto, and a member of the Commission from the Boards of Trade of Toronto, Halifax and St John, which had previously visited the West Indies: —

'. . . there is another point in connection with flour that is well worth stating The great body of consumers in the West Indies are of a much lower class than the great body of consumers in Canada. This met us principally in our investigations at Trinidad. The rate of duty on everything called flour in the West Indies has been the same, whether it is the cheapest or the best. In this country I am glad to say we are rather particular along the lines of what is allowed as food products, far more particular than in the West Indies. In this Inquiry at Port-of-Spain some question arose between some of the people there, we had no part in it, regarding the fairness of the incidence of their specific duty on flour. We were interested in seeing how they worked that out, and one gentleman said: I went once to Guelph to buy some flour. Guelph is a city 45 miles north-west of Toronto. He continued: I was shown there fine brands and I was very much pleased with them, but the price was beyond what I could pay. The miller took me to the different floors of his mill and I saw on one of the floors something that he called mill feed. I said to him: What will you charge me a ton for that? A price was mentioned. I bought that and sent it to the West Indies and sold it as flour at a very much better rate of profit than I was ever able to get on any regular flour that I imported. It was interesting to us to hear that. But I said there is this about it – the same thing came up also in connection with butter and imitations of butter, oleomargarine – I said the Government of Canada does not allow us to adulterate any foodstuffs, and if we are going to do a trade with you in that way, as flour, we will either have to get permission to do so, we will have to lower ourselves to your level of civilisation, and that was all that we said.

'. . . We were shown butter called Morlaix that is very much consumed When they said· Can you compete with this? I looked at the stuff and it looked as if it was mixed with yellow ochre. I said: No I should be sorry to see us making up anything of such a low nature . . .

'. . . So far as the textile stuffs were concerned we examined them in one or two places, and I came to the conclusion that the class of textiles used for the coloured and coolie trade was of so low a nature that we would probably never participate in that trade. It was simply the lowest kind of material, and I wondered at people buying it at all'

The question now inevitably arises. Was Indian immigration necessary?

In the opinion of Sir Henry Alcazar, Mayor of Port-of-Spain, it was not necessary. In a memorandum presented to the West Indian Royal Commission of 1897, on February 28, 1897, he had this to say:

'It must be granted, however, that as far as quality is concerned the sugar planters are the worst served of all employers. This is due to two causes. First the treatment on most estates is such that no man of any spirit will submit to it unless pressed by most dire necessity. Next, while the rate of pay in other occupations was up to quite lately 1s. 8d. and upwards, the sugar planter offers 1s. 0¼d. Under such circumstances it is not strange that preference is as a rule given to other occupations and that men in the employment of sugar planters leave them as soon as they find an opening elsewhere. It will be ascertained on inquiry that almost every complaint on the part of the sugar planters that creole labour is unreliable, may be traced to the fact of their labourers having thus left to better themselves, while even the worst employers have seldom met with any serious difficulty in filling the places so left vacant.

'Wages have during the last 30 years risen all over the civilised world. Even in ultra conservative India there has been a marked increase, as Lord Roberts not long ago reminded us. In Trinidad and the West Indies generally wages have, during the same period, fallen greatly, in some occupations by fully one-half, on an average certainly not less than 25 per cent No doubt the price of sugar has also fallen considerably, but so has the price of iron, of wheat, and of every staple product of the very countries in which there has been a rise. I am justified therefore in contending that the fall in Trinidad is due, not to unavoidable economic causes, but to the operation of a system which places absolute command of the labour market in the hands of the employers As far as the workers are concerned, industry is thus kept artificially in a constant state of extreme depression.

'To these baneful material results must be added still more deplorable moral effects. It is recognised that by making him brutally callous to the rights of others and blunting his moral sense generally, slavery does at least as much harm to the slave owner as to the slave himself. Now, however akin to slavery the coolie's indenture may seem, it has on him no marked degrading effect, because what above all demoralizes the slave is the hopelessness of his lot, while the coolie knows that at the end of his five years he must be set free. On his employer, however, the effect is much more similar to that of slavery, for if one-fifth of his bondsmen are set free every year, a fresh fifth at once take their place, and he has thus permanently about him a large number of his fellow men bound to do his bidding under penalty of imprisonment. In fact, with regard to its effect on the employer, the system is not very different from slavery, with the gaol substituted for the whip. And one of the worst consequences of Indian immigration in Trinidad has been to keep its educated classes at the moral level of slave owners.'

Alcazar attacked the system of indentured immigration on the ground that it was semi-servitude, and his arguments were essentially the same as those advanced by Sewell. Guppy attacked it on the ground that it was a mistake in the first place to give priority to sugar production, that the priority should have been given to cocoa instead, and that cocoa did not require indentured immigrants. This was what he said in evidence before the Royal Commission of 1888:

'But it is said that Lord Harris, by means of Indian Immigration, saved the Colony. For years and years, as the ground of any argument in favour of making the general tax-payers support Indian Immigration for the purposes of the sugar planters, I have been asked to admit that this Immigration saved the Colony. I have always replied, "I do not admit it. First, tell me who or what you mean by the Colony? and next who and what was saved?" Those questions remained unanswered to this day. In fact Trinidad never required a "saviour". That title is indeed usually assumed by destroyers, or given to them by their interested partisans.

'The fertile soil and favourable climatic conditions of Trinidad have saved her throughout the unceasing depredations and misgovernment which she has undergone at the hands of her "saviour." Montserrat is a proof of this. Without any capital beyond the earnings of their daily labour, not only without any assistance from authority, but in disregard of the Proclamations and denunciations of Governors and Attorneys-General and Magistrates, the squatter-pioneers carried their axes beyond the domain of the sugar planters into the trackless forest, and there, not only raising from the soil their daily subsistence but patiently and laboriously striving for future wealth, by planting cocoa trees, for the fruit of which they had to await many years, they laid the foundations of one of the most beautiful, most productive and most valuable Districts of the Island.'

Guppy was adamant that, instead of sugar saving the colony, sugar had ruined it and by sugar he meant the control of the sugar planters in the Crown Colony legislature which was responsible not the people of Trinidad but to the Secretary of State for the Colonies. As one indication of the price that the colony had had to pay for sugar cultivation, which was the justification of Indian indentured immigration, he cited the Trinidad Government Railway. For many years in the recent past great concern has been expressed, and quite rightly, about the expensiveness of the Railway, and a great argument has developed as to whether it should be preserved at all. It is useful for us to remember the origin of this question, as stated in caustic terms by Mr Guppy in 1888:

'The absence of beneficial control, in the general interest of the Island, is shown in nothing more than in the Railway system as adopted. We have had forced upon us a line which can never be so useful or so remunerative as if it had been run some miles to the eastward in the interior. In neglect of warnings and for the benefit of a few favoured sugar planters, the line has been run along the coast where sea-borne craft come into competition with it and through a series of barren lands, bordering on unhealthy swamps which forbid Europeans and offer no inducements for Africans or Indians to settle on them. The result of the blunders made in this line, and in the great cost and uselessness of the line joining the

Williamsville Station with Princes Town, has been that the interior of the Island which it was most desirable to reach, remains untapped, and the Government is powerless to continue the work.'

Dr de Boissiere, a third opponent of the indentured system, argued in 1890 not now that indenture was semi-servitude, not now that sugar should never have been given priority, but rather that the labour should have been sought not in India but in Barbados. He wrote:

'History will pen a terrible indictment of neglect against the administration of the last 30 years for not having organized a system by which this natural and free Immigration, involving as it does scarcely any cost, would have been taken advantage of, and efforts made to retain it'

The Barbadian, however, would as soon accept a contract as slavery. But de Boissiere had a powerful argument. The real paradox of Indian immigration is that it coincided with an even larger wave of Negro emigration. Thousands of labourers, not only from Barbados, but also from Jamaica, emigrated to the Panama Canal, to the banana plantations of Costa Rica, to the United States, and, disproving the argument that the West Indian would not cultivate sugar, to the sugar plantations of Cuba. In 1913, Jamaica emigration totalled 15,096 – 1,510 to Cuba, 9,728 to Panama, 2,313 to Costa Rica. From 1901 to 1917, the net emigration from Jamaica amounted to 24,643, to which must be added 60,200 West Indians who emigrated to the United States – a total of 84,843. During the same period the net immigration from India into British Guiana and Trinidad – subtracting repatriates from immigrants – was 24,260. As many Indians came in as West Indians left Jamaica. Remittances received through the Barbadian Post Office in the years 1900, 1901, 1906, 1907, 1909 and 1910 from Barbadians abroad totalled £515,934 in money orders and registered letters; in the year 1910, £93,361 was remitted in money orders alone, £66,162 from the Canal Zone, £15,078 from the United States, and £12,518 from British Colonies. This compares with the remittances from Indians to India between 1890 and 1912 totalling £65,187 from Trinidad and £52,975 from British Guiana.

Thus, for every Indian added to the British West Indian labour force before World War I, three West Indians were subtracted. For every pound sent out of the West Indies by Indians, seventeen were sent in by Barbadians alone.

By the turn of the century, five years after the consolidated Immigration Ordinance of 1899, which gave the impression that Indian immigration would continue in Trinidad until the end of time, the argument ceased to be whether Barbados could supply the necessary labour instead of India, but became whether there was any shortage of labour at all. Sir Henry Alcazar, Mr Lechmere Guppy and Dr de Boissiere were all white men, directly engaged or connected through their families with agriculture. The fourth great opponent of indentured Indian immigration in Trinidad was neither a white man nor a planter. He was a Negro lawyer, Prudhomme David, a Nominated Member of the Crown Colony Legislative Council Year after year Mr David, in a minority of one as he was wont to say, opposed the annual vote for immigration. This was the speech of Mr David on Monday, November 7, 1904 in the Legislative Council as reported in *Hansard*.

'The Honourable C. P. David said, as this motion was postponed on the last occasion it was brought forward, at his instance, he thought it right that he should address a few remarks to the Council stating in some detail his reasons for opposing it. He was about, therefore, to address a few remarks to that Council explaining the grounds upon which he objected to the motion which had just been introduced. The Hon. The Protector of Immigrants had described this as a formal matter, and from the tone of his remarks he had evidently imagined that the motion would be carried as a matter of course. Perhaps he was right, as motions of that kind had been carried annually with perfect regularity for a series of years, and he was bound to confess that although he offered some opposition to the resolution, he had no hope whatever of convincing a Council, composed as that Council was, that his view of the matter was right and that the common view of the matter was wrong. No one considering the matter from a broad point of view could, however, fail to be struck by the anomaly of a Colony like Trinidad – a purely agricultural Colony with a large agricultural population – spending annually a large sum of money for the purpose of importing labour from such a distance from Trinidad as India is. A step of that kind could only be justified by strenuous necessity, and he had no doubt that, if the Government were to be persuaded that there did not exist a real demand for labour in this Colony, the Government would feel that an expenditure of this kind was not justifiable. The question, therefore, was largely one of whether there does or does not exist in the Colony a supply of labour sufficient for the needs of all classes of employers. The planters of the Colony – the sugar planters, and, more lately the cocoa planters – had, he was aware, been constantly representing that there was not in the Colony itself a supply of labour sufficient for their needs, and that their prosperity, nay the very life of their industry, depended upon the importation of these labourers from India. He would like to see the Government make good that assertion of the planters by something like an independent enquiry into the matter In his opinion it was not sufficient for the Government in that easy fashion to go on year after year listening to what he might describe as interested cries for more labour, and at the same time not taking the steps which would establish clearly, not only to the Government and the sugar planters themselves, but to members of the public connected with other industries – the persons called upon to subscribe to the establishment of these immigrants in the colony – that this scarcity or deficiency which the planters declare to exist, and which could be the only *raison d'être* of the policy of the Government with regard to the labour question really existed. Now he said that the time had come when there should be a change; that the supply of labour in the colony was not short of the legitimate demands of the employers of labour, and he said, moreover, that the cry of scarcity rested upon only this foundation – that the planters by means of this artificial means of drawing their labour supply from India had grown so much accustomed to paying a low rate of wage, that the real fact of the matter was not that there was a scarcity of labour but that they could not get that labour on account of the insufficiency of the remuneration they had grown accustomed to pay and, therefore, would not like a change. He took it that was what the whole question hinged upon, and he thought the Government would be wanting in its duty if it did not institute an independent enquiry for the purpose of dissecting this demand which was constantly being made by the planters of their being a scarcity of labour in the Colony, in support of his argument he would appeal to the experience of persons not connected with the industries of sugar or cocoa. To begin with they never found the Government complaining of any difficulty in obtaining labour. They found large enterprises being carried out by the Public Works Department, the Railway Department and other departments in the Colony, and they never heard that these departments experienced any difficulty in getting the requisite quantity of labour for their enterprises. They saw again companies and firms not connected with agriculture carrying out enterprises, not so large perhaps as those carried out by the Government, but in themselves very important – the establishment of the electric tramways, telephones on a large scale over the island – they saw enterprises of that kind being carried out by private firms without any allegation being ever heard that any difficulty presented itself on account of the deficiency in the supply of labour. The cry of insufficiency of labour was confined to the sugar planters, the cocoa planters and those engaged in the pursuit of agriculture, and these people alone were they who were saying that they could not get the resident population to work, and he suggested that, if they experienced any difficulty, it was not because the labourers were not forthcoming, but because the sugar planters had got so accustomed to being able to procure this class of cheap, artificial agricultural labourers and to paying such low wages because of the existence of this immigration system, because they could get from general revenue a contribution towards importing labourers all the way from India, because the law of the Colony fixed a low remuneration to the labourers so imported, and not wishing to deprive themselves of the advantages to be derived from such a system they continued to assert that there was not a sufficient supply of labour on the spot for their various requirements Not long ago they saw that one of the Honourable Members of that Council started an enquiry with reference to the needs of the planters with a view to getting information about this question, and no doubt some of them had read the interesting letter of one who until recently was a member of that Council – he referred to the Hon. Charles Leotaud, a gentleman who had large cocoa interests in the Colony and whose family was largely interested in cocoa and who had many opportunities of familiarising himself with the state of the labour market. In answer to a letter of inquiry addressed to him by a member of this Council Mr Leotaud stated – and was good enough to publish his reply – that he, a large employer of labour, did not suffer from any scarcity of labour; neither did his sons nor the estates which were entrusted to his management. The Hon. Member who had addressed Mr Leotaud and who was present at that Board as he spoke had not up till now given the public the benefit of the results of his enquiry But, whatever these results might be, he thought the Council ought to attach some importance to the statement of such a large employer of labour as Mr Leotaud, and when he said that in his particular department he could not complain of any want of labour he thought they might fairly presume that many other employers were in the same position, and that itself ought to suggest the desirability of an enquiry as to whether there really existed a *bona fide* demand for labour on the part of the planters of this colony He had said that Trinidad was a country peopled almost entirely by agricultural labourers. The last census taken in 1902 gave the number of agricultural labourers in the Colony at nothing less than 62,946. The report of the Hon. The Protector of Immigrants himself gave the number of Indian Immigrants at over 94,000 and it was an undoubted fact that the majority of these were nothing but agricultural labourers and did it not strike one as being curious that in face of these figures there should still be demand for more labourers?'

These were the arguments against the system of indentured Indian immigration. It is necessary to emphasise that not one single argument was based on racial considerations. The argument was rather that thousands of labourers had been brought in from a distant country, where labourers might have been obtained closer at hand, in order solely to maintain and develop the sugar industry, and that these labourers were brought in because, in the opinion of the sugar planters, they, more than any other group of workers, could be kept in a condition of semi-servitude and compelled to accept sub-human wages and living conditions; and all this was at the expense not of the sugar planter but of the general community, which had to subsidise this system of semi-servitude.

One could well understand the strong feelings on the subject expressed by the agriculturists who did not produce sugar. Forty per cent of the indentured Indians worked on sugar plantations and merely five per cent on cocoa and coconut estates; yet, between 1881 and 1885, the Legislative Council, dominated by the sugar planters, reduced the export duty which was levied to finance in part the cost of the immigration system from 80 to 60 per cent on sugar, whilst on cocoa it was raised from 20 to 37 per cent.

Indian indentured immigration was thus in the final analysis a political question, from which the chief beneficiaries were the English sugar interests in the colony. In 1896, there were 56 sugar plantations in Trinidad of which 36 were owned by non-residents. Eight of these were owned by the colonial Company in England and five by W. F. Burnley and Co. The average sugar estate exceeded 500 acres in size as compared with the average cocoa estate, which was from 10 to 50 acres Trinidad's exports of sugar increased from 10,334 tons in 1833 to 53,847 tons in 1896.

It is quite wrong, however to say that the contribution of the Indians to Trinidad was that sugar exports were five times as much as they were in 1833. The price that the community had to pay for this increase in 1836 in sugar production was semi-servitude, sub-human wages, the degradation of labour, and the perpetuation of the Crown Colony system of Government. The Indian contribution to Trinidad society and Trinidad economy was of a totally different nature. It was that, in the age-old battle which the planter had fought against the small farmer, the sugar planter who had defeated the small white farmer, who had prevented the emancipated Negro slave from becoming a small farmer, that same sugar planter had to compromise with the Indian indentured immigrant, and in the social sense the outstanding result of indentured Indian immigration was the emergence, for the first time in the history of Trinidad, of a class of small farmers.

This was not because the sugar planters liked small farming any more after 1833 than they liked it before 1833. It was not because they liked the Indian indentured immigrant any more than they liked the emancipated Negro slave. It was a simple question of finance, and it applied not only in Trinidad but also in British Guiana and Surinam.

In 1850 the Combined Court of British Guiana protested against the stipulation of a return passage at the expense of the colony as a part of the immigration contract. In 1852 the Governor of Trinidad stated that the prospect of returning home at an early period had a tendency to unsettle the immigrants, and he, too, regretted the requirement of a return passage. Up to 1924, the number of Indians who returned home from British Guiana was 67,320, or a proportion of more than one out of every four who had been introduced. In Trinidad, the number who returned was 27,853 – about one out of every six who had been introduced Thus, of 383,000 Indians introduced into both colonies, 95,173, or more than one-quarter, had returned home by 1924. For every four immigrants, therefore, five free passages had to be found. The two-way traffic reached a point where the number of workers who departed annually exceeded those who were introduced. In 1905, for example, 2,704 Indians came to British Guiana on contract; 2,726 departed. In 1897, arrivals numbered 1,194; departures 1,529. In 1904, 1,314 arrived; 1,625 departed. It was a most expensive method of recruiting labour.

Consequently, the colonies made every effort to induce the inden-

E

tured workers to renew their contract, or, at least, to remain at the
end of their term. With reindenture, they were unsuccessful. Reindentures numbered 6,096 in British Guiana from 1874 to 1895; new
arrivals totalled 105,205. For every 100 who came, only six who had
served their term agreed to a renewal. In the three years 1903–1905,
reindentures aggregated 133 in Surinam, one-tenth of the new arrivals
in 1902 The governments then tried inducements to remain. The chief
inducement was a grant of land. Between 1891 and 1913, in British
Guiana, a total of 31,917 acres was granted to 844 Indians as free
grants or homestead grants, with restrictions on alienation for a period
of ten years In 1898–1899 the number of acres thus granted was
5,922; in 1903–1904, 95 Indians received grants. In addition, 201
leases, involving 10,957 acres, were issued from 1991 to 1913. The
value of landed property held by Indians in British Guiana was
assessed at $972,761 in 1911–1912; in that year Indians owned 13,384
head of cattle and 3,022 sheep and goats.

In Surinam, between 1903 and 1911, over 200,000 acres of land
were allotted to 3,068 immigrants, either in free use, in lease, or by
outright purchase, six out of every ten acres were purchased outright, at a total cost of 589,184 florins. In Trinidad, between 1885 and
1895, a total of 22,916 acres was sold to Indian immigrants; between
1902 and 1912, 4,450 grants, totalling 31,766 acres, were distributed,
the Indians paying £72,837 for them, or over $9.60 an acre.

It will be recalled that in 1841 the Trinidad planters had protested
loudly against any disposal of Crown land in quantities of less than
320 acres. That Indians receiving wages of 25 cents a day could buy
any land at all is a tribute to their well-known capacity for thrift. The
number of Indian depositors in the Government Savings Bank in
Trinidad increased from 5,646 in 1902 to 9,973 in 1912, and the
amount deposited each year rose from £59,725 to £81,403.

Thus by a curious irony, the sugar planter who, in the seventeenth
and eighteenth centuries, refused to grant land to the white indentured
servant, who, after emancipation, tried to prevent the purchase of
land by the former slaves, found himself obliged in the 19th century
to grant land to the indentured immigrant in order to reduce the expense of immigrant labour. Indian immigration, designed to compete
with the Negro landowners, ended in the establishment of a class of
Indian landowners.

But the greatest victory of the Indians was that they established
their right themselves to grow cane. The planters who had brought
in Indian workers at public expense in order to make sure that sugar
would remain a plantation industry, were compelled fifty years later
to recognise the very Indian immigrants as small producers of cane.
The quantity of canes purchased from cane farmers in Trinidad increased from 35,459 tons in 1895 to 75,262 tons in 1896. In 1896 this
production came from 3,712 cane farms. Of these cane farms, there
were 73 at Woodford Lodge, 59 at Aranguez, 1,236 at Usine Ste
Madeleine, 550 at Reform, 94 at Brechin Castle, 29 at Caroni The

highest quantity purchased from any one farmer was 605 tons on the estate belonging to Sir Charles Tennant. The smallest quantity was 4 cwt. produced by a cane farmer on Lothian's estate.

Thus it was that the Indian indentured immigrant was able to raise in Trinidad one of the fundamental questions posed by the West Indian sugar industry – that is, whether sugar cultivation required the combination of ownership of land and factory in the same hands, or would, certainly for social reasons, possibly also on grounds of superior economy, be better organised on the basis of a distinct separation of the ownership of land from ownership of the factory, of the cultivation of the cane from the manufacture of the sugar. The question was posed by Victor Schoelcher in the report which prepared the way for emancipation in the French islands, and Schoelcher came out openly for the separation of cultivation and manufacture. The problem has also been familiar to the Spanish areas, Cuba and Puerto Rico, where much of the difficulty attendant on the development of the sugar industry in the 20th century has revolved around the invasion of large-scale American capital not only producing the sugar in gigantic factories, but also expropriating the native Cuban and Puerto Rican peasantry On a much smaller scale this distinct emergence of the cultivator of canes as a separate class in the society was a familiar phenomenon in the 19th century history of St Lucia and Tobago, where it was known as the *metairie* system.

The Indian cane farmer in Trinidad, cultivating cane on a small plot of land which he had been allowed to buy in exchange for a return passage to India, represented a challenge in Trinidad to the traditional method of production in the British sugar colonies in the West Indies To that extent the indentured Indian immigrant, the last victim in the historical sense of the sugar plantation economy, constituted one of the most powerful social forces for the future in the struggle for the establishment of a proper social structure and modern industrial relations.

CHAPTER 10

Colonialism in Tobago in the 19th Century

We have already seen how Tobago in the 19th Century lived in a state of betweenity, buffeted about from pillar to post, changing national flags and political allegiance. By the beginning of the 19th century it had passed finally into British hands, but Trinidad and Tobago, 18 miles apart, remained separate British colonies not related one to the other, until in 1889 the Governments of the two Islands were amalgamated, to be followed in 1899 by the Act of Union which made the two islands one single colony. We must now turn our attention therefore to the tribulations which Tobago suffered in the course of this transformation whereby an island which at the beginning of the 19th century had supported Bonaparte's dictatorship in France became at the end of that century a Ward of the Crown Colony of Trinidad.

The history of Tobago in the 19th century is the story of a steady economic decline and of the absurdity of self-governing institutions in an island of some 12,000 people.

The slave economy in Tobago was completely bankrupt at the time of emancipation in 1834. As an example may be taken the income and expenditure of a plantation in 1822 which contained 250 slaves, which may be regarded as representative of all the plantations in the island. The expenses of the operations – including salaries of attorney, manager, three overseers, and doctor, purchases of clothes, medicines, staves, lumber and salted fish, and the slave tax of 31 shillings per head – amounted to £4,345 10s. in Tobago currency. The sale of the plantation products, 100 hogsheads of sugar and 60 puncheons of rum, amounted to £3,400 The plantation therefore suffered a loss of £945 10s., exclusive of the interest on the mortgage and the debts due in England.

Thus it was that the House of Assembly of Tobago, could state in a petition to the Parliament of Great Britain on January 17, 1823:

'This Colony has now arrived at a pitch of distress of a deeper nature than we can possibly detail. It is a fact we earnestly submit to the serious consideration of your Honourable House, that there are few, if any estates, now in this Colony, which make any profitable return to their owners. The crops of very many of them, indeed, in spite of the utmost retrenchment possible in their expenditure and of every effort to increase both the quantity and quality of their produce have not been sufficient to pay their Colonial Taxes, and the price of their supplies, leaving the holders of mortgages on them without any payment, even of Interest, and their proprietors without any Income, while the very cultivation of other estates is only carried on by the continued sacrifice of additional capital. Nor is the evil likely to be of a local or temporary prevalence; on the contrary, we fear that under the present system it will and must extend till it attains its consummation in general ruin.'

The economic difficulties of the planters were intensified after emancipation. As everywhere else in the West Indies, the emancipated slaves preferred to set up on their own small plots of land as peasant proprietors. The planters, like their colleagues in other islands, contemplated a new labouring population through immigration. The general economic problem was aggravated by a disastrous hurricane which hit the island on the night of Monday, October 11, 1847. The hurricane appears to have tracked from south west to north east, taking within its sweep the northern part of the island of Trinidad, and proceeding in full force to Tobago. The devastation amounted to 26 persons killed on the night of the hurricane, 30 estate dwelling houses and 26 sugar factories demolished, 31 estate dwelling houses and 33 sugar factories damaged, 456 labourers's cottages razed to the ground and 176 severely damaged, 126 houses of all descriptions blown down in Scarborough and 84 severely damaged. The entire roof of the barracks at Fort George was blown away and some of the walls thrown to the ground. The estimate of the private property destroyed was $720,000.

This tremendous disaster intensified the demand of the planters for immigrants in order to proceed with the work of rehabilitation and reconstruction. As in Trinidad, their tastes were catholic. The immigration schemes proposed included the importation of labourers from England and Europe, English convicts, Barbadians, Africans from Sierra Leone, Indians and emancipated slaves and free people of colour from the United States of America. In 1846, 600 labourers emigrated from Barbados to Tobago and the House of Assembly of Tobago voted £2,000 sterling for immigration purposes. In January, 1860 the House of Assembly requested an imperial guarantee of a loan of £30,000 sterling to be employed in bringing Indian immigrants to Tobago. The British Government took the view that since the rate of wages in Tobago was 16 cents a day, nearly 25 per cent less than in Barbados, and about 50 per cent less than in British Guiana and Trinidad, no immigrants could be authorised until the minimum rate of wages was raised to 24 cents a day.

An Act of the Legislature of May 15, 1861, made provision for African immigrants who had been captured by British cruisers from ships prosecuting the slave trade. On arrival the immigrants were to be lodged in comfortable houses, and given a year's clothing, an iron pot, a spoon, a common clasp knife in the case of a man, one pound of soap per month, and one pound of tobacco. Each African over fourteen years of age was to be granted a quarter of an acre of land for the cultivation of ground provisions. The rate of wages was fixed at 16 cents a day, which a Chief Justice of the Island, Henry Wood-cock, in his little book *The History of Tobago* published in 1867, justified on the ground that the Negro 'is of an enduring nature; he can bear long abstinence, eats sparingly, and is sustained chiefly on vegetable food.' In this way Tobago, which had received 292 captured Africans from St Helena in 1851, received a further shipment from the same place of 225 Africans in 1862. The term of service was three years. With this increment to the population, the census of April 1861 showed a total of 15,410 inhabitants, an increase of 1,032 over the 1851 census.

But Tobago's economy could not really have stood the strain of a large scale immigration of workers, and everyone knew that The population was much too small to include any substantial number of small farmers, who could have been made to finance, as in Trinidad, a part of the cost of persons deliberately introduced to compete with them. Thus many of the planters were compelled to fall back on a system which had become very popular after the hurricane of 1847 when the plantation owners had neither the capital nor the workers to develop their plantations and nobody in England seemed anxious to buy plantations in Tobago That system was the *Metairie* system

Under the *Metairie* system, which was an old and well-known custom in many parts of the Continent of Europe and had been brought to the West Indies to such territories as St Lucia and Antigua, a landowner who had not enough money to carry on the cultivation by wage labour, agreed with his workers that they should work without wages on the promise of sharing the crop with the owner. This system continued to spread in Tobago and to work fairly well until 1884, when another disaster hit the islands and the West Indies generally. That was the bankruptcy of the London firm of Gillespie Brothers, on whom more than half the Tobago sugar estates depended for supplies and advances.

This was the situation when on February 10, 1890, shortly after Tobago's association with Trinidad, the Chief Justice of Trinidad, Sir John Gorrie, delivered one of the most famous judgments in the social history of the West Indies.

The plaintiff in the case, Joseph Franks, was a *metayer* on Castara Estate, the property of the defendant, R. B. Anderson. The plaintiff, 73 years of age, was born in slavery on the estate, and had been a *metayer* growing canes for 45 years, drawing in addition wages as the estate carpenter until 1886. Anderson quite suddenly decided to charge rent for Franks' provision ground against the terms of his agreement as a *metayer*, and to stop his wages as a carpenter, and ultimately turned him off the estate by a simple notice to quit. Franks thereupon sued Anderson for damages.

Sir John Gorrie in his celebrated judgment emphasised that the *metairie* system had developed after emancipation in Tobago under the pressure of two causes. The first was the fear that the emancipated Negroes would abandon the estates and seek other occupations. The second was the fear that the protection which West Indian sugar had enjoyed in the British market would soon cease, and that something had to be done to make the working of estates cheaper in view of the heavy fall in the price of sugar as a result of the competition with foreign slave-grown sugar. Hence the *metairie* system developed in Tobago, the share of the crop going to the owner being one-half as compared with one-third in Antigua.

The Chief Justice concluded that an arrangement of that nature raised the actual cultivator of the soil into a very different position from that of a mere labourer. He had become a contributor to a common fund with the proprietor and shared with him the profits or loss of the enterprise. The Chief Justice continued:

'So in Tobago, if there is any soul of goodness in the *Metairie* system it is because the number of the metayers who have undertaken to grow sugar for themselves and the estates gives a value to the property, and becomes a source of credit by which sufficient means can be raised to tide over the out-of-crop season until the cane has become ripe and has been made into sugar.'

As the Chief Justice understood the system, there was no time specified for the determination of the arrangement, no term expressed for the agreement coming to an end as both parties desired it to continue so long as the conditions are fulfilled. If either the proprietor could cut short the arrangement by a notice to quit or the *metayer* could get rid of his obligations by a similar notice to the proprietor, the whole value of the system would have been destroyed. In other words, as Sir John Gorrie put it, 'if it be good for the proprietor to have his *metayers* assured to him for the purpose of raising money to work with, it is equally good for the *metayer* to have fixity of tenure, because otherwise there would be no inducement to him to lay out his labour and sweat upon another man's land without wages, and only on the precarious chance of reaping the sugar from a year or two's labour.'

Thus did Sir John Gorrie arrive at the determination of the issue placed before him, the notice to quit issued by the defendant to the plaintiff on January 29, 1889. Sir John Gorrie's judgment was as follows:

'It is clear to me the defendant had no right to give that notice. Whether the metairie agreement between the proprietor and the metayer may involve a lien on the land for the purposes of the contract, so as to require to be marked on a Certificate of Title under the new Real Property Ordinance, or does not, it is, at all events, far too serious and important an arrangement, and goes much too deeply into the lot of individuals and families, the prosperity of estates, and the safety of the fund of credit by which the whole agricultural resources of a province are fed and stimulated, to permit one party or the other to bring it to an end at their own will and pleasure. There is no provision in the custom for a termination, nor for any notice. There are obligations on both sides, and if these obligations are systematically disregarded, it would give the sufferer by the fault the right to come to this Court for redress, and if desired, to require that the arrangement as between him and the wrong-doer might be dissolved, whether that wrong-doer were the proprietor or *metayer* Damages, moreover, can be recovered in this Court for isolated and specific breaches of the agreement, which might not amount to such a continuous abuse as to warrant an eject-ment on the one side, or a freeing from the trammels or metayer-ship on the other. But it does not lie in the hands of one party or the other to determine this for themselves, and to terminate at will a contract which, in its nature, is one of continuance while the con-ditions are fulfilled. This being the case it is not necessary to go into the miserable allegations which the defendant has made against this poor, broken-down old man of 73 years of age, whose best days from the age of 28 until now have been given to the cultivation of the estate of Castara Even were all he alleges true, it is for a Court of competent jurisdiction to decide upon them. I do not envy the state of mind of that man who could come into a Court of Justice and ask without a blush that the Court should use its power to punish an old man for the frailties of old age, and to throw out on the roads perhaps the one only person on the estate who had such ample titles to be treated with consideration and respect '

A Daniel come to judgment! The defendant had not only forced the plaintiff to leave his land which he held as a *metayer* by a notice to quit which he had no right to give, but he had also for some years been charging the plaintiff rent for his provision ground. He claimed that the plaintiff had agreed to this. Sir John Gorrie refused to accept this argument. In his opinion, as the security of tenure was one of the mainstays of the *Metairie* system, one of its greatest defects was its lack of pliability and adaptability to the wants of the hour. The sub-sidiary conditions of the contract could be changed by mutual consent, but if any substantial change in the conditions of the arrange-ment were desired, such, for example, as a change from cane to bananas, it would, in the Chief Justice's opinion, be necessary to come to the Court where all parties would be heard and the change, if agreed upon or decided, would be judicially sanctioned and recorded. But in all instances of smaller changes, mutual consent would have to be clearly proved. The Chief Justice continued:

'Now here the defendant, wishing to alter one of the main con-ditions of the arrangement which had endured forty-five years, the burden of proof of the mutuality of the consent to such an altera-tion must be on him. In those cases which frequently occur when consent is alleged on the part of one who is too young to govern well his own affairs or a female not conversant with affairs, or any one in the power of another, or any very old or weak person, or any one enfeebled by disease, or a very rustic and ignorant person, and in various others, a Court of Law will take special care to be advised that the consent of such a person was perfectly free and unforced.'

The defendant had taken the case to the Magistrate's Court, and it was against the Magistrate's decision that the plaintiff appealed to the Chief Justice. The Chief Justice denied that the Magistrate had any jurisdiction to entertain a question of this kind. Its importance could not be measured by the sum of $48 00, which was the limit of the Magistrate's civil jurisdiction. The issue involved was a question of the plaintiff's privilege as a *metayer* on the Castara Estate, and no Magistrate had jurisdiction to try a question so serious and so mixed up with questions affecting real estate

The Chief Justice then turned to the plaintiff's claim for his wages as a carpenter which had not been paid for some years. The defendant's reply was that anything the plaintiff was properly entitled to had been credited to the rent account. The Chief Justice, having denied that there was any right to charge such rent, ruled that the wages had to be paid. In memorable words, therefore, deeming the whole proceedings of the defendant 'to have been not only illegal, but harsh and rapacious,' Sir John Gorrie assessed the damages at $96 00 with $15.00 costs, and fees of Court.

Sir John Gorrie was not merely dealing with a case that had come before the Chief Justice. He was defending the rights of people in Tobago who had never been regarded as having any rights at all. Sir John Gorrie openly and deliberately challenged the entire plantocracy of Tobago, as follows: —

'It is most lamentable to see the want of cultivation of this Island, and I cannot but fear it has occurred from the Courts not knowing their powers, or the various parties to the contract being ignorant how to enforce their rights I shall be prepared while in the Colony to hear applications from the proprietor or metayers of the defendant's estate or of any estate similarly situated.'

The general consternation was indescribable The Governor of Trinidad and Tobago, Sir William Robinson, had already become involved with the Chief Justice in a conflict with the Chief Justice not unusual in West Indian history On March 8, 1889, the Governor forwarded to the Chief Justice a communication from the Commissioner of Tobago to the effect that: —

'. . . the labouring classes of the Island are in an unsettled state and that this condition of affairs is attributable to an impression which has been created amongst them, with which your Honour's name is unfortunately associated, that as one of the immediate results of annexation they should be placed on the same footing in regard to wages as the Trinidad labourer, and that unless this is done, the Trinidad wages being much higher, they are the victims of oppression.'

The Governor added that he had been made personally aware of the existence of such a feeling on a recent visit to Tobago, and had taken the opportunity of endeavouring to undeceive a large body of labourers and artisans whom he had granted an interview. The Governor advised the Chief Justice that 'the next session of the Supreme Court that it may be necessary to hold in Tobago should be presided over by one of the Puisne Judges.'

Sir John Gorrie replied on the same date blaming the trouble on a land speculator from Trinidad who had purchased Studley Park Estate and had refused to grind the canes of *metayers* at his mill in accordance with the custom of the colony. The Chief Justice continued:

'. . . In place of pledging myself in the beginning of March, according to Your Excellency's unheard of request not to go to Tobago in May, I now, as Chief Justice of the Colony, advise Your Excellency that the legal question should be put to rest at once, and by myself, in whom the people have proclaimed their confidence as a Judge, and that it ought not to remain unsettled one day longer than necessary.

'I offer to embark at once, as soon as Your Excellency provides me with the means of conveyance and to hold a special Court under the Judicature Ordinance 1879.'

The Governor, however, saw no necessity for a special Court, and therefore, declined to provide the Chief Justice with the means of conveyance to Tobago.

Three months after Sir John Gorrie's judgment, the Governor appointed a Commission of Enquiry known as the Tobago *Metairie* Commission. The members were the Attorney General of Trinidad, the Commissioner of Tobago, and Rober Aucher Warner, Barrister-at-Law and Bachelor of Arts Of Sir John Gorrie's judgment the Commission wrote as follows:

'This Judgment produced a profound impression among the planters. For the first time in the history of the System it was there suggested that the metayer in Tobago has fixity of tenure of the portion of the Estate on which he is permitted to grow the canes under his Contract . . .

'No such contention was raised during the enquiry between 1884 and 1888, and what appeared to us good reasons were adduced why such a right could not have ever been, and should not now, be a part of the Contract. The metayer in Tobago exercises no rights of ownership over his lot beyond using it for the planting of canes and the growing of some vegetables on the cane banks. He does not live on his lot His home is not there. He pays no land or occupation tax, and does not want to continue his occupation a moment longer when the land ceases to bear fruitful cane. He puts no permanent improvements into the land – he seldom if ever even manures it. When one bit of land is exhausted he moves on to a new one though he may go back to an old lot when it has been again in bush and lain, so to speak, fallow for some time. He moves from one Estate to another, and so far as we can learn expects nothing beyond the right to exhaust the crops he has planted. If it can be said that in respect of the quasi-partnership in the fruits of transient crops (for canes do not rattoon for ever) he is to be endowed with a portion of the freehold, there must be some corresponding obligation on his part not to leave the Estate; but this he has always been at liberty to do, and he would be the first one would suppose, to object to an approach to serfdom of this kind. It would sound strange to a Tobago metayer if he were told that he could not leave his holding without paying compensation to the proprietor of the Estate. We find no warrant in the facts and history of the Contract to import such a right as fixity of tenure into the Contract, nor do we think it would be politic to introduce it '

And what could the Commission itself recommend? In 1890 it could only recommend what had been recommended in 1850, the introduction of Indian immigrants. If this was beyond Tobago's means, the Commission suggested that the Agricultural Board in Tobago and the Government of Trinidad and Tobago should consider whether some scheme was not feasible for inducing some of the Indians who had completed their indenture in Trinidad to try their fortunes in Tobago.

By this time, however, the old Tobago planter society was no more. In the very year in which the *Metairie* Commission reported, 1890, Tobago's revenue had reached the lowest figure recorded since 1865 – £8,657, a mere $40,000, approximately one-half the revenue of 1881. In 1885 the bad state of the colony's finances had demanded wholesale retrenchment The volunteers were disbanded, Churches were to be gradually disendowed, the number of the Police Force had been reduced. When the West India Royal Commission of 1897 arrived in Tobago, the island was bankrupt. The collective value of the exports of sugar, rum and molasses declined from £42,437 in 1882 to £5,209 in 1896. Exports of rum, 20,400 gallons in 1882, were 400 gallons in 1894. Exports of sugar, 2,518 tons in 1882, were 599 tons in 1894. Imports of flour declined from 3,383 barrels in 1882 to 2,093 in 1894; imports of rice from 233,800 pounds to 43,384 pounds; of kerosene from 7,483 gallons to 3,612 gallons; of tobacco from 1,566 pounds to 12,600 pounds; of beef and pork from 107,190 pounds to 31,230 pounds; of salted and pickled fish from 357,004 pounds to 152,688 pounds. The total import trade was £46,927 in 1882 and £15,403 in 1894. The value of exports declined from £48,245 in 1882 to £15,872 in 1894. Making all necessary allowances for the incompleteness of the figure from 1889, the date of the association with Trinidad, the general economic decline of Tobago under British rule is immediately obvious.

So much for the economic side of the story in the 19th century. Now for the political.

Tobago was superior to its sister colony in Trinidad because, as one of the older British colonies, it enjoyed representative institutions. It had its own bicameral legislature with its Governor and Commander-in-Chief. As a self-governing colony and not a Crown Colony, it had the usual quarrels with the British Government over legislation affecting the slaves One example was the British Government's opposition in 1818 to a Tobago Act to establish a public chain gang. The British Government proposed the following amendments to the Act:

'1st—The weight and length of the Chain to be established by Law, as well as the form and nature of the Irons.

'2nd—Females and infirm persons to be treated differently, during confinement, to others.

'3rd—No slave to be subject to this mode of punishment before conviction.

'4th—There ought to be separate rooms for male and female Slaves, as well as for those convicted of crimes and those not under sentence.

'5th—Proprietors or Masters of Slaves ought not to have authority to confine them even for four days, as the Act does not specify any limitation to the interval that may elapse between the expiration of one imprisonment for four days and the commencement of another.

'6th—Proprietors or Masters of Slaves ought not to be entrusted with the power of inflicting the same disgraceful punishment upon them as the Magistrates are authorised by Law to inflict on Public Criminals.'

The Tobago Legislature protested indignantly to the United Kingdom Parliament against the British Government's policy of 1823 for the amelioration of the treatment of the Slaves As in Jamaica and in Barbados, they objected to any measures 'that shall, either directly or indirectly, diminish the authority of their own colonial legislature,' and argued in favour of local knowledge and local competence They condemned the prohibition of the flogging of female slaves as 'tantamount to unqualified emancipation from this hour,' and asserted that in respect of allowing to the female slaves immunities which the male slaves did not possess, 'it is no more in the power of Legislation to raise them at once to a state of moral excellence, than to legislate the blossoms of spring into autumnal fruits.' The British proposal that the slave should be allowed resort to the law courts for redress was rejected by the Tobago Assembly as tantamount to immediate freedom for the slaves. And like their colleagues throughout the West Indies, they called on the British Parliament for compensation.

They beg to remind your Honourable House that neither they nor their ancestors were called upon to view the justice or injustice of slavery as an abstract question. They found it established here and on the faith of Royal Proclamations and Acts of Parliament, embarked their capital in property in this country, and if it is now found that the establishment of slavery in the West Indies has been a National sin, the loss should be National also and they are entitled to a full remuneration for their property.'

Relations between the Tobago Assembly and the British Government became increasingly strained after 1823 This was reflected in the conflict between the Governor, Sir F. E. Robinson, and the House of Assembly. These conflicts culminated in the submission of a petition to the King in which the Assembly laid 43 charges against the Governor and asked for his instant removal. In the absence of prompt action from the British Government the Assembly forwarded two supplementary petitions to the King pressing even more beligerently for the Governor's immediate removal.

In 1833, the British Government decided on a fundamental change. Tobago, with Grenada and St Vincent, were placed under the Governor of Barbados who was raised to the rank of Governor-General. The British Government hoped by this measure to reduce the expenses of the smaller colonies. But the bicameral system remained, and something approaching a Ministerial form of Government even emerged with the development of an Executive Committee whose members were chosen from the Legislature and who ceased to hold office as soon as they ceased to enjoy the confidence of the popular branch The germ of the party system inherent in this development was frowned upon and discouraged. As Woodcock wrote:

'There is not the material in any West Indian community to form either a Ministerial party or a healthy Opposition. We may find, upon some stirring occasion, certain members of a Colonial Assembly joining together to carry a measure they may deem essential to the public welfare, or to oppose what they may consider injurious; but in the detail we shall hardly find them acting in concert. Every man has his own opinion, and he will not relinquish it to adopt that of any party. His feelings of individual independence are much too strong for this; and his daily occupations are such as to preclude him from devoting the necessary time and thought to the organisation of a party, or the conduct of party measures.'

But the representative system was a farce The franchise in Tobago was the prerogative of a mere handful of people. The Lieutenant Governor, in his address to the Assembly on March 10, 1857, spoke as follows:

'The Act by which the elective franchise is at present limited is a relic of the time of slavery, which a free people must long have desired to expunge from their statute-book. It cannot be referred to for the purpose of settling a contested vote without reviving feelings which ought not to exist in a community from which all distinctions of colour and race have long since been practically abolished. The very idea of it must be offensive, suggesting, as it does, that the exercise of the franchise is a privilege conceded for the relief of certain classes, instead of a right, co-relative with the possession of property and the duties of citizenship, and in practice the Act excludes the majority of those who directly contribute to the revenue, and thus violates the principles of the English Constitution, which regards the supplies as gifts from the people, voted by their representatives. The whole number of votes on the books of the returning officer is only 102, of whom only 70 are freeholders, or persons qualified to vote in right of their own properties, whilst the whole number of persons who might be assessed on the valuation rolls to pay taxes upon their freeholds appears to be 2,580. This cannot be regarded as a fair representation of those on whom the burthen of taxation falls and public policy demands that a burthen, which is always felt so irksome, should be lightened as much as possible, by giving the people the credit of bearing it of their own free will.'

The result was an Act of June 1860 to 'extend the privileges, and otherwise provide for better representation of the people.' The island was divided into nine electoral districts, each Parish returning two representatives, and the towns of Scarborough and Plymouth one each. The qualification for an elector became the ownership of real property of the value of $48.00 or a position as manager or overseer in occupation of a house valued at an annual rental value of $720. The tenants or occupants of any freehold part of a house having a distinct communication with a public road or street were qualified to vote, provided that they had been in possession for twelve months and their names were on the valuation roll The qualification for a representative in the House of Assembly was the ownership of real property in his own right or that of his wife, or possession of an annual income, to the value of $720.

The result of this new Representation of the People Bill was that the number of voters was increased from 102 to 215. At the ensuing elections 91 voted, and the representatives for St John and Plymouth were returned by the vote of one voter in each district.

The absurdity was obvious In 1865 the Jamaican rebellion was followed by the suspension of the representative institutions and the introduction of the Crown Colony system. Similar changes followed in the Windward Islands, preparatory to the British Government's proposals in 1876 for a federation of the Leeward and Windward Islands and Barbados. Tobago's turn was not far off Lieutenant-Governor Ussher dealt with the problem in 1872 as follows:

'One of the principal obstructions of progress in the island is the present form of government. Its machinery would doubtless be well adapted to a country like Victoria or the Cape, but its adaptation to the conditions of a country like Tobago, an island of 90 square miles in extent, numbering a population of little over seventeen thousand souls is doubtful in the extreme. One of its results has been the creation of a multiplicity of petty offices with salaries attached of the lowest class, rendering it next to impossible to obtain for the performance of the duties thereof qualified and responsible officers, but at the same time sufficing to induce a certain class to look forward to obtaining them, and to avoid being obliged to betake themselves to more profitable but more undignified pursuits entailing upon them the necessity of hard work.'

In 1874 the bicameral system was abolished and a single Chamber Legislature substituted. The new Legislative Council comprised 14 members, 6 nominated by the Governor, and 8 elected by the people. The new Council met for the first time on February 5, 1875. The planters protested. A public meeting in Scarborough denounced the new arrangement as a violation of vested rights and a time honoured system. But their resentment was soon moderated by the Belmanna riots of 1876.

The Belmanna riots broke out in May 1876 in Roxborough. They started with certain fires on the Roxborough Estate attributed to incendiaries. Several fields of growing canes were burnt and the megasse house containing a quantity of megasse equal to the manufacture of 30 hogsheads of sugar was demolished This was associated with signs of dissatisfaction exhibited by the Barbadian workers on the estate. The Governor sent his police officers consisting of Corporal Belmanna and five privates to Roxborough with warrants for the arrests of the alleged incendiaries and generally to keep order. On May 3rd, warrants were issued for the apprehension of five persons. The police, in going to execute these warrants, carried their arms The official report of what transpired reads as follows : —

'Everything seemed to have been peaceable on this morning: — the people had turned out to work and the mill was about.

'Whilst executing the process of Law, a spirit of determined hostility appears to have taken possession of the people, and exhibited itself in the stoning, and other illegal treatment of the Police – on the fifth arrest being made, matters assumed a worse aspect. The Corporal was thrown down more than once by the missiles thrown at him, and wounded – the people became more violent, and in a most unfortunate moment, it appears to have been considered necessary by the Corporal to fire in self-defence. The result of this firing, which no one deplores more than I do, was the death of a woman named Mary Jane Thomas. From this moment riot appears to have reigned supreme. The Manager's House on Roxbro was gutted. The mob surrounded the Court House at Roxbro armed with cutlasses, sticks and other missiles – some of them I understand being armed with guns – the release of the prisoners was demanded – and acceded to – but had no effect in pacifying the rioters. The Court House was attempted to be fired, and Corporal Belmanna –

whose life they were determined to take together with another Police Officer, Allen, rather than suffer death by fire, most bravely faced the mob.

'The Police generally were beaten severely, but Corporal Belmanna most brutally – so much so, that he died from the wounds inflicted on him.'

The Governor sent for a warship from Grenada and 135 persons were sworn in as special constables Indicative of the general dissatisfaction was the fact that several of the special constables had themselves to be arrested as being concerned in the riots.

In Tobago, as in Jamaica, once the planters felt that their privileges were threatened by a vast mass of Negro and coloured voters, they wanted no self-government at all and voted themselves for Crown Colony government. On June 6, 1867, Tobago became a Crown Colony, the leader of the opposition himself introducing the Bill. The Lieutenant Governor wrote of the new Bill:

'That so complete a change in the constitution of the island should be desired after the comparatively recent one to a single chamber in 1874, is to be attributed to the opinion of those who hold the property of the country, and whose capital is embarked in the cultivation of the land, having undergone the most marked and decided changes upon the island being made a crown colony. The late disturbance also made manifest the insecurity of both life and property unless aided by the Imperial Government, hence there is now a leaning for protection and support which it is felt will not be withheld from this old community.'

As the economic crisis worsened, the political crisis became correspondingly more desperate. On March 2, 1880, the Legislative Council, faced with a British Government's decision that Tobago was thereafter to pay the salary of the Administrator which had formerly been paid by the United Kingdom, and faced with an outstanding debt burden of £4,000 at the end of 1879, decided to increase taxation. The export tax on sugar was reimposed, notwithstanding a protest from the unofficial members, and import dues were increased on flour, salted meat, liquor, tobacco and lumber. Three days later the unofficial members protested to the British Government against the imposition of the export tax on sugar, on the ground that sugar constituted two-thirds of the plantations in Tobago, the sugar market was bad, the sugar industry was operating at a loss, and the export tax had originally been imposed for immigration purposes to boost the sugar industry. On March 31 in the same year, therefore, the Council moved the abolition of the export tax and instead increased taxes on land and tenements and on certain articles in the tariff which fell heaviest on the poorest classes.

The general discontent in the island encountered by a British Royal Commission appointed in December 1882, to enquire into the public revenues, expenditure, debts and liabilities of the islands of Jamaica, Grenada, St Vincent, Tobago, and St Lucia, and the Leeward Islands, was well expressed by a humble labourer from Harmony Hall by the name of Alexander Frazer in a communication to the Commission on April 23, 1883. The letter reads as follows, its grammatical errors reflecting the fifty years of education after emancipation:

'We are more than glad when we hear that you has arrived for our benefit, for we are more than opress with the heavy taxes we are squize down with, it is only the mercy of Almighty God why some of us is still remaining in this land of Tobago. My Lord all the taxes are heavy, but the house and horse taxes are more than we are able to pay, but my Lord we are not able to take their lives on account of the tax, and what must we do with them when we cannot pay the two pounds yearly for them.

'When we offer them for sale those that are in better cercomstances or afraid to perches them on account of the imposing taxes, whenever we go to speak to the Administrator towards the opression of the taxes he dosent want to heare nothing, and we like always to submit ourselves to the rules and laws of our island, we dont like our Sovring Lady to heare anything amiss against us, for we know that she will not uphold with any one to impose on us. Our inhabitants is geting smaller and smaller every day, the labourers are going away daily seeking for bread; and also my Lord last week a poor man came to me asking me to lend him two pounds to pay for his horse tax, that he will give me that said horse with two soots of garment to keep untill he is able to pay me the two pounds, but I was more than sory for him, but I was not in a possession so to do, for with all my effort I am not able to pay my taxes as yet. Jentlemen, I must also inform that last year we had to pay for horse colt of one year old one pound, and if we are not able to pay, and we should try to hide them away for a little time, that should they grow the inspector send police officers to search in the bushes untill they are found, and when the owner cant pay for them, the will sacrifice them according to their likeing; there are many more grievances my Lord, but my talent is small, therefore I will say no more at present, trusting and waiting for your kind deliverance of part of our burden.'

The picture presented by the Commission is one of the most pathetic even in the pathetic history of the West Indies. Expenditure on roads in Tobago amounted to £5,401 in the five years 1878 to 1882, about $26,000. The Government could not afford to pay an officer to superintend the 100 miles of main road in the island. All adults were required to pay a road tax of $1 44 per month or to give six days' labour at the rate of 14 cents per day. The salaries of the medical officers were purely nominal; the 1883 expenditure on the Medical Department was £1,972, about $9,000. The sum of $12,000 was voted in 1882 for the establishment of an Alms House; the Alms House could not be proceeded with, owing to the impoverished condition of the Tobago Treasury. The Sergeant of the island received a salary of $24 a month; there were 18 Constables who received a salary of $12 a month and 10 Constables who received $14.40 a month. The Education vote for 1883 was $2,880, an additional sum of $960 being voted for a Grammar School. The Civil Service establishment in Tobago numbered 60, and their annual salaries amounted to $7,072, a little less than $34,000.

The Commission found the Administration struggling against these adverse conditions, and was satisfied that the recent scandals in Grenada and elsewhere were inevitable when officials generally had to accept such low salaries. The Commission emphasised that in Tobago, Grenada, St Vincent, St Lucia, in each one of the islands the whole work had to be gone through of devising, drafting, considering, passing, and amending an Ordinance on every necessary matter. The same quadruplication was seen in all other work whether of correspondence or finance. Barbados had upset the British apple-cart by positively refusing to participate in any federation with the small islands. It wanted neither Little Eight nor Little Four. It was determined to go it alone. The Commission of 1882 therefore recommended a federation of the four islands of St Vincent, St Lucia, Grenada, Tobago, with the possible inclusion of Dominica, with headquarters in Grenada The Commission stated:

'In each of these four islands it has been the custom to maintain an independence of the others, which may have been excusable in former days, when communication was unfrequent and difficult, and when there were neither telegraphs nor steamers, when each Island was actually separate from the others, and when advice or news from or to the mother country occupied months in transit, a state of things entirely superseded in the present day

'The evils of isolation have, however, for long been acknowledged in the Islands themselves, and for more than a century a tendency towards union has manifested itself. In the year 1765 Grenada was the capital Island of a federation including St Vincent, Tobago, and Dominica. In 1771 Dominica, and in 1776 St Vincent, respectively left the federation, so that in 1783 Grenada was united only to the Grenadines. St Lucia became English permanently in 1803. In 1833 one general government was established, to include Barbados, Grenada, St Vincent, and Tobago. In 1838 St Lucia was included in this federation. There has thus for long existed a consciousness in the Islands themselves that isolation was erroneous, and this even before the days of steamers and the telegraph. Hitherto, however, attempts have been confined to forming a federal rather than a united Colony.

'In the year 1876 the lesser Windward Islands were willing to confederate with Barbados on closer terms, but little was accomplished to realise the expressed wishes of leading inhabitants, owing

to the action of the latter Island. Moreover, the former cannot but
have felt that Barbados, in population and wealth, was more than
their equal, and would have acquired, in consequence, a prepon-
derating influence in any joint government.

'It may be pointed out that the true basis of successful union is
identity of requirements. The lesser islands have now become
Crown Colonies, and in so far differ in the matter of constitution
from Barbados; and if we regard these Islands generally we shall
see that in past history, present circumstances, and future requirements St Lucia, St Vincent, Grenada, Tobago, and Dominica stand
in one and the same category, and apart from any other English
Islands so far as domestic requirements are concerned.

'These five Islands are geographically in position sufficiently near
each other to form one Colony. The extreme distance from south
to north from Grenada to Dominica being only 200 miles, a
distance little exceeding the length of Jamaica, and not half the
length of the Bahamas, the West Africa Settlements, or the Gold
Coast Colony.

'Each of these Islands possesses, in addition to small tracts of
cultivated soil, large areas of accessible and fertile, but as yet uncultivated land. In each roads are urgently required to open up the
various districts; in short there is as yet but little cultivation or
population in proportion to area, and ample opportunity and room
for further growth These distinctive features are present neither
in Barbados, which is densely populated and cultivated over every
acre, nor in St Christopher, Antigua, and Nevis, in which there exists
an old established cultivation extending over nearly all accessible
portions of each Island.'

On February 25, 1885, the Governor-in-Chief of Barbados
addressed the Legislative Council of Tobago and introduced a resolution with respect to the proposed confederation of Grenada, St Lucia,
St Vincent and Tobago, which reads in part as follows:

'The Legislative Councils of the said islands would cease to exist
but that Local Boards should be established in each of the said
islands for the administration and regulation of such local matters
as shall be placed under their control by any law or laws to be
enacted by the Governor with the consent of the Legislative Council
of the (entire) Colony . . .'

The Resolution was rejected by the Council and a counter resolution introduced by the unofficial members The proposed union was
regarded as not acceptable to the great majority of the inhabitants
of Tobago and as not advantageous to its interests. The British
Government was not impressed. On March 5, 1885, an Order-in-
Council separated the administration of Barbados from that of the
four islands and constituted the office of Governor and Commander-
in-Chief of the Windward Islands of Grenada, St Vincent, St Lucia
and Tobago.

In 1886 the Governor-in-Chief in Grenada requested the Tobago Legislature to appoint a committee to submit proposals with respect to Tobago for a comprehensive scheme of fiscal requirements, both in customs and internal taxation, on a uniform basis for the four islands.

The Tobago Legislature submitted its proposals which were qualified by two basic considerations:

(a) 'the opinion that a uniformity of customs duties among these Islands however desirable would to a large extent be impracticable owing to the great differences existing in the circumstances of each of these four Islands.'

(b) '. . . as there is a strong probability that our proposed annexation to Trinidad will soon be an accomplished fact, it would be unwise to make any alterations at present in our Tariff as if that very desirable union is carried out our fiscal system will no doubt have to be remodelled on the Trinidad lines.'

In the 18th century Tobago had lived between England, France, Holland and Courland Becoming finally British, it went it alone for a while. Then Britain tacked it on to Barbados, in association with Grenada and St Vincent, and later St Lucia. Then Barbados seceded. Therefore Britain decided to associate Tobago with St Lucia, St Vincent, Grenada and possibly Dominica Betweenity in the 18th century and betweenity in the 19th century. Metropolitan betweenity in the 18th century became colonial betweenity in the 19th century. Tobago would have none of this. If it was one of the eternal verities that Tobago was to be between, it preferred Trinidad to Barbados or Grenada or St Vincent or St Lucia.

CHAPTER 11

The Union of Trinidad and Tobago

The initiative for the union of Trinidad and Tobago came neither from Tobago nor from Trinidad but from the Secretary of State for the Colonies. In December 1886, the following notice appeared in the *Gazettes* and newspapers of both Colonies at the direction of the Secretary of State for the Colonies:

'Her Majesty's Government having had under their consideration the condition and prospects of the Colony of Tobago and, having regard to its geographical proximity to, and means of communication with, the Colony of Trinidad, are of opinion that it would be for the advantage of both Colonies that the Colony of Tobago should be annexed to and form part of the said Colony of Trinidad.

'Such annexation may be effected in either of the two following modes, namely:

'1. The Colony of Tobago may be wholly and completely incorporated with the Colony of Trinidad; or

'2. The Colony of Tobago may be annexed to the Colony of Trinidad as a dependency, having a separate Treasury and subordinate Legislature, holding to Trinidad the same relation that the Turks Islands do to Jamaica.

'The former of these two schemes appears to be preferable: Her Majesty's Government are however desirous of ascertaining the opinions and wishes of the inhabitants of both Colonies upon the subject; and after a sufficient time has elapsed for a full consideration of the question, resolutions in favour of incorporation of Tobago with Trinidad, or, as an alternative, of annexation as a dependency, will be introduced into the Legislative Council of each of the Colonies.'

The merchants and planters of Tobago immediately took up arms. They preferred the second alternative to the first. Accepting the principle of a customs union, a uniform code of laws, and the appointment of a single Governor for both islands, they demanded full control by Tobago of its internal taxes and disposition of its internal revenues. On January 19, 1887, the following resolutions were carried unanimously in the Legislative Council of Tobago.

'That this Council, having had under its consideration the notice published in the Government Gazette under date 2nd December, 1886, is satisfied that, subject to the conditions hereinafter mentioned, it would be to the advantage of both Colonies that the Colony of Tobago should be united to that of Trinidad so as to form one Colony, to be called the Colony of Trinidad and Tobago; and that the Colony so constituted should be governed by one Governor and be subject to one and the same code of laws.

'That as an incident of such Union this Council is of opinion that the duties leviable in Tobago upon articles imported from abroad should be the same as those in Trinidad, and that the traffic and intercourse between the two Islands should be absolutely free; but that the interests of Tobago imperatively require that all internal taxes other than the duties aforesaid should be imposed and adjusted with strict reference to local circumstances, and should not follow the laws of taxation in force in Trinidad, except in so far as the local circumstances may admit of it

'That this Council is further of opinion that all revenues collected in and on account of Tobago should be wholly expended in the administration of the Island, and should not be absorbed in the general revenue of the United Colony; that no part of the public expenditure of Trinidad should be chargeable upon the revenues of Tobago, and no part of the public expenditure of Tobago upon the revenues of Trinidad, except so far as the two Islands may by mutual consent, and upon terms to be mutually agreed upon, enter jointly upon any public enterprise for the benefit of both.

'That the Chief Executive Officer representing the Government of the United Colony in Tobago should have associated with him a local Board, to be termed the Financial Board, whose duty it should be to advise the Governor in all matters relating to the internal taxation and expenditure of the Island, and that no tax leviable in Tobago (other than Customs Duties) should be imposed or altered without the consent of such Board

'That the Financial Board should, in addition to the Executive Officer, consist of three resident householders not being salaried Public Officers, one of whom to be nominated by the Governor, and two to be elected by the general body of householders in the Island.

'That for the carrying out of these proposals this Council do move an humble address to the Crown praying that Her Most Gracious Majesty will be pleased to take such steps as may be necessary to effect the union of the two Colonies and to secure the faithful and lasting observance of the conditions hereinbefore set forth.'

The merchants of Tobago were emphatic in their repudiation of the extension to Tobago of the fiscal laws of Trinidad or of the utilisation of Tobago's revenues for purely Trinidad purposes. Under no circumstances would they agree to a union which made Tobago a ward or district of Trinidad. They sent a petition to the Legislative Council of Tobago which reads in part as follows:

'Of those that should be avoided we consider the most important is any arrangement that would subject us to the fiscal laws of Trinidad.

Taxation in Trinidad is equal to an average of £3 per head per annum of the population whilst that of Tobago does not ordinarily reach 15s. 6d. per head and is capable of reduction to considerably below that amount and we desire to record our solemn conviction that any such arrangement would be ruinous to the people of Tobago and would depopulate the place and reduce it back to the condition of a wilderness.

'We conceive that it would be unnecessary and unfair to subject Tobago to such fiscal union and assimilation because Tobago has no interest in, and can derive no benefit from, some of the heaviest burdens of Trinidad such as Railways – Immigration Service – Interest on a large public debt and others.

'We think that in some particulars our tariff rates might if found necessary for the prevention of smuggling be assimilated to those of Trinidad.

'We believe that practically such a scheme as would include on fair arrangements as to cost weekly or half weekly steam communication with Trinidad and the working of some of our institutions particularly the Supreme Court, the Gaol and Police in connection with those of Trinidad but preserving the locus of those departments in Tobago would be the most advantageous to this Colony.

'We are of opinion that it would not be advantageous to this Colony to be so united with Trinidad as to be made a ward thereof nor to be deprived of its separate administration subordinate to that of Trinidad.'

Notwithstanding what the Royal Commission of 1882 had said or the Secretary of State for the Colonies had suggested, the Legislative Council of Tobago was reluctant to surrender its institutions and powers, however much these may have been truncated by the introduction of the Crown Colony system in 1876. The debate on the resolutions of January 9, 1887, was concluded with a resolution moved by one of the unofficial members, Mr Ebenezer Henderson, which, after slight amendment, was adopted by the Council as follows:

'That inasmuch as the wish of the people of Tobago for union with Trinidad has principally been based on the representations of the Government and the assurances given to the people that material benefits will result to Tobago from such union, the Secretary of State for the Colonies be respectfully asked in the event of such union taking place to afford the people of Tobago a pledge that should it prove disadvantageous to this Colony, or otherwise undesirable to the majority of the inhabitants, this Colony shall on petition have granted back to it the form of self government which now exists here.'

All this of course was quite absurd in the light of the financial situation of Tobago brought out in the report of the Royal Commission of 1882, of the steady economic decline which we have already indicated, and of the message of the Administrator to the Legislative Council submitting the estimates for the year 1887. With a deficit of

£3,000 and an anticipated revenue of £8,000, the Administrator expressed the hope that 'the roads, with judicious watching, could be kept in fair order a little longer, without any large expenditure', and that the hospital, which at one time it was feared might have to be closed, could continue open, limited to twelve beds Even this was only possible because the Government of Grenada had agreed to wait for five years for the repayment of a loan of £1,000 which, according to the original arrangement, should have been repaid in its entirety in November 1887.

What really mattered, however, was not what Tobago thought and said about the arrangement proposed by the Secretary of State, but what Trinidad thought and said. Trinidad, being a Crown Colony, had little freedom to think or say too much, and of course the people of Trinidad were not consulted in the matter. With this reservation, the question of the association of Trinidad and Tobago, whether incorporation or annexation or union, gave rise, on March 5, 1887, to one of the most amusing debates in the history of the Legislature of Trinidad.

On that day the Solicitor General, Mr Maxwell Phillip, an Englishman, moved the following resolution:

'That in view of the opinion expressed by Her Majesty's Government after consideration of the condition and prospects of the Colony of Tobago, and having regard to its geographical proximity to and means of communication with this Colony, that it would be for the advantage of both Colonies that the Colony of Tobago should be annexed to and form part of the Colony of Trinidad, and further of the resolution adopted by the Legislative Council of Tobago at their meeting on the 19th January in which, subject to certain conditions therein specified, they express their concurrence in the proposal of Her Majesty's Government, this Council is of opinion that it is expedient that the incorporation of Tobago with Trinidad in the manner suggested should be completed.'

The Solicitor General's heart was simply not in the matter, and he himself said at the end of the debate that he had addressed the Council for a 'weary hour and a half'. He emphasised that the proposition was the brain child of the United Kingdom Government which, having failed in its efforts some eleven years earlier to pass the baby on to Barbados, was now seeking to place the responsibilities of paternity on the shoulders of Trinidad. Mr Maxwell Phillip commended the proposition to the Legislative Council of Trinidad in the following terms:

'It therefore appeared clear that what was desired by the Government was to take a step which was likely to diminish the expenditure of Tobago as an independent or separate Government, to enable Tobago to economise a large portion of the money which was now spent for the purpose of keeping up a separate Government, to impart or give to Tobago the assistance of some of the public officers of this country, and to impart from our community, as a commercial community, the intercourse which would take place, to enable Tobago to go on conjointly with Trinidad without unnecessarily spending large sums of money on a Government which was now separate and which ought not to be, considering the condition of Tobago and the state of the times. Then, if that be so, he thought we were bound to accept it and that we would do no violence to the feelings that we always entertained towards the English Government – that we were bound to accept this as a scheme emanating from Her Majesty's Government and one which was put forward to be accepted by Trinidad and by Tobago in case there was no detriment done either to the inhabitants of the one or of the other . . .

'Her Majesty's Government was bound to protect her dominions and to devise the best method of governing any portion of those dominions, and it appeared to him that if it was suggested that this portion of the dominions of Her Majesty the Queen would be efficiently and economically governed, and it was delicately left to them to consider the matter and pronounce upon it whether there was any strong and particular reason – a reason arising from the detriment that would be wrought on the community of Trinidad or Tobago – in the absence of any detriment, if they saw no detriment whatever in a scheme of that sort, he had not the slightest doubt that their desire to assist in the proper government of any portion of Her Majesty's dominions especially when the suggestion was made to them, would induce them at once to consider the matter and to adopt the resolution for having Tobago annexed to us.'

The real mover of the resolution, however, was the Governor, Sir William Robinson, who was presiding over the Council. The Governor interrupted the Solicitor General throughout his speech and heckled the unofficial members. The Governor held out the blandishments that the British Government would reduce the establishment in Tobago which would avoid the question of any pecuniary assistance from Trinidad, that the miscellaneous expenses of the Trinidad Government in Tobago would not exceed £50, and that Tobago would require the services of no civil servant in Trinidad except the Governor and the Chief Justice. The Solicitor General added that Trinidad 'won't contribute a rap' to the necessary steamer service between Trinidad and Tobago.

The resolution came under heavy fire from the unofficial members of the Council, principally Mr Fenwick, the nominated member for Naparima representing the sugar industry, Mr Frederick Warner, and Dr de Boissier. Mr Warner warned that the Trinidad member of the Financial Board would be outvoted by the two Tobago members, and that annexation would ultimately involve a greater contribution on the part of Trinidad to the public establishment in Tobago, whilst the public institutions of Trinidad, hospitals, asylums, prisons, would be crowded with Tobago inmates. He was certain that Trinidad would have to bear a very large proportion of the cost of the steamer service. The unofficial members forced an adjournment of the Council, which reconvened on March 8, and was presented with an amended resolution by the Attorney General, Mr Gatty, which reads as follows:

'Whereas Her Majesty's Government have expressed the opinion after consideration of the condition and prospects of the Colony of Tobago, and having regard to its geographical proximity to, and means of communication with this Colony, that it is expedient that the Colony of Tobago should be annexed to and form part of the Colony of Trinidad:

'Resolved that this Council has no objection to the administrative annexation of Tobago with this Government, Tobago retaining, however, a separate Treasury and a separate internal Financial Board, on the understanding that such annexation is approved and desired by Her Majesty's Government, and on the further understanding that no pecuniary charge is now or hereafter to be imposed on the Revenues of Trinidad for any service connected with the Island of Tobago, or the aforesaid annexation for administrative purposes

'Resolved further that as an incident of such annexation there is no objection to the two Islands being governed by one Governor and being subject to one and the same code of Laws and that the duties leviable in Tobago upon articles imported from abroad should be the same as those in Trinidad, and that the traffic and intercourse between the two islands should be absolutely free.'

The main theme of the Attorney General's submission was again the obligation on the part of a Crown Colony Legislature to do what it was told by the Secretary of State for the Colonies. One would have thought that if the Secretary of State for the Colonies had directed the Legislature of Trinidad to cut its own throat, then as far as the Attorney General was concerned, the Colony's throat had to be cut. Mr Gatty's speech on March 8, 1887, was as follows:

'He was speaking now rather not as a public officer or servant of Her Majesty, but rather as if he belonged to the Colony, and looking at it from a Colonial point of view, and it seemed to him that we must recognise the fact that the Secretary of State and the Home Government were more or less compelled to abide by the decision of the people of England. We could see that there was a tendency of the people of England, as expressed in the votes at elections, to insist upon the Colonies being called upon to cut themselves so far adrift as to manifest some energy, and that the old idea of keeping up expensive administrations in such places as the West Indies was gone and would not be assented to by the people of England. What he could easily see was not very far off was that unless the West Indies would consent to being islands confederated together and help the Home Government to get the administration carried on by responsible officers, not in each individual Colony, but unless some assent was given to amalgamations of that sort, probably the Home Government would be forced by public opinion in England to pass some strong measure to place the whole West Indies in one confederate Government ..

'We might want the assistance of other Islands, and he thought that any West India Island that held out to pursuing a selfish policy of isolation against any reasonable scheme of this kind to enable Her Majesty's Government to meet the depression in the West Indies, was not doing any good.'

This was the man who was a year later to be appointed Chairman of the Royal Franchise Commission to consider the question of the introduction of the elective principle into the Crown Colony system of Trinidad.

Mr Fenwick, a diehard to the last, voted against the amended resolution, concerned no doubt with maintaining that the sugar industry had first claim on the resources of Trinidad for the continuation, in part out of public funds, of Indian indentured immigration. Mr Fenwick protested against the annexation of Tobago to Trinidad for the following reasons:

'1 Because the Colony of Tobago is, owing to the low prices obtainable for its principal and almost only staple, in a state of bankruptcy, with no prospect of better times in the near future, and the commercial credit abroad of the Colony of Trinidad will be injuriously affected by extending its protection to another colony in such circumstances.

'2. Because administrative annexation retaining for Tobago a separate Treasury and separate internal Financial Board and all the machinery of a separate Government, while it will admit of some economy in official salaries, will not effect such reductions as to enable Tobago to keep its expenditure within the limits of its yearly diminishing revenue. If the Ordinance to repeal certain duties of Customs now under consideration of this Council be passed, the small revenue of about £8,000 now collected in Tobago will be reduced to less than one half of this sum.

'3 Because if Tobago do benefit by a closer connection with Trinidad it can only be by the introduction into Tobago of Trinidad capital and by the enterprise of Trinidadians, all and more than all of which are urgently needed in Trinidad for the development of its own resources.

'4. Because any attempts to bring about a closer connection between the two Colonies will necessitate the establishment of a steamer service, the expense of which Tobago is unable to bear even in part and which would be altogether unremunerative to

Trinidad if this Colony be called upon to bear any share of it. Though geographically nearer to Tobago than any of the other neighbouring Colonies, Trinidad is not so convenient for purposes of trade as Grenada or Barbados The prevailing winds of this latitude are favourable only for a voyage from Tobago to Trinidad, the return voyage being usually a long and tedious beat up against the wind often occupying seven days.

'5. Because the whole trade of Tobago with the British West Indies is too insignificant, even if Trinidad obtained it all, to benefit Trinidad to the slightest appreciable extent. The bulk of the existing trade with Trinidad, namely, ground provisions, will find no market here in another year or two. If the cultivation of garden lots in Trinidad continues to increase at the same rate as during the past eight or ten years Trinidad will require very soon to export instead of import ground provisions The exportations from Tobago during the year 1886 of an increased number of ponies, goats, pigs and other livestock, so far from being the natural growth of a prosperous trade, is merely an indication of the distress to which proprietors, great and small, of that Colony, are now reduced.

'6. Because Trinidad is put to expense indirectly by Tobago needing the services of certain public officers paid by the Colony of Trinidad to devote their whole time and attention to its own interests If these officers have the time to spare for the work of another Colony it would appear that there has been and is much room for economy in their various departments.

'7. Because by agreeing to the act of administrative annexation this Council commits itself to a policy which must inevitably terminate in a complete incorporation or absorption of Tobago by Trinidad as soon as the futility of the present arrangements is sufficiently demonstrated.

'8. And because the second resolution is not in accordance with fact, it being notorious that an overwhelming majority of all classes in Trinidad strongly disapprove of the annexation of Tobago.

The *Port-of-Spain Gazette* was the mouthpiece of the opposition in Trinidad, as it was one of the principal spokesmen for constitution reform. In a bitter editorial it took the view that Britain could much more effectively help both Trinidad and Tobago by doing something to assist the sugar producers to find a place in the British market – this question will be taken up later The editorial continued:

'We can readily believe that were these Colonies to go from bad to worse, until it became necessary to draw on the Imperial Treasury for the wherewithal to carry on the local Governments, then the Home Government would very speedily look about for any means of saving the pockets of the English taxpayers, and the interest or welfare of the Colonies would be sacrificed without a single moments reflection; but so long as these Colonies can afford to pay their own way the Home Government will, in the future, as they have ever done in the past, leave them to fight their own battles. In fact in our opinion it was the fear that if things got worse in Tobago, an appeal to England for assistance was inevitable, that induced the Home Government to look about for some other means of providing for the carrying on of the Government of Tobago, and the move that has just been sanctioned by the Legislative Council amounts to an admission on our part that our officials have so little to do locally that they can without any inconvenience or expense to this Colony do extra duty in Tobago whenever called upon.'

Thus were Trinidad and Tobago united, by the insistence of the British Government, into what could only be called a confederation. The arrangement was quite novel, but it was an anticipation of what was to come in the next seventy years when the West Indies were to get accustomed to Britain's readiness to propose or support any arrangement, however fantastic, which might reduce financial obligations to the West Indies, relieve it of the burden of administering these small and separate colonies, and make concessions to any vested interest which Britain thought it necessary to placate, as it had throughout the 19th century placated the sugar interest in Trinidad in respect of indentured immigration at public expense.

So there was nothing surprising in the agitation begun in Tobago in 1893 to the effect that a yearly allowance should be made from the Trinidad Treasury to the Tobago Treasury in compensation for the loss of customs duties because of the union of the two islands for customs purposes and the consequent diversion of direct trade from Tobago to Trinidad. In December, 1893, Tobago sent its Commissioner and its representative in the Legislative Council of Trinidad and Tobago to plead Tobago's case. What was Tobago's case? That Tobago residents went to Trinidad, purchased consumer goods like matches and tobacco, and took them back to Tobago to the detriment of Tobago's revenues.

This was too much for the unofficial members in Trinidad. Mr Fenwick, reiterating his opposition to the original association, thought in disgust that it was carrying things a little too far to enter into the question of how much duty was due to Tobago for a hat and a pair of gloves bought in Trinidad shops by Tobago residents. Dr de Boissiere emphasised that annexation had been forced on Trinidad by the British Government, and therefore, if Tobago suffered any loss from the transaction, in the past or in the future, such loss should in fairness be defrayed by the British Government which had guaranteed that Trinidad should not at any time be called upon to defray any expenses on behalf of Tobago. Mr Eugene Lange also opposed the proposition that Trinidad should pay for loss of revenue in Tobago on every hat or umbrella sold to Tobago residents in Trinidad stores, and he denied that Trinidad had done anything contrary to the Order in Council uniting Trinidad and Tobago.

But the vested interests in Tobago stood firm – for what was involved was not the people of Tobago, the vast majority of whom merely wanted to get freedom of movement to Trinidad, to follow those Tobagonians who had already settled in Toco in large numbers. On February 5, 1894, the Financial Board of Tobago decided to forward the following memorial to the Secretary of State for the Colonies, the Marquis of Ripon:

'1 That by section XXIX of the Royal Order in Council of the 17th day of November 1888 it is, among other things, ordered that the Laws of Trinidad relating to Customs and Customs Duties (other than Export Duty) and Excise Duties on Rum and other Spirits shall be in force in Tobago from the 1st day of January 1889 and that the laws theretofore in force in Tobago in relation to the subjects shall thereupon cease to be in force.

'2. That the operation of these Laws in so far as they affect Tobago has been disastrous to the Revenue which fact has already been laid before Your Lordship in certain correspondence which has passed between the Commissioner of Tobago, His Excellency the Governor of Trinidad and Tobago and Your Lordship and which is within the cognisance of the Members of this Board.

'3. That the above referred to correspondence fully sets forth the present position in relation to the operation of the Laws in question.

'4. That by Section XXX of the said Order in Council it is ordered that the Revenue of the Island of Tobago shall be kept distinct from that of the Island of Trinidad and its Dependencies.

'5. That the object of this section has been defeated by the operation of the Trinidad Customs Laws which has caused and is causing a considerable diversion of Revenue from the Treasury of Tobago to that of Trinidad, it being impossible, as has been demonstrated before the Committee appointed by His Excellency the Governor to inquire into the loss of Revenue to Tobago, to arrive at any system by which the said loss can be checked.

'6. That the Members of this Board are unanimously of opinion that Tobago should have the right to manage her own Fiscal affairs, and to make laws for the regulations of the Customs, Excise and other duties which are at present, imposed under the Laws of Trinidad.'

The absurdity threatened to become more absurd. Tobago had been joined to Trinidad on the basis of a customs union which left Tobago autonomy in matters of internal taxation. Now the vested interests in Tobago wanted to abolish customs union and give Tobago the power to impose its own customs and excise duties. The Select Committee of the Trinidad and Tobago Legislative Council expressed the opinion 'that it would not only be more satisfactory to Tobago but altogether a simpler and more equitable arrangement if the free interchange of goods between the two islands were terminated and each permitted to collect and retain its own duties and to fix its own Customs Tariff.'

This was the situation encountered by the Royal Commission of 1897 when it visited Tobago. The Royal Commission reported as follows:

> 'We recommend the complete amalgamation of Tobago and Trinidad, and the abolition of the separate account of revenue and expenditure. Tobago would then become a ward, or district, of Trinidad, and the two islands would have a common exchequer. To this measure objections would, no doubt, be raised locally, though we believe the majority of inhabitants of Tobago are in favour of it. The owners of large tracts of land are afraid that financial amalgamation with Trinidad might lead to the tax on land being raised to the level of that prevailing in the latter island. We are unable to see why this result should necessarily follow, as Tobago, in its present condition, has a good claim for a separate treatment in this matter. The traders seem to fear that amalgamation with Trinidad would reduce their business in connection with the import trade, and possibly with the export trade. This result might follow, but from the point of view of the general interest, no sound argument against the amalgamation can be based upon it.'

The British Government took action in accordance with the recommendation of the Royal Commission. On October 20, 1898, an Order in Council was approved, revoking the Order in Council of April 6, 1889, and constituting Tobago a ward of Trinidad. The Order in Council prescribed as follows:

> 'On and after the date of the coming into force of this Order, the Island of Tobago shall be a Ward of the Colony of Trinidad and Tobago; and the revenue, expenditure, and debt of Tobago shall be merged in and form part of the revenue, expenditure, and debt of the united Colony, and the debt due from Tobago to Trinidad shall be cancelled ...

> 'All future Ordinances enacted by the Legislature of the Colony shall extend to Tobago. Provided that the Legislature of the Colony may at any time by Ordinance provide for the special regulation of all or any of the matters and things dealt with in the several Acts, Ordinances, and Regulations of Tobago enumerated in the Schedule hereto, and of any other and further matters and things in respect of which it may be deemed necessary to enact special and local Ordinances or Regulations applicable to Tobago as distinguished from the rest of the Colony

> 'The Acts, Ordinances, and Regulations of Tobago enumerated in the Schedule hereto shall, until repealed or amended by the Legislature of the Colony, continue locally in force in Tobago, but such Acts, Ordinances, and Regulations shall in every case be construed as amended by and read together with this Order; and

in particular wherever in such Acts, Ordinances, and Regulations any duty is imposed or power conferred upon any specified officer or person, such duty or power shall be performed or exercised by such person or persons as the Governor may from time to time by Proclamation appoint for the purpose '

The British Government washed its hands of the matter and divested itself of any special responsibility for Tobago by making available to the Government of Trinidad the sum of £4,000 in part repayment of a loan of £5,000 which had been made from Trinidad to Tobago

Tobago's humiliation was complete Throughout the 17th and 18th centuries the great powers had fought over Tobago as if it was one of the world's most precious jewels. In 1898 Tobago was virtually sold to Trinidad for $19,200. The £4,000 made available to Trinidad for taking over the responsibility for Tobago's 18,000 people compared with the £226,746 paid in 1834 as compensation to the slave owners for 9,078 slaves in Tobago, exclusive of £7,130 paid as compensation for 1,479 children under six years of age.

This was no case of isolated parsimony It was a part of the general philosophy of the British Government to the West Indian problems caused and aggravated by Britain's sugar policy in the 19th century which brought the West Indies in 1897 to the verge of bankruptcy.

CHAPTER 12

The Bankruptcy of Sugar

'But what good came of it?', as little Peterkin said of the Battle of Blenheim. One is tempted to ask the same question about the efforts to promote the sugar industry by the importation of thousands of indentured Indian immigrants, as one arrives at the crisis in the sugar industry that hit all the West Indian colonies in 1897.

The Indian indentured system meant, in the ultimate analysis, the continued dependence of the sugar industry of Trinidad on cheap manual labour – or, to put it a little differently, the preference for cheap labour over mechanisation. The sugar industry in Trinidad, as well as in British Guiana and the other West Indian islands, was immediately vulnerable in two directions – (a) from countries which, while indicating the same preference for degraded labour, were nevertheless larger, more fertile and infinitely more advanced in factory technology, such as Cuba; (b) from countries which depended on beet rather than the cane for their sugar, and thus, having to cope with the smaller sucrose content of the beet, were nevertheless infinately more advanced in science and technology, both in field and in factory, such as Germany. The combination of competition from these two areas, Cuban cane and German beet, associated with the almost incredibly selfish policy of the British Government, brought the West Indies to the verge of total collapse in 1897.

Let us first consider the position in Cuba where production increased from 223,145 tons in 1850 to 1,054,214 tons in 1894. Until 1880 the Cuban sugar industry was based on slave labour, the difficulties of obtaining which were aggravated by Britain's policy towards the international suppression of the slave trade which we have already noted Notwithstanding this drawback, the Cuban sugar economy made rapid strides in the 19th century as a result principally of two developments – the amalgamation of factories, in which the latest machinery replaced the old cattle mills, and the introduction of the railway, which permitted an expansion of the radius of the plantation. As a result, Cuban output per factory increased from 30 tons in 1792 to 268 tons in 1859, 500 tons in 1870, and 1,330 tons in 1890. The average output per factory in 1894 was 2,635 tons

At the same time, the monster plantation appeared on the Cuban scene. The first sign of this was in 1857, when the largest plantation, *Santa Susana*, comprising 11,000 acres, of which 1,700 were in cane, employed 866 slaves, and produced nearly 2,700 tons of sugar. By 1893, the largest plantation, *Soledad*, owned by United States capital, comprising 12,000 acres, of which 5,000 were in cane, contained 23 miles of private railway and employed 1,200 men in harvest time. Another United States enterprise, *Santa Teresa*, of 9,000 acres, represented a capital investment of $1,565,000 US. *Central Constancia*, the most important sugar factory in the world at that time, produced 19,500 tons of sugar. The Cuban crop of 1894 was valued at over $62 million US. Some $30 million of US capital were invested in the Cuban sugar industry in 1896.

It was simply impossible for Trinidad to stand up against this competition. The Cuban production figure of 1,054,214 tons in 1894 compared with a total British West Indian export of 260,211 tons in the same year, of which Trinidad was responsible for 46,869 tons. Whilst Trinidad's factory system was quite modern as far as the British West Indies were concerned, it required little more than two factories like *Central Constancia* in Cuba to produce the entire crop of Trinidad, with its 56 plantations and factories, with 14,092 workers, and 33,845 acres in cane. Trinidad's output per factory was 1,200 tons, approximately one-half of the Cuban average.

The competition between Cuba and the British West Indies was a competition between the 18th and 19th centuries, and between steam and wind. The central of Cuba was as to the windmill of Barbados as the hare to the tortoise. Outside of British Guiana and Trinidad, the typical British West Indian factory was still producing muscovado sugar, and steam was the exception rather than the rule. James Watt might never have lived for all the effect his invention had on British West Indian sugar production. An observer of British West Indian society in 1835 had noted that the planters objected to the introduction of steam engines because of the scarcity of firewood. In 1894 about one factory in every five in Barbados was equipped with steam; the others were windmills. In Jamaica one in every four factories utilised water power. The proportion of factories using steam was slightly more than half in Tobago, about three-fifths in St Kitts-Nevis, slightly less than half in Montserrat All but one of the factories in Antigua and St Kitts-Nevis, all but eight of those in Barbados, three-tenths of those in Jamaica, all of Montserrat's, one-fifth of Trinidad's, produced muscovado sugar, an indication of poor equipment. As was said in 1835 of West Indian planters, 'if the finest geologist of Europe were to . . . state that indications of coal were evident in the formations of the neighbouring mountains . . . no effort would be made to obtain it'.

A similar 'statu-quoitism', to quote a traveller in 1825, prevailed in field methods. 'The people of Jamaica made no novel experiments', wrote a visitor in 1835; 'they find sugar planted; and where it is they continue to cultivate it'. He added that they found the hoe the ancient instrument of the husbandman, and they had no desire to substitute the plough. In 1840 a Baptist missionary stated that the old methods were the rule, improvements the exception; the planters looked upon the practical knowledge of the 18th century as superior to the experience and science of the 19th. Implemental husbandry was virtually unknown in St Vincent in 1860. The first steam plough was introduced into Antigua in 1863; it was only this 'wonder working implement', as it was described in 1886, that helped the sugar industry of that island to keep going.

The development of central factories, with their tendency to separate manufacture from agriculture, made no headway. In St Lucia it was objected to as involving 'a certain loss of independence and position'; it was rejected elsewhere as involving heavy costs in the transportation of cane. As the planters preferred the man with the hoe, so they remained devoted to the transportation of cane on the heads of workers or the backs of donkeys, and opposed the railway Barbados continued to use up livestock at a rate which required replenishment of the entire stock every four years. As a result the size of the average plantation was 168 acres in Barbados, 178 acres in Jamaica, 193 acres in Antigua, as compared with 604 acres in Trinidad and 1,045 acres in British Guiana.

The results were catastrophic. In St Vincent, in 1897, it was estimated that the sugar produced under the existing system was worth £20,400; with a central factory it would have been worth £29,650, an increase of nearly fifty per cent. In Antigua the existing system required 13.37 tons of cane to make one ton of sugar; a central factory would have required ten tons, a saving of one quarter. Backward methods were costing the island £50,000 to £60,000 a year, representing a loss of about one-half of the total sugar produced. The island chemist of Barbados estimated that the failure to develop central factories represented a loss of six and a quarter pounds sterling per acre and a loss of 43 per cent in total production. An average loss of nearly one ton of sugar per acre was left in the canes after crushing; for every hundred pounds of sucrose in the juice, not more than seventy-five pounds of muscovado sugar were recovered, representing a loss of 25 per cent. If only half of the plantations of Barbados had adopted the central factory system, the result would have been to add £250,000, nearly 70 per cent of the exports, to the value of the sugar produced.

What improved methods of manufacture and machinery meant can be seen from estimates in British Guiana of the percentage of sugar that could be extracted from cane containing 12 per cent of fibre: single crushing, 76 per cent; double crushing (dry), 85 per cent; double crushing (with 12 per cent of dilution), 88 per cent; triple crushing (with ten per cent of dilution), 90 per cent; diffusion (with 25 per cent of dilution), 94 per cent So slow were the British West Indian planters in adopting modern methods that, in 1870, the process of diffusion was installed in only one factory in Trinidad, as compared with 52 beet factories in Austria, 36 in Germany, 7 in Poland, 8 in Russia. The British West Indian planters justified their backwardness, in the words of the Antigua planters in 1897, on the ground that the profits derived from muscovado sugar were, until the nineties, so good that 'the proprietors were content, and had no motive for adopting improved machinery'.

If Trinidad could not compete with Cuba, it could compete still less with Germany. The second enemy of the Trinidad sugar producer was beet sugar. In 1859–1860 total world beet production amounted to 451,584 tons, one-quarter of the world's total sugar production, slightly more than one-third of the world's total cane production, slightly less than two-thirds of total Caribbean production. In 1894–1895 total world beet production amounted to 4,725,800 tons, more than ten times as much as in 1859; it was three-fifths of the world's total sugar production, one-third more than the world's cane production, three and a quarter times the total Caribbean production. Beet sugar production, one-third more than Cuban production in 1859–1860, was four and a half times as large in 1894–1895. Two and a quarter times as much as British West Indian exports in the first year, it was eighteen times as large in the second.

Thus, four hundred years after Columbus' introduction into the Caribbean of the sugar cane which has dominated its history, the world's most important sugar producer was the very country which had signally failed to get a place in the Caribbean sun. Germany produced more sugar than all the Caribbean territories put together.

Austria-Hungary ranked third, after Germany and Cuba, among the world's producers. France occupied fourth place, and Russia fifth. Belgian beet production exceeded British West Indian cane production. Holland produced more sugar than the French, Dutch, Danish territories and Puerto Rico combined.

It is no wonder that it was reported that in the early years of the 19th century, Britain had tried to bribe the French chemist, Achard, in order to get him not to publish his revolutionary discovery of sugar from the beet

The development of the European beet sugar industry was more striking than the developments which had taken place in the Caribbean, and in their day, astounded the world The European beet sugar industry represented the triumph of science and technology Beet was the great school of scientific agriculture. Where the Caribbean planter remained dependent on the man with the hoe, the beet cultivator introduced deep ploughing, substituting a plough that went to a depth often to eleven inches for the conventional plough which went only four to six inches. Beet introduced a new element into the agricultural rotation, and the methods it required stimulated a vast increase in the yield of cereals. Well adapted to small holdings, the industry was based on a separation of the agricultural and industrial phases, brought winter employment to the countryside, checked the drift to the towns, and provided an enormous quantity of cattle feed. Pointing to the more than one million unemployed in England, a propagandist for the beet sugar industry asked in 1911: 'can our Government take a wiser step and find a better remedy for settling the question of the unemployed than by giving the homeless and starving creatures permanent work in a healthy environment by means of an indigenous sugar industry?' By concentrating on producing better varieties, with a greater sugar content, German science was able to reduce the quality of roots needed to make one ton of sugar from 18 in 1836 to 11 in 1868

The developments in the field were eclipsed by the more spectacular progress in the factory. In 1836 Germany's beet production was produced in 122 factories; the average output per factory was less than twelve tons. In 1866 the largest factory, *Waghausel,* worked 66,000 tons of beet; with 12 60 pounds of beets needed to make one pound of sugar in the country as a whole, this represented an output of over 5,000 tons of sugar. There were 296 factories in that year, which produced 201,240 tons of sugar, an average per factory of 679 tons. In 1896 Germany's record production of 1,821,223 tons was produced in 397 factories, an average of 4,587 tons per factory, three-quarters more than that of Cuba. Barbados had more factories than Germany for a sugar export which was one-thirty-sixth of German production. Eleven factories in Germany were needed to produce what Barbados' 440 factories exported in that year; about four to produce what Jamaica's 140 exported. The average output per factory in Trinidad was slightly more than one-quarter of the German average, in British Guiana about one-third.

Austria-Hungary, with 217 factories in 1896, was only slightly behind Germany; the average output per factory was 4,276 tons. The average in France was 2,024 tons. In 1897 there were nine factories in operation in the United States, representing an average output of 4,170 tons.

Beet sugar manufacture required an enormous investment of capital. The editor of the *Chemical Journal* in England estimated in 1870 that it would require an investment of £13,157 for a factory to handle the roots from 500 acres and produce slightly more than 500 tons of sugar. In 1868 the cost of manufacturing 20,000 tons of beetroot – approximately 1,000 tons of beet sugar – was estimated at £30,630. The thirty beet factories in the United States in 1899 represented a capital investment of $20,959,000, nearly $700,000 per factory. It was estimated in 1911 that, in order to make Great Britain self-sufficient in sugar, it would require 500 factories, each costing £80,000

Large profits were made in the beet sugar industry. In 1867–1868 the *Jerxheim* factory, one of the best in Germany, reaped a profit of $39,310 on total costs of production amounting to $101,368 Baruchson in 1868, estimated that a profit of 25 per cent would be obtained from the manufacture of 20,000 tons of beetroot, if 6¼ per cent sugar were extracted; if the extraction was 8 per cent, however, the profit would increase to 48 per cent. The estimates of the editor of the *Chemical Journal* in 1870 were net profits of £6,490 if 8 per cent of sugar were extracted, and £10,090, if 10 per cent; on the capital investment of £13,157, these rates amounted to 50 and 75 per cent, respectively.

It would appear that this combination of science, technology, capital and profits made beet superior to cane. In reality, this was not so. The decisive advantage which cane enjoyed over beet was its superior sucrose content, a gap which European and American science was able to narrow but not close. According to the report of the Commissioner of Agriculture of the United States for 1869, the product of sugar per acre from the cane in the West Indies was nearly twice that from the beet in Europe, the percentage of saccharine matter being as 18 to 10. According to the West India Royal Commission of 1897, the yield per acre was 18 tons of cane in Trinidad and Martinique as compared with 10 7 tons of beet in France and 12.85 tons in Germany.

But superior science and technology discounted natural advantages. The extraction of sugar was 12½ per cent in Germany, nearly 11 per cent in France, 9½ per cent in Trinidad, 9 per cent in British Guiana, 7½ per cent in Martinique. The cost of manufacturing one ton of sugar was as follows:

BEET	Germany (1894)	....	..	.	$49.60
	France (1894)	.	...	..	50.70
CANE	Trinidad (1896) .	. .	.	...	48.70
	British Guiana (1895) ...		...		52.48
	Martinique (1893)	.	..	...	76.32
	Egypt (1893) ...	. ..	....	...	44.16
	Queensland (1893)		...	.	41.90

Thus, despite the superior science and technology of the beet sugar industry, cane was cheaper than beet – though not in the British and French West Indies. The reason why beet threatened to supplant cane in the world market lies in the deliberate encouragement given by the countries concerned to the beet sugar industry, precisely the encouragement which had been given by the metropolitan countries concerned to the Caribbean producers in the seventeenth and eighteenth centuries. Known generally as the bounty system, the policy involved a substantial subsidy on exports which permitted the beet manufacturer to dump sugar on the world market, even below the cost of production, whilst he was assured of a protected domestic market The very monopoly which had built up the Caribbean was now trained against it. Europe, over which Britain, France, Spain, Holland and Portugal had competed for three hundred years for the privilege of supplying it with sugar, became an exporter of sugar on a large scale The German premium on exports rose from 21 per cent in 1876 to 60 per cent in 1884. The German excise on the raw material, reduced by a drawback on exportation, declined from 58 million marks in 1881 to 14 million in 1887.

The struggle between beet and cane was in reality a struggle chiefly for the British sugar market. The British West Indies lost their monopoly of that market in 1852, when the protectionist duties on sugar were repealed. It was the high water mark of Britain's free trade policy. Thereafter Britain's interest was to buy in the cheapest market. The following table indicates the consequences of that policy:

Year	British Imports (tons)	% Beet	% British Cane	% Foreign Cane
1853	1,476,714	14	17	69
1863	2,005,637	23	17	60
1873	2,951,152	38	12	50
1882	3,799,284	47	13	40
1896	1,526,000	75	10	15

Thus it was neither science, nor technology, nor availability of capital, nor the rate of profit which explained the triumph of beet over cane. It was Britain's free trade policy and her desire for cheap sugar. It was that policy and that desire which gave rise to and stimulated the greatest mockery and the very antithesis of free trade, the bounty system. In 1884 it was estimated that Britain's annual gain from the bounty system was £2,750,000, and that, in the thirteen years preceding 1883, Britain had gained £28 million. British per capita consumption of sugar increased from 68.7 pounds in 1890 to 83.7 in 1900. The price of ordinary refined sugar fell from 28/- per cwt. in 1882 to 13/- in 1896. Unrefined beet fell from 21/- to 10/-; unrefined cane from 21/- to nearly 11/-. The British public, refiners, manufacturers of jams and candies benefited

That was the decisive factor. In a report to the Board of Trade in 1884, it was stated:

'The obvious conclusion . . . would be that even admitting the injury to the complaining interests from the bounty system to be as great as alleged, still the interest of the people of the United Kingdom in cheap sugar preponderates so greatly that that injury, in the interests of the majority, and apart from all question as to the intrinsic objectionableness of any possible remedy, should be disregarded.'

Trinidad and the West Indies found a temporary relief in the United States market. British West Indian exports to the United States increased from 630 tons in 1853 to 115,105 tons in 1883. Trinidad became almost completely dependent on the United States market. For the five-year period 1881–1885, 51 per cent of Trinidad's sugar exports went to the United States as compared with 46 per cent to the United Kingdom. For the period 1886–1890, the proportion was 67 per cent to the United States and 32 to the United Kingdom; and for the period 1891–1895, the proportion was 55 per cent to the United States and 44 per cent to the United Kingdom. Never was there a more curious Crown Colony in the world. Trinidad was a colony forced by the British Crown to import thousands of workers from India to produce sugar two-thirds of which had to be sold in the market of the United States of America. It seemed as if, to paraphrase a witticism of Professor Merrivale lecturing to his students at Oxford several years before, the colony of Trinidad was being retained by Britain for the mere pleasure of governing it.

But the foundations of Trinidad's sugar industry were shaky in the extreme. President Hayes of the United States had declared in his farewell address that he believed that, by 1884, the United States would no longer need foreign sugar. The last decade of the 19th century saw tremendous efforts to increase American sugar production: in 1889 the State of Iowa exempted from taxation until January 1, 1910, later extended to January 1, 1917, the property on beet sugar manufactured including the capital investment and the personal property used in connection with the business. In 1895 Minnesota provided a bounty of one cent per pound on sugar manufactured in that State, and Michigan followed suit in 1897 with a bounty of two cents per pound.

The bankruptcy of the British West Indian sugar industry coincided with the 1896 platform of the Republican Party: 'We condemn the present Administration for not keeping faith with the sugar producers of this country. The Republican party favours *such* protection as will lead to the production on American soil of *all* of the sugar which the American people use, and for which they pay other countries more than $100,000,000 annually'. A leaflet of the American Beet Sugar Industry, circulated widely in the presidential campaign of that year, estimated that the production of the 1,804,866 tons of sugar imported by the United States in 1895 would require 920 factories with a capacity of 350 tons of beet each for each working day of 24 hours. Each factory would work up the product of 2,000 acres of beet – thus calling for a total acreage of 1,840,000 acres. The industry would give employment to people who would represent a population of 2,500,000. The farmer would receive $4 20 per ton of beets; the farm payroll would be $77,280,000. The labour pay roll would amount to $17,599,600. The total annual expenditure for the 920 factories would be $122,496,160

The development of the beet sugar industry was marked by a powerful propagandist appeal directed against the cane sugar industry on the ground that cane sugar required slave, 'coolie', contract, or some form of degraded labour, black, brown or yellow, whereas the beet sugar industry was the product of white and free labour. The pattern was first developed in France, in the decade of the thirties. Beet and cane, wrote Lestiboudois, in a memorandum entitled *Des Colonies Sucrieres et des Sucreries Indigenes*, read to the Royal Society of Science, Agriculture and the Arts of Lille in 1839, were *chemically* similar but *industrially* dissimilar. Cane production, he said, was based on 'exceptional and barbaric principles': it regarded the Negroes as 'inert machines for sugar . . . beasts of burden to go to market . . . animate material property'. In the opinion of another writer in the same year, Dehay, cane cultivation was based on 'antediluvian manners . . . (a) social régime antipathetic to our age'.

The moral note enjoyed great vogue in the second half of the nineteenth century, particularly in the United States Every civilised country, wrote the Commissioner of Agriculture in 1868, had 'exerted itself to secure emancipation from slave-grown cane sugar, and to stop the flow of money to a few colonies. Without the United States as a regular customer, Cuba and Brazil might as well give up growing sugar, and direct their attention to a more healthy occupation'. The Commissioner discreetly refrained from referring to Louisiana, which had fought a civil war for four years to prevent 'the United States from emancipating itself from its own slave-grown cane sugar.

H. T. Oxnard, the president of the American Beet Sugar Association, in hearings before the Ways and Means Committee of the House of Representatives on December 30, 1896, distinguished himself by the vigour of his attack on cheap labour contracts, cheap Asiatic and Hawaiian labour and raw material, and the '24 to 48-cent labour in some cases, and coolie labour in other instances', which made it impossible for California or Nebraska to compete According to a United States official, there was a vast difference, from a moral, civic, or philanthropic standpoint, between beet and cane. 'Whenever you see a success of cane sugar production', it was stated in a pamphlet of the British Beet Sugar Council, 'you will notice it is a blight on everything else. You will find the employers in the fields and factory ignorant, degraded, poorly clothed and fed, and with no social advantages whatever. A beet sugar factory presents an entirely different picture. You will find every convenience of a prosperous civilised community, and that it has attracted to itself a busy centre endowed with all modern improvements . . . To the district come all the social and educational advantages that accrue to closer association of population.'

In 1870 the editor of the *Chemical Journal* estimated that the growing of one acre of beet required 46 days of human labour (partly children's) and 14 days of horse labour, whereas one acre of cane in the West Indies required 172 days of human labour.

Much of this propaganda against sugar produced by some slave labour in Trinidad and the West Indies was so much wool drawn over the eyes of the people of Europe and America. According to the Commissioner of Agriculture in the United States, wages for men in Germany were 31½ cents a day for carrying beets and 19 cents for girls for topping and trimming them. In the early 20th century, wages for field labour in the beet sugar industry were 25 cents a day in Russia, 36 cents a day in Denmark, 45 cents a day in Hungary, and 47 cents a day in Germany. A study produced in the United States of America in 1935 showed that the beet sugar industry had become dominated by contract labour from Mexico, and that the average annual income of beet families for the entire season in that year was $340. Those who lived in glass houses in America and Europe had no business throwing stones at Trinidad.

But that is by the way, necessary though it is at all times to defend the people of Trinidad and Tobago against their detractors abroad. It was the economics that mattered and not social considerations. Trinidad and the West Indies could not compete with Cuban cane or

German beet, and the American market became increasingly closed to it. Thus in 1897, after 50 years of indentured Indian immigration in Trinidad and British Guiana, the British West Indies sugar industry was faced with total extinction. So the British Government, as usual, sent out a Royal Commission.

What was the Royal Commission to do? It was bounty-fed European beet sugar that was ruining the West Indies. The Board of Trade had said quite emphatically in 1885 that that was just too bad, it could not be helped. And what did the West India Royal Commission of 1897 think of this?

The Commission disagreed with the Board of Trade. 'The benefit which the British Empire as a whole derives from any lowering of the price of sugar due to the operation of the bounty system is too dearly purchased by the injury which that system imposes on a limited class, namely Your Majesty's West Indian and other subjects dependent on the sugar industry'. The Commission emphasised the certain consequences of the extinction of the British West Indian sugar industry. It contented itself, however, with the modest recommendation that 'the abolition of the bounty system is an object at which Your Majesty's Government should aim, if they should see their way to securing that result, and that the accomplishment of such an end is worth some sacrifice . . .'

But it did not feel itself in a position to make recommendations of practical value towards securing the abolition of the bounty system. The West Indians recommended the imposition of countervailing duties on bounty-fed beet sugar; the Commission doubted the efficacy and wisdom of such a measure which involved 'the danger, direct and indirect, of departing from what has hitherto been considered to be the settled policy of the United Kingdom'. The West Indians urged the extension of the bounty system to West Indian sugar. The Commission found itself unable to recommend this course, which might so stimulate production as to cause a further fall in price which would neutralise its effect. The West Indies found themselves in the position of a patient suffering from a mortal disease, whose physician propounded all the reasons why he could not perform the operation necessary to restore the patient to health.

The British West Indies, with their long practice in crying 'wolf', blamed the bounty system for their difficulties, as if to say that, without bounties, their eighteenth century fossils could have held their own against German technology. But, emphasised the report to the Board of Trade, 'the gain to the people of the United Kingdom by the present excess reduction of prices, according to the calculation of the West India Committee, viz, 5,000,000 l., is more than equal to the whole annual value of the exports of sugar from the West Indies.

What help, then, could the Royal Commission provide? It emphasised that one of the great advantages of the encouragement of a Negro peasantry would have been a greater local production of food and a larger measure of insular self-sufficiency. With respect to Antigua, it noted that the island had imported, in 1896, 8,065 barrels of corn-meal, valued at £3,573, when corn could be grown as cheaply as in any part of the world; 37,157 bushels of corn and grain, valued at £3,296; 637,101 pounds of meat, valued at £6,437; 633,394 pounds of oilmeal and oilcake for manures, valued at £1,423. All of these articles, the Commission asserted, might have been advantageously produced by persons not engaged in the sugar industry.

The Commission therefore made its most famous recommendation:

'It seems to us that no reform affords so good a prospect for the permanent welfare in the future of the West Indies as the settle-ment of the labouring population on the land as small peasant pro-prietors . . . It must be recollected that the chief outside influence with which the Governments of certain colonies have to reckon are the representatives of the sugar estates, that these persons are sometimes not interested in anything but sugar, that the establish-ment of any other industry is often detrimental to their interests, and that under such conditions it is the special duty of Your Majesty's Government to see that the welfare of the general public is not sacrificed to the interests, or supposed interests, of a small but influential minority which has special means of enforcing its wishes and bringing its claims to notice . . . The settlement of the labouring population on the land, and the encouragement of the products and forms of cultivation suitable for a class of peasant proprietors formed no part of their policy .   If a different policy had found favour the condition of the West Indies might have been much less serious than it is at present in view of the probable failure of the sugar industry'

It was nice to know, in 1897, that Britain had backed the wrong horse in 1833. But that was small comfort to the West Indies.

The Commission recommended the growth locally of more of the food that was imported and greater attention to the fruit trade. It further recommended agricultural and industrial education and a department of economic botany to assist the small proprietors; how-ever, it opposed the establishment of agricultural banks and hesitated to recommend any system of state loans to the small farmer on the ground that it was likely to be mismanaged.

The Commission's recommendations in respect of small farming and local food production were admirable, as far as they went. But they did not go very far. As the sequel was to show, they were not worth the paper they were written on, and the British Government to whom they were addressed seems to have done nothing to secure their implementation. In addition, if the British Government needed someone to go to Trinidad and the West Indies to advise it on this score, it had, long before 1897, similar and more powerful recom-mendations from someone more influential than any of the Commis-sioners of 1897. That someone was Charles Kingsley, the distinguished novelist, who visited the West Indies and wrote a famous book *At Last: A Christmas in the West Indies* published in 1871.

If the British Government did not like what Sewell, the American newspaperman, had had to say a decade earlier, surely it might have been willing to listen to Kingsley. Kingsley addressed himself particularly to the question of the peasantry in Trinidad in his consideration of the general problem of the future economic development of the West Indies, and he emerged with this analysis of the problem and these recommendations for the future:

'. . . What will be the future of agriculture in the West Indian colonies I of course dare not guess. The profits of sugar-growing, in spite of all drawbacks, have been of late very great; they will be greater still under the improved methods of manufacture which will be employed now that the sugar duties have been at least rationally reformed; and therefore, for some time to come, capital will naturally flow toward sugar-planting, and great sheets of the forest will be, too probably, ruthlessly and wastefully swept away to make room for canes. And yet one must ask, regretfully, are there no other cultures save that of cane which will yield a fair, even an ample return to men of small capital and energetic habits? What of the culture of bamboo for paper-fibre, of which I have spoken already? It has been, I understand, taken up successfully in Jamaica, to supply the United States' paper market. Why should it not be taken up in Trinidad? Why should not plantain-meal be hereafter largely exported for the use of the English working classes? Why should not Trinidad, and other islands, export fruits – preserved fruits especially? Surely such a trade might be profitable, if only a quarter as much care were taken in the West Indies as is taken in England to improve the varieties by selection and culture; and care taken also not to spoil the preserves, as now, for the English market, by swamping them with sugar or sling. Can nothing be done in growing the oil-producing seeds with which the tropics abound, and for which a demand is rising in England, if it be only for use about machinery? Nothing, too, toward growing drugs for the home market? Nothing toward using the treasures of gutta-percha which are now wasting in the Balatas? Above all, can nothing be done to increase the yield of the cocoa-farms, and the quality of Trinidad cocoa? . . .

'. . . As an advocate of "petite culture", I heartily hope that such may be the case I have hinted in this volume my belief that exclusive sugar cultivation, on the large scale, has been the bane of the West Indies.

'I went out thither with a somewhat foregone conclusion in that direction, but it was at least founded on what I believed to be facts, and it was certainly verified by the fresh facts which I saw there. I returned with a belief stronger than ever that exclusive sugar cultivation had put a premium on unskilled slave labour, to the disadvantage of skilled white labour; and to the disadvantage, also of any attempt to educate and raise the negro, whom it was not worth while to civilise as long as he was needed merely as an instrument exerting brute strength. It seems to me also, that to the exclusive cultivation of sugar is owing, more than to any other cause, that frightful decrease throughout the island of the white population, of which most English people are, I believe, quite unaware.

'. . . The West Indian might have had – the Cuban has – his tobacco; his indigo too; his coffee, or – as in Trinidad – his cocao and his arrow-root, and half a dozen crops more; indeed, had his intellect – and he had intellect in plenty – been diverted from the fatal fixed idea of making money as fast as possible by sugar, he might have ere now discovered in America, or imported from the East, plants for cultivation far more valuable than that bread-fruit tree, of which such high hopes were once entertained as a food for the negro. As it was, his very green crops were neglected, till, in some islands at least, he could not feed his cattle and mules with certainty, while the sugarcane, to which everything else had been sacrificed, proved sometimes, indeed, a valuable servant, but too often a tyrannous and capricious master.

'But those days are past, and better ones have dawned, with better education, and a wider knowledge of the world and of science. What West Indians have to learn – some of them have learned it already – is that, if they can compete with other countries only by improved and more scientific cultivation and manufacture, as they themselves confess, then they can carry out the new methods only by more skilful labour. They therefore require now, as they never required before, to give the labouring class a practical education; to quicken their intellect, and to teach them habits of self-dependent and originative action, which are – as in the case of the Prussian soldier, and of the English sailor and railway servant – perfectly compatible with strict discipline. Let them take warning from the English manufacturing system, which condemns a human intellect to waste itself in perpetually heading pins, or opening and shutting trap-doors, and punishes itself by producing a class of work-people who alternate between reckless comfort and moody discontent. Let them be sure that they will help rather than injure the labour-market of the colony by making the labourer also a small freeholding peasant. He will learn more in his own provision-ground, properly tilled, than he will in the cane-piece; and he will take to the cane-piece, and use for his employer, the self-helpfulness which he has learned in the provision-ground. It is so in England. Our best agricultural day-labourers are, without exception, those who cultivate some scrap of ground, or follow some petty occupation, which prevents their depending entirely on wage-labour. And so I believe it will be in the West Indies. Let the land-policy of the late governor be followed up. Let squatting be rigidly forbidden. Let no man hold

possession of land without having earned, or inherited, money
enough to purchase it, as a guarantee of his ability and respectability, or – as in the case of Coolies past their indentures – as a
communication for rights which he has earned in likewise. But let
the coloured man of every race be encouraged to become a land-
holder and a producer in his own small way. He will thus, not only
by what he produces, but by what he consumes, add largely to the
wealth of the colony; while his increased wants, and those of his
children, till they too can purchase land, will draw him and his sons
and daughters to the sugar-estates as intelligent and helpful day-
labourers.'

Sewell had said as much a decade before. Père Labat, one of the
great Catholic missionaries who lived for many years in the West
Indies, had said as much and more nearly two centuries before Storm
van's Gravesande, Dutch Governor of Guiana, had said as much a
century before about the prospects of economic diversification. The
British Governor of British Guiana had said as much over fifty years
before. The British Government remained wedded to the policy of
production of sugar which they would not buy, and then sent out a
Commission in 1897 to tell them that they should not have encouraged
the colonies to produce sugar, and that where the sugar industry had
died out or was dying out – as in Tobago, Grenada, Montserrat, St
Vincent – nothing should be done to encourage its resuscitation or
resurrection.

In terms of pecuniary assistance, to assist the West Indies in tiding
over their financial difficulties, the Commission's recommendations
were modest in the extreme. They were as follows:

(a) a loan of £120,000 to Barbados for the establishment of central
factories;

(b) a grant of £27,000 for ten years for the establishment of minor
agricultural industries, improved inter-island communications,
and the encouragement of the fruit trade (the Commission's
recommendation could hardly have been described as revolutionary);

(c) a grant of £20,000 for five years to the smaller islands to assist
them to meet their ordinary expenditure of an obligatory
nature;

(d) a grant of £30,000 to Dominica and St Vincent for road construction and land settlement.

So ended the first century of Crown Colony rule in Trinidad and
Tobago Three centuries of Spanish colonialism had ended in nothing.
One century of British colonialism, with all the pomp and power of
metropolitan rule which Britain refused to surrender to the colonials,
with thousands of immigrants permitted to be imported in a state of
semi-servitude at public expense to produce sugar to which Britain
refused to give any special consideration, and which the USA refused

to buy – one century of British colonialism had ended in nothing.

The 1897 Commission emphasised that 'we have placed the labouring population where it is, and created for it the conditions, moral and material under which it exists, and we cannot divest ourselves of responsibility for its future.' Brave and noble thoughts. But what did the Commission have to say about the labouring population introduced with the full approval and at the direction of the British Government to produce sugar with the full approval of the British Government? Merely this:

'If there is a great and sudden reduction in the sugar industry, there might be a considerable temporary expenditure in providing for labourers, and especially for East Indian immigrants. The expenditure would be very heavy if any large number of immigrants claimed, as they might do, to be returned to India at the public expense, but we are disposed to agree . that there would not be any general desire on the part of the Indian coolies to return. In any case it will be more easy to provide at short notice for the settlement of coolies on Crown and other lands in Trinidad than it would be in British Guiana. There is, therefore, less probability of a sudden and overwhelming demand being made on public funds for return passages.

'The question of the assistance given to immigration at the expense of the public revenue is one that requires careful consideration. We are of opinion that if any industry requires immigrants it should pay the whole cost connected with their introduction. It is argued that the introduction of immigrants is a benefit to the whole Colony, and that the whole Colony should pay a proportion of the cost of introducing them. This view as to the introduction of immigrants being a benefit to the whole Colony is not held by those persons with whom the immigrants compete in the labour market, and if the argument were pushed to its logical conclusion it would follow that every industry should get a bonus from the State, as every industry is a gain to the whole community. It has, however, been pressed upon us by evidence which we cannot disregard, that at the present time, and under present conditions, indentured labourers are absolutely necessary to carrying on of the sugar estates. It would be a calamity, not only to the owner of the estates, but to the general community, to take any steps that must have the effect of intensifying the existing depression, and, whatever our recommendation might have been if the question of State assistance to immigration were now raised for the first time, we are not prepared to say that such assistance should now be withdrawn We are, however, of opinion that the number of immigrants to be introduced every year should be reduced to the minimum that will suffice for the working of the existing estates, and that State assistance in air of immigration should ultimately cease.'

So the Crown Colony system had, after sixty odd years, recognised its mistake. And what was its solution? Continue to pour good money after bad – but don't pour so much, and, above all, don't ask the 'mother country' for any aid.

It has become in the last twenty years very fashionable to say that Trinidad is wealthy, and that such financial assistance as is available should be given to poorer countries. As it is now, so it was in the beginning.

The Government Statistician of Trinidad and Tobago made a comparison in 1899 of Trinidad and Tobago, Jamaica, Barbados and British Guiana. He arrived at the following conclusions in respect of the per capita revenue, imports and exports of the four colonies: —

Colony	Revenue	Imports	Exports
Trinidad and Tobago	$10.40	$40.22	$40.90
Jamaica	4.94	11.95	10.99
Barbados	4.61	26.73	19.44
British Guiana	9.00	23.57	30.48

The population of the colonies at the time was: Trinidad and Tobago, 273,655; Jamaica, 727,636; Barbados, 190,000; British Guiana 279,407.

The Commission of 1897 thought therefore that Trinidad could well depend on its own resources. It wrote: 'On the whole, we are of opinion that, notwithstanding the critical state of the sugar industry, the resources of Trinidad will probably suffice to meet the claims against her if they are carefully husbanded, and if no delay takes place in the adoption of measures for enforcing greater economy in public expenditure.' It never dawned on the Commission, or, as we shall see, on the British Government, that the time had come to let the people of the Colony manage their own affairs– if only because they could not have made a greater mess of things than the Crown Colony system had made from 1797 to 1897.

CHAPTER 13

Crown Colony Government

The Royal Commission of 1897 came, saw, and was conquered.
Britain had made Trinidad a Crown Colony in the first instance to
make sure that the Crown could govern without the impediment of
local elected assemblies. The 1897 Royal Commission made it clear
not only that Britain had failed to settle the economic problems of
Trinidad at the expense of the Trinidad taxpayer, but that Britain
could not be expected to do so at the expense of the British taxpayer.
It was power without responsibility. It was power for the mere sake
of power.

In 1884, however, Britain was forced to restore to Jamaica a
measure of the representative Government which had been suspended
in 1865. This was the signal for the initiation in Trinidad of a movement for constitution reform which led to the appointment of the
Royal Franchise Commission of 1888.

It was at this time that James Anthony Froude decided to visit the
West Indies. He left London in December 1886, and arrived in Trinidad early in the new year. Well known for his imperialist outlook
and his hatred of Irishmen and Catholics, Froude has left us an
account of his travels, *The English in the West Indies*, which not only
affords a valuable insight into the official British mentality of the
period but also provided part of the training for British officials in
Trinidad in subsequent years, when a degree from Oxford or Cambridge was still the necessary passport to a career in Parliament, or
the Diplomatic Service, or the Colonial Service.

Political demonstrations and agitation for constitution reform are
an important part of the Trinidadian's heritage. It is useful therefore,
however amusing it may sound today, to read Froude's account of a
political demonstration for constitution reform in the Queen's Park
Savannah. Froude's account reads:

'The political demonstration to which I had been invited came
off the next day on the savannah. The scene was pretty enough.
Black coats and white trousers, bright-coloured dresses and pink
parasols, look the same at a distance whether the wearer has a black
face or a white one, and the broad meadow was covered over with
sparkling groups. Several thousands persons must have attended,
not all to hear the oratory, for the occasion had been taken when
the Governor was to play close by in a cricket match, and half the
crowd had probably collected to see His Excellency at the wicket.
Placards had been posted about the town, setting out the purpose
of the meeting. Trinidad, as I said, is at present a Crown colony,
the executive council and the legislature being equally nominated

167

by the authorities. The popular orators, the newspaper writers, and some of the leading merchants in Port-of-Spain had discovered, as I said, that they were living under what they called "a degrading tyranny". They had no grievances, or none that they alleged, beyond the general one that they had no control over the finance. They very naturally desired that the lucrative Government appointments for which the colony paid should be distributed among themselves. The elective principle had been reintroduced in Jamaica, evidently as a step towards the restoration of the full constitution which had been surrendered and suppressed after the Gordon riots. Trinidad was almost as large as Jamaica, in proportion to the population wealthier and more prosperous, and the people were invited to come together in overwhelming numbers to insist that the "tyranny" should end. The Home Government in their action about Jamaica had shown a spontaneous readiness to transfer responsibility from themselves to the inhabitants. The promoters of the meeting at Port-of-Spain may have thought that a little pressure on their part might not be unwelcome as an excuse for further concessions of the same kind. Whether this was so I do not know. At any rate they showed that they were as yet novices in the art of agitation. The language of the placard of invitation was so violent that, in the opinion of the legal authorities, the printer might have been indicted for high treason. The speakers did their best to imitate the fine phrases of the apostles of liberty in Europe, but they succeeded only in carica-turing their absurdities. The proceedings were described at length in the rival newspapers. One gentleman's speech was said to have been so brilliant that every sentence was a "gem of oratory", the gem of gems being when he told his hearers that, "if they went into the thing at all, they should go the entire animal." All went off good-humouredly. In the Liberal journal the event of the day was spoken of as the most magnificent demonstration in favour of human free-dom which had ever been seen in the West Indian Islands. In the Conservative journal it was called a ridiculous fiasco, and the people were said to have come together only to admire the Governor's batting, and to laugh at the nonsense which was coming from the platform. Finally, the same journal assured us that, beyond a hand-ful of people who were interested in getting hold of the anticipated spoils of office, no one in the island cared about the matter.

'The result, I believe, was some petition or other which would go home and pass as evidence, to minds eager to believe, that Trini-dad was rapidly ripening for responsible government, promising relief to an overburdened Secretary for the Colonies, who has more to do than he can attend to, and is pleased with opportunities of gratifying popular sentiment, or of showing off in Parliament the development of colonial institutions.'

This was in 1887, a mere 75 years before the Independence of Trinidad & Tobago. The Professor of Modern History at Oxford

University could interpret a political demonstration for constitution reform as nothing but a desire on the part of the majority of the crowd to see the Governor bat in a cricket match, or nothing more than a desire on the part of ambitious Trinidad politicians to share in the spoils of office. Not a single word from Froude about the attack on the Crown colony system which Lechmere Guppy was to make one year later before the Royal Franchise Commission. Not a single word from Froude about the demands which were to be presented to the Royal Franchise Commission of 1888 for the extension of the right to vote to Negroes and Indians. Not a single word from Froude about the attack which Sir Henry Alcazar was to make ten years later on indentured Indian immigration before the Royal Commission of 1897. Not a single word from Froude about the economic difficulties of sugar production in the light of Britain's policy to beet sugar which were to dominate the report of the Royal Commission of 1897. Not a single word from Froude about the semi-servitude to which the indentured Indian immigrants were consigned under the laws which were consolidated by the Ordinance of 1899.

As far as Froude was concerned, Crown colony government had nothing to do with economic development, Crown colony government had nothing to do with the training of the inhabitants for self-government, Crown colony government had nothing to do with the participation of the people of the colony in their political affairs. Crown colony government was there, and was there to stay. Froude envisaged no change whatsoever. He continued his narrative of his experiences in Trinidad as follows:

'But why, it may be asked, should not Trinidad govern itself as well as Tasmania or New Zealand? Why not Jamaica, why not all the West Indian Islands? I will answer by another question. Do we wish these islands to remain as part of the British Empire? Are they of any use to us, or have we responsbilities connected with them of which we are not entitled to divest ourselves? A government elected by the majority of the people (and no one would think of setting up constitutions on any other basis) reflects from the nature of things the character of the electors. All these islands tend to become partitioned into black peasant proprietaries. In Grenada the process is almost complete. In Trinidad it is rapidly advancing. No one can stop it. No one ought to wish to stop it. But the ownership of freeholds is one thing, and political power is another. The blacks depend for the progress which they may be capable of making on the presence of a white community among them; and although it is undesirable or impossible for the blacks to be ruled by the minority of the white residents, it is equally undesirable and equally impossible that the whites should be ruled by them. The relative numbers of the two races being what they are, responsible government in Trinidad means government by a black parliament and a black ministry. The negro voters might elect, to begin with,

their half-caste attorneys or such whites (the most disreputable of
their colour) as would court their suffrages. But the black does not
love the mulatto, and despises the white man who consents to be
his servant. He has no grievances. He is not naturally a politician,
and if left alone with his own patch of land, will never trouble himself to look further. But he knows what has happened in St Domingo. He has heard that his race is already in full possession of the
finest of all the islands. If he has any thought or any hopes about
the matter, it is that it may be with the rest of them as it has been
with St Domingo, and if you force the power into his hands, you
must expect him to use it. Under the constitution which you would
set up, whites and blacks may be nominally equal; but from the
enormous preponderance of numbers the equality would be only
in name, and such English people, at least, as would be really of
any value, would refuse to remain in a false and intolerable position.
Already the English population of Trinidad is dwindling away under
the uncertainties of their future position. Complete the work, set up
a constitution with a black minister and a black legislature, and
they will withdraw of themselves before they are compelled to go.
Spaniards and French might be tempted by advantages of trade to
remain in Port-of-Spain, as a few are still to be found in Hayti
They, it is possible, might in time recover and reassert their
supremacy. Englishmen have the world open to them, and will prefer
land where they can live under less degrading conditions. In Hayti
the black republic allows no white man to hold land in freehold.
The blacks elsewhere with the same opportunities will develop the
same aspirations.

'Do we, or do we not, intend to retain our West Indian islands
under the sovereignty of the Queen? If we are willing to let them
go, the question is settled. But we ought to face the alternative.
There is but one form of government under which we can retain
these colonies with honour and security to ourselves and with
advantage to the negroes whom we have placed there – the mode
of government which succeeds with us so admirably that it is the
world's wonder in the East Indies, a success so unique and so
extraordinary that it seems the last from which we are willing to
take example.'

Just what was Froude making a fuss about? At a public meeting in
Port-of-Spain on October 29, 1892, a Reform Committee was set up.
The members of the Committee were: L.A.A. de Verteuil, nominated
unofficial member of the Legislative Council; Mr Lechmere Guppy,
also a member of the Council and ex-Mayor of San Fernando; Sir
Henry Alcazar, Mayor of Port-of-Spain; Mr W. C. Clerk, Mayor of
San Fernando; Mr Francis Damian and Mr H. B. Phillips, Ex-Mayors
of Port-of-Spain; Mr William Howatson, President of the Trinidad
Chamber of Commerce; with Mr Prudhomme David as Secretary.
Mr David, in a memorandum to the Secretary of State for the

Colonies, stressed the aversion of a large number of people in the island to the despotic features of the Crown Colony system of government. At three public meetings held in the principal centres of population at the end of 1892 and in January 1893, the following resolutions were unanimously agreed to:

'(1) That the system of Government at present existing in the Colony is not only injurious to the best interests of the country and its inhabitants, but is a great public grievance and a cause of general dissatisfaction

'(2) That there can be found in the Colony an electorate qualified by knowledge and education to form an intelligent judgment on public affairs and to ensure the fair representation of all interests by returning fit and proper persons to the Council of Government.'

The constitution proposed by the Reform Committee would not be considered in any way revolutionary today. The principal proposals were these:

(1) A Legislative Council of 20 members, twelve of whom should be elected and eight nominated. The nominated members were the Governor, the Attorney General, the Colonial Secretary, the Auditor General, the Director of Public Works, and three other officials nominated by the Governor. The elected members were to be elected for a three-year term. When not less than eight elected members voted together on any matter of finance or of purely local concern, the official vote was not to be used.

(2) The Executive Council was to consist of the Governor, three officials, and two persons selected by the Governor from the elected members of the Legislative Council.

(3) The franchise was to be extended to males only, who were 21 years of age and who (a) owned or rented a dwelling house within a Borough or Town of the yearly value of $72 or upwards, or in an Electoral District not including a Borough or Town of the yearly value of $48 or upwards, or (b) was a *bona fide* lodger paying rent of not less than $72 per annum, or (c) owned or occupied eight acres of land or upwards with a dwelling house thereon of the value of $96, or less than eight acres of land but more than one acre with a dwelling house thereon of the value of $240, or less than one acre with a dwelling house thereon of the value of $480.

(4) No person could be elected to the Legislative Council who did not possess a clear annual income of $1,920 or was not the owner in his own or in his wife's right of real estate of the absolute value of $7,200.

The Reform Committee estimated that their recommendations would enfranchise from 12,000 to 15,000 of Trinidad's population of 200,000. At a public meeting in San Fernando, their proposals were accordingly rejected as involving a franchise too high to be of any value to the general mass of inhabitants; the San Fernando meeting favoured the view that every elector should be eligible to a seat in the Council. The Reform Committee, however, opposed the recommendation of the Royal Franchise Commission of 1888 that no one should be allowed to vote who 'being under the age of 40 years cannot read and write the English language or understand the same when spoken'.

At the time of Froude's visit to Trinidad, the doctrine of imperial federation was very much in the air. The doctrine in more ways than one represented the beginning of a retreat from the British policy of free trade and abandonment of colonial preferences, and was in more ways than one an anticipation of the later concept of the British Commonwealth. One of its principal philosophers was Froude himself, and one of its principal architects was Joseph Chamberlain, who astonished everybody at the end of the 19th century, when he was appointed to a Cabinet post, by asking for the position of Secretary of State for the Colonies. The philosopher sneered at the idea that Trinidad might have some place in this doctrine of imperial federation. Chamberlain, the architect, Secretary of State for the Colonies, not merely sneered, he acted.

In 1896 the Port-of-Spain City Council submitted a request to the Government of Trinidad for financial assistance and for revision of the financial arrangements between the Council and the Government. The Council asked to be relieved of an obligation to make annual contributions towards the maintenance of hospitals, towards education, and for the registration of vaccination cases and of births and deaths. They asked the Government to contribute to the revenues of the Council by paying for the water used in Government Institutions. They expressed willingness to include within the boundaries of the town the suburbs of Belmont, St Ann's Maraval, and St James, on the condition that the Central Government, which was responsible for the upkeep of these suburbs, put their streets and drains in order. And they asked for assistance from the Central Government, by way of loan or grant, towards the revenues of the Town, emphasising that in twenty years their expenditure had exceeded their revenue by some $232,000; the Port-of-Spain City Council was so short of money that in fact it had to sell the Town Hall to the Government for £5,000, of which £4,000 was applied towards repayment of the Council's indebtedness to the Government. The Council asked the Government to assume full responsibility for the maintenance of the Ariapita asylum, and claimed some compensation from the Government for their waterworks system which the Government had used as the basis of expansion to other parts of the country.

The then Governor of Trinidad, Sir Frederick Napier Broome, appointed a Commission on March 2, 1896, to enquire into the representations made by the Port-of-Spain City Council The Mayor of the Town, Mr Newbold, together with Sir Henry Alcazar, a future Mayor, were appointed members of the Commission. The Mayor attended only the first meeting, and Alcazar, as a result of an accident, left for medical treatment in England. The Commission's report indicated a sharp split between the Government members and the Council members, and Alcazar as well as Mr Eugene Lange of the Legislative Council, dissented from the majority report.

Thereupon Sir Henry Alcazar, who had by that time become Mayor, submitted a petition to the Secretary of State for the Colonies on July 6, 1897, on behalf of the Borough Council of Port-of-Spain. The Council protested against the decision of the Government to make financial aid dependent on the agreement of the Council to increase the house rate from 5 per cent to 7½ per cent, the rate that prevailed in San Fernando and in the Wards The Council argued that taxation in Port-of-Spain was greater than that in other parts of the country, because the inhabitants of Port-of-Spain had to pay licences for the sale of meat and vegetables in the public markets, water rates and sewerage rates, as well as a higher licence fee for the sale of liquor. The petition argued strongly that the Council was entitled to some compensation from the Government for the water works which was their property, for the water which the Government had used for the benefit of public institutions, as well as for the water rates which had been collected by the Government since 1875. The Council emphasised that it could not take in the new suburban districts until they had been put in good condition by the Government. It argued as follows:

> 'These suburbs, which are on the outskirts of the town, were not, until a recent date, subject to any building regulations whatsoever, with the result that the buildings in these localities present all the varieties of irregularity which might have been expected under the circumstances. In the chief of them, Belmont, there are no sidewalks, and no system of drainage save by means of open earth trenches along the main streets. Apart from the main road, along which an electric tramway runs (the tramlines being at many points along the route not more than one or two feet from the entrance to the adjoining buildings) the streets are not more than 15 feet in width. The supply of water to premises is confined to those rated at a sum of not less than £60. At nights, the whole locality is wrapped in complete darkness, not a street light having ever been put up in any part of this district
>
> 'The other suburbs proposed to be incorporated are in a similar or worse plight. In these also buildings of every description have been allowed to be erected without the least regard to symmetry safety or sanitary requirements; and for this state of things the Government are entirely responsible, all these places being included in wards which are under direct and exclusive Government control.'

The Secretary of State replied to the Governor on February 8, 1898, rejecting the petition. He demanded that as the price of any assistance from the Government the Council should levy higher rates and refused to accept the Governor's recommendation that the Government should

make to the Municipality a grant of £5,000 a year for ten years out of
general revenue. He expressed the view instead that 'the Council
should, if possible, be reorganised and reformed', and the Secretary
of State for the Colonies, the architect of imperial federation, the
trustee for the people of Trinidad and Tobago, invited the Governor's
views on two questions as follows:

(a) whether a more widely extended franchise would tend to create
    a more efficient council, and a more intelligent management of
    ˙ Municipal matters;
(b) whether the plan which had been adopted in the case of Bombay
    and Colombo of appointing a high officer of the Government
    to be Mayor or Chairman of the Council could with advantage
    be adopted in the case of Port-of-Spain.

The Secretary of State also insisted on the submission of the annual
Municipal budget for the approval of the Governor and an audit of
the municipal accounts by the Auditor-General He indicated finally
that if, after full examination, the Municipality's claims in respect of
waterworks were to be admitted either in whole or in part, 'such admission may very probably be coupled with a demand that the Council
should contribute towards the cost of the police protection of the
Borough, a charge which is in most towns, at least in part, defrayed
from Municipal funds.'

The Governor thereupon appointed another committee of four
persons of which Alcazar was again a member. The Committee was
obviously in a very difficult situation on the basis of Mr Chamberlain's
despatch to the Governor. But the Committee, while supporting the
view that the Municipal franchise should be extended and that any
burgess should be eligible to be a Town Councillor, was absolutely
opposed to the suggestion of the Secretary of State that a paid official,
appointed by the Central Government, should replace the Mayor of
the Council. The Committee wrote:

'With regard to the second suggestion of the Secretary of State,
we are unable to advise that in this Colony any good result would
follow the appointment of a nominated official Mayor. Self government and absolute official control are essentially incompatible: and
unless the officer to be appointed had the power, in such cases as
he thought necessary, to overrule the opinion of the majority of his
Council, his presence at the Board would prove a mere irritant. And
if he had this power then the ultimate responsibility for Municipal
government would be removed from the elected Council and vested
in the nominated Chairman, and in the last result, in the Governor,
to whose orders he would be bound to refer. The Council would
then be an advisory body, free from real executive responsibility,
but invested with very great powers of hindrance and mischief
We also think that such a step would not conduce to the object in
view in the first suggestion, which we take to be the creation and
favouring of conditions, under which the public might be hoped to

take a more intelligent and careful interest in the acts of their elected Municipality.'

The Committee was equally unhappy about Mr Chamberlain's proposals regarding the Governor's approval of the Council's budget On this matter it reported as follows:

'With regard to the condition that the Municipal Budget should be submitted year by year for the approval of the Governor, we feel some difficulty in reporting. Undoubtedly, it is desirable that the soundness and financial accuracy of the Budget should be approved, that is to say, that the Budget should be a real one, not showing asset items that ought not to be credited to current revenue; not confounding capital with recurring expenditure; framed in all respects in such a manner that it can be made the basis of a subsequent efficient audit, and providing adequately for a sufficient balancing of estimated expenditure and revenue That this much ought to be insisted on and legally secured, we all agree; but when the approval of the Governor is made a condition for sanctioning items and estimates for recurrent expenditure, or some expense which the Borough authorities think it desirable to incur for the benefit of the inhabitants, the effect is to take out of the hands of the Borough Council and vest in the Governor the entire responsibility for the management of the Borough business and finances; and although it is impossible to ignore the danger of questionable expenditure being occasionally proposed and estimated for in the Budget, still it would be a very serious thing to remove the responsibility for such an occurrence from the Council, and we cannot see our way to recommend that the approval of the Budget should imply any responsibility for directing before hand the mode of expenditure of the Municipal authority, except that it ought to be competent for the Governor to insist that the estimated expenditure should be kept within the estimated revenue, in any event.

'No doubt, in submitting the Budget, the Council would submit itself at any rate to such remarks as to the advisability of any proposed expenditure which the Government might be advised to make; but to impose the will of the Governor on the Council as to every matter to be done by the Council during the year would be to relieve that body of their responsibility. The Governor ought to be empowered to insist that the estimates should be technically correct, and should balance and should show a sufficiency to be raised from rates for the purpose of expenditure; that expenditure should be cut down to the amount that can so be raised, and that any supplementary Budget necessary in respect of amounts beyond a certain sum not authorised by the general estimate, should be similarly submitted and no fresh loan estimated for or raised except by previous consent of the Governor and Legislative Council.'

The Committee thought that it was only proper that the rates in

Port-of-Spain should be raised from 5 to 7½ per cent. But it opposed any larger increase, and fully supported the Council's case for assistance from general revenues. After all, who would know this case better than Alcazar, who had attacked the Government's policy on supporting immigrants out of general revenues for years and years for the benefit of a few planters? Thus the Commission wrote:

'This relief, if granted, could, we submit, be provided by the Government out of the large surplus to the credit of the Colony in respect of general revenue in recent years, which has to so very great an extent been built up out of the surplus taxation of the inhabitants of Port-of-Spain itself. The chief town of the Island, to a greater extent here than is perhaps quite realised in England, is, for the purposes of taxation, the Island itself. The revenue from direct taxation in the country districts is much more than directly expended in those districts on roads and other matters. Of the indirect taxation of the Colony, a very large proportion is paid out of the pockets of the inhabitants of Port-of-Spain and the immediate suburbs, and these would be the chief sufferers if the Municipality were to break down for want of a comparatively small balance of available funds to carry on its necessary functions.'

The Secretary of State for the Colonies was adamant. Immersed as he then was in his pet project for a grand Teutonic alliance, comprising Germany, Great Britain, and the United States of America, to dominate the world, one would have thought that he would be a little tolerant of a small community of 300,000 persons in which the people through their prinicpal elected assembly, a Municipality in the capital of 60,000 people, were merely asserting their right to have some say in their government. Not at all. Once a Crown Colony always a Crown Colony No concessions. As Froude had preached, Chamberlain practised. On August 31, 1898, the Secretary of State wrote as follows to the Governor, Sir Hubert Jerningham, rejecting again the Council's claims and repudiating the reports of the Governor's Committee. This is the letter:

'Trinidad – No. 179

Downing Street,
31st August 1898.

'Sir,

'I have the honour to acknowledge the receipt of your despatches No. 112 of the 26th of March, and No. 153 of the 25th of April, on the subject of the Borough Council of Port-of-Spain.

'2 I am equally anxious with yourself to see the Municipal Institutions of Port-of-Spain placed on a sound footing, but I regret that I am not satisfied, as the Committee whom you appointed to consider my recent despatch seem to be satisfied, with a verdict as to the past, distributing the blame for what must be styled a discreditable failure equally between the Borough Council and the Colonial Government.

'3. The whole theory and foundation of sound Municipal Government is that the ratepayers through their elected Representatives should have the full responsibility for, as they have the full management of, their own local affairs, and they cannot throw off this responsibility upon any other authority unless they are content at the same time to part with their control.

'4. In the present case the Borough Council has let the expenditure outrun the revenue, and has tried to redress the balance, not by taking powers to increase rates or by better collection of existing rates but by borrowing in order to provide for the annual deficits created under this system. It is now suggested that they must be to some extent exempted from blame, inasmuch as the Government did not interfere as it might have done to prevent their mode of action. I regret that I an unable to accept this as a sufficient excuse for a body which is or ought to be a leading Municipality in the West Indies, and I cannot agree that the Council will be encouraged to do its duty in the future by the grant of a Government subsidy, at the expense of all the inhabitants of the Colony, to provide for deficiencies which are primarily due to its neglect to provide by the ordinary means at the disposal of a Municipality for its own expenditure.

'5. I have no desire to press the suggestion that the Chairman of the Council should be a Government officer, although such an arrangement has worked well in the case of other Municipalities whose record will compare favourably with that of the Borough Council of Port-of-Spain, and would give the Council the advantage of the advice and experience of a trained official.

'6. You inform me that if the Borough Council is to continue as an institution the first step is for Government to come to its direct assistance. I do not wish to obstruct your plans of re-construction, but I regret that I cannot agree in this view of the case I stated in my despatch of the 8th of February last that guarantees of better and sounder finance should be required as conditions precedent to the grant of any relief.

'7. I am glad to note that the Committee whose report is enclosed in your despatch of the 26th March last "all concur in thinking that a statutory obligation to make and enforce a rate of not less than 1/6 in the £ should form a condition for the granting of the relief applied for," and that similar views are expressed in the concluding paragraph of the letter addressed by the Colonial Secretary to the Mayor of Port-of-Spain on the 21st of March last.

'8. It is now time to bring this question, which has been pending for a considerable time, to a definite decision, and I have therefore to request that you will inform the Borough Council of Port-of-Spain.

'(1) That I shall in no case be able to sanction a direct subvention to the Borough Funds from Colonial Revenues. I consider that such a subvention would be most unfair to the taxpayers of the Colony who do not reside in the Borough and who do not profit by the local expenditure

'(2) That the relief offered in my despatch No. 45 of the 8th of February is strictly conditional on the acceptance of proposals for securing better administration especially of the Finances of the Borough. The proposals may be formulated as follows: —

(a) The extension of the Borough Boundaries in the manner and on the conditions specified in the 5th paragraph of my despatch No. 45.

(b) The submission of the Municipal Budget year by year for the approval of the Governor. Such control would not extend to details but would merely secure that the Estimated Expenditure for the year was fairly provided for by the Estimated Revenue, and that the Estimates were in such a form as to facilitate Audit.

(c) The auditing of the Accounts of each year by the Auditor-General with power to surcharge unauthorised or irregular expenditure.

(d) The removal of the limit of 5 per cent, to the amount of the rate; the rate for each year to be such as with the other receipts will produce sufficient revenue to meet the estimated expenditure of the year.

(e) The assessment of the Borough to be made by an officer appointed by the Colonial Government.

'9. If, as I trust will be the case, the Borough Council accept the terms offered them, you should prepare an Ordinance to give effect to the proposed changes with as little delay as may be. In this case, if it should be found that a Loan is absolutely necessary to enable the Municipality to discharge its pressing liabilities, I shall not object to one being raised, provided that a statement of Revenue is supplied showing a surplus over the current expenditure sufficient to provide Interest and Sinking Fund.

I have, &c.,

J. CHAMBERLAIN.'

The Port-of-Spain City Council would not be bullied. It rejected the conditions laid down by the Secretary of State. It was war between the Colonial Office and the Port-of-Spain City Council. But the odds were as uneven as the war between Spanish cavalry and Arawak Indians armed with bow and arrow. The Port-of-Spain City Council was suspended, and the affairs of the City were entrusted to a Board of Town Commissioners. With the total contempt for intellectualism which characterised the Crown Colony system of government, the Governor of Trinidad and Tobago selected, as the Chairman of the Board of the Commissioners, a British merchant who, of all the names in the world that he could possibly have had, had the name of Adam Smith. The great British economist, who has stood in history for *laissez-faire* and the minimum possible interference of government in the life of the country, became the name associated with as arbitrary an exercise of the metropolitan power as the suspension of the Jamaica

Assembly in 1865 or the suspension of the British Guiana Constitution in 1953.

But Trinidad retaliated – as so often, the calypsonian being the mouthpiece. Norman Le Blanc, Richard Coeur de Lion of calypso fame, immortalized Trinidad's resentment at the execution of the Port-of-Spain City Council:

> 'Jerningham the Governor,
> It's a fastness into you,
> It's a rudeness into you,
> To break up the laws of the Borough Council.'

Water had figured prominently in the conflict between the British Government and the Port-of-Spain City Council. Water figured even more prominently in Trinidad's second great experience of the Crown Colony system in 1903 This experience was the water riots which took place in Port-of-Spain on March 23, 1903.

A characteristic of Trinidad life, then as now, was an enormous waste of water, which seemed to be greater the more abundant the supply In 1874, with a population of 25,000 persons, the daily delivery of water in Port-of-Spain was 1¾ million gallons, averaging from 65 to 71 gallons per head, more than twice the allowance of London. It was therefore recommended that meters and other devices should be used for preventing waste Seven years later a Committee which investigated the water problem reported a daily supply of 2 million gallons for a population of 32,000 The Committee stated that the daily supply was 'largely in excess of what was required either for luxury or use,' and that one-third of the supply was wasted either through carelessness or neglect. The Committee added:

> 'It is true that some provisions of the Water Works Ordinance 3 of 1880 aim at preventing waste by rendering it punishable to let taps flow or otherwise cause waste. But the waste is on such a wholesale scale as scarcely to be affected by any legal restrictions. In nearly every yard, and at almost every house, passers in the street will hear the sound of water running, and, as the gutters show, to waste, in addition to which baths of unnecessary and previously unknown dimensions have been constructed, fountains erected, and gardens irrigated to an extent which could not have been contemplated, and certainly was not provided for, when the water supply was brought to Port-of-Spain.'

The Committee however did not recommend meters as a remedy for the waste but instead the general constriction of the size of delivery pipes by the introduction of ferrules so as to reduce them to ¾ inch in diameter. This was accordingly made law in 1883. Instead of reducing waste, however, the measure appeared to have stimulated it, because the water took so much longer to flow through the pipes that taps were left running even more recklessly than before.

In 1892 therefore another Committee was appointed to consider the question. The population of Port-of-Spain had by then increased to 50,000, the Belmont suburb having been included in the water district. The average daily delivery in that year was 2,800,000 gallons, but the supply in the dry season had to be cut off twice daily for a few hours so as to allow the Maraval Reservoir to refill. The Committee proposed that extravagant waste should be stopped and a storage reservoir containing a 30-day supply should be constructed.

Much of this waste was caused by the well-to-do section of the Port-of-Spain population, principally the large houses around the Queen's Park Savannah. On example given in 1893 cited a house in which no less than 8,170 gallons were consumed daily. Every well-to-do person constructed not an ordinary bath or bathrooms fitted with roman baths of wood or galvanised iron of 68 or 80 gallons, but large plunge baths containing as much as 1,000 or 2,000 gallons each, which were filled every day by letting the tap run all night, the tap, in fact, never being turned off, with a view to the water always being fresh. By the turn of the century there were 1,380 baths in Port-of-Spain exceeding 100 gallons in capacity. The 8,000 people who used them were estimated to consume no less than $1\frac{1}{2}$ million gallons daily, an average of 187 gallons per head.

In 1895 another expert, an engineer, Mr Chadwick, was called in. Aware of the political implications of the question, and the danger of reducing a supply to which the people had got accustomed, Mr Chadwick recommended that the emphasis should be placed on the development of three main sources of additional water supply – in the Diego Martin Valley, at the mouth of the Maraval Valley in St Clair, and the acquisition of a part of the Moka estate and the Haleland Park estate through which the Maraval River ran. He further recommended the construction of a service reservoir containing 4 million gallons and the redistribution of existing mains.

As a result of the implementation of Mr Chadwick's proposals, by 1903 an additional 1,600,000 gallons of water had been made available from Diego Martin, St Clair and Cascade. But Mr Chadwick had also strongly recommended the introduction of meters. All Port-of-Spain was up in arms at the Ordinance of 1896 authorising meters to be put upon large plunge baths and providing for increased rates. The Port-of-Spain Municipality took the lead in this agitation, which was so great that the Government bowed to it and advised the Secretary of State to disallow the Ordinance. The matter was taken up again in 1902 and again public meetings were held in protest against this attempt to throw too much power into the hands of the Government and against the meter system 'as being absolutely unreliable and unsuited to the customs and habits of the inhabitants.' As a result of this outcry this Bill also was withdrawn. At the same time steps were taken to prosecute persons for wasting water and to cut off the supply of those who wasted water. This included cutting off a supply of 80,000 gallons a day in February 1903 to the Town Commissioners who had replaced the Port-of-Spain City Council for flushing the gutters, on the ground that the dirt and dust could be better removed by dry sweeping.

This was the background to the publication on March 5, 1903, of yet another Water Ordinance. The second reading was scheduled for March 16. In consequence of the disorderly behaviour of spectators in the Council Chamber, the Council was adjourned to March 23. By then the fat was in the fire, and the Governor added fuel to the flames by insisting on admission by ticket into the Council Chamber.

The notice that tickets would be required by the public for admission to the Council Chamber precipitated the Water Riots. The Red House was burnt to the ground, the police were called out, two ships, the *Pallas and Rocket,* landed blue jackets, in addition to the 250 men of the Lancashire Fusiliers in the barracks in Port-of-Spain. It was war between bottles and stones on the one side and bullets on the other. Whilst it was not possible to ascertain the exact number of shots fired, returns placed before the Commission of Enquiry showed a total of 16 persons were killed on the spot or died of their wounds subsequently and 43 others were treated at the Colonial Hospital for injuries received.

The conclusions of the Commission of Enquiry which was appointed to investigate the disturbance were as follows:

'(1) That the riots are to be attibuted to the public opposition to the proposed Water Works Ordinance, stimulated by the falsehoods and incitement to violence referred to previously and that they were precipitated by the opposition (stimulated in the same way) to the order restricting admission to the meetings of the Legislative Council to those who applied for and obtained tickets.

'(2) That, with the exception noted in the next clause, the firing by the Police and by certain civilians was amply justifiable.

'(3) That there was excessive and unnecessary firing by some individual members of the Police Force, when not under the control of responsible officers, to which some of the wounding and loss of life is attributable.

'(4) That two, if not three, persons were brutally bayoneted and killed by the police without any justification whatever.

'(5) That the Executive Government failed to take adequate measures to correct the misrepresentations about the draft Ordinance with a view to allaying the public excitement.

'(6) That there is, without doubt, a regrettable and serious division between a large influential portion of the Community in Port-of-Spain and the Executive Government regarding public affairs.

'(7) That there has been most deplorable delay (for which there is, in our opinion, no justification) in prosecuting the rioters and those whose conduct was in a greater or less degree responsible for the rioting.

'(8) That it was not foreseen by anyone in authority that the public excitement against the draft Water Works Ordinance and the Ticket Regulations would culminate in serious rioting, and in that view the steps taken to maintain order and preserve the peace were not insufficient.'

The Commission laid the blame for the riots on the Government of the Colony and on the Crown Colony system. It condemned the Government for failing to take the public into its confidence, to explain the legislation, and to show adequate respect for the views of the unofficial members nominated by the Government. Here are extracts from the Commission's report:

'Undoubtedly the more frequent and the more hostile the criticisms, the more careful the Government should have been to take the public into their confidence, with a view to making them grateful instead of suspicious of the great boon about to be conferred upon them Certainly the Legislative Council were entitled to be kept fully aware of every change of design, involving, as it did, the expenditure of money which they would have to vote Instead of this, the attitude of the Government, unintentionally no doubt, bore the appearance of resentment at the too often unfounded and inept criticism to which the Waterworks project was subjected.

'In view of the deep-rooted prejudice against meters (in regard to which we may at once say that we accept Mr Chadwick's views as to the meter system being both feasible and reliable), the fear of high rates and higher payments for plunge baths, the very troublesome and unpopular proceedings in the matter of cutting pipes, and the general suspicion and dislike of Waterworks schemes, coupled with the fact that two abortive Ordinances were withdrawn, one in 1895 and the other in 1902, both after an outcry from the public, there was every reason why the introduction of a new Water Bill should have been engineered with the greatest tact and care, the more so if it contained, as it was bound to contain, the same unpopular provisions. Under ordinary circumstances a Bill dealing with such a question as water would need careful exposition and explanation to those likely to be affected. Ample time for the public and press to criticise should be allowed, every effort made to prove it just and fair, and every disposition shown to meet opponents half way. No doubt had the debates on the second reading been permitted by the mob to continue, assurance to this effect would have been given. His Excellency the Governor had already told a deputation that he had no intention of rushing the Bill through, and his speech, which was abruptly closed, showed clearly his intention to be eminently fair and conciliatory. But unfortunately the system under which legislation is undertaken in Trinidad is unfavourable to a friendly discussion by the public of the provisions of a draft

Ordinance. There is not, as in India and the colonies in the east, a preliminary enquiry through the executive officers of the Government as to the merits of a Bill, or consultations with members of the public likely to be interested in a Bill, as to how the proposed law will work. After the form of the Bill is decided upon there is no publication with it of a Statement of Objects and Reasons for all new clauses, nor are references given in the margin to clauses of the existing law, which are merely redrafted or repeated.

'What happened might have been anticipated. The moment the Bill appeared violent articles were written against it, and still more violent speeches were made at a public meeting held at the race-stand on the Savannah, or public park, on the 14th of March. It mattered not that the speakers had not even read the Bill. Suffice it that it was a Waterworks Bill – and that it contained the hated word meter – and the agitators were up in arms at once. We think, therefore, that the bringing of the Bill without consulting members of the public, informally if need be, at first – and the bringing in of the second reading within ten days after its publication – was very injudicious, and certainly calculated to give colour to the view that the Government cared naught for public opinion. Even the unofficial members of the Legislative Council, who had pronounced so strongly against the first Bill in October, and whom it was desirable to carry with the Government in a matter of the kind, were not consulted.

'. . . The Water Authority was, pending the creation of a body of Commissioners under the Sewerage Act, to consist of the Governor in Executive Council, which, in the opinion of a great number of ratepayers, owing to Mr Wrightson's great personal influence, practically meant himself, and this was bound to be an unpopular provision. No time was fixed by which a separate Water Authority might be created, and as on the passing of the Bill all control over the working of the new law would wholly pass from the Legislative Council, there was not a single unofficial representative of the community, elected or nominated who would have a voice in its administration . . .

'But there is, of course, the further question of the policy of the course taken by the Government in the circumstances of the case, and while admitting that the order was only reasonable in itself and that the Governor was fully justified in refusing to withdraw it, we cannot refrain from expressing our opinion that in the circumstances of the case His Excellency would have been better advised to have given instructions in the first instance that so soon as the available seats (numbering 180) were occupied no further admission to the Council Chamber should be allowed. The agitation on the water question would not then have been added to by a further complaint, however factitious, of unconstitutional action on the part of the Governor, and the arrangements would have prevented any complaint on the part of the public of favouritism as to admission to the Chamber, which though it was in effect provided against in the notification, yet most regrettably was not carried out. The Clerk of the Council had eighty tickets to give to applicants, and he gave "about half of them" to clerks in the Government offices. It is not surprising that a charge of packing the Council Chamber was made against the Government.

'There was further special reason why the Government should have been careful. For some years a group of persons has existed in Port-of-Spain whose main conception of public spirit and independence is to vilify the Government and indulge in personalities regarding the individuals who compose it. Conspicuous among this group are certain coloured lawyers, some of whom have studied law in England, coloured tradesmen doing a substantial business, and some less reputable persons, while a few persons of English birth, including the editors of two newspapers, have thrown their lot in with them. That some of the individuals are actuated by a natural desire to take part in public affairs we have no reason to doubt, but others are inspired by a vague aspiration for a representative Government. They feel aggrieved at the abolition of the elective Borough Council, which was effected on the 20th December, 1898, under the instructions of the Secretary of State, because the Council had failed in their duty and refused to submit their accounts to a public audit. They have formed themselves into a Ratepayers' Association, numbering 185 members, with Mr Newbold, a former Mayor, as President, and at present the Committee of that Association affects to act on behalf of the whole body of ratepayers in Port-of-Spain, 6,793 in number. The influence of such a party is usually neutralised by the much larger body of quiet self-respecting persons, when satisfied that the Government is just and sympathetic. But in Trinidad it appears to us unfortunately true that the Government of the colony have not in the past, by continuously endeavouring to keep in touch with the more respectable and intelligent members of the public, by invariably consulting them as to legislative measures beforehand, and by showing every possible consideration for the views of the non-official members of the Legislative Council, secured for the Government as such, and for their measures, the strong unswerving confidence and support of the community of Port-of-Spain, which would make a few agitators a negligible quantity. We must acknowledge that any Government would have a difficult task in a society where it seems a tradition even for its leading and most respected members to be usually in opposition to the Government. The Government seem in consequence rather to have taken refuge in a policy of stolid, if not unsympathetic, isolation, which has ended in a kind of cleavage existing between rulers and ruled which we think many years will be needed to correct. The Government must have been aware of the feelings of the public towards them, and should therefore have been doubly careful to move warily in grappling with a thorny subject. However excellent and conciliatory their intentions in fact were as to the conduct of the Bill after its introduction, which they never had an opportunity of expressing, they plunged into the contest apparently with a light heart, just as if the Bill had been one of the smallest pieces of routine legislative business.'

The Commission's criticism of the Crown Colony system in operation touched the Secretary of State for the Colonies in a raw spot, and Mr Chamberlain did his best to cover up the deficiencies and to find an alibi He sought to lay part of the blame on the nominated unofficial members and to say that things could not be so bad after all because of the economic stability of Trinidad. This is what he wrote in a despatch on July 21, 1903, to the Governor, Sir Alfred Maloney:

'I have read these words with great regret, and I have equally regretted to read the words which follow, to the effect that it seems a tradition in Trinidad even for the leading and most respected members of the community to be usually in opposition to the Government. The success of Crown Colony government – and no other form of government is suited to the conditions of Trinidad – depends upon the mutual co-operation of the official and unofficial sections The fact that the ultimate power as well as the ultimate responsibility rest, subject to the Secretary of State, with the Governor and heads of the principal Departments of the Executive Government, makes it absolutely imperative to defer, wherever it is reasonable to do so, to the wishes of the Unofficial Members of the Legislative Council, to consult them on matters of legislation and expenditure, to treat them with the consideration and confidence which is due to representative members of the community, and to be at pains to prevent as far as possible such questions as may arise from being treated as party questions.

'On the other hand, it is for the Unofficial Members to respond by recognizing what I will call the strength of their own position. They must be aware that Governors and Secretaries of State alike are naturally reluctant to override the convictions or even the prejudices of men of high standing and independent position, who have been definitely nominated to represent and speak for the community at large; and to constitute themselves a standing opposition is to assume, what is not the case, that the Government of the Colony is adverse to the interests, and indifferent to the wishes, of the general public.

'I must confess, however, that I see reason for thinking that what the Commissioners call the cleavage between the rulers and the ruled may not have been in fact so complete as might appear at the present moment to be the case. I cannot bring myself to believe that Trinidad would have been so conspicuously prosperous, had not officials and unofficials alike been as a rule working hand in hand for the good of the Colony.'

This was, of course, mere eyewash. It might be very easy for the

Commission of Enquiry into the Water Riots to state that, except in one or two instances, the shooting by the police was justifiable. In fact, however, the Crown Colony system rested on the bayonets of the police supported by British battleships and British troops. The water agitation was started by the disfranchised middle and upper classes, though it was the ordinary citizens who got shot down in Sackville Street, or at the corner of Frederick and Prince Streets, or in Abercromby Street, or in Woodford Square. The less fortunate members of the community, whether of African origin or Indian origin, equally felt the weight of the Police Force which protected the Crown Colony system. It is little wonder that the transfer of the Police Force in later years to the control of elected representatives of the people of Trinidad and Tobago provoked a minor political crisis.

The population that did not live in St Clair felt the weight of police repression particularly in connection with their popular celebrations – Carnival and Hosea.

Between 1881 and 1884 Carnival was in serious danger of being stopped altogether by the police. What was involved was principally the *canboulay* – a corruption of *cannes brulees* – the procession of lighted torches which dominated the Carnival in those days On April 1, 1881 – probably an appropriate day – the Colonial Secretary was asked a number of questions in the Legislative Council regarding the Carnival disturbances in that year. The rumours prevalent in Port-of-Spain were that the police intended to put down Carnival by force, they had ordered a number of heavy staves for special use, and that bands had come into Port-of-Spain from Diego Martin, St Joseph, Arouca, Arima, Chaguanas, and even from San Fernando for the especial purpose of creating a disturbance and of beating up the police. The rumours went so far as to say that if the police had not been confined to barracks on Carnival Monday night, the whole of Port-of-Spain would have been set on fire by the crowd. This last rumour may or may not have been so, but the fact is that the Governor gave this reply on March 3, 1881, to a question as to the reasons for the confinement of the police to barracks from Carnival Monday afternoon until 10 o'clock on the morning of Ash Wednesday.

'The Governor stated that looking to the erroneous reports which had gained currency as to his action in this matter he had much pleasure in replying to the question of the Hon. Member: That as the Council were no doubt aware a serious disturbance had occurred early on Monday morning in which several of the Police had been injured: That the Mayor and Town Council had waited on him on Monday and had represented to him that the owners of property and respectable inhabitants of the Town were in a state of great alarm at the excitement which existed: That after some discussion His Excellency enquired whether in the opinion of the deputation good would result from his going to Town and addressing the people in person and was answered that for him to do so would be productive of more good than the presence of 1,000 soldiers: That His Excellency being most averse to the use of further force and the possibility of bloodshed accordingly went down to the Eastern Market and addressed the people explaining to them that there seemed to have been some misconception as to the views of the Government with regard to the Carnival, that there was no wish whatever to stop their amusements if conducted in an orderly manner but that the use of torches in the streets had been forbidden owing to the danger from fire at this dry season of the year and could not be permitted and that he hoped that no more would be carried about: That if the people would promise His Excellency to conduct themselves in an orderly manner and would keep the peace themselves he would believe them and would withdraw the Police: That on this loud cries of "we promise" were raised: That the Police were accordingly withdrawn into Barracks until the morning of Wednesday the 2nd instant when instructions were issued for their returning to their usual duties '

The official view was that the Carnival of 1883 was even more disorderly than that of 1881. The reports tell of fighting, throwing of stones and bottles, much obscenity, and unmasked bands of disorderly persons marching through Port-of-Spain armed with long sticks. The Governor was of the opinion that it was not for the most part Trinidadians who were involved but bad characters from the neighbouring islands. So in preparation for the 1884 Carnival, legislation was rushed through to prohibit *canboulay* as the principal source of disorderliness.

It was in the same year, 1884, that serious disturbances took place in and around San Fernando in connection with the Hosea celebrations on October 30, 1884. So serious were the disturbances that the Governor of Jamaica, Sir Henry Norman, was appointed on special duty to investigate them.

The disturbances originated in various regulations which had been introduced seeking to confine the Hosea celebrations to the estates, to keep them off the highroads, and to prevent them from entering San Fernando and Port-of-Spain. Over the years the Hosea celebrations had ceased for the most part to have a religious character, to the extent where it was boycotted by the most respectable Muslims, either because they considered it unsanctioned by their faith, or because of the boisterous nature of the procession; as Sir Henry Norman wrote in his report:

'. . . in fact the ceremony, although it is purely appertaining to the Mahomedans, is one in which most of the persons engaged are Hindoos, and the whole celebration has come to be regarded as a sort of national Indian demonstration of a rather turbulent character, and common to both Hindoos and Mahomedans.'

The Indian population simply refused to accept the regulations. They marched in large numbers determined to enter San Fernando. The police prevented them from doing so and opened fire. In all some twelve Indians were killed and over one hundred wounded and treated in hospital. Sir Henry Norman had this to say in his report:

'A few of the wounds were severe, and one man under treatment is not expected to survive, but a large number of the wounds were very slight. All were the result of buckshot, which was issued to the police in lieu of bullets some time back by order of Sir Sanford Freeling. The list of casualties is very heavy, and is probably far more numerous than would have been the case if rifle bullets had been used, although, in the latter case, at close quarters, if the police had fired low, their forty-five shots would probably have killed more men and mortally wounded more men than the fire of buckshot. The question of whether rifle bullets or buckshot should be used when it is unfortunately necessary to fire upon rioters is not one upon which any opinion I can give will be of value, and must be decided upon general considerations as to humanity and effectiveness.'

The Water Riots Commission had emphasised the total lack of relationship between governors and governed and the total contempt on the part of the Government for local public opinion. The *canboulay* disturbances involved, at least in the minds of the people of Port-of-Spain, a total lack of understanding on the part of the Inspector of Police, Captain Baker, who was even alleged in the 1881 disturbances to have drawn his sword and severely wounded one or more persons. The 1884 Hosea disturbances showed the same lack of understanding of and sympathy with the population by the Colonial Government. The Government had simply passed regulations and proceeded to enforce them. Sir Henry Norman was at great pains to argue that the Indian population could not have been unaware of the regulations and must have understood them, and therefore those who proceeded with the procession were determined to disobey them. This may or may not have been so, but Sir Henry Norman's report emphasises again the failure to establish any harmony rapprochement between governors and governed.

Disregarding the contemptuous references to the Indian immigrants and the opprobrious epithets used to designate them which was conventional at that time, this was Sir Henry Norman's condemnation of the whole system of Crown Colony government in its relation with the human beings for whom it was supposed to be the trustee:

'It was not, as I think, want of information that led to this deplorable collision, but want of influence over the Coolies, and there was no authority in the Island who possessed this influence If there had been, as protector, an officer whom the Coolies were often accustomed to see, who could speak to them thoroughly in their own language, and who they knew was well acquainted with their customs, I think there might have been a great effect produced by the visit of such an officer to as many of the estates as possible prior to the festival of the Mohurrum. I think any experienced well-selected officer of Indian experience would have visited the estates, and have addressed the Coolies with good results; but then such an officer would, probably by personal intercourse and by intimate knowledge of the Coolies, have acquired an amount of influence over them which could not be expected from a gentleman who, however zealous he may be, and though, like the present Protector, he may be most anxious to do his duty, has not had the advantage of an Indian training in a position of authority with natives, and who cannot speak fluently to the immigrants in their own language.'

And yet Joseph Chamberlain was able to say in 1903 that no other form of government but the Crown Colony system was suited to the conditions of Trinidad, and Froude, in similar vein, was able to sneer at the agitators for constitution reform in 1887. Disturbances in 1881, disturbances in 1884, disturbances in 1903, riots and police shootings on three occasions in 20 years, involving whites, Negroes, and Indians, and yet England's leading Professor of History could sneer at constitution reform, the Secretary of State for the Colonies could suspend the principal elective assembly in Trinidad, and, after twenty years of shooting, could say that only the Crown colony system, which had produced the shootings, was suited to the conditions of Trinidad.

A Trinidadian, Mr J. J. Thomas, replied to Froude in a well-known Trinidad classic entitled 'Froudacity: West Indian Fables by James Anthony Froude.' Mr Thomas enlarged on the scandal of the Public Works Department and the rubbish that had been sent out by the Colonial Office in the form of Governors in reply to Froude's argument that Trinidad's affairs had not been ill-managed and possibly in anticipation of Mr Chamberlain's argument that things could not be so bad in Trinidad after all because the economy had been developing. Thomas sneered at the whole long succession of Governors after Sir Anthony Gordon – a good Governor in his view – with whom the colony had been afflicted until the arrival of Sir William Robinson – whom he considered another good Governor – who was in Trinidad when Froude arrived. He sneered at Sir James Longden with his slavish adherence to red tape and his total lack of initiative. He sneered at Sir Henry Irving with all his vulgar colonial prejudices, his abject surrender to the sugar interests and his conviction that sugar growers alone should be possessors of the lands of the West Indies, under whose régime the scandalous mismanagement of the Public Works Department had become a warning to the whole of the West Indies.

Irving was particularly distinguished by his ostentatious hostility to creoles in general and to coloured creoles in particular, and it was Irving who insisted that the Arima Railway was not to have its terminus in the centre of Arima but was to be diverted 'by only a few yards' from the originally projected terminus, which would save the colony £8,000. Instead Arima found that the terminus was nearly a mile outside of the town, and the population of Trinidad found that they had to pay an extra £20,000 for the Governor's few yards. Thomas sneered at Irving's San Fernando Waterworks, which saddled San Fernando with a debt of £17,000 for water, which half the inhabitants could not get, and which few of the half who did get dared venture to drink.

Thomas was particularly savage on Sir Sanford Freeling, the Governor of the colony who in 1884 sanctioned the shooting down of Indian immigrants at the Hosea festival. He sneered at Sir Anthony Havelock, a dandy, whom the historian might well by-pass.

With this catalogue of the woes of Trinidad under Downing Street rule, Mr Thomas turned on Professor Froude. This is Thomas' defence of the political reformers in Trinidad:

'This brings us to the motives, the sordid motives, which Mr Froude, oblivious of the responsibility of his high literary status, has permitted himself gratuitously, and we may add scandalously, to impute to the heads of the Reform movement in Trinidad. It was perfectly competent that our author should decline, as he did decline, to have anything to do, even as a spectator, at a meeting with the object of which he had no sympathy. But our opinion is equally decided that Mr Froude has transgressed the bounds of decent political antagonism, nay, even of common sense, when he presumes to state that it was not for any other object than the large salaries of the Crown appointments, which they covet for themselves, that the Reform leaders are contending. This is not criticism: it is slander. To make culpatory statements against others, without ability to prove them, is, to say the least, hazardous; but to make accusations to formulate which the accuser is forced, not only to ignore facts, but actually to deny them, is, to our mind, nothing short of rank defamation.

'Mr Froude is not likely to impress the world (of the West Indies, at any rate) with the transparent silly, if not intentionally malicious, ravings which he has indulged in on the subject of Trinidad and its politics Here are some of the things which this "champion of Anglo-West Indians" attempts to force down the throats of his readers. He would have us believe that Mr Francis Damian, the Mayor of Port-of-Spain, and one of the wealthiest of the native inhabitants of Trinidad, a man who has retired from an honourable and lucrative legal practice, and devotes his time, his talents, and his money to the service of his native country; that Mr Robert Guppy, the venerable and venerated Mayor of San Fernando, with his weight of years and his sufficing competence, and with his long record of self-denying services to the public; that Mr George Goodwille, one of the most successful merchants in the Colonies; that Mr Conrad F. Stollmeyer, a gentleman retired, in the evening of his days, on his well-earned ample means, are open to the above sordid accusation In short that these and such-like individuals who, on account of their private resources and mental capabilities, as well as the public influence resulting therefrom, are by the sheer

logic of circumstances, forced to be at the head of public movements, are actuated by a craving for the few hundred pounds a
year for which there is such a scramble at Downing Street among
the future official grandees of the West Indies! But granting that
this allegation of Mr Froude's was not as baseless as we have shown
it to be, and that the leaders of the Reform agitation were impelled
by the desire which our author seeks to discredit them with, what
then? Have they who have borne the heat and burden of the day in
making the Colonies what they are no right to the enjoyment of
the fruits of their labours? The local knowledge, the confidence
and respect of the population, which such men enjoy, and wield
for good or evil in the community, are these matters of small
account in the efficient government of the Colony? Our author,
in specifying the immunities of his ideal Governor, who is also ours,
recommends, amongst other things, that His Excellency should be
allowed to choose his own advisers. By this Mr Froude certainly
does not mean that the advisers so chosen must be all pure-blooded
Englishmen who have rushed from the destitution of home to batten
on the cheaply obtained flesh-pots of the Colonies.

'At any rate, whatever political fate Mr Froude may desire for
the Colonies in general, and for Trinidad in particular, it is nevertheless unquestionable that he and the scheme that he may have
for our future governance, in this year of grace 1888 have both
come into view entirely out of season. The spirit of the times has
rendered impossible any further toleration of the arrogance which
is based on historical self-glorification. The gentleman of Trinidad,
who are struggling for political enfranchisement, are not likely to
heed, except as a matter for indignant contempt, the obtrusion by
our author of his opinion that "they had best let well alone." . . .

'All of a piece, as regards veracity and prudence, is the further
allegation of Mr Froude's, to the effect that there was never any
agitation for Reform in Trinidad before that which he passes under
review. It is, however, a melancholy fact, which we are ashamed
to state, that Mr Froude has written characteristically here also,
either through crass ignorance or through deliberate malice. Any
respectable, well-informed inhabitant of Trinidad, who happened
not to be an official "bird of passage", might, on our author's honest
inquiry, have informed him that Trinidad is the land of chronic
agitation for Reform. Mr Froude might also have been informed
that, even forty-five years ago, that is in 1843, an elective constitution, with all the electoral districts duly marked out, was formulated
and transmitted by the leading inhabitants of Trinidad to the then
Secretary of State for the Colonies. He might also have learnt that
on every occasion that any of the shady Governors, whom he has
so well depicted, manifested any excess of his undesirable qualities,
there has been a movement among the educated people in behalf
of changing their country's political condition.

'We close this part of our review by reiterating our conviction that, come what will, the Crown Colony system, as at present managed, is doomed.'

But the Crown Colony system took no heed of Thomas' warning or of the continued agitation for political reform. This, in its simplest form, meant nothing more than the conviction of ordinary people in Trinidad that the only way to have their affairs properly administered was to select their own elected representatives It was not only people like Guppy, or Stollmeyer, or Rev. Morton, or Rev. Grant, or Dr de Verteuil, or Mr Rostant, or Mr Rapsey, who argued for constitution reform and who attacked colonialism. It was the ordinary man in the street, like Alexander Wood of Fifth Company, 63 years of age, owning 16 acres or growing cocoa, or Mr Juppy, an ex-indentured Indian immigrant, who had been in Trinidad for 34 years, who supported constitution reform. In Mr Wood's view, constitution reform meant better roads. This was his evidence before the 1889 Franchise Commission ·

'Well, I really wants a road first of all, to convey my produce to market, and that we may able to pay our taxes Secondly, my children goes to school. The road is so very bad sometimes the teachers have to send them back; and thirdly, to see that the immigrants has been lately come and wherever they forms they flock they have good roads, and we are the natives here we suffering; and by this reason I really think that if we have a Council of our own, to help us very much, because I have been travelling to other islands and I have been seein' the Black have a Council as well as the White, but here, in this part of the Vineyard, we partly stifle down, suffering If one of the Europeans stand up and said "That man is to go to prison", without any crime, no one would bid against him; right away to prison. So I looks into all these reasons, which causes me to agree with the Petition.'

Bad grammar but good politics. Mr Juppy was just as simple, just as eloquent, and just as explicit. Here is Mr Juppy's evidence before the Commission:

'Well, then, you have not talk to people much about this Reform Petition at all, about changing the Government; at present it is the Queen; you know who the Queen is, Mr Juppy? – Yes, I know the Queen, because Queen brought me down here . . .

'The Queen brought you down, and the Queen makes the laws; that is to say she names some gentlemen to make the laws out here then they go to her and she confirms them. Now some gentlemen in the Colony say, "Oh don't let the men who the Queen names make the laws; let every one in the Colony who knows about it, let them choose some gentlemen to make the laws; let all the Indians choose their man and send him up to make laws;" do you think that would be a good thing? – No, sir, this country belong to here gentlemen, they live here, make children here, and what gentlemen here, four, five, or ten, twelve agree to make law, me agree for um same law too.

'But, Mr Juppy, do you wish yourself, and do you think your countrymen wish to be choosing a gentleman to go and make laws? – Me-self can't choose-um me-self. Some like-um this man; some no like-um this man All man no got-um same opinion. Some 'gainst one another.

'Mr Wilson: Now the Queen appoint-um. You like better that all the people shall round choose-um, instead of Queen make-um?

'Witness: If me tell-um me choose-um?

'Mr Wilson: You think that better?

'Witness : No; more better for here people 'point-um.

'The Chairman: I must ask for a little silence.

'A Voice (Mr Maisonneuve): We are public here.

'The Chairman: I must ask for silence, or the room must be cleared. Better the People 'point-um than the Queen?

'Witness: Yes; because they people the gentlemen live here and appoint higher people, and higher people make-um law. Because meself can't go see Queen. Me know all-you sabbet point it out.

'Dr de Verteuil: He means he cannot see the Queen but he can see the people here.

'Mr Garcia: He means he cannot advise the Queen who to nominate because he cannot get to her, but if he is asked to nominate he knows who to nominate.

'The Chairman: Is that what most of your countrymen think too?

'Witness: I don't know, sir, because me know for me-self, but me no know, for any countryman but me-self.'

Mr Juppy would not have passed an English examination in Standard I, but his political acumen was absolutely impeccable. He wanted to appoint the members of the Legislative Council himself and he did not want the Queen to do so. He could see them but he could not see the Queen. Mr Wood agreed; with his own representatives he would have a better chance of getting better roads. What Mr Wood and Mr Juppy were attacking, together with their white colleagues among the cocoa planters and the mercantile community, was the Crown Colony system under which an official of the Government was *ex-officio* a member of the Legislative Council. As such he had no freedom to vote as he pleased. As the Secretary of State, the Duke of Buckingham, stated in a circular despatch on August 17, 1868, 'the power of the Crown in the Legislature, if pressed to its extreme limit, would avail to overcome every resistance that could be made to it.'

Thus it was that when in 1862 the Governor of Trinidad complained that the Chief Justice had openly disagreed with him in the Legislature in the course of a debate on sewerage works in Port-of-Spain and had twice voted against him, the Duke of Buckingham stated the official obligation with the utmost clarity:

'. . . an Officer, whose seat in the legislature is by law insepar-able from his office, could not be continued in the office and the seat if his conscience should not permit him to give the Crown such a measure of support as may be necessary to enable the Governor to carry on the business of Government in the Legislature on the principles and according to the intentions with which the Legislature was constituted.'

Only minor changes were made in the 19th century to the Crown Colony legislature established in Trinidad in 1831. In 1862, two un-official members were added on the understanding that, should the unofficials outvote the officials by voting together habitually and as a party, two official votes would be added. In 1886 the unofficial mem-bers complained about their lack of control over expenditure; a Finance Committee was therefore established to enable them to par-ticipate in the framing of the estimates, to examine each item of the estimates before they were submitted to the Legislature, and to make recommendations thereon to the Governor. This, however, did not prevent the Governor from recommending to the Secretary of State the cancellation of a vote unanimously agreed upon by the unofficial members.

In 1880, as a substitute for the elected members representing fixed constituencies as recommended by many people before the Royal Franchise Commission, the unofficial members were assigned by the Governor to represent the counties into which the island was divided. The Secretary of State for the Colonies, however, disallowed this arrangement in 1898, and gave orders that in future the selection of unofficial members should depend entirely on their fitness for that position. The single exception to this rule was to be Tobago. The Secretary of State directed that Tobago should always be represented by an unofficial member in the legislature. But the communications with Trinidad were so poor that for the next quarter of a century no resident in Tobago was able to spare the time to attend meetings of the Legislature in Port-of-Spain.

In 1898 the membership of the Legislative Council was 21, of whom 11 were unofficial members and 10 official members including the Governor. In that year the number of official members was increased to 11 and the Governor was given both an original and a casting vote to ensure that there should always be an official majority.

It is in this context that we must see the action of the Legislative Council of Trinidad and Tobago in 1917 in passing an Ordinance to authorise the raising of money as a contribution to His Majesty to-wards the expenses of World War I The sum involved was £100,000. In a speech remarkable for its understatement on March 9, 1917, one of the nominated unofficial members, Dr Laurence, considered it 'remarkable that this small island should have to contribute towards the expenses of the war undertaken by the most powerful financial Empire that the world has known.' There was nothing remarkable about it in a Crown Colony On August 28, 1918, the Secretary of State for the Colonies wrote to the Governor expressing the sincere thanks of His Majesty's Government for so generous a contribution and for such a generous and patriotic gift.

It was no wonder that the Royal Commission of 1897 could have taken the view that Trinidad had no need for financial assistance from Britain in the economic difficulties occasioned by the development of the sugar industry in the West Indies. It was no wonder that Joseph Chamberlain could have stated in 1903 that only the Crown Colony system of government was suited to Trinidad. It was no wonder that Froude in 1887 could have sneered at the agitation for constitution reform as nothing more than a desire on the part of certain Trinidadians to share in the spoils of office.

Under the Crown Colony system of government Britain's control was supreme. The colonials were expected to obey the fiats from London, to thank London for those fiats, to finance London's policy out of its own pockets, to produce commodities which London would not buy, and finally to contribute to the defence of London. One can now see in better perspective the anger of the King of Spain some centuries before when he protested to his advisers that they were criticising him as if he was stealing their or somebody else's property.

CHAPTER 14

The Education of the Young Colonials

Four centuries of colonialism, from 1498 to 1897, had made of Trinidad and Tobago a great workshop rather than a miniature state. A race had been freed, but a society had not yet been formed. The people were denied all representative institutions and were considered unfit even to operate a Municipal Council in their capital. The Crown Colony system was considered the only suitable form of Government, in 1903 as in 1810, when the decision was taken on the two grounds that the majority of the free persons were non-white In such a colony, both in order to form a society and develop a spirit of community and in order to train the people for self-government, education would have an important role to play. The importance of education was enhanced by Chacon's emphasis on racial disunity and national divisions in 1796, both of which were necessarily intensified by the introduction after emancipation of thousands of workers from all parts of the world, the large majority from India.

The question of education was taken up by the Governor, Sir Henry MacLeod, in a despatch to the Secretary of State for the Colonies on October 13, 1841. The Governor wrote:

'. . . There is perhaps no British Colony, where, from the mixed nature of its inhabitants, which I have before stated, the necessity of some general plan of Education is more required than in Trinidad.

'The number of Immigrants we are receiving renders the demand of an extension of the means of Education of greater consequence every day, and while there appears a willingness and readiness on all sides to aid in this desirable object, yet the differences of languages and religion make it more imperative that the system to be adopted should be one under the control of the Government, not only with a view to make it accessible to all parties and creeds, but to cause the language spoken to be that of the Country to which this Colony belongs.

'Your Lordship will not fail to think this most essential when I tell you that two thirds of the natives still speak exclusively either Spanish or French, and I conceive it absolutely necessary that people living under British rule and claiming the benefit of British subjects should be able to read the laws by which they are governed'

The Secretary of State, Lord Stanley, replied at length on January 8, 1842. His reply raised issues fundamental to education in Trinidad over the past century and a quarter, and is therefore reproduced in its entirety:

'. . . The question of Education, embarrassing enough in any of the Colonies, is surrounded in Trinidad by peculiar difficulties, arising out of the differences of language and of Religion; the majority of the population being foreign in language and Roman Catholic in religion, the bulk of property being English and Protestant. As to the former point of difference, I think it quite clear that it should be a leading object with the Government to encourage by every means in their power the diffusion of the English language; and it would not appear unreasonable to require that instruction in the language should be made a *sine qua non* in every school applying for aid from public funds. Difference of Religion presents a more formidable obstacle; and some regulations appear obviously desirable to prevent the establishment of three or four schools, set up for the mere purpose of rivalry, by different denominations, all claiming and all receiving the aid of Government, in a district the population of which would be abundantly supplied by a single school On the other hand I much doubt the possibility of laying down and adhering to a rule, in such a society, of withholding aid from all schools which shall not be conducted according to a single scheme laid down by the Government. The system introduced into Ireland was founded upon the necessity arising out of circumstances in some degree analogous to those which you describe; and was intended to communicate to Children of all denominations a religious education without shocking the prejudice of those who dissented from the Church of England, or introducing doctrines at variance with the opinions of that Church. But, although Schools upon this principle have rapidly multiplied in Ireland, the system has met with a very decided opposition from various quarters, and especially from the Clergy of the Church of England: and I fear it must be admitted that in few instances has it effected that combined Education which was one of its main objects, but the different Schools, taking their colour from their respective local Superintendents have become for the most part exclusively Roman Catholic, or Presbyterian, or Church of England, the latter being comparatively a very small number. Now this is not the effect which I am desirous of producing in Trinidad; and although I am of opinion that if a Board could be constituted in which the various religious denominations were fairly represented and if the system were taken up in a spirit of cordiality and mutual good understanding by their respective Clergy, such a system might be productive of great good in Trinidad, I am afraid that it would hardly be justifiable to calculate upon such a contingency. The refusal of the Clergy generally of any one denomination, especially of the Established Church, to co-operate in such a system would be a serious obstacle to its introduction; and still more so to the exclusion from the benefit of public aid, of all schools not conducted under it. In conformity however with your wish expressed in your Despatch to my Predecessor of the 1st May 1840, I have given directions for supplying you with the principal rules and regulations

under which the Irish system is at present carried on, and a copy of
the Scriptural books which have been prepared for general use in
their schools, under the united sanction of the Government Board:
You will endeavour to ascertain by private and personal enquiry how
far the Clergy of the various denominations might be expected to
co-operate in such a scheme; and I shall await with much anxiety your
report upon this interesting question. Should the result be such as
I am afraid must be anticipated, it will be necessary to take steps for
restricting within reasonable limits the liability of the Government to
be called upon to aid in the establishment of schools of an exclusive
character; and perhaps no better course could be pursued than that
which has been adopted in this Country of taking an annual grant to
a limited amount in aid of Education, and receiving, through certain
authorised channels, applications for participation in the grant,
delegating to a Committee of the Privy Council the examination
separately of the merits of each particular application, and laying
down at the same time certain indispensable conditions with reference
to the amount of local contribution, the number of scholars anticipated, the right of Government inspection, and other points to which
it is unnecessary now to avert In the absence of any general system
under the superintendence of the Government, I see no other mode
likely to be productive of equal advantages with that which I have
thus generally indicated, respecting which, if necessary, I shall have
pleasure in furnishing you more particular details.'

Lord Harris, who assumed the Government of Trinidad in 1846,
found an irregular system of some forty religious schools in operation,
aided but not supervised by the Government, attended by some 1,000
children. He announced to the Legislature on February 1, 1847, however, that he would shortly propose an ordinance to empower the
Government to establish a system of general instruction and 'to carry
out nothing more than what is generally termed secular instruction'.
This departure from the admonitions issued by Lord Stanley was
presented to the Legislative Council on April 2, 1851, and was thus
introduced by the Governor:

'I decided on this plan with considerable anxiety and in no spirit
of pride but rather that of deep humiliation; for I am obliged to come
to the conclusion that the unfortunate differences which exist in
religion would prevent any united action if that subject were introduced; and though I acknowledge to the fullest the immense importance of this subject in developing the powers of man, I thought it
better, under the circumstances, that it should be left to be provided
for by other means.'

The fundamental principles of Lord Harris' system were as follows:
(a) That no religious instruction whatever was to be imparted in
the schools.
(b) That under no circumstances were the schoolmasters to give
the religious instruction.
(c) That the religious instruction of the children was to be com-

mitted to their respective pastors who upon a day set apart for the purpose in each week – the schools being closed on that day – were to impart such instruction in the churches or elsewhere.

(d) That the instruction in the schools was to be of such a character as not to offend the religious susceptibilities of any of the inhabitants of the colony.

(e) That no school fees were to be charged

(f) That the school expenses were to be met by local rates.

(g) That the entire management and control of the schools, the appointment and dismissal of teachers, the determination of the course of instruction and of the books to be employed, were to be vested in a Board of Education.

A Committee of the Council adopted the same year the following resolutions for the establishment of schools in Trinidad:

First: A Board of Education was to be formed, consisting of the Governor, with such members of the Legislative Council and other persons, being laymen, as may be appointed from time to time by the Governor.

Second: An Inspector of Schools was to be appointed with a salary.

Third: A training school, with a master and mistress, was to be established for the educational training of teachers; the expense of maintaining such school, with suitable accommodation for the teachers, was to be defrayed from the public funds of the colony.

Fourth: Public schools were to be established at once in each ward of the colony, and at such places most suitable for the convenience of the population.

Fifth: The training and primary schools were to be under the control of the Board of Education, and subject to the supervision of the Inspector

Sixth: The expenses of erecting and maintaining the school-houses, with suitable accommodation for teachers, and the salaries, were to be defrayed from the funds of the wards.

Seventh: No person was to be appointed master or mistress unless such person had produced a certificate of good character to the satisfaction of the Board of Education, and until such person had undergone an examination by the Board, and had received a certificate of efficiency.

Eighth: At the primary schools instruction was to be provided for day scholars, and for evening and adult classes

Ninth: Admission to the primary schools was to be free.

Tenth· Instruction to be given at the training and primary schools was to be secular, and without direct religious or doctrinal teaching.

The 1851 population of 69,609 included 10,812 persons born in other British colonies; 8,097 born in Africa; 4,915 born in foreign colonies; 4,169 born in India; 729 citizens of the United Kingdom. Roman Catholics predominated – 43,605; followed by adherents of the Church of England – 16,246. Other denominations included –

Wesleyans, 2,508; Presbyterians, 1,071; Baptists, 448; Hindus, 2,649; Moslems, 1,016 French was the dominant language, and services in the Roman Catholic cathedral in Port-of-Spain and in other Catholic Churches were normally preached in either French or Spanish. The Catholic children normally learned their catechism in French or Spanish. There were in the colony 19 French interpreters, 9 Spanish, one German and one Hindustani.

The next few years saw the establishment, under this system, of 30 ward schools, a model school for boys and one for girls as well as a normal school for training of teachers in Port-of-Spain. Of the 30 ward schools, thirteen were the property of the wards – in Laventille, Arima, La Brea, Cedros, Icacos, Mayaro, St Joseph, Couva, Naparima, Iere Village, Indian Walk, Guapo and Arouca. The others together with the model schools in Port-of-Spain were operated in rented buildings in Maraval, Santa Cruz, Maracas, Tacarigua, Victoria Village, Carenage, Diego Martin, San Juan, Caura, Chaguanas, Savonetta, Pointe-a-Pierre, St Madeleine, Canaan Village, Oropouche and Erin.

On February 10, 1869, the Governor, Sir Arthur Gordon, appointed Patrick Keenan to make a diligent and full inquiry into the state of public education, whether secular or religious, in Trinidad. Mr Keenan's report is a devastating criticism of the state of education under the Crown Colony system.

Eighteen years after the establishment of the Board of Education, only thirteen school buildings, as has been indicated, were publicly owned Mr Keenan described 17 of the ward schools as buildings 'which would bring discredit upon any country that recognises civilisation as a principle of Government' Generally speaking, the design of the school buildings had no reference whatever to school purposes. Sanitary facilities were primitive where they were provided at all; some schools were entirely destitute of them. The school furniture was of the rudest kind Keenan found a total lack of 'everything that gives character and tone to a well-worked school in Great Britain or Ireland' Attendance was poor; not more than one pupil in four attended school for 100 days a year.

On the general suitability of the school books in use in Trinidad Keenan commented as follows: —

'The books which I found in use were chiefly the publications of the Irish National Board. For elegance of style; for correctness of information; for acquaintance with the best prose and poetical compositions of the English language; for a general course of useful and interesting knowledge; for the high, manly, and moral tone of the selections; and for the didactic skill exhibited in the arrangement of the lessons, no set of primary school books ever previously published in the English language could surpass, or even equal them But notwithstanding their recognised excellence and reputation, I should desire to see them superseded by a set of books whose lessons would be racy of the colony – descriptive of its history, of its resources, of its trade, of its natural phenomena, of its trees, plants, flowers, fruits, birds, fishes, &c. The pitch lake and the mud volcanoes, for instance, would supply materials for an attractive series of lessons. So would the growth, manufacture, value, and uses of sugar. And so, again, would the cacao, the bois immortelle, the cocoa-nut, the coffee plant, the cotton plant, the cannon-ball tree, the mora, the pine-apple, the mango, the star-apple, the sapodilla, the orange, the shaddock, the cashew, the guava, the plantain, the different varieties of palms, &c. – objects all familiar to the Creole. Interspersed amongst a number of such chapters there might be selections from the prose and poetical extracts in the Irish National school books – local matter forming, say, one-half, and general literature the other half, of each volume of the new series. The books would then possess the same general characteristics as the revised edition of the Irish series. As the Irish element preponderates in the Irish books, so the Trinidad element ought to preponderate in the Trinidad books, which would then be as popular with the Trinidadians as the Irish books are with the people of Ireland. Lord Harris evidently contemplated such a series of books, for in his original instructions to the Board of Education he said – "Still it is my opinion that, on some subjects, books might be written especially adapted to the children of this island." No attempt, I regret to say, has hitherto been made to carry out Lord Harris' views. So far as I have been able to ascertain, the only publication of a local character that has emanated from the Board, or from any of its staff, is a little volume descriptive of the geography of the island, by Mr Fortune, master of the Eastern Market Borough school.'

Mr Keenan recommended the abandonment of state control over education and the introduction of what has come to be called in Trinidad the denominational system. His recommendation was as follows: –

'. . . I propose that the plan now in force of exclusive management on the part of the State shall be abolished; and that, in future, all schools shall be placed under the care of responsible persons having local relation or connexion with the places in which the schools are situated. The person who, in the first instance, applies to establish a school in connexion with the Board of Education should be recognised as the local manager If the applicant be a clergyman, so much the better; because the duties and opportunities of a clergyman peculiarly qualify him for the government of schools. If the applicant be a layman, he should be a person of station or property

'(a) The managers should have the power of appointing the teachers subject, as to character and professional qualifications, to the approval of the Education Board.

'(b) When there is but one school in a locality, the teacher should be of the same religion as the majority of the people of the locality.

'(c) The manager, on his own authority, should have the power of dismissing the teacher without notice, provided he state in writing, to the Board of Education, the grounds of dismissal, and that the Board approve of so extreme a step being taken.

'(d) The manager, should, however, have the power of dismissing the teacher upon a three months' notice without being required to state to the Board of Education his reasons for the dismissal.

'(e) He should have entire control over the use of the schoolhouse, and have the right to employ it for any lawful purpose, before and after school-hours.

'(f) He should have the determination of the religious instruction of the pupils, subject only to the provisions I have already laid down on the subject.

'(g) He should have the right of selecting the books to be used by the pupils.

'(h) He should have the right of fixing the rate of school-fees to be paid by the pupils, provided the Board of Education be satisfied that the fees are not fixed at so high a rate as practically to exclude the poor from the advantages of the school.

'(i) He should have the right of appointing the subjects of instruction, and of arranging the general details of the school business, provided the Board of Education be satisfied that due attention is paid to the cultivation of the essential subjects – reading, writing, arithmetic, and industrial instruction.

'(j) He should have the right to give holidays, vacations, &c. to the masters and pupils, provided the school be kept open for a certain minimum number of days in the year – say 200 . . .

'. . . The great, indeed the only, rule that I would insist upon is that no child should on account of class, creed, or colour be refused admittance to a school aided by the State; and that no child be exposed, directly or indirectly, to the danger of proselytism.'

With respect to secondary education, Lord Harris, in his message, to the Legislative Council in 1847, had said that his education plan 'would be rendered complete by the establishment of a college, to which those scholars who might be found fit might be passed on, so that in fact every encouragement would be given to all, however humble their birth, to place themselves in such a position as their talents and their industry would show them capable of supporting.'

The question of establishing a college remained in abeyance until 1857, when the Board of Council passed the following resolutions:—

1. That in order to place within the reach of the youth of the Colony the opportunity of obtaining a classical education at a moderate charge, there be established in the town of Port-of-Spain, at the public expense, a collegiate school.

2. That such collegiate school be open to students of any religious denomination, and that there be no direct religious teaching, but that attendance at some place of worship be the condition of admittance to, and continuance at, such collegiate school.

3. That for the purpose of encouraging emulation among the

students, there be annual public examinations, and that the two successful candidates for honours at such examinations be entitled to exhibitions, each of £150 for three years, to assist them in prosecuting their studies in Great Britain or Ireland.

4. That such collegiate school be under the superintendence of the Board of Education, and that the Governor with the advice of such Board, have power from time to time to make rules for the government of such collegiate school – such rules to be approved by the Board of Council before they are put in force.

5. That for the purpose of maintaining such collegiate school, there be charged annually on the public funds the sum of £3,000 sterling, and that the income from the fees from students be paid into the Colonial Treasury.

The Queen's Collegiate School was formally inaugurated in 1859 in a rented building. In the first ten years, 206 pupils were admitted, and the school promptly began to concentrate on the Cambridge examinations Less than a fifth of the students in 1869 were coloured, none was black, none was Indian.

The Roman Catholics, who had been operating since 1836 St Joseph's Convent in Port-of-Spain for girls, promptly attacked, in a petition to Queen Victoria, the college and the resolutions on which it was based as 'opposed to the convictions of all Roman Catholics who cannot admit to be beneficial to any system of education which is not founded on religion.' The Roman Catholics kept their children away, and instead, by public subscription, organised a college of their own in 1863 which they entrusted to the Fathers of the Congregation of the Holy Ghost, and which they called the College of the Immaculate Conception.

The conflict between the two philosophies and the results of the two systems were thus indicated by Keenan in his report in 1869: —

'Upon the subject of secondary education, feeling runs high in the colony. There are some who would rank it next to sacrilege to touch a penny, or disturb even a form, of the Queen's Collegiate school. There are others who, if they could, would with a single stroke annihilate it. Similarly, the Catholic College has its champions and its foes . . .

'The first thing likely to strike a person . . . is the strangeness of the fact that whilst the white population, which is only between 5,000 and 6,000, furnishes 142 pupils to the collegiate establishments, the coloured population, which, exclusive of the Coolies, numbers from 60,000 to 70,000, furnishes only 37 pupils. Twenty-four of the coloured pupils are in the Catholic College, and 13 in the Queen's Collegiate School.

'Lord Harris provided, as I have already stated, that every encouragement should be given to all, however humble their birth.

No such encouragement, however, is afforded to the poor in the Queen's Collegiate school, for the high rate of fees effectually bars the door against them; and at the Catholic College the authorities plead that they derive no aid from the State to enable them to give places on moderate terms to the poor.

'The next conclusion which a person reading the reports will probably arrive at, is that the Queen's Collegiate school has not obtained the confidence of the people generally Of the 68 pupils on its rolls, 28 are the sons of members of the Civil Service. This is a large proportion of the whole attendance. The children of the public officers receive a most excellent education, which, however, is mainly paid for by the taxes of the people The Queen's Collegiate school is therefore a great boon to the public servants of the colony. But is the interest of the public servants to be primary and paramount in the consideration of this question?

'In measuring the relative acceptability of the two colleges to the people of the colony, I have to turn to the other classes – the merchants, the planters, and the professional men. And how does the case appear from this point of view?

'At the Queen's Collegiate school there are 14 sons of merchants; at the Catholic College there are 41 At the Queen's Collegiate school there are 13 sons of planters or of proprietors; at the Catholic College there are 41 At the Queen's Collegiate school there are 10 who are the sons of professional men or of others; at the Catholic College the number is 29. The Queen's Collegiate school has 28 sons of members of the public service, exclusive of 3 who are the sons of rectors; whilst the Catholic College has only 6.

'These facts are conclusive. They require no comment. The people flock to the non-endowed college; not because its education is better than that which the Queen's Collegiate school affords, but because the principle of its foundation – the introduction of the religious element – is more acceptable to them.

'In the Queen's Collegiate school there are 17 Catholic pupils – but 8 of them, as the sons of deceased public servants, are receiving a free education. The measure of spontaneous Catholic support given to the Queen's Collegiate school is therefore represented by 9 pupils. From a population of something like 50,000 Catholics, this is a poor expression of confidence or favour.

'At the College of the Immaculate Conception, on the other hand, there are 111 Catholic pupils.'

One of the principal difficulties presented by Keenan's recommendations related to the dominant position of the French language among the Roman Catholics Keenan was at great pains to minimise these difficulties. In respect of his proposal for the introduction of denominational managers, he wrote:

'Some of the priests are unacquainted with English. This is, no doubt, a drawback; for it must be a *sine qua non* that English shall be the language of the schools. I have been assured, however, by the Archbishop that should the Government – as I think it ought, after the lapse of a reasonable time – require the managers to be acquainted with English, that they may be able to conduct the examinations of the schools in English. His Grace would be prepared to enjoin upon the priests the duty of immediately mastering the language. But I should add that the non-English-speaking clergymen are gentlemen of rare intelligence and accomplishments, and bent beyond measure upon promoting the education of the people. That they thoroughly understand the people – their language, their ways, and their faults, is a circumstance which, perhaps, outweighs the temporary inconvenience resulting from the reverend gentlemen's imperfect acquaintance with the English language.'

Of the Roman Catholic College at secondary level and the prominence accorded to French, Keenan had this to say:

'. . . The fact that such prominence is given to French in the system of instruction; that the community who conduct it are a French order; that half the professors are Frenchmen; that nearly half the pupils are the children of French families; and that the discipline and ceremonials of the school are founded upon French models, have all contributed to inspire the designation of the "French College" by which the institution is popularly known. Indeed, the fact that the college is a Catholic college would be quite reason enough to suggest to the people to call it the "French College" just as they call a Catholic church the "French church".

'In an English colony it would seem only natural to expect that a great public school like this, advancing a claim on Governmental consideration for its support, and appealing for the popular favour to its success in turning out intelligent and enterprising citizens, should be conducted on what are recognised as English principles – that is, that the language, the tone, and the social atmosphere of the school should be English. To a certain extent I sympathise with such an expectation. Every person I met with in Trinidad, including His Grace the Archbishop, the leading Catholic clergy, Dr de Verteuil, Mr Farfan, and the professors themselves of the college, sympathised with it. But I cannot close my eyes to the difficulties of – and even the objections to – a sudden metamorphosis I have before me, as I write, the name of every boy in the school, with the nationality of his parents or family.

'Of the 111 boys—

48 belong to French families.
33 „ „ Spanish „
30 „ „ English „

'Would it be rational to attempt to extinguish the instincts of vernacular speech in the vast majority of the children? Would it be philosophical to fail to cultivate the mind, and fill it with stores of knowledge, in the language most natural to it? I do not, therefore, condemn the college because it is so French in its character; nor do I venture to advise the suppression of the French element; but, at the same time, I think that, without being made less French, the college could be made much more English than it is The professors themselves are of this opinion, and have expressed their readiness to act upon it '

The Governor, acting on Keenan's recommendations, proposed to the Legislative Council important modifications to the system established by Lord Harris These involved the provision of State aid for schools established by private persons, on the following conditions:

(1) That the property and control of the schools were vested in a local manager, or managers, having the power (a) to appoint the teacher, provided he or she was duly certified by the Board of Education, (b) to make use of the schoolhouse for any lawful purpose, before and after school hours; (c) to grant holidays and vacations, provided the school was kept open not less than 200 days annually.

(2) That the teacher of the school was duly licensed by the Board of Education.

(3) That the school was open to all children, without distinction of religion or race.

(4) That no child received any religious instruction objected to by the parent or guardian of such child; or was present whilst such instruction is given.

(5) That free access was given, under regulations approved by the Board of Education, to all ministers of religion who might desire to afford religious instruction to children of their own persuasion who were pupils in such schools

(6) That the school was to be, at all times, open to inspection.

(7) That the rules and books used in secular education were subject to the approval of the Board of Education.

(8) That the aid to which such schools were to be entitled should consist of: —

(i) provision for the remuneration of teachers, by (a) a fixed salary dependent upon the possession of a first, second, or third class certificate, obtainable by examination, (b) a capitation grant, paid proportionately to the educational results certified annually by the Inspector of Schools; (c) a capitation grant paid proportionately to the attendance of pupils, certified quarterly by the local manager or managers;

(ii) grants in aid of the erection of buildings and supply of necessaries proportionate to the amount obtained from private sources.

Further modifications were made by the Ordinance of 1875 in the principles governing State aid to denominational primary schools. The new conditions, summarised, were as follows: —

(1) That provision, to the satisfaction of the Board of Education, was made for the control and management of the schools by the local manager or managers.

(2) That the school was open at all times to inspection or examination by the Inspector of Schools, or by any officer appointed by Government for the purpose.

(3) That the average daily attendance at the school, computed on a period of a year, was not less than twenty-five.

Subject to the provisions of the Ordinance, the aid to which any school became entitled consisted of a certain annual capitation grant, according to the results of an annual examination of the school in secular instruction by an Inspector of Schools, such annual capitation grant being at the rate of: —

(i) $4.80 for each pupil passed in the First and Second Standards;

(ii) $6 00 for each pupil passed in the Third and Fourth Standards;

(iii) $7.20 for each pupil passed in the Fifth and Sixth Standards.

At the end of 1880 there were in operation in Trinidad a total of 96 schools – 3 secondary, 2 normal with model schools, 52 government primary schools, and 39 assisted primary schools. There were 332 students in the secondary schools – 80 at the Queen's Collegiate School, 142 at the College of the Immaculate Conception, 110 at St Joseph's Convent. There were 408 pupils in the Model and Normal Schools. The government primary schools had 3,964 pupils, and the assisted schools 3,807 In addition, where were 590 Indian children in estate schools.

In 1889 the Governor, Sir William Robinson, appointed a Committee to consider and report on the working of the education system in Trinidad. The Committee found that very few of Sir Patrick Keenan's suggestions had been implemented, and that Government schools had been fostered and Assisted Denominational Schools discouraged. It laid the whole blame on the Board of Education. More important it attacked the philosophy enunciated by Keenan twenty years before and came out boldly for what was tantamount to the virtual abolition of Government schools. The Committee advocated an educational system based on the following considerations and requirements:

'That the State considers it desirable in the interests of the Commonwealth that the people should be educated.

'That it is the duty of the parent to educate his child, and not that of the State.

'That the State should compel a parent to perform this duty, if neglected, and should pay for the Education of a child on being satisfied that the parent is unable to do so

'That a child should be educated at the cost of the parent and not at the expense of the tax-payer who if he educates his own children has enough to do without having to educate those of others. But in helping to pay for the Education of the poorer classes generally the tax-payer is performing a simple duty and in contributing to assist Education he discharges an obligation imposed in the interests of the common weal.

'That the State in giving effect to the law of compulsion, and in imposing taxation or expending public moneys for purpose of Education, respects the natural rights of the parent to educate his child as he likes, and in providing Education for those unable to pay for it, the State only imposes necessary safeguards to ensure its moneys being properly applied for the purpose.

'That the Education required by the State does not extend beyond reading, writing, and arithmetic, commonly called the three Rs., but the State is willing to assist Education beyond this, in the general interests of the community.

'That in giving assistance the aim is to encourage parents and those interested in the subject, and the latter consist in this Colony almost entirely of Ministers of Religion, to provide their own schools, the conditions of a grant being that a school is properly conducted under certain rules.

'That in places where no schools are provided, the State will establish them on the secular model, but such schools will only be established when there is no prospect of any other school being provided, and withdrawn when any voluntary school is ready to take its place.

'That the influence to be exercised by the State over the schools, in consideration of the Grant, will be directed in encouraging Managers to afford a simple and sound system of Education suitable to the character of the people and their surroundings, advising Managers and Teachers, requiring the Rules to be observed, and seeing that proper results or guarantees are obtained for the moneys granted.

'That it is not practicable to set up any idol of uniformity or national system of Education under the circumstances existing in the Colony, and therefore it seems desirable to rely on parents to discharge their duty towards their children, aiding them and compelling them to perform it in cases of neglect, and to trust to the assistance of religion to aid in disciplining the minds and morals of the children.'

Mr Justice Lumb, a member of the Committee, disagreed sharply. He advocated the retention of the dual system·—

'. . . The strongest objection to the above Report is, that its main effect would result in the complete extinction of Government Schools with the substitution of Assisted Schools only. This is the thread that runs through the whole fabric . . . and is in distinct opposition to the first two principles agreed upon by the Committee on the 12th December, 1887 . . . Being strongly in favour of both systems of Education working side by side in such a heterogeneously composed population, in my opinion, to destroy either one would be a huge, lamentable, dangerous and unjust mistake.

'Whatever scheme is adopted, it is undesirable that it should be for the benefit of one portion only of the community, on the contrary it should be in accordance with the time-tried principle – the greatest good for the greatest number – and without the moral power of public confidence behind it, it will be certain to end in disaster and failure.'

As always under the Crown Colony system, the ball was passed to the Secretary of State for the Colonies. Lord Knutsford gave his ruling in a despatch to Sir William Robinson on November 27, 1889:

'I have come to the conclusion that I should not be justified in assenting to the abolition of the system of Grants-in-Aid to Denominational Schools and a return to the system of purely secular Schools maintained by the Government, which is advocated by the representatives of Protestant denominations in their Memorial of August last, as to which it is to be observed that, as Sir P. Keenan has pointed out, the opinion of the Memorialists has undergone a very recent change, but that the system of Government Schools and Assisted Schools working side by side must be continued . . .

'It is of the first importance that the Board of Education should actively fulfil its duties. It is clear that much of the present evil has arisen from the Board's neglect of its proper functions, and I cannot acquit successive Governors, who have been *ex-officio* Presidents of the Board and Members of the Executive Committee, of large responsibility for the present disorganisation of the Education system. Your action in suspending the operations of the Board for two years pending the recent enquiry, appears to me to have been of questionable validity, and you should, if you thought such action necessary, have obtained authority for it by a special Ordinance . . .

'One of the most difficult questions, in connection with the Public Education and one which was most hotly contested before the recent Royal Commission on Elementary Education in this country, turns upon the point whether a new Assisted School or Schools should be allowed to be established in the near neighbourhood of an existing Government School. I am not disposed in this matter to approve of the enforcement of the absolute rule expressed in the 8th condition of the draft Ordinance, but I would leave it to the Board to decide in each case. They must be trusted not to permit the waste of public money by allowing a number of small rival schools to be started . . .

'I am of opinion that a Government School should not be established in any particular District where the Board is satisfied that sufficient accommodation is provided, or will within a reasonable time be provided, by an Assisted School or Schools fulfilling the conditions which will be required by the new Law . . .

'Children whose parents are unable to pay School fees, and children of indentured Indian Immigrants should be admitted to Government or Assisted Schools free of charge, but I agree with you in thinking that the time has not arrived for making education either compulsory or gratuitous, and that except when inability to pay is proved to the satisfaction of the School managers, fees at such reduced scale as may be thought advisable should be retained, and their payment enforced by the Wardens

'Children of indentured Immigrants should be educated gratuitously and, if necessary, special Government Schools should be established for Indians . . .

'If a sufficient supply of qualified Indian teachers cannot be obtained in the Colony, the question of importing some from India should be considered.

'I cannot agree in your view that teachers in Assisted Schools (or even in Government Schools) should be treated as public servants for pension purposes, but I incline to approve Mr Lumb's scheme for a Superannuation Fund to be formed by deduction from salaries.

'The model Schools in Port-of-Spain should be abolished or converted into Industrial or Training Schools.

'The greatest defect in the system of elementary education in Trinidad, as in other West Indian Colonies is the want of properly trained teachers. Mr Lumb's Bill and draft Rules contain sufficient provisions for a Government training School, and I think that one such institution will be enough. It would however be inconsistent, under a system of assisted denominational Schools to require all teachers to pass through a Government undenominational School, and some provision should be made for the recognition of other training Schools.'

In 1895 a Commission was appointed to enquire into the question of free and compulsory education in the primary schools of Trinidad. The Commission recommended that primary education should be made free, and that the Assisted Schools should receive, by way of compensation for the loss of school fees, a payment of $1 80 a year for each child in average attendance. It recommended further that education should be compulsory for children from the ages of six to ten, that Local Attendance Committees should be established in each town, ward, or school district, the duties of Attendance Committee Officer being executed by the Sanitary Inspectors in the towns and the Ward Officers in the ward on the basis of some addition to their substantive salaries. One member of the Committee, Canon Trotter, advocated the introduction, simultaneously, of free and compulsory education in the entire island.

This was the Crown Colony system of education in a colony that was twice as wealthy, from the revenue point of view, as Jamaica or Barbados, and which had been able, for half a century before 1900, to finance the introduction of indentured Indian immigrants partly at public expense, purely for the benefit of the sugar planters. The Government's expenditure in 1896 on immigration and other aids for the sugar industry – medical department, police, jails, railway – represented approximately 40 per cent of the total expenditure. Expenditure on police and prisons alone was one-half larger than the expenditure on education.

The worst victims of colonialism in this respect were the children of the indentured immigrants. Until the arrival of the Canadian Mission to the Indians in the 1860's, no attention was paid to them at all, and they boycotted the ward schools set up by Lord Harris. Rev. Morton, at the time Presbyterian Minister of Iere Village, pleaded with Keenan for the establishment of schools in the sugar areas. Keenan himself commented on this aspect of the education system of the colony: —

'The Government has exhibited a paternal solicitude for the physical wants and comforts of the indentured class of Asiatic immigrants; it has required that hospitals shall be provided for them on the estates; that medical attendance shall be every week at their service; and even – in compliance with an Ordinance passed during my stay in the colony – that cooked food shall be provided for them during the first six months after their allotment to an estate. But the solicitude of the State ended here. The moral and intellectual necessities were overlooked. The Coolie's mind was left a blank. No effort was made to induce him, through the awakening intelligence and dawning prospects of his children, to associate the fortune or the future of his family with the colony. It is therefore that – collaterally, and I believe legitimately – I connect the magnitude of the periodical exodus of the Asiatics with the educational system, which fails to provide for their children acceptable schools. I cannot call to mind any other case of a people who, having voluntarily come to a strange land which they enriched by their labour, were – morally and intellectually – so completely neglected as the Coolies have been during the past twenty-four years . . .

'I would recommend that the proprietors of estates should be encouraged to open schools for the special accommodation of Coolie children. As regards salaries, religious instruction, &c., I would treat such schools in exactly the same way as the ordinary schools. The two fundamental principles characteristic of the proposed system of public education should be strictly applied to the Coolie schools, viz. (1) they should be open to all comers, and (2) all comers should be protected from even the suspicion of proselytism. If the observance of these fundamental rules were guaranteed, the Coolie might then be safely entrusted with the secular and religious training of the children of his own caste.'

The whole emphasis, therefore, was on separation and division of the two major racial groups, in much the same way as the Government of the day, in 1890, prescribed separate latrine accommodation for Negroes and Indians on the sugar plantations. Rev. R. H. Moor, who established an Anglican School in Belmont in 1888, endeavoured to set up a separate school in Belmont for some 30 or 40 children of Indian labourers, in addition to the separate schools he had established in Peru Village, Rose Hill, Phoenix Park, Cedros and Columbia, two miles from Cedros. Rev. Moor justified the racial separation as follows:

'In my Mission Report for 1887–88 I gave it as my emphatic opinion and this opinion is being strengthened every day, that a mixed school, i e. for Creoles and Indians will be a mistake. An Indian will not send his child to a Creole school He is afraid of injustice being done his child from the Creole teacher, and of ill-usage from the Creole pupils. The Creole, as a rule, looks down on the Indian: he is a semi-civilised being, he speaks a barbarous language, and his manners are barbarous. He comes to Trinidad to make money for there is no money in his own country, so he thinks. He takes work cheaper than the Creole will do, hence he must be ill-treated where he can be ill-treated with impunity.'

The grim reality of the Crown Colony system, in so far as education was concerned, was revealed in the evidence of two sugar planters, Mr E. A. Robinson and Mr C. Knox, in evidence before a Select Committee of the Legislative Council appointed in 1926 to 'enquire whether it is desirable to introduce legislation to fix or restrict the hours of labour in any particular trade, business or industry in the Colony'. The Committee included two of the first elected members in the Legislature of Trinidad and Tobago, Capt. Cipriani and Mr A. V. Stollmeyer. L. A. P O'Reilly, a nominated unofficial, was also a member of the Committee.

Here is the evidence of Mr E. A. Robinson:

'Mr O'Reilly: With regard to children?

'Mr R.: We have none in the factory, but 120 work outside. They are from 10 years of age up to 20; they work from 7 a m. to 5 p.m.

'Mr O'Reilly: Do you think it is satisfactory to have a child of 10 working that number of hours?

'Mr R.: This is an agricultural country. Unless you put the children on to working in the fields when they are young, you will never get them to do so later. If you want to turn all these people into a lot of clerks, caneweighers, and people of that sort, all you have to do is to prevent them working in the fields until they are 16 years old; then I guarantee you will have but very few labourers in the Colony, but if you train them to work in the fields you will never have any difficulty.

'Mr O'Reilly: You agree that the present system shuts them off from education?

'Mr R.: They are well-fed!

'Mr O'Reilly: I am talking of their education. If they are educated they won't want to be labourers?

'Mr R.: No. Give them some education in the way of reading and writing, but no more. Even then I would say educate only the bright ones; not the whole mass. If you do educate the whole mass of the agricultural population, you will be deliberately ruining the country.

'Mr O'Reilly: From the health point of view, is it satisfactory to have children working for such long hours?

'Mr R.: I cannot tell you, except that physically they are far better off than the children who idle in the street.

'Mr O'Reilly: Are they doing regular work during their hours of labour?

'Mr R : Yes; but they are working in the open air, not in a stuffy factory Even then they do not work when it rains. They are accustomed to the sun, which does not hurt them; they do not physically suffer at all

'Mr Stollmeyer: What do you say to the suggestion that they are cheaper to employ than adults?

'Mr R.: I do not say so at all, but if you did not employ them, I am certain there would not be enough labourers. They are paid quite in proportion. They get about 20 cents a day . . .

'Mr Cipriani: You say that all the children should be sent to work in the fields and not sent to school?

'Mr R.: Not all: give the bright ones a chance to win as many scholarships as they can; give the others 3 hours education a day.

'Mr O'Reilly : You do not suggest that you could, by giving a child 3 hours' education a day make it proficient at the age of 10 years? My view was that a convenient age would be 12.

'Mr R.: I have no objection to 12; but if you keep them longer you will never get them to work in the fields.

'Mr O'Reilly: You would not object to a maximum of 12 years?

'Mr R.: No; but if you want agricultural labourers and not dissatisfaction, you must not keep them longer.'

Mr Robinson was followed by Mr Knox, whose evidence in relation to child labour was as follows:

'Mr O'Reilly: Do you think it is satisfactory to employ children under 12?

'Mr K.: What are you going to do with them?

'Mr O'Reilly: Send them to school.

'Mr K.: They prefer to work in the fields.

'Mr O'Reilly: You suggest that a child should go to work before 10?

'Mr K.: They should go as soon as they are able to work, as long as this is an agricultural country.

'Mr O'Reilly: A child of 10 would not get very proficient even before 12, in the normal way, so don't you think it would be more satisfactory to say that a child under 12 should be sent to school?

'Mr K.: It would be of no use to them.

'Mr O'Reilly: Then they are to be without any education at all?

'Mr K.: As long as this is an agricultural country. Personally I prefer to deal with adults because they have more experience.

'Mr O'Reilly: Well, if that is so, why don't you?

'Mr Fraser: Mr Knox means that if children were not employed now, there would not be enough agricultural labourers in years to come.

'Mr K.: I will say 12 if you like; there's not much difference.

'Mr O'Reilly: I think there is.

'Mr K.: Of what use will education be to them if they had it?

'Mr Fraser: They would be better citizens.'

The Crown Colony system was based on sugar workers and needed only sugar workers. It did not need citizens. If Trinidad aspired to citizens instead of sugar workers, it necessarily had to achieve the destruction of the Crown Colony system That was the object of the movement for self-government which moved into a new phase at the end of World War I

CHAPTER 15

The Movement for Self-Government, 1921 to 1956

By the end of the First World War three decisive changes had taken place in Trinidad.

The first was the discovery of oil in commercial quantities in 1910. Trinidad, producing sugar which was of no interest to the British Board of Trade, became an oil colony of enormous importance to the British Admiralty. The output of crude oil increased from 125,112 barrels in 1910 to 2,083,027 barrels in 1920.

The second decisive change that took place in Trinidad was the abolition of the indentured system of Indian labour, based very largely on the opposition of the nationalist movement in India. On March 20, 1916, Pandit Mohan Malaviya moved in the Indian Legislative Council that 'early steps be taken for the abolition of the system of Indian indentured labour'. This motion reflected the persistent agitation that was going on throughout India for the immediate abolition of recruiting for indentured labour. At mass meetings held in all the great centres of population the indentured system was attacked on the ground that it was based on fraudulent statements made by the recruiter and that the direct result of the system was the slavery of the men and the prostitution of the women. The agitation was also based on the superior opportunities available in India itself for employment as compared with the low wages paid in the colonies The Viceroy himself, Lord Hardinge, gave expression to this point of view in his speech before the Indian Legislative Council on March 20, 1916:

> 'Why should the labourer have to journey thousands of miles over the "black water" to settle in a strange country and to place himself for a long period under conditions often of an undesirable, and in some cases of a revolting nature in order to achieve the desired end, when he can obtain in India the choice of either better paid labour, as for instance, in the big jute areas of Eastern Bengal, or almost equally well paid labour with the prospects of obtaining in a very few years a home and a piece of land on the Assam tea gardens? It seems rather absurd to find a man going to Fiji for a wage of 26/- a month with rice at 2½ seers to the rupee, when he can readily earn 6/- or 7/- a week during the jute season in Eastern Bengal with rice selling at a third of the price prevailing in Fiji, with the additional advantage that he can, if he likes, with far greater ease, take his family with him to add to his earnings than in the case of distant Colonies. It is clear then that the cooly himself does not stand to gain much by emigration.'

In Trinidad itself the system was on its last legs. In 1915 there were in Trinidad 8,827 Indians not indentured as compared with a total Indian population in the 1911 Census of 121,895 Indians who had completed their indenture. These Indians had 90,314 acres under cultivation – of these 56,414 were in cocoa; 9,698 in ground provisions; 9,488 in rice; 9,368 in sugar-cane; 3,081 in corn; 1,740 in coconuts; 408 in coffee; 117 in fruits

The third change that came over Trinidad in the war years was the emergence of the working class movement, assisted quite accidentally by the overseas service of the British West Indian Regiment. The Regiment won no startling successes and achieved no startling acclaim except in so far as the Secretary of State for the Colonies was able to advise the Governor on August 30, 1917 that the West Indian boys stationed in Egypt had developed good fellowship with the Australians, New Zealanders and men from all parts of the Empire, had shown their prowess at cricket and sports, and at two athletic meetings had carried all before them. Apart from this, the West Indian boys did their marching behind the lines and were put to patrol the railway and pipe lines; on one occasion, when a hostile aeroplane landed behind the lines in an endeavour to destroy the railway, the enemy was engaged by a patrol of the British West Indian Regiment, and pilot and passenger were obliged hurriedly to return to their plane leaving their explosives behind them.

But the West Indian soldiers brought back explosives of their own to the British West Indies, principally Captain Arthur Andrew Cipriani, who on his return was asked to revive the Trinidad Working Men's Association. Thus did Cipriani enter politics in Trinidad, ultimately forming the Trinidad Labour Party with a programme of socialism, in close communication with the British Labour Party.

The discovery of oil, the abolition of indentured servitude, and the organisation of the Trinidad Labour Party formed the background to an intensification of the demand for constitution reform at the end of the war The movement was West Indian in scope and not limited to Trinidad. The British Government sent out the Parliamentary Under-Secretary of State for the Colonies, the Honourable E. F. L. Wood, on a visit to the West Indies and British Guiana.

By the time Major Wood reached Trinidad, he found two fundamental changes in the situation which Froude and Joseph Chamberlain had encountered in the previous quarter of a century. In 1887 and 1903, the principal advocates for constitution reform were members of the upper class, planters, merchants, white or coloured, but some of them, progressive in their thinking, demanded votes for Indians and the extension of the Municipal franchise in Port-of-Spain. In 1887 and in 1903 the movement for constitution reform was as national in scope as any movement in the Crown Colony period could be national.

Major Wood encountered a totally different situation. The principal opponents of any change in the constitution were the Trinidad Chamber of Commerce who, in their representations to Major Wood, regarded the demand for constitution reform as largely inspired by movements external to the colony; and they pointed, just as Chamberlain had done in 1903, to the prosperity of Trinidad under its existing form of government which, in their view, afforded adequate representation to every interest. These were the very people who had taken the most prominent part in the agitation against the Crown Colony system which led to the Water Riots of 1903. The Agricultural Society was also not in favour of changing the existing form of government. In 1903 it was Joseph Chamberlain, the Secretary of State for the Colonies, who stated that the Crown Colony system was the best form of government for Trinidad. In 1889 Thomas, in attacking Froude, had emphasised the respectability and the status of the commercial and agricultural advocates for constitution reform. In 1921 it was the commercial and agricultural interests in Trinidad, some of the very people who had objected to the suspension of the Port-of-Spain Municipality in 1898, who were echoing Joseph Chamberlain's words and agreeing that the Crown Colony system of government was the best for Trinidad.

In 1889 before the Royal Franchise Commission, in so far as it was possible for the two major racial groups submerged by the Crown Colony System to express an opinion, both Negroes and Indians supported the demand for constitution reform. By 1921 Major Wood encountered a division between Negro and Indian as well as a split in the Indian ranks. One group, the East Indian National Congress, advocated communal representation of the Indian community as one group, on the ground that otherwise there was a danger of their being outvoted, As Major Wood wrote:

'They claimed that religious differences in the East Indian population did not create any political issue in the Colony between the Christian, Hindu, and Mohammedan, and could not fairly be adduced as a reason for refusing separate representation to them as a race. They recommended that everyone who paid direct taxes, however small, should exercise the franchise. They were opposed to any educational test, which they did not consider would be required if proof of payment of taxes was given. They agreed, however, that if any test were to be imposed, it would meet their wishes if literacy in any language were regarded as adequate. They would have no objection to the representation of particular industries.'

The other section of the Indian community was represented by a deputation of Indians who opposed any change in the Crown Colony system, and claimed that the system of nomination was a good one because it permitted representation for the various and widely differing nationalities which comprised the colony of Trinidad and Tobago Their views as stated by Major Wood were as follows:

'The chief reason for their opposition was the fact that the complete substitution of election for nomination might operate to the disadvantage of the East Indian community and deprive them of the only representative whom they now had in the Council. They asked that this representation on the Legislative Council should be increased. In their view, the fact that East Indians were not in a position to return members under the representative system was ultimately due to the lack of educational facilities available for the East Indian community, for which they could not be blamed. It was not, therefore, reasonable to expect the East Indian community to be properly represented in proportion to its members. They were asked if they would have the same anxiety as to the prejudicial effect of a system of election if any literacy test imposed were not confined to English. They admitted that their position would be improved, but this would not remove their objections to any change. They stated that the advocates of communal representation were few, that their deputation represented the chief section of the East Indians, and that the wealthiest and best-educated East Indians were among them. Most of their supporters belonged to San Fernando and the southern district of the Colony.'

The principal advocates of constitution reform were the Trinidad Working Men's Association. It proposed an income qualification for a voter of $20.00 a month or payment of an annual rent of $96.00, and qualifications for membership of the Legislative Council of an income of $100.00 a month or a capital of $2,400.

Major Wood's recommendations were not in any sense revolutionary He opposed responsible government and did not consider that such a demand could rightly be considered 'within measurable distance of time'. In his view four principal factors militated against it: the mixed character of the population and the backwardness of large sections; the absence of a leisured class, independent of local ties; the necessity of the Secretary of State to retain the controlling influence in order to secure uniformity of administration among the adjacent colonies; and the small proportion of the electorate who in fact exercised the franchise in those colonies with representative government. He emphasised also:

'The risk, which is no small one, that the only effect of granting responsible government might be to entrench in power a financial oligarchy, which would entirely dominate the Colony and use their power for the sole purpose of benefiting one class instead of the community as a whole.'

The new Legislative Council as recommended by Major Wood included 26 members. The unofficial side of the Council was increased from 11 to 13, seven of whom were to be elected and six nominated. The official members of the Council were increased in number from 10 to 12, whilst the Governor retained his original and his casting vote to ensure an official majority.

Major Wood rejected the communal system of representation. His views on this matter are important for the subsequent constitutional and political history of Trinidad and Tobago. They are as follows:

'It will be seen from the above that I have not adopted the system of the election of members by particular interests or any system of communal representation. We came to the conclusion that the objections to the first were insuperable on the ground of the difficulties of determining what the constituency would be and of drawing the line between bodies which should, or should not, be represented. Moreover, the concession would not satisfy those who are clamouring for a change. As regards communal representation, apart from the objection that this arrangement would be opposed by the chief advocates of constitution change, there would again be great difficulty in deciding what the constituencies were to be, and, moreover, it would accentuate and perpetuate the differences which, in order to produce a homogeneous community, it should be the object of statesmanship to remove. The East Indians are an important element in the community, and it would be a great misfortune if they were encouraged to stand aside from the main current of political life instead of sharing in it and assisting to guide its course Finally, if a concession of this kind were granted to the East Indians, there would be no logical reason for withholding it from persons of French, Spanish or Chinese descent, a situation which would become impossible. By retaining the system of nomination by the Crown, it will always be possible to secure representatives on the Council of races or important interests not otherwise adequately represented by direct election.'

Thus, for the first time since 1797, for the first time in 128 years of British rule, the people of Trinidad and Tobago, in a limited number had the right to elect a small proportion of their own representatives. The limitations seem almost ludicrous 40 years later. In accordance with the recommendations of the Franchise Commission appointed to work out the details of Major Wood's recommendations, candidates for election to the Legislative Council were required to own real estate of a minimum value of $12,000 or from which they derived an annual income of $960; alternatively they were required to have an income of over $1,920 per annum from any source. Candidates must have resided in their constituency for one year or own there real estate of $24,000 in value or from which they derived an annual income of $1,920. Only male candidates able to read and write English were eligible for election. Members of the Council were unpaid, although a subsistence allowance of $5.00 was granted to the elected member for Tobago when attending meetings of the Council; not until 1939 did unofficial members of the Council receive payment at the rate of $720 per year, which was increased to $1,800 in 1947 and again to $3,840 in 1949.

The franchise was limited by high property and income qualifications – occupation as owner for one year of property of $60 rateable value in a borough or $48 elsewhere; occupation as tenant paying $60 per month rent in a borough or $48 elsewhere; or payment as a lodger for one year of $60 rent or $300 rent and board combined; or occupation as owner or tenant under agreement of property paying at least $2 40 per annum land tax; or annual salary of $300.00. The age limit was 21 years in the case of male voters and 30 years in the case of female voters, and voters were required to understand spoken English. Any one who had received poor relief within six months before the date of his registration as a voter was disqualified from voting

If this was the representative system after 128 years of British rule, it was certainly the representative system with a difference. It was the domination of property and wealth, influenced by Wood's emphasis on taking no action which would disturb the confidence felt by outside capital in the stability of the government.

Thus did Trinidad and Tobago come to its first election on February 7, 1925 The seven constituencies were Port-of-Spain, the County of St George including the town of Arima, the County of Caroni, the County of Victoria including the town of San Fernando, the County of St Patrick, the Eastern Counties, and Tobago. In a total population of 364,828, the number of registered voters was 21,794, 6% of the total population. Two of the seats, Victoria and the Eastern Counties, were uncontested. For the other five seats, with a total population of 244,551, there were 15,632 registered voters, of whom 6,832 voted.

But it was the first election in Trinidad – there had been elections in the 19th century in Tobago. The election has been made famous in Trinidad calypso: 'Who you voting for? Cipriani.'

The composition of the Legislative Council which Cipriani entered did not permit the implementation of any socialist programme. The Governor, as the Queen's representative, was in complete charge and he presided over the Council. To criticise the Government was in fact to criticise the Queen's representative. It was difficult for him to be impartial, or even to appear to be impartial, in debates. He could always count on the votes of his nominated official members in law, and on the votes of his nominated unofficial members in fact. One of the latter, Sir Lennox O'Reilly, once protested vigorously, on March 6, 1931, against the insinuation that he was a government stooge and he would either have to obey instructions of the Governor or quit his seat, as Cipriani taunted. O'Reilly stated:

'Nothing of the kind! The day a Governor tells me that, he can have my resignation . . . I could not of course accept nomination at the hands of the Government if I did not in my humble way approve the general policy of the Government. That is as far as it goes. It has been said over and over again by us and by Government that under our constitution we, nominated members of this House, are entitled to express our views and not the views of

Government . . . We are not, it is true, in direct touch with the people, because under our constitution we have not yet attained that stage of political development when the legislators fully represent the people. We are in the position of trustees, to see that justice is done to all sections of the community.'

But all Trinidad knew what happened to another nominated unofficial member, Sir Gaston Johnston, who, as a Roman Catholic, voted against the divorce bill. Sir Gaston made heroic efforts to reconcile his conflicting loyalties to the Government and to his Church, and to render unto Caesar the things that are Caesar's and to God the things that are God's. He failed. He was not renominated, and everyone knew that he was not renominated because he had voted against the Government

In addition the Legislative Council, with its minority of elected members was nothing more than a debating assembly, and the Government took the view that the elected members were there to express their views and not to oppose the Government. Sir Selwyn Grier, when he was acting Governor, expressed on November 29, 1929, the following conception of the functions of the Council:

'May I say that I look upon this . . . as a deliberative Council, one in which there will be sincere differences of opinion and in which the general discussion of our difficulties may lead to definite progress . . . As far as this Council is concerned I would ask honourable members that where there are definite differences of opinion they should be discussed on both sides in a calm spirit and that as far as possible we should avoid making assertions which cannot in my opinion promote real progress in our discussions.'

On another occasion, on April 21, 1933, when one of the elected members accused certain Government contractors of dishonest practices, Grier developed his conception of the role of the elected member in the Crown Colony legislature. He stated:

'What I feel very strongly, is that it is the manifest duty of honourable members, when definite instances of dishonesty come to their notice, to bring them to the notice of Government so that an investigation can be held, rather than to make them the means of attacking the Government in the Legislative Council . . . I would suggest that we ought to regard ourselves as a deliberative assembly gathered together for the purpose of considering constructive proposals for the general good of the community.'

Cipriani was not impressed. He considered it his duty to attack or censure the Government whenever the opportunity presented itself.

In this he was expressing his own opinion and not that of his elected colleagues. One of them, T. M. Kelshall, was particularly careful to repudiate Cipriani's view in a speech of April 27, 1925, as follows:

'The idea seems to be gaining ground that some of us on this side of the House are *de facto* in opposition . . . I am not a member of the Opposition; I am proud to be a member of the Government on the Unofficial side.'

Cipriani operated through three forums – (a) the Legislative Council; (b) the Port-of-Spain City Council, of which he was a member continuously from 1926 to 1941 and earned the distinction of serving as Mayor eight times, a record in the Council's history; (c) the organ of the Trinidad Labour Party, *The Socialist*, the first issue of which appeared in October 1935.

The greatest value of his membership of the Legislative Council to him was that what he said there was privileged He once explained to Sir Murchison Fletcher on November 6, 1936, that

'The only place where I can say anything which is privileged is in the Legislative Council. If I dare say anything outside, I am liable to be brought up under the libel laws of the Colony and to find Government and the police taking part in my prosecution, so that this is the only place where I can really make representation.'

The Governor contradicted Cipriani and asserted that the law of libel did run in the Council. Worse than this, the same Governor once threatened him with prosecution and referred his speech to the Attorney General. Cipriani was in 1938 making his annual speech in opposition to the local volunteer force, specifically against the expenditure of $40,000 on rifles and ammunition. After being called to order by the Governor, Cipriani continued:

'We have in this Colony too long been accustomed to be ruled by an employer Government, and I have no doubt, Sir, that as long as that Government is Tory or Conservative – call it which you will – still it is employer, and as long as employees in this country are the friends, the relations and the wire-pullers of the Colonial Office, that condition of affairs will remain here. It is the arming of class against class and the depriving of that section of the community, whose inalienable right it is to live, to live in the country of his birth or adoption.

'I, Sir, will not today or ever will agree to the expenditure of any more taxpayers' money in the purchase of rifles or ammunition.'

The Governor, Sir Murchison Fletcher, at once intervened to say:

'The Colony has received full warning that Government will not tolerate propaganda which is calculated to set class against class and which is subversive of law and order There is no privilege in this House. The Member for Port-of-Spain rose to tell us that we are buying rifles to set class against class. I refer the matter to the Honourable Attorney General.'

The Socialist claimed that it was this speech which culminated in the dismissal of Sir Murchison Fletcher. Possibly the Governor thought better of it, but in any case Cipriani was not arrested or prosecuted.

Cipriani was the only member, in the early years of the Council, to identify himself solely with labour. He agitated for old age pensions, minimum wages, against the employment in the colony of persons from abroad, particularly South Africans and Americans, and against the nomination system.

The limitations imposed on him by the composition of the Legislative Council led Cipriani to use his City Council forum as the centre of opposition to colonialism. In doing this he sought to extend the sphere of municipal government to an extent perhaps that could not really have been justified. It was Cipriani in the Port-of-Spain City Council for example, who fought the Crown Colony government on the question of the electricity franchise in Port-of-Spain.

A foreign company, the Trinidad Electric Company, had been given the monopoly of electric lighting and tramway services in Port-of-Spain and its environs in 1901 for 30 years, with the proviso that if the Company applied for an extension of its rights at any time within one year before it expired, the Governor-in-Council might extend the Company's rights for a further 20 years, but that should the application be refused, the Governor-in-Council should purchase the Company's undertakings. When the question of the extension of the Company's franchise came up in 1930. The Company adopted the strange attitude that it had perpetual rights and intended to file an action to have a declaration of these rights. The Company's claim was rejected by the Supreme Court of the Colony and the Company appealed to the Privy Council in England. The Port-of-Spain City Council protested against an assurance given by the Governor to the Company that it could continue to operate the service pending the Privy Council's decision. The Port-of-Spain City Council claimed the right to take over the Company's undertaking, which it eventually did, though the Government reserved the right itself to assume control over the extension of electricity to other parts of the country outside Port-of-Spain.

Cipriani and the Port-of-Spain City Council also took the lead in the attempt to take over the telephone undertaking from private enterprise, and it was against Cipriani's protest that the Ordinance of 1939 was passed giving a private Company the right to operate the telephone system under very favourable conditions which were not altered until the Company's undertaking was acquired by the Government of Trinidad and Tobago in 1960, at a cost of some $13 million, in accordance with the formula for purchase prescribed by the Ordinance of 1939.

Outside of the Legislative Council and the Port-of-Spain City Council, Cipriani was the leader of the Trinidad Labour Party and a prominent writer in *The Socialist*. Through *The Socialist* Cipriani's speeches in the Legislative Council were made available to the Trinidad working classes, as well as Cipriani's international contacts, particularly with the British Trade Union movement and the British Labour Party. Some idea may be gained of the attitude of the Trinidad Labour Party to colonialism from an article in *The Socialist* in July 1938, opposing the West Indies Royal Commission appointed in that year:

'The people of these small countries are just about fed-up with Commissions and the manner and methods employed by them in the taking of evidence and carrying out of their jobs which to them merely appears to be out to deceive and to evade the important issues which mean so much to them with a view to appease and smooth things over by a process of make-believe and the employment of the played-out and time-worn policy of Marchand de promesses and manana.'

Cipriani claimed at that time a membership of 120,000 in the Trinidad Labour Party or nearly one-third of the whole population. He stated also that the Party had 126 affiliated sections, comprising every type of worker, both male and female.

Cipriani, himself a white man of Corsican descent, was completely devoid of racial antipathy and prejudices. From the very outset he worked easily with prominent Indians in the political sphere. The first issue of *The Socialist* carried an article by C. B. Mathura, 'Why should Indians and Negroes Unite,' in which Mathura stated:

'I have been called a political agitator and a foolish one, because of my desire to awaken the political consciousness of the East Indians, and to get them to join the Trinidad Labour Party, the only Political Organization in the West Indies'

Another Indian leader, Rienzi, before he joined the Civil Service, had assisted Cipriani in the formation of the Trinidad Working Men's Association, organised a San Fernando Branch of the Association, and in 1924 became President of the Branch and the Association's chief organiser for southern Trinidad

In the Legislative Council Cipriani also formed a loose alliance with two Indian members of the Council, Teelucksingh and Roodal, both of whom were Vice Presidents of the Trinidad Working Men's Association. On Cipriani's death in 1945, Roodal became head of the Trinidad Labour Party, the name which the Association had adopted in 1932. With these Indian colleagues Cipriani brought into the working class movement a substantial section of the Indian working class, giving to the Trinidad movement for self-government an inter-racial solidarity which augured well for the future.

Cipriani deserves in full measure the esteem in which he has been held by large sections of the population of Trinidad, and was justly honoured a few years ago by a statue erected to him by the Port-of-Spain City Council in the very centre of Marine Square facing Frederick Street which the Port-of-Spain City Council has decided to rename 'Independence Square.' But by 1938 the leadership of the working class, both political and in the trade union field, had passed into other hands.

This was the result of the economic development of the country in the two decades after World War I, in respect of the colony's two principal industries, oil and sugar.

In 1927 the Governor of Trinidad and Tobago appointed Sir Thomas Holland to make a survey of the oil industry, the particular problems referred to him for investigation being:

(1) the development policy designed to promote the maximum and most efficient exploitation of the Island's oil resources without impairing the Crown's policy of leasing oil in its own possession only to interests under British control;

(2) the taxation of oil;

(3) compensation for surface rights;

(4) the organisation of the Mines Department of the Colony.

In that year, 1927, Trinidad's oil production had attained the figure of 5,380,178 barrels, more than $2\frac{1}{2}$ times the production in 1920. Holland's report, which was laid before the Legislative Council on October 19, 1928, made two points of great significance for the future of the oil industry. The first was this: 'compared with the term granted in most countries, there is no doubt about the leniency of the royalty rates hitherto demanded by the Government in Trinidad.'

The second point stemmed from a debate in the Legislative Council on April 9, 1926, when the following resolution was adopted:

'That the Government be pleased to take steps to consider in what way additional revenue can be derived from the oil industry.'

On this matter Sir Thomas Holland wrote as follows in his report:

'During my stay in the Colony I have received views from various sources, firstly regarding the justification for increased taxation, and secondly regarding the methods by which additional revenues from the industry might be obtained. During the discussion on this resolution expression was given to what appears to be, from the evidence that I have obtained, a prevalent impression in Trinidad, namely, that oil working displaces and in other ways injures the staple agricultural and planting industries, without contributing from its profits a sufficient compensation by way of revenue. The form of additional taxation most commonly proposed is an export duty, on oil and its products.

'The impressions referred to appear to have grown, without close analysis of the facts; they are, however, worth critical examination, although it is beyond my province to discuss the merits of the more extreme assertions made to the effect that, in displacing locally the planting industry, the development of the oil-fields is economically a drawback rather then an advantage to the Colony. Obviously, it adds to the stability of the community to increase its variety of industries instead of remaining dependent on one type which is seriously affected by secular variations of the climate; but the intrusion of a new industry on any substantial scale naturally disturbs the equilibrium of the local complex, and complaints are therefore not unexpected I assume, however, that any questions of taxation are to be considered only on the assumption that the development of the oil resources is definitely accepted to be the public interests, and my observations are limited therefore to the problem of obtaining for the State a fair share of compensation for the inevitable depletion of a wasting asset, without, at the same time, discouraging the inflow of capital or forcing the established leaseholders to limit their activities to the high-grade parts of the field.'

The second development affected the sugar industry. In 1929, as in 1897, the British West Indian sugar industry was bankrupt and was faced with almost total extinction. The explanation, in 1929 as in 1897, was world over-production and the consequent low prices. Whilst all producers suffered more or less from this, the position of the British West Indian producer was aggravated by the fact that he received only a small tariff protection of 89 cents per cwt. in the British market. The 1897 Royal Commission had indicated that Britain would do nothing and had made, with the exception of the recommendation about peasant land settlements, insignificant recommendations. So in 1929 the British Government sent out another Commission to make another investigation and to make other recommendations.

The situation that faced the Commission of 1929 was very straightforward The world surplus of sugar at the end of 1929 amounted to over five million tons. As result of artificial stimulus to the cane sugar industry due to a protective tariff in certain countries, cane sugar production in the five-year period 1924 to 1929, as compared with the 5-year period 1919 to 1924, had risen 50 per cent in Puerto Rico and Hawaii, 79 per cent in Australia, and 100 per cent in the Philippines. In a total world production of 28 million tons in 1929, the poor British West Indies and British Guiana combined produced a mere 380,000 tons as against five million in Cuba alone. Cuba's costs of production were 1.8 cents per pound, and Java's 2 cents per pound. Compared with these, British West Indian costs of production were 2.63 cents per pound, and these were much lower than in other producing areas; the cost in Hawaii was 2.9 cents per pound, in Germany 3.4 cents, in the United States beet sugar industry 4 cents, and in Australia 4.93 cents.

The British West Indies sugar industry employed directly 176,000 persons in a total population of approximately 2 million. The percenage of the population directly involved varied from 33 per cent in St Kitts and 31 per cent in Antigua, to 20 per cent in Barbados, 16 per cent in British Guiana and 3 per cent in Jamaica. In Trinidad it was 10 per cent. The Commission of 1929 estimated that, in the event of the abandonment of sugar production, the working population would be affected to the extent of 100 per cent in St Kitts and Antigua, 66 per cent in Barbados, 50 per cent in British Guiana, 25 per cent in St Lucia, and 10 per cent in Jamaica; the figure for Trinidad was 33 per cent.

The West Indian territories were dependent on sugar for their export trade and their earnings of foreign currency to the extent of 97 per cent in Antigua and 95 per cent in Barbados; 86 per cent in St Kitts; 60 per cent in British Guiana; 45 per cent in St Lucia, 19 per cent in Jamaica and 20 per cent in Trinidad: 9 per cent in St Vincent – a total of 35 per cent for the British West Indies and British Guiana combined.

The commission brought to light once more one of the worst features of the colonial system: its inability or its unwillingness or its indifference to implement the recommendations of the Commissions of Enquiry or Investigation which it had appointed. The principal recommendation of the 1897 Royal Commission related to the settlement of the workers on the land principally for the purpose of providing some of the large quantities of food which were imported. The 1929 Commission drew attention to the fact that imports of food, drink and tobacco were approximately $26 per head of the population in Trinidad and $24 in Barbados. In other territories the figure was smaller: nearly $18 in St Kitts, $16 in Antigua, $14.40 in British Guiana, and $10 in Jamaica.

One of the great advantages of a Commission is that it lays the foundation for yet another Commission. So it was that the 1897 Royal Commission permitted the 1929 Commission to reiterate its recommendations, with some slight expansion:

'We are convinced, however, that, while schemes of land settlement cannot relieve the present emergency, the increased settlement of labourers on the land as peasant proprietors offers the best prospect of establishing a stable and prosperous economy in the West Indian Colonies We regret that, with exceptions to which we refer more particularly elsewhere, so little has been done to carry out the strong recommendations of the 1897 Commission in this direction. We desire to reiterate those recommendations as an essential part of the general policy for the progressive solution of the present difficulties of the West Indian Colonies. In addition, we strongly recommend that every attention should be given to the development of co-operation among the smaller producers and to assisting them with credit facilities and in the preparation and marketing of their crops. Without such co-operation peasant production can hardly establish itself against the competition of larger units.'

But the 1929 Commission differed from its predecessor in 1897 in one important respect. The 1897 Commission had merely thrown up its hands in despair and said that nothing could be done to help the West Indies to compete with the beet sugar producer because the British people and the British Government wanted cheap sugar. The

1929 Commission emphasised that West Indian sugar production was not particularly inefficient and a grant of direct financial assistance could place it upon a stable footing and defend it in the future from further vicissitudes of the character which had repeatedly affected and crippled it in the past. It warned the British Government that it should insist on raising the standards of cleanliness and sanitary conditions both in the sugar factories and in the housing of sugar workers, and emphasised that any withdrawal of the then limited preferences would lead to the infallible deterioration of even the limited progress that had been made and inevitable pressure to reduce wages which were already at a bare subsistence level.

The problem was therefore a problem for the British Government which the 1929 Commission placed squarely at the door of the British Government; by implication it attacked Britain's entire policy in the 19th century to the West Indies, and the *laissez-faire* attitude of its 1897 predecessor:

'It has become increasingly difficult for us to imagine how anyone can suppose – if anyone does – that it would be of advantage for the people of Great Britain, for the British Empire, or for the world, that British consumers of sugar should be enabled to buy their sugar at an advantage of perhaps a farthing a pound through the acceptance of tribute from the taxpayers of other nations or the under-paid labour of Cuban colonos, Haytian primitives, or congested Javan peasants, at the cost of destroying old-established and valuable organic British communities successfully developing the solution of the problems of racially mixed populations, such as those we have been surveying in the West Indies. Very great damage would be done to the inhabitants and societies of those communities themselves, which, on ethical or Imperial grounds, it might well be judged imperative to avoid: but on material grounds alone the economic argument of the possible interest of British consumers would appear to us to be quite inadequate to commend such a proposal. If the loss to British export trade which the destruction of the West Indian market, so far as it depends upon sugar production, would cause is taken into consideration, and if it is admitted that there would be an obligation upon the Imperial Government to provide at least the expenditure necessary for the relief of distress, and for carrying on the institutions of local government in those Colonies which would chiefly suffer, it cannot but be recognised that the pecuniary balance of profit to the British community, as taxpayers, consumers and producers, which would accrue through the reduction of the price of all the sugar they buy to the lowest competitive open market rates at which it could be obtained, would be either on the wrong side or at best very small.'

The world economic depression of 1929 hit this crazy West Indian structure like a thunderbolt, and showed up in all its nakedness the hollowness of the Crown Colony system.

The 1929 Sugar Commission had particularly stated that Trinidad produced upon a visitor, especially after a tour of the Lesser Antilles and British Guiana, 'a pleasant impression of general prosperity.' There has always been a tendency, when foreigners look at Trinidad, and especially foreigners representing the British Government, to say that Trinidad's oil economy differentiates it from its agricultural neighbours, and to ignore, behind the outward signs of limited prosperity, the grim social realities It is almost as if such observers come to Trinidad with preconceived views of the standard of living that should be attained by a colonial population, and having seen superior standards in Trindad, they simply say that Trinidad is wealthy and needs no further attention

The grim realities in Trinidad were displayed in all their starkness by the Commission that investigated the disturbances in 1937. This is an analysis of the position encountered by the Commission:

(1) Sugar production had almost doubled in the 10 years, before 1936. 'During this period of rationalisation, labour contributed its share by continuing to accept a standard of wage and living conditions far below what is desirable. It would appear that during the period in question the resources of the estates must have been almost exclusively utilized in carrying out the programme . '

(2) Cocoa production had declined from an average of 57 million pounds in the three-year period 1927 to 1929 to an average of 33 million pounds in the three-year period 1934 to 1936: 'there would appear to be no prospect of the cocoa industry recovering to its former position as the principal agricultural staple of the Colony.'

(3) With respect to coffee: 'At present it is only possible to grow coffee profitably if the cultivation and overhead expenses are borne largely by the cocoa crop.'

(4) With respect to citrus: 'We understand, however, that in view of the extensive cultivation of this crop in Palestine you consider the future outlook offers such poor prospects for a profitable market price for grapefuit grown in Trinidad that you have deemed it necessary to issue to the Colony a warning not to extend unduly the acreage under this crop.'

(5) As far as oil was concerned, production had increased from 5,380,178 barrels in 1927, the year immediately prior to Sir Thomas Holland's Report, to 13,237,030 barrels in 1936. Trinidad had thus become the leading Empire producer of oil, accounting for 62.8 per cent of Empire production in 1936. This, however, was less than 1 per cent of world production for the same year.

(6) With respect to asphalt, average production for the five-year period 1932–1936 had declined to 44 per cent of the pre-depression average.

That was the economic picture presented in 1937. The social side of the picture is as follows. The Indian population in particular was riddled with hookworm. The incidence of infestation was 79 per cent in the Cunupia district, 80 per cent in Capara and Todds Road, 80 per cent in Guaracara district. Post mortem examination of Indians performed at the Colonial Hospital in Port-of-Spain revealed that the worms were found in enormous numbers in 50 per cent of all adult Indian patients, the incidence being highest in women. The commission concluded:

'It appears from the evidence that hookworm must be a major factor in reducing efficiency among the East Indian community. Generally, we understand that the Health Department, in considering such evidence as is at present available, is tending more and more to the opinion that malaria and hookworm will be found to be the cause of the greater part of the debility and sickness in both East and West Indians in country districts.'

Here are the Commission's strictures on the general housing conditions in the colony:

'It is hardly too much to say that on some of the sugar estates the accommodation provided is in a state of extreme disrepair, and thoroughly unhygienic . . .

'Nor is the type of dwelling referred to confined to the agricultural districts. We visited "barrack" dwellings in Port-of-Spain which are indescribable in their lack of elementary needs of decency and for which, we learned, monthly rents varying from twelve to fifteen shillings a room are paid . . .

'We visited the Waterloo sugar estate and were shown the plans of an admirable scheme of rehousing, but were subsequently advised that since the scheme was prepared the undertaking had been converted into a public company (which, we understand, is mainly United Kingdom personnel), and that the shareholders' money could not be used for the carrying out of the scheme, which must now depend upon the profits made by the company. As some of the worst type of barrack dwellings are to be found on lands belonging to this company, we could only conclude that the Directors were failing to realize that the claim of the workpeople for the common decencies of home life should be one for primary consideration, and that by maintaining the existing conditions they were providing ground for justifiable discontent . . .

'In general, our view is that up to the present there has been a lack of a co-ordinated and definite policy for the decent housing of labour on the sugar estates . . .

'If housing of workers resident in agricultural estates leaves much to be desired, the conditions in some of the villages are even more unsatisfactory. An example of this is to be seen in the case of Fyzabad, a village which has grown up on the edge of the oilfields without any apparent regulation or control or observance of elementary rules as to structure, space, or sanitation, and which forms a suitable rendezvous for all the undesirable elements which congregate in the neighbourhood of new industrial developments where men obtaining comparatively high wages are to be found. In the recent disturbances Fyzabad was the centre of activity of the hooligan element which played so conspicuous a part in the attempts to provoke riot and damage to life and property. Similar examples of the worst village housing conditions adjacent to oilfields exist at Frisco Village, Point Fortin, and Cochrane Village, Guapo.'

But the Crown Colony system was seen at its worst in the field of labour relations.

The Crown Colony Legislature, before the addition of the minority of elected members, had in 1920 provided by law for the establishment of an Industrial Court. The President and members were to be appointed by the Governor, some – including the President – to be 'independent persons', some to represent the employers, and some to represent the workers. The President was appointed but no Court was established. So the President never functioned and the Ordinance remained inoperative right down to 1937. As the 1937 Commission wrote: 'It is clear to us that at no time has the Industrial Court Ordinance been regarded as a serious factor in the Colony's industrial system.'

The Trade Union Ordinance of 1932 contained no provisions safeguarding the right for peaceful picketing or giving unions immunity against action in tort. Accordingly the Trinidad Working Men's Association, which had two branches operating as Trade Unions, the Railway Union and the Stevedores Union, refused to register as a Trade Union. When the Commission of 1937 arrived in Trinidad, there were only two Trade Unions registered – the Federated Workers' Trade Union and the Amalgamated Building and Woodworkers' Union. After its arrival two other Unions were registered, the Oilfield Workers' Trade Union and the All Trinidad Sugar Estates and Factories Workers' Trade Union.

In April 1935, in pursuance of the International Labour Convention on minimum wage fixing machinery, the Labour (Minimum Wage) Ordinance was passed in Trinidad. It was only an enabling Ordinance and up to 1937 no action had been taken under it

The Workmen's Compensation Ordinance in force in 1937 did not apply to agricultural workers, except those employed in connection with any engine or machine worked by mechanical power. The original intention to cover all agricultural workers was abandoned on the representation of the Agricultural Society of Trinidad and Tobago that this would impose a heavy burden on large numbers of peasant proprietors.

In November 1935, the Secretary of State for the Colonies addressed a circular despatch to all Colonial Governments regarding the creation of Labour Departments. The Government of Trinidad and Tobago took no action on this despatch, and sent no reply at all until after the 1937 disturbances.

This was the background to the disturbances of 1937. On the one hand, there was the expansion of the oil industry and the sugar industry combined with depression or depressing prospects in other branches of agriculture. On the other hand there was an explosive social situation arising out of the discontent of the workers who had no legitimate means of expressing their grievances, who had no legal protection for ordinary trade union activities, and who found themselves, especially in agriculture, with the removal of the legal obligations of the employer during slavery and indenture, dependent solely upon the goodwill of the employer As the Commission of 1937 wrote:

'In the absence of any means of collective bargaining, the measure of the labourer's well-being and contentment depended upon the manner in which that goodwill was exercised. While, as we have indicated above, it is true that there are today employers who are giving a lead in the adoption of a more enlightened policy, the fact remains that the present condition of a large section of agricultural workers justifies the view that many managements display a surprising indifference to the welfare of their labour '

This general condemnation applied not only to sugar but also to oil where the oilfield workers had the special grievances of the 'Red Book' and the triplicate 'discharge ticket' used by Trinidad Lease-holds, both of which were regarded by the workers as instruments designed to facilitate 'blackmailing' procedure. There was further the marked hostility to the employment of South African staff on the oilfields. But the workers had no means of bargaining for better conditions or even of expressing their point of view. The 1937 Commission emphasised:

'The advent of the oil industry has without doubt been a disturbing factor in the economic and social life of the Colony, but in no sphere is the effect more pronounced than in that of agricultural labour. At the same time, labour in this new field of industry has been as little equipped as labour in the agricultural areas with the means of articulating grievances, or of discussing, through recognized machinery of collective bargaining, matters relating to its terms and conditions of employment
'Among many other matters complained of were alleged unfair discrimination between white and coloured employees, inadequate ambulance provision, lack of a satisfactory apprenticeship system for young workers, excessive fines, and so on: all matters making their contribution to the sum of discontent, but which in industry in Great Britain would, in so far as they had any substance, have found ready and early adjustment by friendly collaboration between the men's representatives and the management.

'Unfortunately, though there seems to be some evidence since the disturbances of a more enlightened outlook, it can safely be said that prior to the outbreak employers generally had been slow to realize the importance of the development of machinery for conciliation or collective bargaining on modern lines, and that, indeed, their attitude had been the reverse of encouraging.'

The oilfield workers in particular were very concerned with the rise in cost of living; by April 1937, the cost of living in Fyzabad and surrounding areas had increased by 17 per cent over the 1935 figures. The oil companies claimed that there was no demand for wage increases. The 1937 Commission repudiated this alibi:

'We are not impressed by the statement made by the employers in the course of our inquiry that there was no general demand for a wage increase. Where no organized machinery existed for collective representations and joint discussion, what the work-people were thinking could only find expression by individual complaints, and as those were not likely to be too sympathetically received, the number in fact put forward cannot be regarded as a safe indication of the measure of discontent . . .

'Had there existed in the oilfields and elsewhere organised means of collective bargaining through which the claims or grievances of the workpeople could have found ample means of expression, there can be little doubt but that the disturbances which subsequently arose might have been avoided.'

All this explains not only the violence of the eruption but its widespread nature. The 1937 disturbances were a close approximation to a general strike. They began in Fyzabad on June 19, 1937, when the police with the general contempt for public opinion which we have already noticed in the Carnival disturbances of 1881, the Hosea riots of 1884, and the Water Riots of 1903, attempted to arrest the leader of the oil workers, Uriah Butler, originally from Grenada. The police had a warrant for Butler's arrest, but no Government responsible to the people or sensitive to public reaction would ever have authorised the arrest of a popular leader when he was addressing a meeting in the very centre of the disturbed area.

Butler's emergence emphasised that working class leadership had passed from the hands of Cipriani and Port-of-Spain. A former employee of the oilfields, who had been made permanently lame as a result of an accident on the job, Butler was the emotional mass leader crying out for action. He had been expelled in 1936 from the Trinidad Labour Party, whereupon he had formed his own party, the British Empire Workers and Citizens Home Rule Party. He claimed to have 100 paying members and 900 others at the time of the disturbances. The disturbances of 1937 arose out of his threat to stage a sit-down strike on the oilfields.

The day of the strike passed off peacefully enough until the police tried to arrest Butler when he was addressing a meeting in Fyzabad.

Butler asked the Police Officer to read the warrant Whilst it was being read Butler asked the crowd whether they were going to allow the police to arrest him. The crowd replied 'No, they can't take you,' and rushed the police. Butler got away, and a plainclothes policeman, Corporal King, who followed him in an attempt to arrest him, was set upon by the crowd and compelled to seek refuge in a shop. Jumping from the shop window, he broke his leg, and whilst he lay upon the ground he was beaten, oil was poured upon him, and he was burnt to death. A Police Inspector was also shot. Thereupon the Trinidad Light Horse, a mechanised volunteer unit in San Fernando, was mobilised and the Governor telegraphed to the Commander-in-Chief in Bermuda for the despatch of a cruiser.

Thereafter the disturbances spread to Point Fortin, to Usine Ste Madeleine, to San Fernando, to Penal, to Port-of-Spain, to Rio Claro, and to Dinsley Village; as a result of rumours of disturbances in Tobago, a warship proceeded to that Island and scattered leaflets from its seaplane. The Port-of-Spain workers attempted to hold up the departure of a train to San Fernando containing a large supply of rifles and ammunition. The Governor sent for a second cruiser, and the H M.S. Ajax and H.M.S. Exeter arrived in Trinidad on the 22nd and 23rd June. The Government had at its disposal a total of 2,200 men, including Police, Special Police, and Volunteers, some of whom had machine guns. In addition Navy reinforcements supplied 210 men.

Many persons were arrested, though Butler himself evaded the net. A reward of $500 was offered for information leading to his arrest. It speaks volumes for the unity of the people of Trinidad and Tobago and the loyalty to Butler that no one volunteered to claim the reward, and Butler himself was arrested only when he came out of hiding on the basis of a promise from the Government that he would be free to give evidence before the 1937 Commission. It was a united front of all the workers in the colony, irrespective of occupation and irrespective of race.

The Government of the colony appointed on June 26 a Mediation Committee to receive representations from all concerned and to make recommendations to the Governor A glaring commentary on the state of industrial relations at the time was the proposal of the oil companies, with the approval of their Head Offices in London, that the Government and the oil companies should agree on terms and present them to the workers. The Mediation Committee refused to agree to this procedure, but the procedure ultimately adopted by the Government was not much of an improvement on the oil companies' proposals This was the notice published by the Governor on July 5, by which time most of the workers had returned to work ·

'The Oilfields.

'It is proposed to adopt the following procedure for the purpose of settling outstanding questions in the oilfields.

'The managements will discuss with representatives of the workers any representations which the latter may wish to make.

'The managements will thereafter confer among themselves and will then make to their workers a pronouncement of the steps proposed by them to meet the representations which have been made by the workers.

'Any differences thereafter outstanding may be referred either by the employers or by the workers to the Committee of the Executive Council which has been appointed by the Governor for the purpose.

'Either the employers or the workers may invite the assistance of the Committee at any period of the negotiations.

MURCHISON FLETCHER,
Governor'

Butler had become a national hero, and Trinidad and Tobago had received a new political leader. But the war generally and Butler's internment interfered with his freedom of action, and his place was taken by his lieutenant, Rienzi, who split sharply with Cipriani on the attitude to Butler and the significance of June 19 in the history of the workers of Trinidad and Tobago. The real problem, however, was that Butler proved inadequate to the task either of forming a political party or of organising the oilfield workers, and whilst his popularity was undoubted and was fully deserved, and whilst he never swerved in his demand for self-government for Trinidad and Tobago, he proved as inadequate as Cipriani had proved before him in the sense of mobilising the mass movement that he had helped to develop and guiding it along the inevitable organisational channels for the capture of political power and for the use of that power when it had been captured. His Election Manifesto issued for the General Elections of 1946, which were the first to be held on the basis of universal suffrage, gives a clear picture both of the strength and of the weaknesses of the man, both of the strength of the mass movement and its problem of leadership.

'Comrades, . . .

'On this very great and glorious date in the history of our struggle for the liberation of the land from the Spoiler, the Oppressor and the Exploiter of our people, I, as Commander-in-Chief of Trinidad's Great Army of Liberation, salute you and your immortal deeds of valour, service and sacrifice on the battle fields of nine years ago. Nine years ago today, together we faced an enemy with all the Imperial might and military power of Imperial Britain behind him Then, as now, we had nothing but our great faith and confidence in God, and in the rightness and justice of our cause. Then, as now, we were denied elementary human rights and were prepared to die fighting for these rights, then as now we looked to heaven as the great Arsenal of all those who have laboured and still continue to labour for the rich who have kept back by fraud their hire.

The Workers of the Colony for the past few months have been counselled to clear the decks and to stand by for action to win a fairer share of the very great wealth they create by the sweat of their brows, action to ensure for all Workers everywhere in the Colony better living and working conditions. The time for such action has quite definitely arrived. To those who do not think so, I beg to submit the following for their considerations:

'1 Every day whole bunches of workers are being reduced to give one man work that was formerly done by five or six men with the result that the Crown Colony Employers . . . Created Army of Sufferers (unemployed workers not in receipt of a dole) pledged by Churchill and the late Pres. Roosevelt to enjoy freedom from want now suffer untold misery and want. 2. More work and less pay seems to be the order of the day in the ranks of the enemy. 3. Even now plans are about complete for the cutting down of wages, the removal of the war bonus which in our view should be left just where it is for ten years or until rice, flour, salt fish, pork, cooking oil, Milk, Sugar, etc , return to prewar prices, whichever is the shortest period. In these great and trying circumstances I am to order you to stand firm and await the results of new demands that shall, before election day (which is comparatively speaking of little concern to Uriah Butler while the many hundreds of frail Indian women are given impossible tasks which take four and five days to perform) on the sugar fields of the colony with impossible rates per task (40 & 50c) be made on the employees of Oilfield, Sugar Estate, Cocoa Estate, Stevedore and Waterfront labour, plus Shop, Store and Grocery labour with special serious demands for Bungalow, Parlour, Government and private Bus Service Company Labour not forgetting Hospital, Railway, Housing and Planning (where Gomes made a mess of things) and every other known type of labour in the colony of Trinidad and Tobago to ensure for each and every one of these a fuller, better, brighter and a more abundant life of progress, happiness and prosperity . . . And, as your Commander-in-Chief under God, I shall not hesitate to take action, Constitutional action, to win for our country and its people the same rights and the same privileges enjoyed by the Workers and Citizens of Great Britain itself.

'May the next Anniversary of our historic June Revolution (from which date we date the New and ever-growing interest now taken in our General condition by the Government and the people of Great Britain) find our country still under the Union Jack but recognised and treated by Imperial Britain as the equal of Canada, Australia, New Zealand, South Africa (whom we fought to bring under the Union Jack) and all the other self-governing portions of the British Empire

'The zeal of the Lord God of Host . . . the only giver of Victory – and our United Strength and Indomitable Spirit will perform it.

GOD BLESS YOU ALL'

Butler himself was defeated in the 1946 Elections, where, perhaps stupidly, he decided to contest a seat in Port-of-Spain. He had to wait until the 1950 Elections to achieve his ambition to represent his Party and his country in the Legislative Council. By that time, by a species of chicanery which the Constitution permitted, the leader of the party who won a majority of the elected seats was kept out of the power which rightly belonged to him by a combination of his elected opponents and the nominated and official members who then formed part of the Legislative Council. Thus instead of the first Party Government in Trinidad and Tobago, which might have failed but also might well have succeeded, Trinidad and Tobago, for six long years from 1950 to 1956 had to tolerate a coalition government of five individuals with no Party affiliations or no Party programme, portraying the notorious individualism of the Trinidad character and the Trinidad society in its worst possible light.

By the time that Butler's light was dimmed in 1946, another political figure appeared on the Trinidad and Tobago scene in the movement towards self-government. He was Dr Patrick Solomon, a physician in private practice, who had helped to form with a Grenada colleague, Dr David Pitt, the West Indian National Party, an inter-racial Party, which had achieved some success in the 1946 Elections. The West Indian National Party however failed to curb the individualism of its members, and never really functioned as a Party. Its outstanding and most dynamic figure was Dr Solomon, who later formed the Caribbean Socialist Party, which had even less success than the West Indian National Party.

The enduring contribution of these two parties was Dr Solomon's Minority Report on Constitution Reform in 1948. Differing sharply and fundamentally from the innocuous and wishy-washy report of the Constitution Reform Committee which had been appointed with Sir Lennox O'Reilly as Chairman, Dr Solomon produced what will always remain a decisive document in the political and constitutional history of Trinidad and Tobago.

Dr Solomon attacked first the composition of the Committee. He wrote as follows:

'It would have been too much to hope for the deliberate appointment of a progressive assembly to draft the new constitution and, in point of fact, most people would have been satisfied with a representative one; but the official charged with the responsibility of selecting persons for this important task seems to have disposed of his task quite summarily, by the simple expedient of choosing the unofficial members of Legislative Council, adding some diehards from the old Franchise Committee and rounding off the whole by the addition of a few persons chosen at random from among those whose names occasionally appear in the press.

'There was no attempt to ensure that public bodies or active groups of the Colony were represented, an ommission which was

bound to result in a general dissatisfaction with the personnel of
the Committee, as well as with its recommendations. It is purely
by accident that any trade unionists gained membership on this
Committee, though the very nature of the trade union movement
made such a choice abundantly obvious. The same applies to
political parties. Cultural groups, Literary and Debating Societies,
Young People's Clubs, the Co-operative Movement, the Youth
Council and the Municipalities were all similarly ignored. Worst
of all, the County Councils, which are the most democratically
elected public bodies in the country, were given no opportunity,
once they had come into being, to share in the discussions surrounding so very important a matter as a new constitution for the Colony.'

In the second place Dr Solomon attacked the findings of the
Majority Report as unreasonable and illogical. He refused to accept
the proposal that the Governor should preside over the Executive
Council with a casting vote, and that the Executive Council should
include three *ex-officio* members and three nominated members
elected by the Legislative Council, or the proposal that the Governor
'should appoint a Leader of the Executive Council chosen from those
members who were not *ex-officio* members. He poured scorn on the
proposal that members of the Executive Council should be 'associated'
with administration. Dr Solomon wrote:

'There is no boldness of outlook, no freedom of thought, no sign
of individuality in any of these recommendations. The desire has
been, as far as possible, to base their ideas on the Jamaican constitution, without pausing to consider whether the conditions which
obtain in Trinidad today are identical with those which obtained
in Jamaica in 1944, or even whether the quasi-ministerial system
has indeed proved an unqualified success in Jamaica The recommendations, therefore, are merely negative; the one positive thought
that again emerges is the wish at all times to give favoured treatment to the nominated elements in that, while it has been made
compulsory for the legislature to elect 3 of 6 nominated members
to the Executive, it is not similarly compulsory that these persons,
once elected, should hold portfolios and make the necessary sacrifices of time and energy which the elected members are called upon
to bear. The fact that there are people willing to be on the "inside"
without the corresponding willingness to shoulder the burden of
work usually associated with the inside position, is in itself the
strongest condemnation of the system which protects the privileged
position of such people.

'The allocation of portfolios by the Governor in consultation
with the Leader of the Executive emphasises the anomaly of the
Governor's position. If it is intended that the selections should
actually be made by the Leader of the Executive and endorsed by
the Governor as His Majesty's representative, then we must be
prepared to accept the position that the Leader of the Executive

is, in effect, the Prime Minister and should preside over all meetings of the Cabinet.

'A Prime Minister, however, in a country without responsibility is like a king without a throne. If on the other hand we are to assume that the Governor makes the selection, or that, in any event, he has the final say, one wonders just what is the purpose of appointing a Leader of the Executive. This playing with high-sounding names might be suitable enough for parlour games, but is certainly out of place in the responsible business of framing a constitution for the Colony.

'It is further recommended here that, except under certain circumstances, the Governor and he alone should have the authority to summon the Executive. To make such a body the principal instrument of policy and ordain at the same time that it should be summoned to business only at the behest of the Governor, is but another of the ridiculous contradictions which face us at every turn in the recommendations of this committee. Apart from the fact that this is a matter which should be covered by the Standing Orders and not embodied in the Constitution at all, it further emphasises the desire that the bulk of power should, in fact, still reside in the hands of the Governor, making the Prime Minister merely a name – to be written in small letters – and the quasi-ministers something less than figure-heads. The whole constitution, in fact, is but an empty mockery, and, if accepted by the people without demur, would certainly brand them as being totally unfit for responsibility of any kind.'

Dr Solomon further opposed the Committee's proposal to elect a Speaker from outside of the House and to give him a casting vote. In one of his finest passages he attacked the continuation of the nominated system, as follows:

'The insistence on the retention of the nominated system cannot be justified on any ground whatever. Several arguments were brought forward by those who oppose this point of view. It was stated that the nominated elements are the ones who made the finest speeches recorded in *Hansard;* that the nominated elements consisted of people of sterling worth and ripe experience in important matters, who would be of extreme value to the Council in its deliberations; that in the absence of the nominated system, certain important interests, which have a right to be represented would never gain representation by the elected route; that the desire of those who, for years, had been excluded from representation is to exclude, in their turn, those who for years had occupied privileged positions on the Council; that Adult Suffrage was a failure and that the only counter to the excesses which would be practised by the people's elected representatives is a solid block of the saner elements of society. These arguments condemn themselves by their very flimsiness. The duty of a legislator is not so much to dot his i's and cross his t's as to bring to bear on the deliberations of the House the point of view of the people he represents; and while history will make scant reference to the polished phrases of the otherwise useless scholar, real cognisance will be taken of those who, by their sincerity of purpose and honesty of intentions help to lay the foundation of a better community. Again while we do not deny the undoubted talent and ability of these elements of the community usually associated with nomination on the Council, we do not at all agree that they are the only talented people to be found; and even where the elected member has proved to be of inferior ability to his nominated counterpart, his obviously less selfish perspective, his genuine sincerity of purpose and the disciplinary action of the vote, are collectively a guarantee of more satisfactory service to the community as a whole. The problem as regards the nominated members is not whether they lack talent but rather in whose interest they will utilise that talent.'

Dr Solomon summarised his own proposals as follows:

'Confident in the knowledge that the people both need and desire Responsible Government, I now make the following recommendations, with regard to a new Constitution for Trinidad and Tobago, for the consideration of His Majesty's Principal Secretary of State for the colonies:

'1. A fully elected single-chamber Legislature of 25 members, elected on the basis of adult suffrage as at present.

'2. Representation to be on a population basis of approximately 1–20,000 and a committee to be appointed to determine the precise boundaries of the electoral districts, special consideration being given to Tobago, the Borough of Arima, San Fernando and the Eastern Counties.

It is here recommended that the Committee be requested to provide a report within 30 days and, in order to avoid interminable delays, that it be given executive powers within its terms of reference. The Census Officer and the Electoral Officer should both be members of this Committee which should not exceed three persons, but should have powers of co-option.

'3. (a) A speaker to be elected by and from the House and removable on a vote of no-confidence.

(b) The Speaker to have a casting vote only.

'4. An Executive of at least nine members elected by the Legislature from among its members, the Executive to be the principal instrument of policy, and the Governor to be obligated to act on its advice in all internal matters.

(I consider that although the Executive cannot expect to control foreign policy, it ought nevertheless to be consulted on external affairs and especially in the matter of inter-Caribbean relationships.)

'5. The members of the Executive to have full ministerial responsibility for specific Departments of State; the Executive or Cabinet to be collectively responsible to the Legislature, by which it should be removable on a vote of no-confidence.

'6. Where there is a majority party in the Legislature, the leader of that party to become the Prime Minister; where there is no majority party the Prime Minister to be elected by the House.

'7. The Prime Minister to allocate portfolios and the Governor to appoint the ministers on his advice.

'8. Where national expediency demands it, the Prime Minister to be empowered to create new ministries.

'9. The Prime Minister to preside at all Cabinet meetings.

This memorable document was concluded with a peroration which was the finest statement of the nationalist aspirations up to that time and which will always find a place in the documentary history of the people of Trinidad and Tobago. The peroration reads as follows:

'Such is the Constitution that I believe to be best suited to the needs of the people of this country; and in this connection I feel that Trinidad is but blazing the trail along which the other Caribbean territories must follow. This is the type of constitution at which each must aim if federation of the West Indies is to become a workable practical reality and not a tragic farce.

'The keynote is "responsibility" which every people must shoulder sooner or later. That we shall make mistakes, I have no doubt; but we claim that we should be free to make those mistakes; that our mistakes will be no worse than those of other peoples in similar circumstances – and need not necessarily be as bad – and in any event would be less costly than those of past administrations in this country.

'Under such a constitution the broad masses of the people can at last realise that this country is *their* country and that they have an obligation to contribute to its welfare; that they have the opportunity freely to aid in its economic recovery without the fear of exploitation; and that ultimately, *their* country, by *their* efforts, will make its own particular contribution to the sum total of world progress and of human happiness.'

CHAPTER 16

The Road to Independence

Cipriani, Butler, Solomon – these three will go down in our history as the great trinity in our movement for self-government. Cipriani gave dignity to the barefooted man. Butler brought the inarticulate masses on a national scale on to the political stage. Solomon introduced the intellectual element and dignified the constitution reform movement by placing it squarely in its world democratic context. All three were defeated. Cipriani ended up justifying World War II and opposing Butler. Butler ended up in sonorous platitudes, not all of them intelligible, in the Legislative Council, in which he lost his seat in the 1961 Elections. Solomon was repudiated by a Port-of-Spain Constituency in the 1950 Elections Cipriani, Butler and Solomon ended up in the almost unbelievable fiasco of the first Ministerial system under the 1950 Constitution. Cipriani, Butler and Solomon laboured, each in his own way in the vineyard, only to produce the barren fruit of Albert Gomes.

This was the depressing situation in Trinidad and in Tobago when in January 1956 the political scene was revitalised with the formation of a new political party, the People's National Movement, with Learie Constantine as Chairman, and Dr Eric Williams as Political Leader. Dr Patrick Solomon, persuaded to come out of retirement, was subsequently elected Deputy Political Leader. The People's National Movement won 13 of 24 seats in the Elections of September 24, 1956, and became the first Party Government in Trinidad and Tobago. They followed this up by winning 20 out of 30 seats in the General Elections of December 4, 1961.

The People's National Movement represented the first manifestation of Party politics in Trinidad and Tobago on a national scale. For the first time the electorate of Trinidad and Tobago were presented with a Party which had a written Constitution. The Constitution provided for the setting up of Party Groups all over the country with a line of communication leading up to Constituency Groups, the General Council of the Party, and ultimately the Annual Convention. Breaking sharply away from precedents in other countries, the People's National Movement Constitution provided for a separation of the political leadership from the administrative control of the Party. In the almost indecent indiscipline which characterised political life in Trinidad and Tobago, and drawing largely on the bitter experience of its predecessors, the People's National Movement placed great emphasis on the promotion and maintenance of discipline within the Party. And for the first time in the history of the country, a political party prescribed in its Constitution the procedure for the selection of its candidates not only in General Elections, but in all elections in the country.

Thus fortified with its Constitution, the People's National Movement made the first plank in its platform the political education of the people. It organised what has now become famous in many parts of the world, the University of Woodford Square, with constituent colleges in most of the principal centres of population in the country. The political education dispensed to the population in these centres of political learning was of a high order and concentrated from the outset on placing Trinidad and Tobago within the current of the great international movements for democracy and self-government. The electorate of the country was able to see and understand its problems in the context of the ancient Athenian democracy or the federal systems of the United States and Switzerland, in the context of the great anti-colonial movements of Nehru and Nkrumah, and in the context of the long and depressing history of colonialism in Trinidad and Tobago and the West Indies. The voter in Trinidad and Tobago was quite suddenly invested with a dignity for which he was obviously, by his response, well-fitted.

The second plank in the platform of the People's National Movement was Nationhood. From the very outset, in unambiguous language, the Party stated its clear and uncompromising stand on self-government and independence – independence within a federation of the British Caribbean, but if that was not attainable, independence outside the Federation. There was never at any time any misunderstanding on the part of any of the voters in Trinidad and Tobago as to the repudiation by the People's National Movement of the constitution inflicted on the country by the Colonial Office in 1956 or the constitution agreed to by West Indian representatives with the blessing of the Colonial Office in respect of Federation at the London Conference in February 1956.

The third plank in the platform of the People's National Movement was morality in public affairs, the emphasis on honesty and integrity among Party members and their representatives in the elected Assemblies, the elimination of graft and discrimination in public life and in public appointments. This constituted a veritable revolution in a country circumstanced as Trinidad and Tobago had been under the Crown Colony system.

One of the outstanding achievements of the People's National Movement was the emancipation of the women of the country and their incorporation with equal rights on an equal footing with men in the political life of the country. The Movement stood from the outset for inter-racialism and the reduction of racial tension in the community, its flag, black, brown, yellow and white, symbolising the union of the principal ethnic groups which had suffered under colonialism and which had at various times fought for constitution reform.

When in July 1962 over 300 delegates of the People's National

Movement drawn from all parts of the country assembled in Special
Convention to revise the Party constitution in accordance with the
requirements of the Constitution itself, and spent seven days on this
exercise to which most serious study had been given for well over 18
months by a variety of representatives of the Party at different levels,
that more than anything else constituted a dramatic manifestation of
the extent to which in 1956 the Movement had established the system
of party politics in the traditional land of unrestrained and undisci-
plined individualism.

In its six years of power the government of the People's National
Movement has also been able to satisfy the aspirations of so many
people in the country for such a long period of time and virtually to
revolutionise the society and the economy.

Its first achievement was the abolition of the Crown Colony system.
On the very morrow of its victory in the 1956 Elections, the Colonial
Office, in accordance with precedents previously set in Malaya and
Singapore, agreed to its request to modify drastically the system of
nomination by including among the five nominated members two
People's National Movement members selected by the leader of the
Party who had become Chief Minister. This was followed in 1959 by
the introduction of the Cabinet system, under which the Premier (the
new title of the Chief Minister) presided over the Cabinet (the new
title of the Executive Council), the Governor ceased to be a member
of the Cabinet, and the *ex-officio* members, retained for the sake of
continuity and on the basis of their experience, were not allowed the
right to vote The next step was full internal self-government attained
after the General Elections of December 1961 Old Joseph Chamberlain must have turned in his grave. Fifty-eight years after his boast
that the Crown colony system was the only form of government suited
to Trinidad, Trinidad and Tobago assumed absolute and untram-
melled control of its internal affairs. This was associated with a
dramatic reversal of the Crown Colony pattern of Legislature In
accordance with the election pledges of the People's National Movement in 1956, a bicameral legislature was introduced, the Lower
House fully elected and the Upper House fully nominated.

The second achievement of the new Government was the introduction of the concept and techniques of planning in the national life.
Before the People's National Movement there had been a five-year
plan, which was nothing more than a collation of the individual wishes
of individual Ministers. Within one year of assuming control of the
Government, the new Government had ready for general discussion
a five-year plan of the order of $191 million, providing for the exten-
sion of roads, the increase in hospital accommodation, the construction
of new schools, the expansion of the Airport, the development of
neglected and maligned Tobago, the construction and encouragement
of hotels, the organisation of new markets, the expansion of electricity,
the modernising of the sanitation system, and a vastly extended water
supply.

Subsequent revisions raised the cost of the five-year programme to $248 million. Now in its final year, the success of the programme has been obvious to all. It greatest achievement has been that it has been financed to the extent of 98½ per cent from purely local resources, surplus revenues or local loans, without assistance from outside. New factories which have grown up in the last five years have testified to the success of the Industrial Development Corporation established in 1958. The small farmer, bypassed and despised in the age of colonialism, received aids and subsidies which he had never received before. The fishing industry, neglected and ignored under previous governments, received special attention. The New Port-of-Spain Town Hall, replacing the one destroyed by fire in 1948, the new and imposing Hilton Hotel, elegant and commodious new blocks at the Port-of-Spain Hospital, the Navet Dam, the Mausica Teachers College, the John S. Donaldson Technical Institute, a large number of new Primary and Secondary Schools, the introduction of free secondary education, the paving of the Tobago runway, the new Terminal Building at Piarco, two new ships for the Tobago service, street lights and village lights in many communities, a vast sewerage scheme under way, an extensive north coast road under construction in Tobago, the extension of the Trinidad North Coast Road from Maracas Bay to Las Cuevas Bay– the entire population has been able to see, to hear, to touch and to feel these and kindred developments, and to understand that where Spanish colonialism had signally failed to develop the country, where British colonialism had signally failed to develop the country, Trinidad and Tobago nationalism had been able to achieve where the others had not dared to aspire.

The third major achievement of the years since 1956 was in the field of finance. The income tax system was revised by the introduction of the Pay-as-you-earn system. Local savings were tapped as never before, not for war loans or depression loans to the British Government, but for the development of local resources. A Central Bank now in process of formation will be the apex of the banking structure. With the establishment of a Minister of Finance by the new Government in October 1956, financial autonomy was achieved and the people of Trinidad and Tobago, through their elected representatives, assumed responsibility for their financial affairs on which they had been formerly dependent on the approval of the Colonial Office.

In respect of relations of Church and State in the field of education, the new Government signed a Concordat with the denominations ensuring the denominational character of the schools, incorporating the denominational schools into the Government's policy of free secondary education, and, subject to the overriding authority of the Public Service Commission, giving assurance to the denominations in respect of the appointment, transfer, or dismissal of teachers in denominational schools considered by the denominations unsuitable on grounds of faith or morals.

The Government purchased the telephone system from a private Company. It also purchased British West Indian Airways from the British Overseas Airways Corporation to prevent its liquidation and the retrenchment of several hundred workers that that would have entailed, to ensure that the vital field of air transport would not fall entirely into foreign hands, and to preserve for the West Indian people the rights and privileges which had accrued to them from British West Indian Airways. British West Indian Airways is conceived by the Government of Trinidad and Tobago as a National Carrier for the West Indian area as a whole, and steps are now being taken to implement this policy.

In accordance with its Election Manifesto pledges of September 1956, the new Government also reformed drastically the electoral procedure. The two principal innovations, under which the General Elections of 1961 were contested, were the introduction of personal permanent registration, involving an Identification Card carrying photograph, signature, and basic particulars of the voter, and the use of the Voting Machine.

A fundamental reorganisation of the Public Service was initiated in 1959, based principally on the necessity for the integration of Ministries and Departments of Government. A complete reappraisal of existing classifications with the consequent readjustment of salary grades and salary scales is now being made.

New legislation in the past five years has drastically changed some of the essential features of the old colonial régime. The cane farmers of the society have been incorporated and given a recognised place in the sugar industry. Security of tenure has been provided for small farmers, and provision made for a number of agricultural tribunals to settle disputes. Preliminary steps have been taken for the establishment of a Public Utilities Commission to fix rates for all essential public utilities. The Government has taken steps to rationalise and improve the system of public transport by bus. Town planning legislation has given the Government the necessary powers to deal with the better use of land and protect the interests of the citizens from selfish individuals in a society becoming increasingly complex The health laws have been drastically revised in respect of doctors, dentists, nurses, pharmacists, and private hospitals. A Port Authority has been established to replace the Government Department previously responsible for port operations.

The labour movement in the country has been given increasingly important responsibilities, and the Government has set the lead in the fields of collective bargaining and civilised industrial relations procedures. It has encouraged the formation of a Joint Industrial Council comprising all the Unions and all the Government employing bodies connected with Government daily-paid employees Boards of Enquiry have been set up to deal with the disputes which have arisen in a number of basic industries such as asphalt, cement, telephones and sugar.

The increasing control by the elected representatives of the people of Trinidad and Tobago over their own affairs and particularly their own economic affairs, in anticipation of their control of external affairs with Independence, has been nowhere better reflected than in the broad scope of the expert advice which the Government has been able to make available to the people of Trinidad and Tobago. Experts have come from the United States of America in the field of oil, from Canada in the field of income tax and legal drafting, from Canada and the United States of America in the field of housing, from India in the field of planning, from the United Nations in the field of port development. The International Bank for Reconstruction and Development has advised on the whole question of electricity expansion in connection with a loan of $40 million recently provided by it to the Government of Trinidad and Tobago. More recent international contracts have produced agreements to make available to the Government of Trinidad and Tobago experts in the field of vocational education, agricultural marketing and water winning and distribution from Israel, experts from Switzerland in the field of railway operations, tourist promotion, and hotel management.

The results of this expansion, both physical and psychological, have been twofold. In the first place, the political stability and the economic potential of Trinidad and Tobago have increasingly been recognised as differentiating the country sharply from most of its neighbours. This has had the result in the private sector of the economy of large-scale private investment principally in oil, where the take-over of Trinidad Leaseholds by Texaco, an American Company, in 1956, with the approval of the British Government, has been the principal factor in the expansion of the production both of crude oil and of refined products—crude oil production averaging 130,000 barrels per day, and refined production 305,000 barrels per day. Investment in oil in drilling operations, in refining operations, and in by-products such as lubricating oils, has formed the largest part of the substantial capital investment which has taken place in Trinidad in the past few years. It is largely because of oil, and the substantial revenues derived by the Government from oil, that the per capita national income of Trinidad and Tobago for 1960 was about $850, and is estimated to have increased to approximately $1,000 in 1961, a figure larger than that of the vast majority of its Caribbean and South American neighbours, and very much larger than that of the majority of the newly independent countries of Africa and Asia.

The second result of the expansion has already begun to emerge in the field of art and culture. A sugar economy, governed from abroad, dominated by slave or semi-servile labour, talked and thought as we have seen, in terms of slaves and sugar, and was entirely destitute of learned leisure, liberal and scientific intercourse, and even of liberal recreations. No love or appreciation of the arts, nor artistic traditions, could develop in such sordid material circumstances, and until recently, the young writer or the man who wrote poetry, or the

I

painter or the sculptor was regarded as little more than a freak, a disappointment to hard-working parents who looked to him, either as a professional man who had won a scholarship or as a civil servant, to raise the family status and to occupy a higher rung on the social ladder than his father and grandfather had occupied.

With the increase of population in recent years, the new confidence of the people, and the broadening of their horizons, coupled with the relative improvement in material conditions and standards, there has been a flowering of the native forms of culture and a marked increase in popular interest and appreciation. The calypso and the steelband, both products of the underprivileged members of the society, have gained a well-deserved reputation for Trinidad and Tobago among the folk arts of the world, and the enormous enthusiasm, capacity for improvisation, and zest for living which constitute the Trinidad Carnival have more and more brought themselves to the attention of the outside world.

Trinidad art, in painting and sculpture, is coming forward, though it has not yet begun to achieve anything of the reputation of Mexican art or the Haitian primitives The folk dances and the folk songs are being revived and preserved, and there is the nucleus of a native theatre, constantly struggling against the harsh criticism of those in the society who seek to parade their superior knowledge by continuing in the well established colonial tradition of depreciating local efforts and disparaging local forms.

Trinidad and Tobago has as yet produced nothing remotely approaching the world-famous poetry of Aime Cesaire of Martinique, but in the field of prose writing it has produced two of the outstanding novelists of the Caribbean of the last decade, Vidia Naipaul and Samuel Selvon, both of whom, as Indians, testify to Trinidad's achievement in the abolition of the Crown Colony system. They are the children of those who, as we have seen, were towards the end of the last century not sent to school, of those who were to be found, as the saying went, either in the field or in the hospital or in jail, of those of whom the sugar planter contemptuously asked in 1925, 'Of what use would education be to them if they had it?' Naipaul and Selvon write about their own experiences in Trinidad, the streets they knew, the people they mixed with, their family customs and traditions; Naipaul's novel on the first fruits of universal suffrage and the ministerial system, or his novel dealing with the birth of a colonial politician – whilst the illustration is Indian, the subject and scope are Trinidadian, and they will always remain as outstanding landmarks in the political evolution of Trinidad

These, broadly speaking, have been the developments in the political, economic and social field in the past six years. A political party, a relatively new phenomenon in the history of Trinidad and Tobago, drawing a considerable measure of mass support, had released the latent capacities and pent-up energies of the people of Trinidad and Tobago and was leading them inexorably on the road to independence.

It was inevitable that this political drive and these economic prospects would clash with British efforts to establish a federation of the West Indies. It was not that the new Government and the new mass movement were opposed to federation. Quite the opposite. They were both in the vanguard of federation. But it was that the British idea of Federation was so much behind the times and so redolent of the old colonialism, so wedded to the policy of Caribbean consolidation in order to facilitate the government of the Caribbean, either directly or indirectly, from outside.

Britain's concern with federation of the West Indies, fundamentally a progressive step and a sound proposition, went back, as we have already seen, to the year 1876. But what was involved was nothing more than an administrative consolidation of separate governments to suit Britain's purposes, particularly in respect of defence. The Secretary of State for the Colonies, the Earl of Kimberley, made this quite clear to Governor Rawson of Barbados in a despatch on May 1, 1873: —

'No one can dispute the advantages, for purposes of defence, of union between weak neighbouring communities. Moreover, it cannot be expected that the governments of a number of small Islands independent of each other should possess the experience and information necessary to enable them to deal with questions which in times of war or other emergencies may arise with foreign powers, and on which there may be no opportunity to refer home for instructions. It must be apparent to all the colonists under your Government that the Imperial Government may justly call upon them to adopt any improvements in their system of administration which without prejudicing their local interests may increase the efficiency of the Colonial Government in reference to these serious matters.'

The administrative consolidation envisaged was unpretentious and ridiculous in the extreme. The specific proposals submitted by the Governor to the Assembly of Barbados in 1876, the six points as he called them, were as follows: — (1) the appointment of the Auditor of Barbados as Auditor-General of the Windward Islands; (2) the transporting of prisoners between the islands when necessary; (3) the admission of lunatics from the other islands into a new asylum in Barbados; (4) a federal leper asylum for all the islands; (5) the appointment of a Chief Justice of the Windward Islands and the centralisation of the judicial system in Barbados; (6) the creation of a police force for the Windward Islands.

Thus federation eighty years ago meant freedom of movement for lunatics and prisoners, and the federation of lepers and policemen. The Colonial Office alone could find that attractive.

The only hint of an economic side to federation came from the Governor of Barbados who linked federation with freedom of movement. The Governor said: —

'Our redundant population will find a natural outlet in the neighbouring Islands when by a uniform political system, the same laws, the same tariff, and constant means of rapid communication, the now unoccupied Crown Lands and half-tilled estates will be available for their labour, and they can come and go from the various islands as readily as they now pass from parish to parish in Barbados.'

Barbados refused to have anything to do with these proposals or any other proposals for federation. It wished to have absolutely nothing to do with the smaller territories governed as Crown Colonies, which they feared would mean the downgrading of their own political status to that of the Crown Colony system; the fear was a legitimate one, in view of what had happened to Jamaica a mere ten years before. So the Barbados sugar planters made overtures instead for joining the Canadian Federation, which they hoped would give them a duty free market for their sugar and an outlet for their surplus population. Britain, therefore, had to abandon its proposals and, as we have indicated, to substitute the smaller federation of Grenada, St Vincent, St Lucia and Tobago, which Tobago itself rejected in favour of union with Trinidad, thereafter, the British Government maintained an intermittent interest in the subject of federation, an interest which was distinguished by an incoherence that stemmed from a total lack of policy towards the West Indies; one gets the impression that nobody ever had time to sit down and work out some sort of policy, good or bad, for the West Indies as a whole.

In the first place there was complete confusion as to the scope of the federation. The British proposals of 1876 involved the federation of the Leeward Islands, which then included Dominica, and the Windward Islands, which then included Barbados and Tobago. The headquarters of the federation was to be Barbados. In 1893 a commissioner investigating the affairs of Dominica recommended 'an administrative union of all the British Antilles under one Governor-General.' The Royal Commission of 1897 opposed this and limited federation to Barbados and the Windward Islands, with Dominica transferred from the leeward to the Windward Group. The early years of the twentieth century saw proposals by the Administrator of St Vincent for a federation of all the territories excluding British Honduras and the Bahamas, while Sir Samuel Hoare, later Foreign Secretary of the United Kingdom, who had economic interests in British Honduras, included both British Honduras and the Bahamas in his proposal for the appointment of a single High Commissioner for all the West Indian territories. Major Wood was lukewarm in support of a federation and limited his proposals to a suggestion that the possibility of a federation of Trinidad and the Windward Islands should be explored.

This was opposed by the Closer Union Commission of 1932, which proposed instead a loose federation of the Leeward and Windward Islands with a single Governor but with no federal legislative or execu-

tive councils, and with headquarters in St Lucia. The Royal Co
sion of 1938, while emphasizing that the federation of the entire
was the ideal to which policy should be directed, repeated the propo.
of the Closer Union Commission for a federation of the Leeward an
Windward Islands.

There was a similar confusion as to the necessity or desirability of
federation. The British Government's proposals of 1876 were based
on the argument that federation would be more economical and more
efficient. But the Royal Commission of 1882 limited itself to a recognition of the importance of joint consultative action on such matters
as the civil service, taxation, customs duties, reporting of trade statistics, administration of justice, telephone and postal communications
and was very careful to state that this should be done 'without infring-
ing on the constitutional independence of any one colony.' The Royal
Commission of 1897 opposed the proposal for a unified West Indian
Civil Service on the ground that no appreciable evil or inconvenience
necessarily arose from the existing system, and that no substantial
economies would be effected by its modification which would not be
equally possible under the system then existing. Major Wood, however, took the view that separation involved excessive overhead charges
by requiring the full paraphernalia of administrative machinery for
communities whose population was so small. The Closer Union Commission recorded that the witnesses that appeared before it made it
clear that for any federation or closer union to be acceptable it must
achieve economy in administration, but the Royal Commission of
1938 condemned as short-sighted policy the rejection of the principle
of federation merely because in its initial stages it would not secure
savings on salaries or other administrative expenses.

This confusion as to the necessity or desirability of federation is
well illustrated by the question of transportation. As far back as 1860
a Colonial Office official expressed the view that federation was
demanded by what he called the 'modern facility of communication'
available a hundred years ago. The 1897 Commission, on the other
hand, rejected federation principally because, in its view, the Governor
General, apart from the waste of time and the physical strain that
would be involved in the necessary journeys to the different territories,
would have to be furnished with a special vessel and establishment,
which would cost a considerable sum, while the task of bringing the
Federal Council together in order to arrange for its constitution and
for the conduct of its business would also involve great difficulties.
Major Wood in 1921 also regarded as the most serious impediment
to federation the distances separating the colonies and the absence
of the necessary transportation facilities He pointed out that Jamaica
was separated from the Lesser Antilles and British Guiana by a
journey longer in time than that from England to Jamaica, stressed
that his mission was made possible only by the fact that a British warship had been specially detailed for his use, and cited the case of an
official letter addressed from Trinidad to the officer commanding the

troops in Jamaica which had taken five and a half months to reach its destination. The postal authorities in Jamaica were in those days usually compelled to send mails for Trinidad, Barbados and British Guiana via England, New York and Halifax.

Neither the 1897 Commission nor Major Wood stopped to consider that distance has not prevented either the political dependence of the British Caribbean territories on the United Kingdom or the representation of the French West Indies in the Parliament in Paris. Distance did not prevent Barbados which objected in 1876 to British Caribbean Federation from proposing in 1884 that it should be admitted into the Canadian Federation.

In its federation policy the British Government was faced with the opposition of powerful vested interests. The Barbadian planters of 1876 refused to surrender their ancient constitution under which they enjoyed a large measure of self-government. The opposition in later years came principally from Trinidad, which was described by the Closer Union Commission of 1932 as being unsympathetic to the idea.

The British Government forced Nova Scotia into the Canadian Federation but allowed the ruling class in Barbados and Trinidad to get away with their opposition to Caribbean Federation. This was only another illustration of its tenderness to the West Indian ruling class. The tenderness was particularly evident in Major Wood's report in 1921. Major Wood was more impressed with the differences between the territories than with the similarities. He considered, for example, that Barbados with its uninterrupted and unchanged constitution and its land and industry almost exclusively in the hands of European large proprietors, was, historically, socially and politically, poles asunder from the Crown Colonies of St Vincent and St Lucia where there was a considerable coloured and Negro peasant proprietary. Influenced by the difficulty of obtaining contributions from some colonies towards the establishment of what used to be the Imperial College of Tropical Agriculture in Trinidad, Major Wood wrote as follows:

'The establishment of West Indian political unity is likely to be a plant of slow and tender growth. If any advance in this direction is to be achieved, it can only be as a result of a deliberate demand of local opinion, springing from the realisation of the advantages of co-operation under modern world conditions. Such development is likely only to be prejudiced, if ground were ever given for the fear that it was being imposed upon reluctant communities from without . . .'

This was the position when in 1932 a conference of West Indian leaders was convened in Roseau in Dominica to consider the question of federation, in the light of the appointment of the Closer Union Commission. All the West Indian islands except Jamaica were included in this conference. The Conference was dominated by Capt. Cipriani of Trinidad. There was nothing particularly revolutionary about the draft constitution drawn up at this conference, the principal features of which were as follows: —

(1) A single chamber legislature comprised of 27 elected and 6 official members.

(2) A Federal Executive comprised of the Governor-General, 3 officials nominated by the Crown, and 6 elected members elected by and from the Federal Assembly.

(3) The Governor-General was to act on the advice of the Federal Executive and 'the functions now exercised by the Colonial Office in relation to the British West Indies Colonies shall, as far as practicable, be transferred' to him.

(4) 'Reconstitution of Island Legislatures: It is necessary and desirable that in each island the nominated and unofficial element should disappear and be replaced by elected members; and that the number of elected members should be increased so as to provide for a clear elected majority; in case of conflict between the Island Government and the Island Legislature in any matter of paramount importance the issue to be referred to the Governor-General'.

(5) The qualifications for membership of island legislatures were to be a clear annual income of $960, or ownership of real property of at least $2,400 clear of all charges and encumbrances, or occupation of land of an annual rental value of at least $240.

(6) 'Qualifications of Voters:
For the time being the question of voters' qualifications shall be left to the local Legislatures, it being understood that no adult who pays any direct tax shall be deprived of a vote, and that any property or income qualification that may be imposed shall be sufficiently low to provide for the free expression of opinion of all classes, and that adult franchise is the ultimate aim of the Federation: The qualifications of voters to be reviewed triennially in each unit with a view to bringing adult suffrage gradually into general operation.'

(7) The establishment of Municipal Councils or Boards in all towns or villages, 'with a controlling elective element, wherever practicable, the enjoyment of a full measure of municipal autonomy by every centre of population being regarded as essential to the ultimate realization of Dominion Status.'

There the matter rested until in 1947 the British Government convened a conference in Montego Bay in Jamaica of all the West Indian Islands, British Guiana and British Honduras to discuss the question of a federation of the West Indies. A Standing Closer Association Committee was appointed under a British Chairman and with headquarters in Barbados to work out the details of a constitution. The Committee was concerned purely with two questions: first, to reduce the revenues of the Federal Government – it came up with a ridiculous proposition for a revenue of $864,000 most of it to be eaten up by the Governor General's establishment. Second, arguing the case against economic aid from the United Kingdom.

A draft Constitution in 1953 was prepared on the basis of the Committee's findings and this was modified by an amended Constitution in February 1956. Both Constitutions were similar in that they gave the Governor General enormous powers. He presided over the Executive which included *ex-officio* members. In 1956 in the month of February, the West Indian people were being asked to set up a federation in which the Governor General was to have reserve powers in the field of defence, foreign relations, international obligations, currency, constitutional amendments, imposition of differential duties, measures affecting the security of the federation and involving financial assistance to the federation from the British Government. Even in 1856 nothing worse could have been perpetrated, but in 1856 unlike 1956 there would have been no West Indian leaders of the various territories to draw up and sign the report that was drawn up and signed in 1956.

The Constitutions of 1953 and 1956 were absolutely innocent of any economic perspectives They ran away from the great question of customs union and internal free trade and postponed them for five years. They ran away from the equally great question of freedom of movement among the territories of the federation, and postponed that to the time of their reconsideration of the question of free trade. They reduced federation to a laughing stock by limiting it to a fixed revenue of $9,120,000 derived from a mandatory levy of all the territories compounded on considerations based on revenue and population – as a compromise between Jamaica with half the population of the area. By this time British Guiana and British Honduras had ceased to take part in the exercise.

The West Indian leaders were not able to agree among themselves as to the location of the federal capital. In 1953 they selected Grenada. In 1956 they had second thoughts and decided against Grenada. But they could not agree on an alternative location. Therefore, they decided to ask the British Government to send out a commission of three persons to decide on the location of the capital. The commission subsequently recommended that the capital should not be located in a small island as a matter of principle, and that among the three larger territories, the order of merit should be (1) Barbados, (2) Jamaica, (3) Trinidad. The commission urged that, under no circumstances, should the capital be located in Trinidad, because of the low tone of political life in Trinidad at the time, the absence of regular political parties, the pronounced individualism of the place, and the racial divisions between the two major groups in the Island, Negroes and Indians.

This anaemic infant, showing all the conventional signs of malnutrition, took its bow on the world stage on April 22, 1958 By that time, however, the People's National Movement had emerged as the governing party in Trinidad and Tobago. The party had always stood for federation and had demanded independence for the Federation in a period of not more than five years from its inception. It won its first victory when it discarded the report of the Capital Site Mission into the waste paper basket where it belonged and secured the acceptance of Trinidad as the Capital Site of the Federation. It won its second victory over its West Indian colleagues in the Federal party of which it was an affiliate member, the West Indian Federal Labour Party, when in 1959 it secured acceptance of the proposal that immediate steps should be taken to convene the conference envisaged in the 1956 Constitution, to revise the Constitution within the five year period stipulated and achieve full independence for the Federation.

At a series of conferences convened by the Federal Government between 1959 and early 1961, a sharp division of opinion emerged between Jamaica and Trinidad and Tobago. Jamaica wanted a loose confederation with limited revenues and limited powers, based on a customs union among the territories which excluded significant products of its own. Jamaica advocated a federal government whose revenues were derived from import duties, and which had no powers whatsoever over income tax and industrial development. Trinidad and Tobago, on the other hand, led the fight for a strong central government with full powers to organise and shape the national economy, and with adequate revenues to carry out the inescapable responsibilities of a new independent State. The Government of Trinidad and Tobago advocated customs union, freedom of movement of labour and capital throughout the Federation, a single West Indian currency, a Central Bank, and federal powers over income tax and industrial development. The concrete proposals of the Government of Trinidad and Tobago were outlined in the *Economics of Nationhood* published in 1959, the only document in over eighty years in which the concept of federation was analysed and rationally presented. The philosophy underlying the document was contained in the following paragraph: —

'These islands have a long history of insularity, even of isolation, rooted in the historical development of their economy and trade and the difficulties of communications for centuries. No amount of subjective, that is to say historical, cultural or other activity of the time can be expected to overcome this heritage. Only a powerful and centrally directed economic co-ordination and interdependence can create the true foundations of a nation. Barbados will not unify with St Kitts, or Trinidad with British Guiana, or Jamaica with Antigua. They will be knit together only through their common allegiance to a Central Government. Anything else will descredit the conception of Federation, and in the end leave the islands more divided than before'.

In this conflict between the two philosophies of federation Trinidad and Tobago was ready to compromise with Jamaica in respect of conceding to Jamaica, on the basis of its population, some 48% of the seats in the House of Representatives, to delay customs union for nine years, and to impose on the Federal Government a moratorium for nine years on the exercise of the power to levy income tax and direct industrial development of the region. Even this was unable to reconcile the profound differences between the two concepts. When, at the Lancaster House Conference in London in June 1961, the Colonial Office and the other Territories sided with Jamaica against Trinidad and agreed to a Constitution which gave Jamaica or any other Territory a perpetual veto on the exercise by the Federal Government of its powers over income tax and industrial development, whilst limiting the moratorium on freedom of movement, which was of vital concern to Trinidad, for a period of nine years, this was not, as so many observers thought, the beginning of the end of Federation, it was rather the end of the beginning

The Jamaica Government had agreed to a referendum to decide the question of Jamaica's future in relation to the Federation. The governing party fought the referendum on the basis that the weak Federation could not possibly harm Jamaica's development. The opposition party fought the referendum on the clear issue of secession and Jamaica having nothing to do with its Eastern Caribbean neighbours. The Opposition won the referendum by a small margin, with approximately one-third of the population abstaining from voting The Jamaica Government decided to secede from the Federation and the Colonial Office agreed.

Thereupon, the Government of Trinidad and Tobago took the stand that the secession of one territory meant the abandonment of the 1956 compact for the Federation of ten territories. The Trinidad and Tobago slogan was '1 from 10 leaves 0'. This stand was subsequently upheld and the Federation was dissolved by an Act of Parliament.

Trinidad and Tobago, like Jamaica, decided to proceed to national independence by itself. Unlike Jamaica, however, Trinidad and Tobago did not exclude association with its neighbours. But that association was to take two forms – the first, related to the smaller territories, was that, following the example of Tobago in 1899, the association must take the form of the expansion of the unitary state of Trinidad and Tobago. Much nonsense has been written in abuse of Trinidad and Tobago for this decision. The whole history of Trinidad and Tobago and the West Indies, as presented above, is an exemplification of the fundamental soundness, from both the political and the economic point of view, of the decision of Trinidad and Tobago.

The second form of association proposed by Trinidad and Tobago involved the attempt to integrate the economies of the entire Caribbean area not restricted as with the Federation to British territories It appeared to Trinidad and Tobago that, if the European countries in the Common Market could subordinate their political jealousies and economic rivalries to integration of their complementary economies, there was no reason why, especially with Britain's anxiety to join the Common Market, the Caribbean countries traditionally associated with European countries which were part of the Common Market could not themselves get together and try to organise, under the European umbrella, something approximating a Caribbean Economic Community. Towards this end, the Governments of Trinidad and Tobago and Surinam have already embarked on profitable discussions, and it has been announced that the Government of France has agreed to explore with the Government of Trinidad and Tobago the possibilities of such association in respect of their overseas departments of Martinique and Guadeloupe which are themselves, through France, integral parts of the European Common Market.

Only time can tell what will be the outcome of the initiative of Trinidad and Tobago in these two directions. Suffice it to say that, with the achievement of independence on August 31, 1962, Trinidad and Tobago stands out today as the standard bearer of the idea and ideal of Caribbean integration.

If the advent of the People's National Movement on to the West Indian political stage inevitably foreshadowed, for a Party whose constitution and programme were based on the philosophy already indicated, a challenge to the whole concept of administrative consolidation based on the Crown Colony mentality of 1876, it was just as inevitable that a powerful Nationalist Government would have come into conflict with a weak Federal Government located on its Territory and deriving its sustenance from the Colonial Office. What appeared to superficial observers as a conflict of personalities in the inglorious career of the Federation stemmed in reality from a conflict between a powerful nationalist idea with roots deep in a people who were the most cultivated and politically conscious in the area, and a weak Government looking for its inspiration to the British Colonial Office and the American State Department. Right from the outset a conflict developed between the Government of Trinidad and Tobago and the Federal Government in the field of foreign affairs. Two issues in particular were involved, the Venezuela 30% surtax and the American Naval Base at Chaguaramas.

The Venezuela 30% surtax was originally aimed by the Government of Venezuela at British manufactures transhipped from Trinidad and Tobago to Venezuela. This trade had from the outset of Trinidad's annexation of the Colony, as we have seen, dominated Britain's interest in Trinidad. The intention of the Government of Venezuela was, by this measure, to force British firms to establish subsidiaries in Venezuela and ship direct to Venezuela. Some indication of the strength of public feeling in Trinidad on this measure is provided in a report of the Government Statistician to the Legislative Council in 1888 as follows:—

'I cannot conclude these remarks without expressing my regret that, as yet, no way has been found of convincing the Venezuelan Government of the impolicy, as well as the injustice, of such an

unwarrantable impost as this 30 per cent additional duty. It is quite
true that it is scarcely possible for any artificial barrier to entirely
stem back or dry up a trade following so natural a channel as did
that between this Colony and Venezuela, but the natural results
of the imposition of such a barrier can never prove one-sided, but
must inevitably be equally injurious and demoralising to the trade
of both countries. In the best interests of both I would therefore
urge that some further steps be taken to endeavour to secure the
repeal of this unfair and unjustifiable impost.'

The Venezuela surtax was of no particular importance except to
a few Trinidad merchants so long as Trinidad remained a Crown
Colony, dependent principally on sugar, and even the discovery of
oil in Trinidad was of no particular significance to Venezuela relations because Venezuela itself had even more substantial oil resources.
With the emergence of a Nationalist Government in Trinidad, which
was followed by the emergence of democracy in Venezuela and the
overthrow of the traditional dictatorship, the political situation automatically changed. A Nationalist Government in Trinidad could not
possibly acquiesce in a discrimination against a British Crown Colony,
over 80 years old, whilst a democratic Government in Venezuela
would obviously want to maintain friendly relations with a neighbour
in its backyard, if only to ensure that the overthrown dictatorship
would not find an asylum on Trinidad's soil or would not be allowed
to abuse Trinidad's soil by hatching conspiracies against the lawful
government of the people in Venezuela. The political consideration
was reinforced by an economic consideration. The Venezuela surtax
was imposed on British goods shipped from Trinidad. The development of the Trinidad economy by the Nationalist Movement diversi-
fied the Trinidad and Tobago economy, and the Venezuela surtax
imposed on British goods ended up by discriminating against goods
produced in Trinidad and Tobago by workers of Trinidad and Tobago
from, for the most part, the resources of Trinidad and Tobago.

The Government of Trinidad and Tobago, therefore, immediately
sought to establish good neighbourly relations with the democratic
Government of Venezuela, and to have the surtax removed Goodwill
missions were exchanged on both sides and the foundations of a new
and harmonious relationship were laid. These were suddenly disrupted
when the Colonial Office entrusted to the Federal Government, which
had at the time a lower constitutional status than that of Trinidad and
Tobago, complete power in the field of Venezuelan relations. The
Government of Trinidad and Tobago saw in this entrustment yet
another attempt to hamstring the Nationalist Movement for independence by subordinating it to a federal power, destitute of financial
resources, with limited constitutional powers, but very responsive indeed to the influence of the Colonial Office. The Venezuelan Government, at best confused by having to deal with two parties, at worst
presented with opportunity for dividing the two parties in order the

better to ensure a continuation of the discrimination behind which certain vested interests had inevitably been built up, temporised. The dissolution of the Federation and the achievement of independence by Trinidad and Tobago have restored the status quo. The Government of Venezuela finds itself in the unenviable position today of being one of the only Governments in the world which perpetuates a colonial discrimination against an independent country, whose friendship must mean more than that of the friendship of many other countries. It is not difficult to predict the outcome of this massive contradiction.

The other issue in the field of external relations which embittered relations between Trinidad and Tobago and the Federal Government was the American Naval Base at Chaguaramas. Chaguaramas, as we have seen above, has always occupied an important place in the economic and social life of Trinidad and Tobago, either as the Spanish Naval Base when Trinidad was annexed by Britain or as the centre of one of the most serious slave revolts in the history of Trinidad when it was still one of the most important sugar producing areas of the Island. In 1890 a respectable and long established family, the Siegert family, which today enjoys an international reputation in respect of its products, principally Angostura Bitters, submitted a proposal to the Government of Trinidad and Tobago for establishing a deep water harbour in Chaguaramas Bay for the coaling of vessels, and the construction of a railway from Chaguaramas Bay to link up with the terminus in Port-of-Spain.

The proposition was submitted to the consulting engineer to the Government of Trinidad and Tobago, Sir John Coode. Sir John Coode warmly commended Mr Siegert's proposals in the following terms:

'Summarising the foregoing recommendations I may remark that the construction of a satisfactory Quay, the formation of the reclaimed area and the provision of adequate berthings for vessels of deep draught in Chaguaramas Bay, are from an engineering point of view perfectly feasible.

'The formation of a Railway from such Quay to the Port-of-Spain, is in my opinion a matter of absolute necessity for the proper and convenient working of the goods traffic in connection therewith. Further the site selected is capable of affording extended Quay and Wharf accommodation when required hereafter on the lines indicated.

'I have not considered whether the project will be financially successful, as this is no part of my duty, but should it be carried into effect the trade and prosperity of the Colony generally cannot fail to be considerably benefited thereby.'

Mr Siegert's proposal was at once attacked by vested interests in Port-of-Spain, principally British merchants who saw in Chaguaramas an unwelcome rival. In a most astonishing argument the Chairman of the Dock Basin Committee in Trinidad claimed that it was not at

all certain that Chaguaramas would be universally accepted and used
as a port of entry, that it would be expensive to establish Chaguaramas
as a port of entry, that the erection of warehouses at Chaguaramas
for the storage of goods would very seriously depreciate the value of
warehouses in Port-of-Spain, and that, since it would take some time
to construct and complete the works at Chaguaramas the colony
should duplicate the expenditure by proceeding with improvements
and modifications in the Port-of-Spain harbour which were then under
consideration. The fight was on. The Governor, Sir William Robinson,
supported the Siegert proposal and opposed any Government expenditure on the Port-of-Spain harbour which would compete with private
expenditure on the development of Chaguaramas. Eventually, towards
the end of 1892, a draft contract with Mr Siegert was agreed to and
accepted by the Governor and Legislative Council. The Chaguaramas
Bay Agreement, a formidable document of 80 pages, with an index
of 11 additional pages, was presented to the Legislative Council in
Council Paper No. 167 of 1894.

The cost of the proposed quay of 920 feet in length, and the
reclamation of some 16 acres, including the erection of a coal shed
and the provision of the necessary fittings for the convenient berth-
ing of vessels, together with the dredging work involved, were estimated to cost £121,600. The estimate for the construction of the
railway from Chaguaramas to Port-of-Spain with stations, rolling
stock, etc., was £138,200. The total cost of the scheme, therefore, was
£259,800, approximately $1¼ million. The promoter, however, was
unable to raise the necessary finance for his proposal and the scheme
was abandoned.

A Government of Trinidad and Tobago which was able to find
year after year thousands of dollars from the public treasury to finance
the immigration of thousands of workers for the benefit of the sugar
planters, was unable either to finance or assist the promoter in financ-
ing a proposition which was regarded by the experts as being of the
utmost importance to Trinidad. The Colonial Office, which was very
shortly to intervene to demand that the municipality of Port-of-Spain
should raise its rates and get the Governor's approval of its expenditure, which used its power year after year to divert a substantial part
of Trinidad's revenue from education to immigration, could not use
its power to promote a scheme that was of the greatest benefit to
Trinidad and Tobago. Within three years of the draft Chaguaramas
Bay Agreement the West Indian Royal Commision of 1897 was to
emphasise the danger to Trinidad and to all the West Indian islands
from the reduction or extinction of the sugar industry, and could
only say that if Trinidad rigidly controlled its public expenditure and
spent less on immigration, it would be able to tide over the difficulties
faced by the sugar industry. Within four years of the draft Chaguaramas Bay Agreement the Colonial Office was to pay £4,000 to Trinidad for relieving it of the burden of Tobago. Nowhere, at any time,
was there any suggestion, either by the Government of Trinidad and

Tobago or by the Colonial Office, that this beneficial Chaguaramas scheme, warmly commended by a British consulting engineer, could have been financed by way of loan or directly by the Government, or by some form of assistance to the promoter. That was the Crown Colony system. It thought only of sugar. Its vision was limited by the circumference of a sugar plantation. Sugar meant cheap labour as far as it was concerned. The Colony's revenues could not be diverted from the introduction of cheap labour to the construction of a deep water harbour and the promotion of the colony's trade.

This was the first Chaguaramas Agreement in the history of Trinidad. The first agreement having aborted, Chaguaramas remained a playground for the people of Port-of-Spain until 1941, when it became the subject of a second Agreement, this time with a foreign power, this time for the utilisation of its remarkable deep water facilities for a naval base. To understand the full significance of this distortion of the normal course of Trinidad's history, which would inevitably have made the North West Peninsula a natural outlet for the population of Port-of-Spain which had to spill over instead into the heavily congested areas of Diego Martin, Carenage, Point Cumana, Glencoe, and La Horquette, we must now consider the expansion of the United States of America into the Caribbean area.

That a new star had been added to the Caribbean firmament was strikingly and dramatically brought out in 1895, when a fifty-year old boundary dispute between British Guiana and Venezuela came to a head. The United States, to whom Venezuela had repeatedly appealed for support of its claims, decided to press the issue vigorously. The United States Secretary of State, Richard Olney, sent a despatch to the British Government which contained three essential points. The first may be stated in his own words: 'today the United States is practically sovereign on this continent, and its fiat is law upon the subjects to which it confines its interposition.' The second was that the three thousand miles of ocean which separated Europe from America were a physical fact which made any 'permanent union between a European and American State unnatural and inexpedient.' The third was that the dispute fell within the competence of the Monroe Doctrine and, as such, affected the interests of the United States, which was within its rights in demanding that the truth be ascertained. 'Being entitled to resent and resist any sequestration of Venezuelan soil by Great Britain, it is necessarily entitled to know whether such sequestration has occurred or is now going on.' Then followed the threat that, unless Great Britain consented to submit the entire matter to arbitration by an independent tribunal, 'the transaction will be regarded as injurious to the interests of the United States as well as oppressive in itself.' The doctrine of manifest destiny could not have been more incisively or arrogantly stated

The British Foreign Secretary, Lord Salisbury, replied with similar incisiveness to the United States Secretary of State. His reply, too,

consisted of three main points. The first was a virtual rejection of the
Monroe Doctrine. Salisbury wrote:

> 'International law is founded on the general consent of nations;
> and no statesman, however eminent, and no nation, however power-
> ful, are competent to insert into the code of international law a novel
> principle which was never recognised before, and which has not
> since been accepted by the Government of any other country.
> The United States have a right, like any other nation, to interpose in
> any controversy by which their own interests are affected, and they
> are the judge whether those interests are touched, and in what
> measure they should be sustained But their rights are in no way
> strengthened or extended by the fact that controversy affects some
> territory which is called America.'

In his second point Lord Salisbury dealt with Olney's criticism of
the unnatural and inexpedient union between a European and an
American state:

> 'The necessary meaning of these words is that the union between
> Great Britain and Canada; between Great Britain and Jamaica
> and Trinidad; between Great Britain and British Honduras or
> British Guiana are "inexpedient and unnatural" . . . Mr Olney
> lays down that the inexpedient and unnatural character of the union
> between a European and American State is so obvious that it "will
> hardly be denied." Her Majesty's Government are prepared
> emphatically to deny it on behalf of both the British and American
> people who are subject to her crown.'

Thirdly, while stressing that the question of arbitration was a matter
for the two parties concerned, that Britain had repeatedly indicated to
Venezuela its readiness to submit the issue to arbitration, and that the
claim of a third party, unaffected by the controversy, to impose this
procedure on the others could not be reasonably justified and had
no foundation in the law of nations, Salisbury added that the British
Government was 'not prepared to admit that the interests of the United
States are necessarily concerned in every frontier dispute which may
arise between any two of the States who possess dominion in the
Western Hemisphere; and still less can they accept the doctrine that
the United States are entitled to claim that the process of arbitration
shall be applied to any demand for the surrender of territory which
one of these States may make against another.'

President Cleveland of the United States breathed defiance. In his
famous message to Congress on December 17, 1895, he proposed the
appointment of a United States Commission to investigate the facts,
after which it would be the duty of the United States 'to resist by every
means in its power, as a wilful aggression upon its rights and interests,
the appropriation by Great Britain of any lands or the exercise of
governmental jurisdiction over any territory which, after investigation,

we have determined of right belongs to Venezuela.' War loomed on the horizon.

But in January, 1896, the German Kaiser sent his telegram to President Kruger of the Transvaal congratulating him on the frustration of the Jameson Raid. With the Boer War on its hands, with Joseph Chamberlain as Colonial Secretary flirting with his dream of an alliance between the three great Anglo-Saxon powers, Great Britain, Germany and the United States, Britain adopted a conciliatory attitude and agreed to arbitration by an international tribunal, whose decision followed, in the main, the British claim.

The Venezuela boundary dispute provides the setting for the American incursion into the Caribbean with the Spanish-American War of 1898. There were four factors involved.

The first was that, by 1898, the United States had achieved a position of leadership in the industrial world and had supplanted Great Britain, the leader in the nineteenth century race. In 1835, Richard Cobden, the leader of nineteeth century British capitalism, viewing the Monongahela Valley flowing north to Pittsburg, had prophesied: 'Here will one day centre the civilisation, the wealth, the power of the entire world.' Sixteen years later, on March 8, 1851, Britain's distinguished journal, *The Economist,* had predicted: ' . . . the superiority of the United States to England is ultimately as certain as the next eclipse.' By 1898 the predictions had been fulfilled, and the leading circles in the United States knew it. 'We hold now,' said the president of the American Bankers' Association, in a speech at Denver in 1898, 'three of the winning cards in the game for commercial greatness, to wit – iron, steel and coal. We have long been the granary of the world, we now aspire to be its workshop, then we want to be its clearing-house '

The following table provides the statistical demonstration of these proud but justified boasts with respect to the three leading countries of the world:

Countries & Commodities	1880	1900	1913
COAL million tons			
Great Britain	149	229	292
Germany	47	109	190
U.S.A.	65	245	517
IRON million tons			
Britain	8	9	10
Germany	2	7	19
U.S.A.	4	14	31
STEEL million tons			
Great Britain	1	5	8
Germany	1	6	19
U.S.A.	1	10	31

The second factor which explains the Spanish-American War was the growth of an unmistakably belligerent spirit in the United States of

K

America. 'We are face to face with a strange destiny,' wrote the *Washington Post* in 1899. 'The taste of empire is in the mouth of the people even as the taste of blood in the jungle.' The incarnation of this spirit was Theodore Roosevelt, Governor of New York State, soon to be Assistant Secretary of the Navy, Vice President of the country, and, when President McKinley was assassinated, President. In a speech delivered at the opening of the naval War College in New-port, Rhode Island, on June 2, 1897, a speech which was widely praised all over the country, Roosevelt said:

> 'A really great people, proud and high-spirited, would face all the disasters of war rather than purchase that *base prosperity* which is bought at the price of national honour . . . *Cowardice* in a race, as in an individual, is *the unpardonable sin,* and a wilful failure to prepare for danger may in its effects be as bad as cowardice . . . As yet no nation can hold *its place in the world* or can do any work really worth doing unless it stands ready to guard its rights with an armed hand . . . Tame submission to foreign aggression of any kind is *a mean and unworthy thing* . . . If ever we had to meet defeat at the hands of a foreign foe, or had to submit tamely to wrong or insult, every man among us worthy of the name of America, would feel *dishonoured* and *debased* . . . We feel that no national life is worth having if the nation is not willing, when the need shall arise, to stake everything on the supreme arbitrament of war, and to pour out its blood, its treasure, and tears like water rather than submit to the loss of *honor* and *renown.*'

This was not mere jingoism, which was a characteristic of the first Roosevelt. It was the underlying philosophy of a plan to repeal the Papal Donation of 1493 and its amendments. On February 9, 1898, he wrote to a correspondent:

> 'I should myself like to shape our foreign policy with a purpose ultimately of driving off this continent every European power. I would begin with Spain, and in the end would take all other European nations, including England.'

Roosevelt added that it was even more important to prevent any new nation from getting a foothold, and pointedly referred to Germany in this connection. Ten weeks after this letter the Spanish-American war broke out.

A third factor in the situation was the preoccupation of the European powers. 1898 was a black year in Europe; the outbreak of World War I hung in the balance. At Fashoda, in that year, Anglo-French rivalry over Egypt brought both nations to the brink of war, and France was allied with Russia. In the same year Britain and Russia, at loggerheads over Persia, Afghanistan and Tibet, almost came to blows over Port Arthur. The battle of concessions in China was at its height, pitting nation against nation and the Chinese nationalist movement against all foreigners. The German Kaiser had launched his vigorous programme for a powerful navy, saying that Germany's future lay upon the water. Europe was thus too busy to pay too much attention to what was happening in the Caribbean.

The final factor in the Spanish-American conflict was the value of Cuba to the United States. As early as 1881 a United States Consular Report had stated that Cuba was a commercial dependency of the United States but a political dependency of Spain. The sugar of Cuba, stated the United States Minister to Spain to the British Minister, was as vital to the people of the United States as the wheat and cotton of India and Egypt to the people of Great Britain. According to Secretary of State Olney in 1896, United States investment in Cuba totalled fifty million dollars, the greater part in the sugar industry; one of the leading United States investors has stated that Olney was always willing to listen to what he had to say about the Cuban situation. These investments were seriously affected and endangered by the outbreak of the second war of independence in Cuba. Olney was afraid that, once the power of Spain was withdrawn, Cuba would be partitioned into two parts, a white republic and a black republic, which raised the spectre of a race war.

The outcome of the Spanish-American war was never in doubt. But what was involved far transcended the question of Cuban independence to which the United States was officially committed and which the United States public warmly espoused. On June 12, 1898 Theodore Roosevelt wrote to Senator Lodge: 'You must get Manila and Hawaii, you must prevent any talk of peace until we get Porto Rico and the Philippines as well as secure the independence of Cuba.' Whilst the question of Oriental annexations falls outside the scope of Caribbean history, the first and major result of the war was not only the independence of Cuba but United States annexation of Puerto Rico. The United States had acquired its first colony, and that colony, following the tradition set by Europe in previous centuries, was in the Caribbean. The once proud Spanish empire sanctioned by Papal dispensation in 1493 had ceased to exist. The first step had been taken towards making the Caribbean Sea, in the phrase that has become popular in the United States, 'the American Mediterranean' As the Assistant Secretary of State stated in 1904, 'no picture of our future is complete which does not contemplate and comprehend the United States as the dominant power in the Caribbean Sea.'

This is the background to the United States action on the Cuban question. Cuba's independence was recognised, but it was limited by the famous Platt Amendment which passed the United States Congress after a mere two hours of debate in March, 1901, and which led European statesmen to coin the phrase, to 'cubanise' a country. The Platt Amendment was as follows:

'(1) That the Government of Cuba shall never enter into any treaty or other compact with any foreign power or powers which will impair or tend to impair the independence of Cuba, nor in any manner authorise or permit any foreign power or powers to obtain by colonisation or for military or naval purposes or otherwise, lodgment in or control over any portion of said Island.

'(2) That said Government shall not assume or contract any public debt, to pay the interest upon which and to make reasonable sinking-fund provision for the ultimate discharge of which, the ordinary revenues of the Island, after defraying the current expenses of government, shall be inadequate.

'(3) That the Government of Cuba consents that the United States may exercise the right to intervene for the preservation of Cuban independence, the maintenance of a government adequate for protection of life, property and individual liberty, and for discharging the obligation with respect to Cuba imposed by the Treaty of Paris on the United States, now to be assumed and undertaken by the Government of Cuba.

'(4) That all acts of the United States in Cuba during its military occupation thereof are ratified and validated, and all lawful rights acquired thereunder shall be maintained and protected.

'(5) That the Government of Cuba will execute, and as far as necessary extend, the plans already devised or other plans to be mutually agreed upon, for the sanitation of the cities of the Island, to the end that a recurrence of epidemic and infectious diseases may be prevented, thereby ensuring protection of the people and commerce of Cuba, as well as to the commerce of the Southern parts of the United States and the people residing therein.

'(6) That the Isle of Pines shall be omitted from the proposed constitutional boundaries of Cuba, the title thereto left to future adjustment by treaty.

'(7) That to enable the United States to maintain the independence of Cuba, and to protect the people thereof, as well as for its own defence, the Government of Cuba will sell or lease to the United States lands necessary for coaling or naval stations at certain specified points, to be agreed upon with the President of the United States.

'(8) That by way of further assurance the Government of Cuba will embody the foregoing in a permanent treaty with the United States'.

In 1906 the United States intervened, in accordance with the Platt Amendment, in a Cuban revolutionary movement which had developed.

If the Platt Amendment changed Cuba from a political dependency of Spain into what was universally regarded as a protectorate of the United States, the Reciprocity Treaty of 1902 was designed to maintain the commercial relationship which had developed notwithstanding the Spanish sovereignty. The Treaty was presented to the House of Representatives of the United States in this entrancing vision of its sponsor:

'Sir, let Cuba become prosperous, with closer trade relations with the United States, making the conditions down there stable for five years or as much longer as this treaty shall remain in force. Let American capital go down there to develop the island and employ the islanders. Let there be a demand for better things and more of them. Multiply the buying capacity of the people as we have multiplied it in the last five years in the United States under the Dingley tariff law, so that the people want more, buy more, and are ready to give bigger prices, because they get larger wages. Under such improved conditions what shall be the figure of our imports into Cuba? Shall the amount be barely $60,000,000 as during the past year, for all imports, running up to $100,000,000 in the days preceding the war; or shall it be what Colonel Bliss of the United States Army, a careful and impartial observer, says in his report on Cuba – $300,000,000 a year bought from the United States to supply the needs and capacities of the people down there? Why there are millions in this bill to the farmers and manufacturers of the United States'.

Thereafter the United States of America intervened during the First World War to establish a military protectorate over Haiti and the Dominican Republic, independent States, in order partly to ensure against the establishment of any German naval bases in either of these Republics, and partly to take control of the customs of both Republics as a guarantee of payment of their debts. At the same time the United States of America purchased the Virgin Islands from Denmark at a cost of $25 million, having endeavoured to acquire these islands as far back as 1867. As a result of considerable opposition in subsequent years in the South American countries to what came to be described as 'Yanqui' imperialism and dollar diplomacy, the U.S.A., under President Franklin D. Roosevelt, withdrew its marines and announced the Good Neighbour Policy of non-interference in the domestic affairs of Latin America.

This was the situation in the Caribbean when the Second World War broke out in 1939. The immediate result as far as the British West Indies in general and Trinidad and Tobago in particular were concerned was the Anglo-American Agreement of 1941 by which, in return for 50 antiquated destroyers, the British Government conceded to the United States of America 99 year leases on certain areas in Antigua, St Lucia, Jamaica, British Guiana and Trinidad – the principal area in Trinidad being Chaguaramas, the north west peninsula.

Some information on these transactions, presenting the American point of view, has recently been made available in the Department of State publication, *Foreign Relations of the United States*, for the year 1941. The background to the transaction was stated in a letter from the President to the Secretary of State, Cordell Hull, on January 11, 1941:

'There is always the possibility of their putting up their sovereignty to and over certain colonies, such as Bermuda, the British West

Indies, British Honduras and British Guinea (Guiana?). I am not
yet clear in mind, however, as to whether the United States should
consider American sovereignty over these islands and their populations and the two mainland colonies as something worth while or
as a distinct liability. If we can get our naval bases why, for
example, should we buy with them two million headaches, consisting of that number of human beings who would be a definite
drag on this country, and who would stir up questions of racial
stocks by virtue of their new status as American citizens?'

A conference was convened in London on January 28, 1941 to discuss the details of the entire transaction. The Government of Trinidad
and Tobago was represented at the conference, along with other
Colonial Governments. The reaction of the Colonial Governments
to the claims and propositions put forward by the United States representatives was well expressed in an account transmitted by the United
States Chargé d'Affaires in London to Cordell Hull on January 21
with particular respect to Bermuda. This account reads as follows:—

'While the Colonial Office is hopeful that the Governor may
accomplish their purpose, they are apprehensive that if the backs
of the Bermudans are put up too much the legislature will refuse
to meet the Imperial Government's views. It was explained that
the Imperial Government is in an entirely different position vis-
a-vis Bermuda and the Bahamas to any other of the West Indian
Island Governments; that the Imperial Government cannot by executive action force the Bermuda legislature to pass any law or
to implement any obligation of the Imperial Government. The only
machinery for overriding the Bermuda legislature would be an act
of Parliament – a last resort which they are most reluctant to invoke
as it would arouse extreme hostility in Bermuda and in their opinion
would have bad repercussions elsewhere as well as affording
material for German propaganda. The Under Secretary and all
his officials most earnestly assured me, and I am sure it is true, that
the Colonial Office and the Government in London desire to meet
our views as quickly as possible. We will take account of the difficult
political situation with which they are faced in Bermuda and not
try to push matters to an immediate conclusion. One of the officials
present, who was a former Governor of Bermuda, said the single
thing that was most alarming the legislature and people now was
a clause in the draft lease which would give, in their opinion, blanket
authority to the United States to take over in the future any other
site on the island they wanted and that they therefore felt that they
had no protection; that what they are clamouring for now is some
assurance that as to where the United States' requests would stop.
The Colonial Office hopes that the meeting shortly to take place
here with United States officials will be able to eliminate all serious
points of difference and many of the minor ones.

'I pointed out to the official that while I could understand that the Bermudans would feel upset at such great changes in their way of life, that nevertheless our officials were under the urgent necessity to begin their programmes, that the purposes for which they were there were obviously of overriding necessity and that my Government necessarily had to look to the Imperial Government to implement the agreement contained in our exchange of notes of last September. The Colonial Office readily admits that we must look to the Imperial Government for action, but says they hope the statements which have been outlined above will convince the Department that the Government is doing all it can in a practicable way to effect a speedy solution and they hope we will understand their desire to obtain action through the consent of Bermuda and not through the Imperial Government being forced to override them by an act of Parliament.'

The British Government, with its back to the wall at the height of the war, put up what resistance it could – but this was not much – to America's claims which seemed to it, as to the Colonial Governments, far in excess of what was required for military defence. The British Embassy in Washington put up the case for the colonials in a memorandum to the Department of State on February 26, 1941, as follows: —

'the question to be solved would seem to be how to arrange that the United States authorities in the various territories shall obtain adequate powers to defend, control and operate their bases with the minimum disturbance to the existing British administrative and jurisdictional arrangements.

'There is, of course, no suggestion that the United States Government should be denied any powers which they consider necessary for the proper defence or use of the bases. At the same time, it is felt that it is most important that the fullest consideration should be given to the interests and feelings of the local inhabitants and that the existing administrative and jurisdictional arrangements should only be disturbed if this is really essential for the proper defence of the American bases. While the British authorities are naturally particularly concerned to protect the interests of the local inhabitants for whose welfare they are responsible, it is felt that it is equally to the advantage of the United States authorities to see that the leases are drawn up in such a manner as to reduce to the minimum the possible causes of friction between the various parties concerned. The leases are to run for a period of 99 years, and that being so it is clearly necessary that their long term effect upon the well being of the local inhabitants should be taken into account. It would seem however, that the instructions sent to the United States Delegates in London make it difficult for the latter to pay due account to the interests of the different territories and their inhabitants, and compel them to put forward demands for concessions or facilities which would not seem to be essential for the defence control of the bases.'

The British Government agreed with the American proposals only with the greatest reluctance; and it was only Sir Winston Churchill's personal decision which eventually allowed the Agreement to go through. This is well brought out in a report by the United States representatives at the Conference to President Roosevelt: —

'The agreement embodies a number of concessions by the British, particularly with respect to the specification of rights, defence and jurisdiction which they were most reluctant to make. They were finally secured yesterday at a meeting attended by the Prime Minister, Lord Moyne, Admiral Sir Dudley Pound, Chairman of the Chiefs of Staffs' Committee; Sir Alan Burns, the Ambassador and ourselves. The Prime Minister indicated that our requests in some respects went beyond the intent of the exchange of notes of September 2, 1940, but that he had no desire to restrict our necessary military requirements and that in view of the general situation he was prepared to accept our views. He considered, however, that the concessions given represent the maximum which the British could give. He held that any further concessions would probably necessitate an act of Parliament to override Colonial legislatures and would be difficult to defend in Parliament should the need for such an act arise.

'The Prime Minister attaches great importance to the fourth clause of the preamble which he considers truly represents the spirit in which the whole base lease project was conceived and should be carried out. Without it he said the agreement would be more of a "capitulation" than a friendly arrangement between great powers. He holds that this clause sets the tone of the whole agreement that the British Government could agree on the understanding that our rights would be exercised in that spirit to a number of points which they could never otherwise concede and that his presentation of the agreement to Parliament will be based upon the spirit of the preamble.'

The American Ambassador in London, John Winant, thus summed up the American view of the 1941 Agreement: —

'The Base Lease Agreement has been signed. I think it contains everything we need to use these bases effectively.

'The rights and powers it conveys are far-reaching, probably more far-reaching than any the British Government has ever given anyone over British territory before. They are not used to giving such concessions and on certain points they have fought every inch of the way. While they have intended all along to give us everything we really needed – they could do no less and had no desire to do less – it was a real struggle for them to break habits of 300 years. The Prime Minister has been generous throughout. Certain powers, notably those in article XII, are so sweeping that the British would never have granted them except as a natural consequence of the original agreement and the spirit which it embodies.

'It is important that the agreement be carried out in that spirit. The Colonies have been lightly touched by the war, their point of view is local and their way of life will be greatly changed by the bases In the main the changes will benefit them but it may take them some time to find it out.

'In the negotiations both sides have tried to avoid anything which would wall off the bases from the local communities Our people and theirs are to live together without even a fence, much less a frontier, between them.

'The character of the men in command of the bases is of tremendous importance, especially in the beginning. If they are the right kind and ready to carry out our part of the agreement in a friendly and understanding spirit they can do much to inaugurate 99 years of good neighbourliness.'

This is the American story. The Trinidad and Tobago story has not yet been told. The United States representatives concentrated on the British Government and ignored the representatives of the Crown Colony legislatures. The Trinidad story, which will certainly be told one day, will supplement the American narrative, correct the distortion, and present, what is totally excluded in the American document, the point of view of the Government and people of Trinidad and Tobago.

That point of view was one of almost total resistance to the American demands. The centre of the opposition was the Governor, Sir Hubert Young. Conventionally regarded as an autocrat, Sir Hubert Young was one of those strange characters that one encounters in the colonial history of the West Indies, ready to resist at all times any demands of the people for self government, but in the foreground of their defenders when certain of their rights were threatened.

The main points of the Trinidad opposition were as follows. The first, was that, if any base was to be granted at all it should not be at Chaguaramas. Chaguaramas was the obvious area for the future development of Port-of-Spain. It provided the best beaches close to Port-of-Spain, and from the standpoint of future economic development of the country, Chaguaramas occupied a key position Sir Hubert Young was convinced that the United States of America should seek an area which would not deprive Trinidad and Tobago of any of its assets, but which, if the Americans developed it, would add to the assets of Trinidad and Tobago and thus make a contribution to the development of the society and the population. He suggested the Caroni Swamp, and went on a personal mission to Washington to try to convince the Americans. The Americans simply would not listen to him and the American Press gave him a rough time. They claimed that reclamation of the swamp would be too costly both in time and money, and against the Governer's protest rushed through their selection of Chaguaramas in some ten days. The Governor also protested against dispersal of the American locations in so many spots over the island that, based on the supplementary leases which the Agreement permitted them to obtain, a committee subsequently appointed by the Government of the People's National Movement claimed that, if the war had continued much longer, the people of Trinidad would have had to live in the Gulf of Paria.

The opposition to the 1941 Agreement from the West Indian Colonial Governments and Governors centred around, in the second place, the 99-year lease. Governor after Governor, and particularly Sir Hubert Young, issued stern warnings of an unavoidable conflict with the nationalist movement when the West Indian movement for self government had achieved its aspirations. The United States of America would not listen and Britain, perhaps, could not.

The third feature of the 1941 Agreement which provoked intense dissatisfaction in the Colonies was the fiscal and customs privileges extended to the American Forces. The Government of Trinidad and Tobago, in particular, which had to bear the major brunt of the American Army of occupation, was particularly concerned about the many incidents which, from the start, developed in violation of customs laws and currency controls, in the absence of even a fence, much less a frontier, separating the Bases from the local territory.

The fourth point of colonial resistence to the 1941 Agreement was the extra territorial rights extended to the American Forces. This ultimately involved, as many West Indians foresaw, serious difficulties between the Colonial Government and the American Command in relation to offences of one sort or another committed by the occupation troops. The general situation was not assisted by the obvious concern with questions of race and colour which dominated the highest American circles in this matter.

The final bone of contention emerged at the end of the War when the Americans retained control of large areas of Trinidad which they obviously did not need.

The situation was bound to come to a head sooner or later. It came to a head in 1957 when the representatives of the West Indian territories selected Chaguaramas as the most suitable site for the location of the Federal Capital. Thereafter, in the course of patient research, a long train of abuses was brought to light – agricultural cultivation for profit on the naval base in competition with local producers; sales to the local residents in violation of local laws of prohibited foreign imports or of imports brought in free of customs duty for consumption by American troops; repeated infractions of the local currency control system; expansion of the American facilities accorded in 1941 as, for example, the construction of a missile tracking station. With the increase in international tension the suspicion was engendered that Trinidad and Tobago was being brought within the scope of nuclear weapons and nuclear war. With the emergence of a local concern with foreign relations, the apprehension grew that the naval base would be utilised by the United States of America for purposes which could not be regarded as being in the interest of the people of Trinidad and Tobago – as, for example, the hostile reception of a United States Vice President in Venezuela. Without any agreement at all, and without the approval of the Government of Trinidad and Tobago, the American Military Command had virtually made the Piarco Airport in Trinidad a United States Military Airport.

The entire situation was embittered by the public knowledge that officials of the United States Naval Station in Chaguaramas were intervening in local politics.

Public feeling was aroused and all the bitterness of the days of 1941 revived. The general feeling was expressed by the Premier of Trinidad and Tobago in a speech at Arima in July 1959 : —

'The whole West Indian movement is moving towards control of its own affairs. I, too, would like to know the clause in Adam's will which denies the West Indian people a share of the world, especially a share of the world that rightly belongs to them. And what progress have we made if, instead of the fortress in Havana, guarding the treasure fleets in the 16th century (you could see in St Kitts a tremendous fortress built by slave labour, Brimstone Hill, symbolising the time when that tiny island of St Kitts was divided up, half to the French and half to the British, with constant warfare until the British took the whole island over), what progress have we made, if we have substituted Chaguaramas, the naval base of the 20th century, for Brimstone Hill, the military base of the 18th century, and Morro Castle, the military base of the 16th century? Are we still to be bases defending Spain's treasure fleet on the one hand, British sugar lifeline on the other, and, in this case, the lifeline of the United States of America? Historically speaking, where are we going? We come to the population and we say: Cabinet Government as the step towards full internal self-government. But how could you have full internal self-government if you don't have control over a part of your territory, if people are allowed to land a plane here without permission, if they could claim all sorts of economic privileges that you cannot guarantee to your own population?

'It is the Americans who have to answer the question; it is we in Trinidad who ask the question, it is their answer. And the first question that they have to answer is: are they for colonialism or against it? This was British colonialism, this was Spanish colonialism, this was French colonialism; if the Americans do the same thing it can only be defined as American colonialism. All over the West Indies this movement is breaking out, Venezuela, Cuba, and Cuba has a base, Guantanamo Bay, imposed in 1906, by a permanent treaty with the United States. Ours is 99 years like the Philippines. Theirs is permanent. What sort of thing is this? What is sacred about 99 years? One of the Kings of England, King Charles the II, I believe, gave a contract to a company which he dignified by permitting it to use the title "Royal", gave the Royal African Company a contract for the monopoly of supplying slaves to the West Indies for 1,000 years We should still be slaves today. The contract should come to an end in the year 2,663. (Laughter.) And look at us here in 1959 enjoying some sort of Cabinet Day. That we have to decide. The 99 years don't mean a thing, really. Because as you know, I think we have said it before, let's say it again for the record, tonight, they are not committed to the development of the areas. You should see Waller Field We are supposed to maintain Waller Field. There are parts of Chaguaramas today which have been allowed to revert to jungle. Scotland Bay and Teteron Bay, they are not supposed to keep it up. They could move from Chaguaramas tomorrow and they would say they must get it back on 48 hours notice – but we will have plenty to say about that They are under no obligation to defend, they don't have to employ a single West Indian. They don't have to have anything standing down there, they were just given areas for 99 years. And we have to ask ourselves, what is this? The British Government in the colonial period left large parts of the West Indies undeveloped and unexploited – Dominica, St Vincent, Grenada, Tobago. Are we, with a Cabinet, are we with self-government, going to have large parts or large areas, like Waller Field or Tucker Valley, lying undeveloped, lying unexploited, when you can't get enough land for the people of Trinidad and Tobago, when you require all sorts of opportunities, when you require to exploit all sorts of opportunities to develop our limited resources and for finding employment for our population? They are going to have to decide that. And then somebody comes to tell us if we behave badly, we won't get American aid.

The Government offered the United States of America an alternative site for a base in Trinidad. As a result of its insistence it was able to secure the appointment of a four party commission, the United Kingdom, the United States, the Federal Government and the Government of Trinidad and Tobago, to consider the question of an alternative site. The commission reported to the effect that, whilst Chaguaramas was the best site for a naval base, an alternative base could quite easily and quite conveniently be located in Irois Bay in the south west part of the island. The alternative site was rejected by the United States Government, and when the Federal Government indicated a readiness to accept assurances and compromises that were unacceptable to Trinidad and Tobago, the weak Federal Government was further weakened by another conflict with the Government of Trinidad and Tobago in which the Federal Government fell into the worst possible mistake any Government could find itself, supporting the American Government and pleading with the British Government for support against the Government of a unit Territory which had enormous mass support. When on April 22, 1960, the People's National Movement staged a demonstration in Port-of-Spain in which thousands marched in a steady downpour in manifestation of their support for full national independence and for the revision of the 1941 Agreement, it was quite clear that the Federal Government was doomed.

Persistent pressure from the Government of Trinidad and Tobago forced the American and British Governments to agree to a conference to consider the 1941 Agreement. The Americans and British decided that it would be a tripartite conference, with Trinidad and Tobago forming part of a federal delegation. The Trinidad and Tobago Government insisted on its separate, direct and equal representation in a matter which it had raised, in a matter in which its views were notoriously divergent from those of the Federal Government, in a matter in which, under the 1941 Agreement, it and it alone was involved in respect of customs, or restoration of its lands, or rights and duties under that Agreement, in a matter finally which it alone knew and of which the Federal Government had no knowledge whatsoever. Eventually, after protracted and unnecessary negotiations, it was decided that the conference would be held in three stages. In the first, the formal stage in London, there would be speeches and protocol for press and radio. In the second, the effective stage, which was eventually held in Tobago, the Territory concerned would negotiate directly with the American Government, with the British and Federal Governments on the sideline, observing. In the third stage, held in Port-of-Spain in Federal quarters, the Agreement was to be signed

The Government of Trinidad and Tobago had previously made proposals to the United States authorities for the reduction of the 99 year term to a maximum of 10 years, for the immediate restoration of areas at Waller Field and Carlsen Field which were not being utilised, and for the reduction of the leased area in Chaguaramas in the north west peninsula by the restoration of areas growing citrus and dedicated obviously to non-military uses. This submission formed the basis of the discussions in Tobago in which the Trinidad and Tobago delegation, which was prepared to accept a phased restoration of the military areas over a period extending to 17 years, submitted that if through Chaguaramas the people of Trinidad and Tobago had been able to contribute freely to the preservation of the American way of life, the Americans in the new Agreement should undertake to contribute to the preservation of the Trinidad and Tobago way of life and to the development of the self governing Trinidad and Tobago society.

Five specific projects were put forward by the delegation under this head to be financed by the United States of America: —

    (1) The construction of an alternative road from Diego Martin to Chaguaramas to ease existing congestion which would obviously be enormously aggravated in time of emergency if the base

were to be called upon to perform the functions for which its retention was requested by the United States Government.

(2) The reclamation of the Cocorite Swamp as an integral part of the new road to Chaguaramas, which would incidentally make available a large area of land for low cost and middle class housing for the benefit of the people of Trinidad and Tobago.

(3) The improvement of the port facilities in Port-of-Spain, not only to assist the Territory, but also as an insurance in the event of war in the light of the experience in 1941 when the port was almost entirely taken over for United States military purposes.

(4) The rehabilitation of the Trinidad Government Railway which had been taken over by the military authorities in 1941, which would serve conceivably a similarly valuable purpose in the event of another emergency, and whose notorious deficits originated with American control during the Second World War.

(5) The establishment of a College of Arts with an excellent library endowed with a collection of *Americana* as the most appropriate contribution that America could make to Trinidad and Tobago and which Trinidad and Tobago would always want to associate with America.

The delegation also raised the question of a sugar quota for Trinidad and Tobago in the United States market, on the principle that America cannot be the military friend and the economic enemy of Trinidad and Tobago.

The new Agreement was worked out in Tobago in an atmosphere of rare good will and friendship; Trinidad and Tobago's first diplomatic success in the field of international relations. The Agreement, however, has remained so far, largely on paper, as a result of the American claim that they agreed only to participate in and not to provide the five projects indicated above, and as a result of the American attempt to inject into the Agreement considerations of the national income of Trinidad and Tobago and Trinidad's prosperity as compared with other Caribbean Territories which were quite foreign to the Tobago discussions and quite irrelevant to a military agreement. The situation has not been improved by the American refusal to date to consider any of the conventional forms of economic aid to developing countries such as was requested officially by the Government of Trinidad and Tobago in October 1961 in the field of housing, not only to raise the standard of living in the country but also to provide much needed employment. And there the matter stands – for the present.

This was the general situation in which Trinidad and Tobago found itself at the beginning of 1962. The Federation was dead. The Government of the country was committed to independence for Trinidad and Tobago. The success of the programme of economic development had established the economic and political stability of Trinidad and Tobago in the eyes of investors. The country proceeded rapidly on the road to independence; a draft Constitution was submitted to popular discussion, both written and oral, in a manifestation of democracy perhaps unprecedented in modern times.

The opposition element in the country expressed grave apprehension about the draft Constitution even after extensive modifications as a result of popular comments. The Parliamentary Opposition, led by Dr Rudranath Capildeo, called for greater safeguards in a number of fields with particular reference to the Judiciary, appointments to the Public Service, the control of Elections, the protection of human rights, and provision for consultation with the Opposition. Some sectional interest advocated proportional representation and the Constitution of Cyprus. It was alleged that racial discrimination prevailed in public appointments and in the award of scholarships. This was shown to be without substance, and Trinidad and Tobago and the world at large were given evidence of an integration possibly without parallel in the world, certainly unequalled in many other multi-racial communities, in the public service generally, in the teaching profession, in professions like law and medicine and dentistry, and in other fields.

The Independence Conference opened in London in Marlborough House on May 28, 1962 and ended on June 8, a great success for the two major Parties and for the country as a whole. Carefully eschewing to divide the major racial groups in the community, a constitution was achieved which kept Trinidad and Tobago as a monarchical state in the Commonwealth, provided for the independence of the Judiciary, ensured the rights and privileges of the Parliament and its Members, guaranteed equality of opportunity and the removal of discrimination in the public service, ensured the independence of the Auditor General, and provided for the control of Elections and delimitation of constituencies. Under the benevolent and efficient chairmanship of the United Kingdom, whose goodwill and sincerity in respect of independence were never in doubt, the leaders of the two political parties publicly pledged themselves to associate on their return to Trinidad in bipartisan discussions designed to prevent the disruption or jeopardising of national unity on national issues.

What for centuries the people of the colony together had aspired to, the two political parties together achieved in London.

To the rejoicing of all the people of Trinidad and Tobago, Independence Day was fixed for August 31, 1962.

Conclusion

Independence Day, August 31, 1962, finds Trinidad and Tobago no longer a great workshop operated by slave or semi-servile labour, but a miniature state. Two races have been freed, but a society has not been formed. It takes more than national boundaries, a National Anthem however stirring, a National Coat of Arms however distinctive, a National Flag however appropriate, a National Flower however beautiful, to make a nation. The task facing the people of Trinidad and Tobago after their Independence is to create a nation out of the discordant elements and antagonistic principles and competing faiths and rival colours which have produced the amalgam that is today the approximately 875,000 people of Trinidad and Tobago.

In assuming this enormous responsibility the people of Trinidad and Tobago have two decisive advantages, provided only that they appreciate them and act accordingly.

The first advantage is the fundamental underlying unity of the society of Trinidad and Tobago. A foreign student, with all the impetuosity of youth rushing in where angels fear to tread, may talk glibly of an Indian village in Trinidad not being West Indian, and predict that the Indians will never be assimilated. It is certain, however, that he did not have to paint his white face black or brown to ascertain this, as a compatriot of his had to do in respect of his native country. The fact of the matter is, however, that in Trinidad the Negro, the Indian, French and Spaniard, English and Portuguese, Syrian and Lebanese, Chinese and Jew, all have messed out of the same pot, all are victims of the same subordination, all have been tarred with the same brush of political inferiority. Divergent customs and antipathetic attitudes have all been submerged in the common subordinate status of colonialism. All have been maligned for centuries – the Amerindians as subhuman, the Africans as closer to the ape, without manufactures, arts, or sciences, the Indians as savages, without a history of their own, objects of commerce and conquest, the Chinese as a passive people and a negative element, the European reformers as disreputable persons courting Negro suffrages. Cipriani, Butler, Solomon, the same epithet was applied to all – 'agitators'.

Whether it was carnival or hosea or water, the same blank wall of governmental indifference faced the people, the same gulf separated governors and governed. Froude in 1887 repeated the Secretary of State for the Colonies, Lord Liverpool, in 1810, in opposing any form of government which would subject a white minority to a coloured majority. Joseph Chamberlain, the Secretary of State for the Colonies, repeated in 1903 substantially what Froude had written in 1887, that external control was alone suited to the conditions of Trinidad. The continued separation of the separate racial groups was the principal aim of policy; they were kept separate by law in respect of schools, in respect of latrines, in respect of location, insofar as the Indians were virtually tied to the plantations to which they were indentured. Portuguese indenture was hardly distinguishable from African slavery, and Indian indenture differed from Portuguese only in its greater intensity and in the larger numbers involved. Together the various groups in Trinidad and Tobago have suffered, together they have aspired, together they have achieved Only together can they succeed.

And only together can they build a society, can they build a nation, can they build a homeland. There can be no Mother India for those whose ancestors came from India; the young Trinidad novelist, Ismith Khan, in his recent novel *The Jumbie Bird*, has described the disappointment of the Indians when the first Commissioner of the Government of India arrived in Trinidad some 11 years ago, not to arrange their repatriation as they had hoped, but to advise them to stay in Trinidad and become good Trinidad citizens. There can be no Mother Africa for those of African origin, and the Trinidad and Tobago society is living a lie and heading for trouble if it seeks to create the impression or to allow others to act under the delusion that Trinidad and Tobago is an African society. There can be no Mother England and no dual loyalties; no person can be allowed to get the best of both worlds, and to enjoy the privileges of citizenship in Trinidad and Tobago whilst expecting to retain United Kingdom citizenship. There can be no Mother China, even if one could agree as to which China is the Mother; and there can be no Mother Syria or no Mother Lebanon. A nation, like an individual, can have only one Mother. The only Mother we recognise is Mother Trinidad and Tobago, and Mother cannot discriminate between her children. All must be equal in her eyes. And no possible interference can be tolerated by any country outside in our family relations and domestic quarrels, no matter what it has contributed and when to the population that is today the people of Trinidad and Tobago.

The second decisive advantage with which the people of Trinidad and Tobago assume their Independence status is that they cannot conceivably do worse than their former metropolitan governors. Spanish colonialism in 1797 was bankrupt; Spain reigned but France governed, and Britain took over without firing a shot. British colonialism in 1941 was bankrupt; Britain reigned but America governed, and America took over Trinidad without firing a shot. Spanish colonialism was absolutely powerless to develop Trinidad's economy, and European colonialism could only treat Tobago as waste land. British colonialism was equally powerless. It denied Trinidad African slaves to develop the sugar industry but authorised Indian semi-slaves to develop the sugar industry. It compensated British planters out of British funds for the slaves emancipated, and utilised Trinidad's revenues as further compensation to British planters to enable them virtually to enslave thousands of Indians. It protected Trinidad's sugar in Britain's market only in 1845 to cast it adrift in a hostile world; Trinidad turned to the United States of America until with the closing of the American door it sought refuge in Canadian reciprocity; brought back into the British fold shortly after, Trinidad's sugar now faces with Independence the uncertainties of the European Common Market. A population brought in indiscriminately without any thought for the future, four being brought in to do the work of three, with an outward migration exceeding an inward migration and raising the sceptre of possible forced repatriation in later years, laying the foundation of an inevitable explosion in a society in which official-dom has always encouraged population growth, pressing more and more on economic resources which have not expanded in the same proportion, that population that was told by the Royal Commission of 1897 that it had been placed where it was by the British Govern-ment which could not divest itself of responsibility for their future, that population which in its Independence Constitution has through its political parties specially entrenched Trinidad and Tobago in the Commonwealth, that population is now discriminated against solely on grounds of race and colour by the Commonwealth Immigration Bill as it has been kept out for decades by other Commonwealth countries and by the United States of America. Always the metro-politan interest has dominated and the colonial interest was subor-dinated or ignored. If Trinidad was to be united with Tobago it was because of the paramountcy of British interests. If Trinidad was to be associated in a Federation with the other territories, it was because of the paramountcy of British interests in respect of defence and administrative consolidation.

The population of Trinidad and Tobago must be made of the poorest stuff if it cannot improve on more than four and a half centuries of colonialism.

Unless of course the metropolitan countries take the view that Independence is a penalty imposed upon a refractory people. Unless of course the metropolitan countries continue to take the view that Trinidad's wealth makes economic and financial assistance unneces-sary. Unless of course the metropolitan countries take the view that Trinidad is to relieve Britain of its responsibility in other parts of the Caribbean as it was required to do in 1898 with Tobago. Unless of course the metropolitan countries take the view that metropolitan interests are better served by Independence than by colonialism, by ridding them of two million headaches, and by merely controlling the local population and defending metropolitan interests by con-verting sugar colonies into naval bases, as the Americans did in 1941. Unless of course the metropolitan countries take the view that the independent country must continue, on the basis of its colonial antece-dents, to subserve metropolitan ends, must cease therefore to grow sugar which embarrasses the metropolitan countries in its search for markets, as they had for generations been commanded to grow sugar, and must concentrate, as was recommended some eight years ago by an Assistant Secretary of Commerce in the United States at a Trade Promotion Conference in Trinidad held under the auspices of the Caribbean Commission, the quintessence of metropolitan ineptitude, on the production of flavours and essences for the American ice cream industry. Unless of course the metropolitan countries continue to find it difficult, as Froude and Trollope found it difficult or as the Chaguaramas Agreement of 1941 indicated that it was difficult, for them to treat the people of Trinidad and Tobago as their political and intellectual equals.

Against these two decisive advantages the people of Trinidad and Tobago face one overwhelming disadvantage. That is the national character, as developed and encouraged by generations of slavery and colonialism, by harsh pressures, political, economic and social, to which they have been subjected, by the domination in theory and in fact of the metropolitan organisation and the metropolitan civilisation personified by the expatriate officer who ruled Trinidad and Tobago without any reference whatsoever to the wishes or opinions or needs of the people of Trinidad and Tobago In this climate, political rather than physical, social climbing has become the major industry of Trinidad and Tobago – invitations to cocktail parties, and appearing in the photographs and social columns of the newspapers. Legal slavery and political slavery implicit in the nominated system have led to a capacity for individual ingratiation with the political powers or the social arbiters that make Trinidad and Tobago a byword even among the West Indian territories. The pronounced materialism and disastrous individualism have spread to all parts of the fabric of the society; Vidia Naipaul has dissected them mercilessly in his recent book *The Middle Passage: The Caribbean Revisited*. The political parties are riddled with individualism. The trade unions are riddled with individualism. The professions are riddled with individualism. Each seeks aggrandisement at the expense of his neighbour, giving rise to attitudes that threaten equality of opportunity and jeopardise political democracy. Some of those who protest against colonial exploitation seek in the same breath to demand the perquisites enjoyed by the expatriates, seeking thereby not only to foist upon the people of Trinidad and Tobago a perpetuation of colonial standards and colonial privileges, but also to maintain the same distributive injustice which precipitated the nationalist movement; as if a parasite ceases to be offensive because it is indigenous. Some of those who were despised and ignored by the former colonial system have as their main anxiety to place themselves in positions where they could bask in the sunshine of those in authority, and if their advice is not accepted or their own inflated assessment of their importance not shared by others, they rush off in a huff and attack or form a rival union, or form a rival party, or indulge in the lowest form of intrigue and machinations. The whole society lived in the colonial period on a colonial making himself *persona grata* with a particular big shot who could make or break him, and the tradition of the

colonial service as well as of private employment in the colonial service as well as of private employment in the colonial days is one of the
rankest forms of discrimination; there are those today who see in
nationalism and self government nothing but an opportunity for
establishing their own little clique and having around them a mass
of clients and protegés whom they push forward at the expense of
others.

Their history was in the past made for the people of Trinidad and
Tobago. They were the subjects and the objects of that history. With
Independence, the people of Trinidad and Tobago will make their
own history; they will be active and no longer passive. There are
many injustices to correct and many indignities to remove. But if
colonialism meant the exploitation of the people of Trinidad and
Tobago with others growing fat on the fruits of their sweated labour,
Independence means not that they must work less, but that they must
work more, not for others, but for themselves. The slave could idle
when he was working for his master, and the indentured worker could
feign sickness and go to hospital. This was passive resistance, the
retribution exacted by the weak majority from the strong minority.
The slackers and the thieves and the confidence men in the age of
Independence are the enemies of the people of Trinidad and Tobago.
If a man must steal, as long as he is in his right mind he will not
steal from himself.

On August 31, 1962, a country will be free, a miniature state will
be established, but a society and a nation will not have been formed.
After August 31, 1962, the people of Trinidad and Tobago will face
the fiercest test in their history – whether they can invest with flesh
and blood the bare skeleton of their National Anthem, 'here ev'ry
creed and race find an equal place'. That is their challenge. They may
fail. Others more important and better endowed than they have failed
conspicuously. That would be no justification for their own failure.
But merely to make the attempt, merely to determine to succeed,
would be an enormous tribute to their capacity, a powerful inspiration to frustrated humanity, a wonderful opportunity for self-gratifica-
tion. This will be their final emancipation from slavery, this will be
their final demonstration that slavery is not by nature and that the
Humblest antecedents are not inconsistent with greatness of soul.

*For I will make you a name and a praise among all people of the
earth, when I turn back your captivity before your eyes, saith the
Lord.*

Brief Bibliography

The most important source for the history of Trinidad and Tobago is a collection of 999 documents published by the Historical Society of Trinidad and Tobago and covering approximately the period 1498–1840, and including a number of documents on Tobago. These documents, unfortunately, are not published in sequence – a valuable document relating to 1593 is likely to follow a number of documents relating to 1841. In addition, much of what has been reproduced is of no value whatsoever and merely a waste of paper. But if one has the time and the background knowledge to separate what is valuable from what is inconsequential, then this collection of documents is unique in the history of the West Indies and constitutes an important source book for the student of the history of Trinidad and Tobago.

There are no histories of Trinidad and Tobago, using 'history' in the acknowledged sense. Gertrude Carmichael's recent *History of Trinidad and Tobago* is a compilation which, making the necessary reservation for its emphasis on Governors as the line of demarcation between periods, is full of useful facts, which demonstrate assiduousness on the part of the compiler that is to be highly commended. Apart from this there are two ancient histories of Trinidad, one by L. M. Fraser in two volumes – Vol. I for the period from 1781–1813, published in 1891; Vol. 2 for the period from 1814–1839, published in 1896; and a French *History of Trinidad under the Spanish Régime*, from 1498–1797, by P. G. L. Borde, published in Paris in 1882. Of some value from a constitutional point of view is Hewan Craig's *The Legislative Council of Trinidad and Tobago*, published in 1952. A former Chief Justice of Tobago, H. I. Woodcock, has left us a small *History of Tobago*, published in 1867. To these must be added the popular narratives of Carlton Ottley: *An Account of Life in Spanish Trinidad (from 1498–1797)*, published in 1955, and *The Complete History of the Island of Tobago in the West Indies*, which carries no date of publication.

The Historical Society of Trinidad and Tobago has also published two volumes, edited by the author, which are of particular importance for the period immediately preceding the abolition of slavery: *Documents on British West Indian History*, 1807–1833, which covers Jamaica, Barbados and British Guiana as well as Trinidad, published in 1952; and *The British West Indies at Westminster – Part I – 1789–1823*, published in 1954.

Nos. III–IV of the *Caribbean Historical Review*, December 1954; another publication of the Historical Society of Trinidad and Tobago, includes a number of selected documents on the historical background of the British West Indies Federation.

Together with the 999 documents published by the Historical Society of Trinidad and Tobago the Reports of Commissions of Enquiry over the past century and a quarter constitute the principal source for the history of Trinidad and Tobago. The most important of these reports are as follows: —

Accounts of Slave Compensation Claims, 1838.

Report from the Select Committee on West India Colonies, 1842.

Reports of a House of Commons Committee on Sugar and Coffee Plantations, 1847–1848.

Sugar Growing Colonies, Part III, Trinidad, 1853.

Report upon the state of Education in the Island of Trinidad, by Patrick Joseph Keenan, Dublin, 1869.

Report of the Royal Commission appointed in December, 1882 *to enquire into the Public Revenues, Expenditures, Debts and Liabilities of the Islands of Jamaica, Grenada, St Vincent, Tobago and St Lucia, and the Leeward Islands*. C.– 3840, 1884.

Report of the Board of Trade entitled 'Progress of the Sugar Trade', by T. H. Farrer, August 7, 1884.

Report on the Coolie Disturbances of Port-of-Spain, Trinidad, 1885.

Report of the Royal Commission to consider and report as to the Proposed Franchise and Division of the Colony into Electoral Districts, Trinidad, 1889.

Tobago Metairie Commission, 1890.

Railway Enquiry Commission, Trinidad, 1894.

Roads Enquiry Commission, Trinidad, 1894.

Report of the West India Royal Commission, C. 8655, 8657, 8667, 8669, London, 1897 – Appendix C., Vol. II, Parts II–V. *Evidence in British Guiana, Barbados, Trinidad and Tobago*.

Correspondence relating to the Re-adjustment of the Finance of the Borough of Port-of-Spain, Trinidad, 1898.

Report of the Commission of Enquiry into the Recent Disturbances at Port-of-Spain, Trinidad, 1903

Further Papers relating to the Disturbances at Port-of-Spain, Trinidad, in March 1903. Cd. 1988, 1904.

Report of the Royal Commission on Trade Relations between Canada and the West Indies, 1910.

Report by the Honourable E. F. L. Wood, M.P. (Parliamentary Under Secretary of State for the Colonies) on his visit to the West Indies and British Guiana, Cmd. 1679, London, 1922.

Oil Industry of Trinidad, Report of Sir Thomas Holland, Trinidad, 1928.

Report of the West Indian Sugar Commission, Cmd 3517. 1930

Report of the West Indian Unofficial Conference in Roseau, Dominica, 1932

Report of the Closer Union Commission (Leeward Islands, Windward Islands, Trinidad and Tobago), 1933, Cmd. 4383, London. 1933.

Report of Commission on The Trinidad and Tobago Disturbances,
1937, Cmd. 5641, 1938.

The records of the Legislative Council of Trinidad and Tobago
provide invaluable material. The Chaguaramas Bay Agreement is
Council Paper No. 167 of 1894. The Immigration Ordinance of 1899
will be found in the *Immigration Ordinances of Trinidad and British
Guiana,* Cd. 1989, presented to Parliament in April, 1904. The debates
of the Legislative Council provide much material on Immigration and
Tobago. Valuable records have been preserved in Tobago including
Despatches and Minutes of the House of Assembly. These, together
with the files of the *Port-of-Spain Gazette,* are the best source for the
relations between Trinidad and Tobago which culminated in union
in 1899.

There are five important accounts of the British West Indies after
emancipation, three of them hostile and two sympathetic, which are
essential for any analysis of British West Indian history in the nineteenth century. These accounts are as follows: —

> *An Occasional Discourse on the Nigger Question,* by Thomas
> Carlyle, London, 1848.
> *The West Indies and the Spanish Main,* by Anthony Trollope,
> London, 1860.
> *The Ordeal of Free Labour in the British West Indies,* by W. Sewell,
> New York, 1860.
> *At Last: A Christmas in the West Indies,* by Charles Kingsley,
> New York, 1871.
> *The English in the West Indies, or the Bow of Ulysses,* by J.
> A. Froude, London, 1887.

To these must be added J. J. Thomas, *Froudacity; West Indian
Fables by James Anthony Froude,* published in Philadelphia in 1890.

On Captain Cipriani the best material is his speeches in the Legislative Council and the files of the *Socialist.* There is also a *Life of Captain Cipriani,* by C. L. R. James, 1932.

Three general books dealing with the West Indies, though not
exclusively with the West Indies, are of value for the history of Trinidad and Tobago They are: —

> N. Deerr, *The History of Sugar,* two volumes, London, 1950.
> *The Spanish Struggle for Justice in the Conquest of America,* by
> Lewis Hanke, University of Pennsylvania Press, 1949.
> Eric Williams, *Capitalism and Slavery,* University of North
> Carolina Press, 1942. André Deutsch, 1964.

For the Amerindians, only two works need be consulted. They
are: —

> *Origins of the Tainan Culture, West Indies,* by Sven Loven.
> Goteborg, 1935.
> *The Aborigines of Trinidad,* by J. A Bullbrook, Trinidad, 1960.

Attention may also be invited to two essays by the author on separate issues dealt with in the context of: —

'The Negro Slave Trade and Anglo-Spanish Relations', in the *Caribbean Historical Review*, No. 1, December 1950; and 'The Intercolonial Slave Trade after its Abolition in 1807' in the *Journal of Negro History*, April, 1942.

In respect of Africa's importance for the history of Trinidad the work of Basil Davidson is all that is needed: *Old Africa Rediscovered* London, 1959; *Black Mother*, London, 1961. *Trinidad Village*, by M. J. and F. S. Herskovits, New York, 1947, is very valuable. So is P. J. C. Dark's, *Bush Negro Art: African Art in the Americas*, London 1954.

In the general field of Race Relations, with particular reference to Trinidad, attention is directed to Eric Williams, *The Historical Background of Race Relations in the Caribbean*, Havana, 1957.

With respect to the depreciation of Indian civilisation which formed the background to Indian immigration to Trinidad, a useful introduction is the author's Tagore Centenary Celebration Address delivered in Port-of-Spain on May 6, 1961.

The publications of the People's National Movement are of importance for the Chaguaramas issue. The two most important are *From Slavery to Chaguaramas*, 1959, and the *History of Chaguaramas*, Authorised *Version*, *U.S.A.*, a reprint of articles appearing in the *Nation*, the official organ of the People's National Movement. Both are the work of Eric Williams.

A useful analysis of the background of the British West Indies Federation, with particular reference to Trinidad and Tobago, is *Federation, Two public lectures*, by Eric Williams, published by the People's National Movement in 1956. Attention is directed also to the *Economics of Nationhood*, published by the Government of Trinidad and Tobago on September 11, 1959.

Index

ACTON, Lord, 110

AFRICA, natives of compared with Amerindians, 3; to rescue of Trinidad, 29; ancient civilisation of, 30–9; contribution of to Trinidad customs, 38–9; immigration to Trinidad from, 76, 98–9

ALCAZAR, Sir Henry, 112–13, 169–70, 172–6

AMERINDIANS, civilisation of, 1–4; enslavement of by Spaniards, 5–6, 10, 22–5; in Tobago, 8; conflict as to nature of, 8–9, 111; Raleigh's speech to, 18; slave trade in, 23; revolt in Trinidad, 25–7; population of in Trinidad, 47, 76

ANGUIANO, Mateo de, 26

ANTIGUA, 65; slave compensation in, 83–4; metairie system in, 124–5; sugar industry in, 152–3, 226–7; food imports in, 160–1, 227

ARIMA, 3, 189

BARBADOS, English grant of, 19; Caribs in, 23; policy of to Tobago, 53, 55–6, 58; slave revolt in, 63; attempt to join Canada, 63, 66; migration from to Trinidad, 74–5, 98–9; slave compensation in, 83–5; federation disturbances in, 84; sugar industry in, 109, 152–3, 155, 226–7; emigration from, 115; associated with Tobago, 131; opposes Windward Islands Federation, 136–7, 250; compared with Trinidad, 166; food imports in, 227; and Federation, 249–55

BENTINCK, Lord George, 98

BERRIO, Antonio de, 11, 13, 17, 21, 27

BOISSIERRE, Dr de, 115, 143, 147

BROOME, Sir Frederick Napier, 172

BROUGHAM, Lord, 68–9

BULLBROOK, J. A., 1–3

BUTLER, T. U. B., 233–5, 236, 237, 242

CABILDO, on defence of Trinidad, 17; description of in 1757, 28–9; Chacon's reform of, 46; on constitution reform, 68; powers of, 72; revenues of, 82; and slaves, 82

CANADA, Barbados' efforts to join, 63; trade with Trinidad, 112; federation in, 252

CANNING, George, 66

CARIBS, civilisation of, 1–4; threat to Trinidad, 17–18; enslavement of, 23; threat to Tobago, 52; in Tobago, 59

CARLYLE, Thomas, 89

CASAS, Bartolome de las, attitude to Amerindians of, 9, 22–5; white colonisation plan of, 20; on Amerindian slave trade, 23; on Negro slave trade, 27

CASTLEREAGH, Lord, 72–3

CATON-THOMPSON, Dr Gertrude, 33

CHACON, Jose Maria, 11; reorganisation of government of, Trinidad, 43–4; land reforms of, 44–5; slave code of, 45–6; and Cabildo, 46; expansion of Port-of-Spain, 46–7; on defence of Trinidad, 47–9; on slave danger, 49; trial and condemnation of, 49–50; on colour problem, 49, 67

CHAGUARAMAS, sugar cultivation in, 46, 82; Spanish fleet in, 49; suitability of for naval base, 82; First Agreement on, 259–61; Anglo-American Agreement on, 267–76

Lightning Source UK Ltd.
Milton Keynes UK
UKHW020639080321
379980UK00008B/1337